"十二五"普通高等教育本科国家级规划教材

新世纪高等院校英语专业本科生系列教材（修订版）
总主编 戴炜栋

圣经文化导论
An Introductory Course of Biblical Culture

学生用书

任东升 张德禄 马月兰 / 编著

上海外语教育出版社
外教社 SHANGHAI FOREIGN LANGUAGE EDUCATION PRESS

图书在版编目（CIP）数据

圣经文化导论学生用书 / 任东升，张德禄，马月兰编著. -- 上海：上海外语教育出版社，2013 (2024重印)
新世纪高等院校英语专业本科生系列教材. 修订版
ISBN 978-7-5446-3311-6

Ⅰ. ①圣… Ⅱ. ①任… ②张… ③马… Ⅲ. ①英语－高等学校－教材 ②《圣经》－宗教文化 Ⅳ. ①H31

中国版本图书馆CIP数据核字（2013）第049930号

出版发行：**上海外语教育出版社**
（上海外国语大学内）　邮编：200083
电　　话：021-65425300（总机）
电子邮箱：bookinfo@sflep.com.cn
网　　址：http://www.sflep.com
责任编辑：张传根

印　　刷：上海宝山译文印刷厂有限公司
开　　本：787×1092　1/16　印张 17.25　字数 460千字
版　　次：2013年4月第1版　2024年8月第10次印刷

书　　号：ISBN 978-7-5446-3311-6 / G・1022
定　　价：31.00 元

本版图书如有印装质量问题，可向本社调换
质量服务热线：4008-213-263

"新世纪高等院校英语专业本科生系列教材"(修订版)

编委会名单

主 任： 戴炜栋

委 员： （以姓氏笔画为序）

文秋芳	北京外国语大学	杨达复	西安外国语大学
王 岚	中国人民解放军外国语学院	杨信彰	厦门大学
王立非	对外经济贸易大学	邹 申	上海外国语大学
王守仁	南京大学	陈建平	广东外语外贸大学
王俊菊	山东大学	陈法春	天津外国语大学
王腊宝	苏州大学	陈准民	对外经济贸易大学
史志康	上海外国语大学	姚君伟	南京师范大学
叶兴国	上海对外经贸大学	洪 岗	浙江外国语学院
申 丹	北京大学	胡文仲	北京外国语大学
石 坚	四川大学	赵忠德	大连外国语大学
刘世生	清华大学	殷企平	杭州师范大学
刘海平	南京大学	秦秀白	华南理工大学
庄智象	上海外国语大学	袁洪庚	兰州大学
朱 刚	南京大学	屠国元	中南大学
何兆熊	上海外国语大学	梅德明	上海外国语大学
何其莘	北京外国语大学	黄国文	中山大学
张绍杰	东北师范大学	黄勇民	复旦大学
张春柏	华东师范大学	黄源深	上海对外经贸大学
张维友	华中师范大学	程晓堂	北京师范大学
李 力	西南大学	蒋洪新	湖南师范大学
李庆生	武汉大学	谢 群	中南财经政法大学
李建平	四川外国语大学	虞建华	上海外国语大学
李绍山	中国人民解放军外国语学院	蔡龙权	上海师范大学
李战子	中国人民解放军国际关系学院		

总　序

　　我国英语专业本科教学与学科建设，伴随着我国改革开放的步伐，得到了长足的发展和提升。回顾这30多年英语专业教学改革和发展的历程，无论是英语专业教学大纲的制订、颁布、实施和修订，还是四、八级考试的开发与推行，以及多项英语教学改革项目的开拓，无不是围绕英语专业的学科建设和人才培养而进行的，正如《高等学校英语专业英语教学大纲》提出的英语专业的培养目标，即培养"具有扎实的英语语言基础和广博的文化知识并能熟练地运用英语在外事、教育、经贸、文化、科技、军事等部门从事翻译、教学、管理、研究等工作的复合型英语人才。"为促进英语专业本科建设的发展和教学质量的提高，外语专业教学指导委员会还实施了"新世纪教育质量改革工程"，包括推行"十五"、"十一五"、"十二五"国家级教材规划和外语专业国家精品课程评审，从各个教学环节加强对外语教学质量的宏观监控，从而确保为我国的经济建设输送大量的优秀人才。

　　跨入新世纪，英语专业的建设面临新的形势和任务：经济全球化、科技一体化、文化多元化、信息网络化的发展趋势加快，世界各国之间的竞争日趋激烈，这对我国英语专业本科教学理念和培养目标提出了新的挑战；大学英语教学改革如火如荼；数字化、网络化等多媒体教学辅助手段在外语教学中广泛应用和不断发展；英语专业本科教育的改革和学科建设也呈现出多样化的趋势，翻译专业、商务英语专业相继诞生——这些变化和发展无疑对英语专业的学科定位、人才培养以及教材建设提出了新的、更高的要求。

　　上海外语教育出版社（简称外教社）在新世纪之初约请了全国30余所著名高校百余位英语教育专家，对面向新世纪的英语专业本科生教材建设进行了深入、全面、广泛和具有前瞻性的研讨，成功地推出了理念新颖、特色明显、体系完备的"新世纪高等院校英语专业本科生系列教材"，并被列入"十五"国家级规划教材，以其前瞻性、先进性和创新性等特点受到全国众多使用院校的广泛好评。

　　面对快速发展的英语专业本科教育，如何保证专业的教学质量，培养具有国际视野和创新能力的英语专业人才，是国家、社会、高校教师共同关注的问题，也是教材编撰者和教材出版者关心和重视的问题。

　　作为教学改革的一个重要组成部分，优质教材的编写和出版对学科建设的推动和人才培养的作用是有目共睹的。外教社为满足教学和学科发展的需要，与教材编写

者们一起，力图全方位、大幅度修订并扩充原有的"新世纪高等院校英语专业本科生系列教材"，以打造英语专业教材建设完整的学科体系。为此，外教社邀请了全国几十所知名高校40余位著名英语教育专家，根据英语专业学科发展的新趋势，围绕梳理现有课程、优化教材品种和结构、改进教学方法和手段、强化学生自主学习能力的培养、有效提高教学质量等问题开展了专题研究，并在教材编写与出版中予以体现。

修订后的教材仍保持原有的专业技能、专业知识和相关专业知识三大板块，品种包括基础技能、语言学、文学、文化、人文科学、测试、教学法等，总数逾200种，几乎涵盖了当前我国高校英语专业所开设的全部课程，并充分考虑到我国英语教育的地区差异和不同院校英语专业的特点，提供更多的选择。教材编写深入浅出，内容反映了各个学科领域的最新研究成果；在编写宗旨上，除了帮助学生打下扎实的语言基本功外，着力培养学生分析问题、解决问题的能力，提高学生的思辨能力和人文、科学素养，培养健康向上的人生观，使学生真正成为我国新时代所需要的英语专门人才。

系列教材修订版编写委员会仍由我国英语界的知名专家学者组成，其中多数是在各个领域颇有建树的专家，不少是高等学校外语专业教学指导委员会的委员，总体上代表了中国英语教育的发展方向和水平。

系列教材完整的学科体系、先进的编写理念、权威的编者队伍，再次得到教育部的认可，荣列"普通高等教育'十一五'国家级规划教材"。其专业技能板块的70多种教材更于2012年首批被评为"'十二五'普通高等教育本科国家级规划教材"。我深信，这套教材一定会促进学生语言技能、专业知识、学科素养和创新能力的培养，填补现行教材某些空白，为培养高素质的英语专业人才奠定坚实的基础。

戴炜栋

教育部高校外语专业教学指导委员会主任委员

国务院学位委员会外语学科评议组组长

序言

摆在读者面前的，是由来自高校英语系的教授任东升、张德禄、马月兰所编写的一部如何阅读、研习《圣经》的著作。读到这样的"圣经文化导论"，自有一种振奋和欣喜，因为本书所传递的直接信息是，圣经文化研究在我国当代学术界和教育界有了其深度和广度上的新拓展、新成就。中国学术走向世界，圣经文化研究乃其不应缺少的重要内容。

圣经文化是世界文化的一大组成部分，它与犹太教文化和基督教文化形成相关叠合，亦涵括了东方和西方文化的许多重要因素。《圣经》迄今仍是世界上各种文字译本最多、印刷量最大、影响最广的著作，其形成的影响已经辐射到世界广大地区和诸多领域，引起了各方持久的反响及回应。千百年来，人们对《圣经》有着各种理解、领会、诠释和评说。作为宗教经典，它始终保持为犹太教、基督教的最重要的读物，为其教义、神学、思想和精神之源。但这部宗教名著并不仅仅为其宗教内容所局限，相反，它所蕴涵的资源、信息揭示出一个更广远的世界、一段更悠久的历史、一种更复杂的图景。正是因为《圣经》起着古代文明百科和现代思想智库的作用，才能够形成其源远流长、绵延不绝的圣经文化现象。我们今天在政治、经济、历史、体制、律法、民俗、哲学、伦理、神话、文学、艺术、语言等领域，仍然能够感受到圣经文化的博大精深和久远魅力。

在对《圣经》本身的研究上，其传统大致可分为两种趋向：一为"内涵式"研究，即《圣经》研究中的"解经学"传统，强调对《圣经》本身章节及其内容和寓意的梳理、解释，以章句考证、训诂和批注为特色，形成对《圣经》内在结构与经文意义的分析、研究和阐释。二为"外延式"研究，即超出《圣经》本身结构而从其产生、演变的大文化背景来辨析、研讨，不再满足于对其经文的章句之考，而更关注其经卷作者、成书年代、书卷真伪、历史背景和其内容的引申、演化、蕴含和预表；由此而形成对不同抄本、版本的考证，对经文意义的回溯和对其发展沿革的追踪，以及对其原初教义的确认和对其神学发展的探索。这后一种开放性、拓展性的研究也被称为"解经原理"，即尝试确立一些基本"原则"来对《圣经》加以正确解释，并以这些"原则"来扩大观察、解读《圣经》的视域。这两种基本研究方法，构成了《圣经》之探的主要思路和解经体系，亦为西方学术界更宽范围的语言文化及哲学思辨的解释学提供了启迪、奠立了基础。

与《圣经》本身研究所不同的，则是更大范围的圣经文化研究。这种研究的视野更为开阔，涉及面亦更为广泛。如果说《圣经》研究有其专业性、特殊性的话，那么圣经文化研究则更体现出其普遍性、普及性，其研究兴趣、研究成果可以雅俗共赏，因而和者甚广、运用颇多。而我们眼前所阅读到的这部《圣经文化导论》，正是从圣经文化研究这一进路来展开的"外延式"、普及性研究。显然，它作为视角颇新、涉猎较广的"通识课"教材，有着其涵括大、易理解等特点，一定能够吸引众多的读者来分享其中的知识、体悟编者的立意。而且在这种轻松、惬意的阅读中，人们也能获得一种认知上的提高，甚至精神上的升华。

中国许多著名的思想家、文学家和翻译家都曾强调，学习和研究语言文学、尤其是西方语言文学的中国人应该读读《圣经》，了解其基本内容和蕴涵。这在英美语言文学的学习和研究中尤为突出。对于大学英语专业学生而言，熟悉《圣经》应该是一种"基本功"，因为在英美作品中《圣经》格言乃耳熟能详，《圣经》典故则俯拾即是，有了对《圣经》的了解会非常有助于对这些作品的阅读、理解，增加自己的领悟、想象。而对于大学其他专业的学生，读点《圣经》书中的内容也是有用的"杂学"知识，是对西方文化之"通识"的必要接触和把握，故而会给自己带来意外的收获或扩大自己的为学眼界。从这一角度来看，这部《圣经文化导论》的价值和意义也就不言而喻了。

仅仅快速浏览了一下这部著作，就发现了它有着不少亮点，屡见珠玑。首先，这部著作中英文并举，选有"钦定本"英文《圣经》来让读者直接阅读、鉴赏，感受其文字之美和经典表述。其次，这部著作重在文学、文字，对与《圣经》相关的古代神话、典故、传说、谚语等都有精彩的解读和恰当的点评，使读者能对《圣经》原文有更深层次的理解，克服其"语焉不详"之疑。第三，这部著作揭示了《圣经》传统对西方文化发展演变的影响，尤其是对美国政治文化理念得以形成的《圣经》根源进行了具体剖析，如"上帝造人神话与美国人权观"的对比、"摩西十诫"与美国第一个政治契约文件"五月花号公约"的关联等均为点睛之笔，颇为精彩。第四，这部著作列举了《圣经》内容在西方文化名著中的普遍运用和理想效果，有助于中国青年学者欣赏、解读这些名著名篇。第五，这部著作亦搜集了中国学者、文人、翻译家对《圣经》的采用、评说和理解，让人们得以学会如何在中国语言文化"语境"和中国社会思想"处境"中"洋为中用"，且能恰到好处。最后，这部著作还以众多的讨论题、思考题、注释、分析、点评和背景知识介绍来丰富其内容，使之成为一本实用、方便的工具书和多用途的教材。其构思、体例、编排乃匠心独到、颇具特色。

综上所述，这部著作适应了在"全球化"信息时代扩大知识内容、改善知识结构的需要，体现了我国大学通识教育中"阅读中外经典、通识人类文化"的指导思想和基本精神。它有利于我们在外语教学中从文字性到文化性的深化、从语言性到社会性的深入，可为我们提供"走向世界"的必要语言文化知识和应该掌握的社会人文学科之基本功。因此，我们应该感谢任东升等老师们的辛勤努力，也衷心感谢出版界的全力支持！

是为序。

卓新平

编者的话

《圣经》不仅是一部宗教经典，也是史学百科、文学巨著、语言宝库。在漫长的中世纪，《圣经》成为西方文明发展的支柱，渗透到意识形态和精神生活的各个领域。到了近现代，《圣经》的影响与日俱增，波及东方各国的文化，甚至成为影响中国近代社会的一百种著作之一。可以说，《圣经》文本的存在及其不断被翻译、传播进而产生广泛的影响，已经成为一种世界性的文化现象。

中国学者认为，以圣经文学为代表的古犹太—基督教文学与古代中国文学、印度文学和希腊文学比肩而立，共同构成世界文学大厦的四根支柱。[1] 对于《圣经》自身的文学价值和基于《圣经》文本的基督教文化，不少西方大文豪和著名学者做过精辟的评价。歌德(Johann Wolfgang von Goethe, 1749–1832)早就预言，世界可以按它的步伐飞速前进，人类的科学可以向着最高的阶段发展，但却没有任何东西可以取代《圣经》的地位。[2] 雨果(Victor Hugo, 1802–1885)曾指出："在所有流传于人们手头的书籍中，只有两本他需要加以研究，那就是《荷马史诗》和《圣经》。因为这两本值得尊敬的书，从其创作的时期和本身的价值来说，都是一切书籍中最重要的两本，它们几乎和世界同样古老，而从精神思想方面来说，它们自己就体现了两个世界。在这两本书里大家几乎可以发现有一种具有双重面貌而又统一共同的创造，在《荷马史诗》中，表现为人类天才的创造，而在《圣经》中则为上帝精神的创造。"[3] 诺贝尔文学奖得主、英国诗人艾略特(Thomas Steams Eliot, 1888–1965)说："人文主义是时隐时现的，而基督教却是延续不断的。我们不必去设想，如果没有基督教，那么欧洲各民族的发展可能是个什么样子。"[4] 在加拿大、美国、英国和中国多所大学担任教授或客座教授的著名圣经学者谢大卫(David Lyle Jeffrey)指出："事实上，《圣经》在西方文学中成了如此基本的文献，以致假如缺少了圣经先例，西方文学几乎不可能出现今天的面貌"。[5]

我们还可以从许多中国著名学者对《圣经》的评论中体察《圣经》的价值和影响。中国圣经学者马佳指出："如果我们把文学视作一条源源不断、生生不息的河流，那么《圣经》对中西文学的影响也将是源远流长的。"[6] 北京大学的刘意青教授指出："几乎所有的西方文学作品，都渗透着基督教或《圣经》的影响，即使没有明显地取用其内容和人物的名字，它们也渗透着基督教的善恶观和为人处世的态度。"[7] 中国社会科学院的叶舒宪教授指出："《圣经》从头到尾都是用比喻和象征的编码方式表达的，前后连结为一个繁复而完整的语码系统，不仅为《旧约》、《新约》奠定了双重蕴涵的叙述模式，而且给后

---

1. 梁工主编：《基督教文学》，北京：宗教文化出版社，2001年，第44页。
2. 转引自刘意青等译：《圣经故事一百篇》，北京：中国对外翻译出版公司、商务印书馆(香港)有限公司，1989年，参见"前言"。
3. 雨果：《〈短曲与民谣集〉序》(1826)，载于《古典文艺理论译丛》(第二册)，北京：人民文学出版社，1961年，第120–121页。
4. 孙彩霞著：《西方现代派文学与〈圣经〉》，北京：中国社会科学出版社，2005年，第4页。
5. 谢大卫的文章："圣经与西方文学"，载于《西方文学与基督教论文集》，北京：北京大学出版社，1996年，第17页。
6. 马佳编：《圣经典故》，上海：学林出版社，2000年，参见"后记"。
7. 刘意青著：《〈圣经〉的文学阐释》，北京：北京大学出版社，2004年，第11页。

世的西方文化奠定了基本的想象构思和文学表达的原型基础。"[1]

事实证明，不了解《圣经》这块"西方文明的基石"(the cornerstone of western civilization, 美国学者 Thomas Cahill 语)，便不能很好地理解西方文化。早在19世纪，反对实用和功利性教育、主张强化人文教育的英国著名学者马修·阿诺德(Matthew Arnold, 1822–1888)就大力提倡在大学开设阐释《圣经》的课程，不是宗教意义上的读经，而是对《圣经》进行文化的和文学的阐释，并把这门课程看成了解英国和西方文化的一个重要举措。直至20世纪80年代，许多西方学者意识到，要想让西方经典文学被读者接受、读懂并欣赏的话，了解和熟悉《圣经》已是"当务之急"[2]。因此，西方几乎所有英语国家的大学都纷纷开设了圣经文学课程。20世纪二三十年代，随着《圣经》汉译本"和合本"的传播，中国学者和青年学子对圣经文学产生了浓厚兴趣。文学青年对《诗篇》、《雅歌》、《约伯记》、《马太福音》等觉得"美不胜收"。[3] 1932年，周作人在燕京大学讲授"新文学"课时，就把《旧约》中的《传道书》和《路得记》作为一个独立的部分讲授，在他为青年学生列出的10部"必读书"中，"汉译旧约(文学部分)"排在第四。1989年，编著了英文版《圣经浅析》(Venturing into the Bible, 南京大学出版社)的郭秀梅教授指出，对于学习英语的中国学生而言，熟悉英文《圣经》(指"钦定本")是 must (必需)。

随着中外文化交流的深入和大学生英语水平的普遍提高，当代大学生已不再满足于阅读中文或英文"圣经故事"的层次，而是想亲自涉猎《圣经》文本，欣赏"原汁原味"的圣经文学和文化。鉴于此，我们根据多年的圣经文化教学经验，汇集已有相关教材的优点，按照全新的教学思路，编写了这部教材。我们采用"圣经文化"(Biblical Culture)的提法，是为了体现《圣经》文本的三重"文化性"：(1)《圣经》的语言，尤其是其原创意义上的语言意象具有独特的文化气质；(2)《圣经》里所描述的民族性事件具有元典意义、原型意义和普世意义，在一定程度上代表全人类的文化现象；(3)从学术界来看，长期以来人们对《圣经》文本的诠释和解读并非局限于语言层面，更多的是一种跨文化的解读。对于本课程的教学而言，以"圣经文化"的宽广视角可以覆盖语言学习、文学赏析和文化比较三个层次。本教材的选文全部采用原汁原味的"钦定本"英文，而且基本涵盖了"钦定本"的精华。这是因为，出现在英语语汇里的《圣经》词汇和典故，外国小说、电影中引用的典故和段落，外国领导人演讲中引用或化用的《圣经》内容绝大多数源自"钦定本"。如果不阅读"钦定本"，就不能准确地识别、把握相关《圣经》引文的妙处，甚至难以把握整个文本的精髓。时至今日，"钦定本"依然是英语国家人民和以英语为第一外语的读者群学习英语语言、了解圣经文化的重要读本之一。

下面我们介绍本教材的编写目的、授课对象和编排体例。

一、**编写目的：**本教材贯彻"阅读中外经典、通识人类文化"的大学通识教育指导思想，知识性、趣味性和学术性兼具，以"圣经文化"的宽广视角覆盖英语学习、文学赏析和文化比较三个层次，引导学生从唯物史观认识《圣经》作为世界文化经典的地位和作用，从而理解西方社会的历史、政治、文学、艺术之圣经底蕴，培养与西方人士进行文化交流的能力。

二、**授课对象：**面向高等院校英语专业高年级本科生，作为专业必修课或选修课，可

---

1. 叶舒宪著：《〈圣经〉比喻》，桂林：广西师范大学出版社，2003年，"前言"第1页。
2. David L. Jeffrey. "The Bible as Literature in the 1980s: A Guide for the Perplexed", Toronto: The University of Toronto Quarterly, Vol.59, No.4, Summer, 1990, p. 570.
3. 朱维之："朱维之自传"，载于王寿兰编《文学翻译百家谈》，北京：北京大学出版社，1989年，第189页。

以有力补充欧洲文化入门、英美概况、英美文学史、比较文学、翻译等课程内容；本教材也适用于通过大学英语三级的非英语专业学生，以英语选修课或文化通识课的形式进行英语技能训练和跨学科文化学习。对于准备报考翻译专业硕士(MTI)、英语教育、世界文学、西方文学、比较文学等硕士相关专业或研究方向的本科生，本教材具有重要参考价值。对圣经文学和宗教文化感兴趣或有研究的社会人士而言，本教材不失为得力的参考书。

三、编排体例：本教材的授课周期为一个学期，除"绪论"外共设16讲，教学进度为每周一讲。每讲包括三个模块共6部分：

1. 导读、选文与注释："导读"高度概括每一讲主要内容并集中介绍相关背景知识；所有选文均为"钦定本"的精华内容，自编顺序，自拟标题；个别含有对话的章节采用了新式标点；表述性文字中所引《圣经》章节的标注法采用通用的简写形式。"注释"对选文中特有的语言现象、偏难的词汇和复杂的表达方式作了较为详细的说明，辅助学生课前预习。我们建议学生在学习过程中参考中文"和合本"《圣经》或英汉对照的《圣经》版本。同时，为了方便学生集中学习、记忆和查读，教材末尾附录了"词汇表"。

2. 圣经文化知识链接、圣经文化专题与圣经典故集锦："链接"涵盖面广，趣味性强，便于学生拓宽本讲的圣经基本知识，提高自主学习能力；"专题"以本讲圣经主题为切入点，就西方文学和文化的难点问题及相关宗教知识展开论述，内容涉及西方哲学、政治、经济、教育、美学、美术、影视等方面，帮助学生从根本上理解西方文化的源头和精髓；"典故"尽量结合具体实例，详细解释西方文学、政治、经济等话语中对《圣经》的引用及其目的。此外，我们还尽量列出中国现代文学作品引用《圣经》典故的不少实例。

3. 课堂讨论题和课后思考题："讨论题"的设计侧重西方文化中核心要素的《圣经》渊源，适于师生互动，激活学生的知识储备，培养思辨能力。"思考题"围绕中西文学和文化方面的对比和分析，引导学生课后查阅相关资料，进行拓展性学习。

为便于学生自学和教师备课，本教材配备了《教师用书》，补充并拓展了圣经文化链接知识和圣经文化专题的内涵，提供了《学生用书》中所有课堂讨论题和课后思考题的详细参考答案。此外，《教师用书》中还附录了五个《圣经》与西方文学、文化、艺术的大型专题讲座稿。

为了方便学生自主检查学习效果，本教材附录了四套课程模拟试题，两套为英语试题，侧重"钦定本"英语学习，两套汉语试题，侧重《圣经》对西方文学和艺术的影响。《教师用书》中提供了这四套模拟题的参考答案。

本教材《学生用书》和《教师用书》第一至五讲由马月兰执笔，第六至十讲由张德禄执笔，其余各讲均由任东升执笔；全书由任东升统稿。

承蒙中国社会科学院学部委员、世界宗教研究所所长、中国宗教学会会长、博士生导师卓新平先生为本教材作序。卓先生的序言视域宽广，言语恳切，不仅给本教材起到"总论"的作用，而且为中国大学生和其他读者通过本教材"通识"西方文化指明了方向。在此，我们对卓先生表示衷心的感谢！

我们谨向圣经文学和圣经文化研究的学界前辈表示由衷的感激！向为本课程提出建议的中国海洋大学、河北师范大学听课专家和全体学员表示感谢！承蒙上海外语教育出版社慧眼及本教材审稿专家的首肯，本教材有幸走进更多的大学课堂，为中国高校的大学素质教育贡献一份力量。本套教材的策划编辑许高女士对本教材提出了宝贵的修订建议，张传根先生为编辑本教材付出了辛勤汗水，在此我们表示衷心感谢！我们感到欣喜的同时，更希望同行、学员和读者不吝指正！

Contents

7　绪　论

16　第 一 讲　希伯来神话故事：《创世记》(上)
　　　　　　The Hebrew Mythical Stories from *Genesis*

32　第 二 讲　希伯来族长故事：《创世记》(下)
　　　　　　Legends of the Hebrew Fathers from *Genesis*

48　第 三 讲　以色列民族的形成：《出埃及记》
　　　　　　Exodus, the Growth of Israel as a Nation

69　第 四 讲　以色列律法集萃：《利未记》、《民数记》和《申命记》
　　　　　　Leviticus, *Numbers* and *Deuteronomy*: Essence of Law

82　第 五 讲　时势造就的英雄：士师
　　　　　　Judges, "Heroes" in the Lawless Period

97　第 六 讲　以色列统一王国：三代君王
　　　　　　Three Kings of the United Kingdom of Israel

114　第 七 讲　正义的呼告者：希伯来先知
　　　　　　The Hebrew Prophets, Spokesmen of Justice

130　第 八 讲　人生苦难的思索：《约伯记》
　　　　　　Job, Probing into Bitterness of Life

144　第 九 讲　田园牧歌：《路得记》
　　　　　　Ruth, an Idyllic Story

155　第 十 讲　宫廷小说：《以斯帖记》
　　　　　　Esther, a Court Story

167　第十一讲　希伯来诗歌荟萃：《诗篇》
　　　　　　Psalms, an Anthology of Hebrew Poems and Songs

179　第十二讲　浪漫爱情歌集：《雅歌》
　　　　　　Song of Songs, Lyrics of Romantic Love

190　第十三讲　以色列民族的绝唱：《哀歌》
　　　　　　Lamentations, a Poetic Peak of the Israel

202　第十四讲　人生经验的浓缩：《箴言》和《传道书》
　　　　　　Proverbs and *Ecclesiastes*, a Treasure of Life Wisdom

215　第十五讲　耶稣形象的多维视角：福音书
　　　　　　Gospels, Multiple Perspectives of Jesus

229　第十六讲　启示文学的典范：《启示录》
　　　　　　Revelation, a Model of Apocalyptic Literature

244　附录1　课程模拟试题

261　附录2　词 汇 表

绪论

一、《圣经》文本及其内容

"圣经"(The Holy Bible,简称The Bible)一词初见于希腊文biblia,意思是"一组书卷"。《圣经》并不是一本书,而是许多卷书的合订本,是不同时代、不同作者的著作的汇编。习惯上人们把66卷本《新旧约全书》称为标准《圣经》。39卷本《旧约全书》简称《旧约》(The Old Testament)[1],原文大部分用古希伯来语写成,少部分章节用亚兰文写成;27卷本《新约全书》简称《新约》(The New Testament),原文全部用古希腊文写成。从学术观点看,用希伯来文写成的《后典》(Apocrypha)(或称"次经"Deuterocanonical)也是《圣经》一个重要组成部分。[2]当代西方基督教《圣经》中的《旧约》,在内容上源自犹太教的"圣经",即《希伯来圣经》(The Hebrew Bible),而《新约》的写作大量参考了《希伯来圣经》。之所以分为"旧约"和"新约",是因为视本民族为上帝的选民的古犹太人把自己的"圣经"当作上帝与人所立的"契约"(Covenant),形成"立约→违约→受罚→悔改→重新立约→守约→违约"的模式。公元一世纪基督教从犹太教中分离出来,继承并发扬了犹太教的"立约"之说,认为"救世主"耶稣在上帝与人之间重立了"新约",因此把原来上帝与犹太人所立之约称为"旧约"。《旧约》大多出自以色列先知和其他哲人之手,《新约》则出自耶稣宗徒和宗徒弟子的记述。简要地说,《旧约》讲述了古代以色列民族的起源、传说、历史、法律、制度,及其民族英雄(族长)、君王、士师和先知在古代以色列民族神权国家的形成过程中和以色列后来的兴衰过程中的作用及他们给予以色列人的道德训诲。《新约》主要记载耶稣的生平及其使徒传道的过程。

1. 《旧约》的编排方式

按照基督教《旧约全书》的分类,39卷书可以分为四类:律法书(又称"摩西五经")、历史书、智慧书(诗歌书)、先知书,如下图所示:

律法书5卷 (摩西五经)	《创世记》(*Genesis*)、《出埃及记》(*Exodus*)、《利未记》(*Leviticus*)、《民数记》(*Numbers*)、《申命记》(*Deuteronomy*)
历史书12卷	《约书亚记》(*Joshua*)、《士师记》(*Judges*)、《路得记》(*Ruth*)、《撒母耳记上》(*1 Samuel*)、《撒母耳记下》(*2 Samuel*)、《列王纪上》(*1 Kings*)、《列王纪下》(*2 Kings*)、《历代志上》(*1 Chronicles*)、《历代志下》(*2 Chronicles*)、《以斯拉记》(*Ezra*)、《尼希米记》(*Nehemiah*)、《以斯帖记》(*Esther*)

---

1. 基督教新教(中国大陆称"基督教")、天主教和东正教对《旧约》所含经卷的篇目有着不同的看法。因本教材为大学通识课教材,着重给大学生介绍《圣经》的大致面貌,不侧重神学视角,故不对此进行细致区分。本书旧约经卷篇目以"新标点和合本"为准。
2. 《七十子希腊译本》译本共有50卷,比《希伯来圣经》多出一部分卷章,即收录了希伯来文本未录的一些卷籍和补编,这些补入的作品后来被列为"后典"。事实上,包括英文"钦定本"在内的不少《圣经》译本都包含"后典"或"次经"部分。当代英国学者Mona Baker、美国圣经学者 Eugene A. Nida 等均主张《圣经》文本包含"后典"或"次经"。"后典"的书目和内容可参见张久宣译《圣经后典》,北京:商务印书馆,1987年。此外,《死海古卷》也是一部很重要的经外书。可参见王神荫译《死海古卷》,北京:商务印书馆,2003年。

智慧书5卷（诗歌书）	《约伯记》(*Job*)、《诗篇》(*Psalms*)、《箴言》(*Proverbs*)、《传道书》(*Ecclesiastes*)、《雅歌》(*Song of Songs*)
先知书17卷	大先知书5卷：《以赛亚书》(*Isaiah*)、《耶利米书》(*Jeremiah*)、《耶利米哀歌》(*Lamentations*)、《以西结书》(*Ezekiel*,)、《但以理书》(*Daniel*)
	小先知书12卷：《何西阿书》(*Hosea*)、《约珥书》(*Joel*)、《阿摩司书》(*Amos*)、《俄巴底亚书》(*Obadiah*)、《约拿书》(*Jonah*)、《弥迦书》(*Micah*)、《那鸿书》(*Nahum*)、《哈巴谷书》(*Habakkuk*)、《西番雅书》(*Zephaniah*)、《哈该书》(*Haggai*)、《撒迦利亚书》(*Zechariah*)、《玛拉基书》(*Malachi*)

2.《新约》的编排方式

《新约全书》正典共有27卷，可以分为四个类型。其中《以弗所书》、《腓立比书》、《歌罗西书》和《腓利门书》这四卷书又被称为"狱中书信"，因为它们被认为是作者在监狱被囚时所写的。

福音书4卷	《马太福音》(*Matthew*)、《马可福音》(*Mark*)、《路加福音》(*Luke*)、《约翰福音》(*John*)
历史书1卷	《使徒行传》(*Acts*)
新约书信21卷	保罗书信14卷：《罗马书》(*Romans*)、《哥林多前书》(*1 Corinthians*)、《哥林多后书》(*2 Corinthians*)、《加拉太书》(*Galatians*)、《以弗所书》(*Ephesians*)、《腓立比书》(*Philippians*)、《歌罗西书》(*Colossian*)、《帖撒罗尼迦前书》(*1 Thessalonians*)、《帖撒罗尼迦后书》(*2 Thessalonians*)、《提摩太前书》(*1 Timothy*)、《提摩太后书》(*2 Timothy*)、《提多书》(*Titus*)、《腓利门书》(*Philemon*)、《希伯来书》(*Hebrews*)
	大公书信7卷：《雅各书》(*James*)、《彼得前书》(*1 Peter*)、《彼得后书》(*2 Peter*)、《约翰一书》(*1 John*)、《约翰二书》(*2 John*)、《约翰三书》(*3 John*)、《犹大书》(*Jude*)
启示著作1卷	《启示录》(*Revelation*)

以上编排是对《圣经》各卷的大致分类。其中，《希伯来书》的作者仍存疑问。《圣经》文本还有很多分类形式，如就文学类别来讲，《旧约》呈现出以下几种文学形式：(1)诗歌，其形式又可细分为庆祝胜利的诗歌、祝福和诅咒诗、哀歌、情歌等；(2)诗化散文，其形式又可细分为神话、奇迹故事和民间故事、寓言和比喻、短篇故事和小说等；(3)历史，其形式又可细分为传说、年鉴、历史记载等。《新约》的文学形式又可细分为传记、书信、家谱等。

3.《圣经》的主要版本

《旧约》早期最重要的译本是出现在公元前3—前2世纪期间的希腊文《七十子希腊译本》(*Septuagint*)，是为了那些只懂希腊文、已经不能读懂《希伯来圣经》的散居的犹太人而翻译的。这个译本成为早期教会使用的权威《旧约》。中世纪在欧洲通行的《圣经》是罗马教父哲罗姆翻译的《通俗拉丁译本》(*Vulgate*)。近代以来影响最大的英文译本是1611年出版的"钦定本"(*The Authorized Version*)，又称"詹姆斯王本"(*King James Bible*)。该版本很快就在英语世界得到普及，在现代也不断被修订。比较著名的现代英文译本有：(1)美国版《圣经》：1952年出版的 *Revised Standard Version*（《美国标准修订本》）；1971年出版的 *New American Standard Bible*（《新美国标准圣经");1990年又推出了 *New Revised Standard Version*(《新修订标准版》);(2)英国版《圣经》:1978年出版的 *New International Bible*(《新国际版圣经》),2002年又推出了 *Today's New International Version*(《今日新国际版》)。这两类《圣经》版本的主要差别不在内容上,只是体现在"英式英语"和"美式英语"的不同风格上。此外,1976年出版的 *Today's English Version*(《今日英语圣经》,又称 *Good News Bible*《福音圣经》)、1982年出版的 *New King James Version*(《新詹姆斯王本》)、1985年出版的 *The New Jerusalem Bible*(《新耶路撒冷圣经》)也很著名。

中文《圣经》版本中,初版于1919年的"官话和合本"《新旧约全书》(简称"和合本",1988年修订)迄今依然是在中国大陆最为通用的新教译本。1968年在香港印行的"思高本"《圣经》迄今仍然是天主教通用的《圣经》译本。分别于1979年和1992年在香港出版发行的《圣经现代译本》和《圣经新译本》,也逐渐为大陆人士所熟悉。

二、《圣经》里的宏观历史脉络

《圣经》文本兼具宗教性、历史性和文学性。《圣经》虽然涉及内容庞多,但是历史线索还是比较清晰的。为了对《圣经》史话有一条清楚的历史线索,我们采用"旧约年表"和"新约年表"的方式分别加以勾勒。

1.《旧约》年表[1]
公元前1950—前1700年左右: 以色列族长亚伯拉罕、以撒、雅各的时代
公元前1700—前1290年左右: 以色列人在埃及
公元前1290—前1250年左右: 摩西带以色列人出埃及
公元前1250—前1225年左右: 约书亚率以色列人征服迦南
公元前1225—前1025年左右: 士师时期
公元前1025—前1010年左右: 扫罗王朝,先知撒母耳
公元前1010—前970年左右: 大卫王朝,先知拿单
公元前970—前931年左右: 所罗门王朝
所罗门死后以色列王国分裂为二: 南部的犹大国与北部的以色列国
公元前931—前722(撒玛利亚失陷): 南部犹大国
公元前931—前586年(耶路撒冷失陷): 北部以色列国
公元前586—538年: 犹太人的"巴比伦之囚"
公元前538年: 返回耶路撒冷
公元前458年: 以斯拉进行宗教改革
公元前445年: 尼希米进行宗教改革

2.《新约》年表
公元前6年: 天使预言施洗约翰的诞生。
公元前5年: 天使向童女马利亚预言耶稣的诞生;施洗约翰出生;耶稣诞生。
公元前4年: 耶稣父母带耶稣进圣殿拜主;耶稣全家逃往埃及;从埃及回到拿撒勒。

---

1. 参考卓新平著:《圣经鉴赏》,北京: 宗教文化出版社,2000年,第61-62页。本年表有所简化。

公元8年：耶稣12岁时进圣殿听道。

公元27年：耶稣受洗；耶稣在旷野受魔鬼试探；耶稣在耶路撒冷过第一个逾越节，在犹太地布道；耶稣经撒玛利亚回到加利利。

公元28年：耶稣在加利利开始公开的传道活动，招收第一批门徒(收彼得等四徒)；耶稣回到耶路撒冷过第二个逾越节；在加利利登山训众论福(登山宝训)；在加利利治病、布道；关于撒种、稗子等比喻；耶稣差遣十二使徒；施洗约翰因责备希律王而被斩头。

公元29年：耶稣在加利利过第三个逾越节；预言自己受难并复活。

公元30年：耶稣往约旦河外去布道；论拉萨路复活；耶稣骑驴进入耶路撒冷，受到民众欢迎；星期一，耶稣洁净圣殿；星期四，最后的晚餐(与门徒一道过最后一个逾越节，设立圣餐)；星期五，耶稣受审，被钉十字架；星期日，耶稣复活；耶稣复活后数次向门徒和义人显现；复活后40天耶稣升天，第50天圣灵降临，门徒们领受圣灵而开始传教，建立教会。

公元35年(一说37年)：大数城的扫罗改宗归主，易名保罗。

公元37年：保罗作为基督徒第一次访问耶路撒冷。

公元37—45年：保罗早期在大数传教。

公元44—46年：保罗在安提阿和耶路撒冷从事传教活动。

公元45年(或60年)：雅各写书信。

公元46—48年：保罗第一次传教旅行。

公元50年左右：耶路撒冷教会会议。

公元51—53年：保罗第二次传教旅行。

公元52年左右：《帖撒罗尼加前书》、《帖撒罗尼加后书》、《加拉太书》写成。

公元54—58年：保罗第三次传教旅行。

公元56年：《哥林多前书》写成。

公元57年：《哥林多后书》写成。

公元58年：《罗马书》写成，保罗被捕。

公元56—60年：保罗被监禁在该撒利亚。

公元60年：保罗向非斯都上诉，保罗被带进罗马城。

公元61年：保罗被监禁在罗马。

公元62年：《以弗所书》、《歌罗西书》、《腓利门书》写成。

公元63年：《腓利比书》写成。

公元63—64年：保罗从监狱获得释放。

公元64年：《提摩太前书》写成。

公元65年：《马可福音》、《提多书》、《彼得前书》写成。

公元67年：保罗第二次被逮捕；《提摩太后书》写成。

公元68年左右：彼得和保罗在罗马遇害殉道。

公元75年左右：《马太福音》、《路加福音》写成。

公元77年左右：《使徒行传》写成。

公元85年左右：《希伯来书》写成。

公元90—100年：《约翰福音》写成。

公元90年以后：《犹大书》、《启示录》、《约翰一书》、《约翰二书》、《约翰三书》、《彼得后书》写成。

三、犹太民族与《圣经》

犹太民族古称希伯来民族(Hebrew)。一般认为,《旧约》里的希伯来民族起源于底格里斯河与幼发拉底河之间的一条狭窄的河谷地带,《创世记》就提到亚伯兰一家曾经定居该地带南部的吾珥(Ur,现今伊拉克南部境内),后来由吾珥北迁到哈兰地区居住了一段时间。根据《圣经》记载,亚伯兰与耶和华神立约后改名为"亚伯拉罕",并按照神的旨意迁居迦南地。古代的迦南(Canaan),又称古巴勒斯坦,地处地中海与约旦河之间(见右图)。

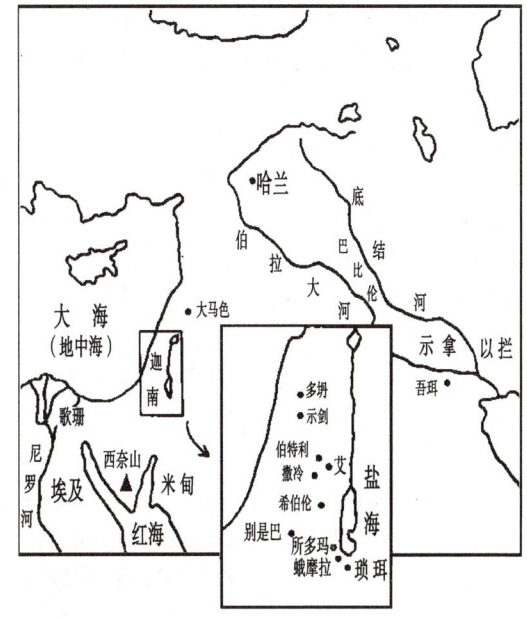

《圣经》里所记载的希伯来民族历史可以分为9个时期[1]:

1. 族长时期 (The Patriarchal Period)

大约公元前18世纪前后,亚伯拉罕离开吾珥进入迦南时,当时受埃及控制的这一地区已经生活着几个民族和部落。西北有腓尼基人,中西部低地平原被迦南本地人占据,稍往东北则生活着亚摩利人。位于约旦河谷地和沿海平原之间的中部山区,人口相对稀少。这一地区虽不宜农耕,但适合放牧,所以亚伯拉罕和他的后代以撒、雅各三代就生活在这里。他们主要通过和当地人立约、协商的方式,和平地占据了一些土地;还有一些则是以武力从亚摩利人手中夺过来的。从亚伯拉罕到雅各的三代人之间,是犹太史上的族长时期,亚伯拉罕、雅各和约瑟即是犹太史上的三位族长。需要注意的一条历史线索是,由于诸种原因,雅各之子约瑟,被哥哥们卖到了埃及。《圣经》与该时期相关的书卷是《创世记》。

2. 摩西时期 (The Mosaic Period)

雅各的后代离开迦南投靠已为埃及高官的约瑟,并在埃及生息约400年。在后一段时间,由于约瑟及兄弟们的后代人数众多,另外埃及法老已经不熟悉约瑟是何人物,便开始剥削压迫希伯来人,让他们做苦力。摩西接受上帝召唤成功拯救族人出埃及。不管有多少神话和不实成分,出埃及标志着希伯来民族历史的转折点。摩西把希伯来族人带回到亚伯拉罕曾居住过的迦南定居下来。当时被称为迦南的这块土地,在以色列人的心目中一直是"以色列故土",被他们称之为"以色列地",自罗马统治后才改称"巴勒斯坦"。公元前13世纪到11世纪之间,以色列人征服迦南时,生活在这一地区的民族除了迦南本地各部落及亚摩利人、腓尼基人外,还有亚玛力人、亚扪人、摩押人、以东人等民族。此外,几乎与以色列人同时进入迦南的海上民族非利士人,占据了迦南西部一片肥沃的平原,在此后的很长一段时间里他们一直威胁着以色列人的安全。对迦南

---

1. 关于希伯来民族历史的阶段划分,参照了许鼎新著《希伯来民族简史》,金陵协和神学院出版发行,2001年,第2版。

的征服是从摩西的继承人约书亚开始的，大约始于公元前13世纪中期。与该时期相关的《圣经》书卷是《出埃及》、《民数记》、《约书亚记》、《士师记》。

3. 士师时期(The Period of the Judges)

从公元前13世纪中期到大约公元前1028年扫罗为王，以色列民族12支派进入士师执政时期，史称"士师时代"。这一期间，以色列没有统一的首领。当某个支派受到威胁时(往往是一次外族入侵)，常常会有一个既有勇气又有智慧的人挺身而出，组织整个支派对外作战并取得胜利，于是他自然而然地被选为该支派的军事首领，并取得其他一些权力。这些人被称为"士师"。和平时期他们的角色类似"仲裁者"。士师所统率的民众往往限于一个或几个支派，其权力在一定时期可能会高于长老会或公众议会，却仍未能凌驾于所有支派之上，成为整个以色列民族的领袖。士师的职位既非世袭继承，也不一定有连续性，一个士师死后，如果社会安定，没有外来危害，很可能就无人继了。与该时期相关的《圣经》书卷《士师记》直接记载了这一时期没有律法、没有国王的混乱局面。另外，《路得记》正是以士师活动的这一时期为背景来折射公元前三世纪的宗教斗争和社会问题。

4. 统一王国时期(The Period of the United Kingdom)

士师权力的局限性和不稳定性决定了他们无法改变以色列各支派各自为政的分裂局面，这种局面在四周敌国虎视眈眈的生存环境中，显然隐伏着灭亡的危机，在与非利士人的战争中，这种危机得到了彻底的显露。在战争中，以色列人遭到非利士人痛击，他们发现对方统一作战具有优势，便要求当时的先知撒母耳，为他们立王。首先被撒母耳立为王的是便雅悯支派的扫罗。自扫罗为王起，以色列人便进入统一王国时期(公元前1028年—前931年)。公元前1006年，扫罗战死，儿子伊施波设继位，而犹大部落则借着撒母耳的支持，推本支派的大卫为王。几年后，伊施波设遇刺，以色列各支派便推大卫为全以色列的国王，大卫建都耶路撒冷，以色列统一王国由此日益兴盛。大卫在位时，继续对外作战。扩大了王国的版图，到大卫停止对外征战时，以色列统一王国的国土已经东临阿拉伯沙漠，西抵地中海，北起叙利亚的加低斯，南到红海岸边的以甸迦别。大卫之后，其子所罗门继承王位。所罗门统治期间，完成了耶路撒冷圣殿的建造，进一步巩固了王权，加强了以色列统一王国以经商为主的对外交往，使以色列统一王国在当时的中东享有很高的地位。

5. 分国时期(The Period of Divided Kingdom)

公元前931年，所罗门去世，其子罗波安继位。以色列民众对这位新王寄以希望，请求他减轻赋税，结果却遭到断然拒绝。民众转而拥立反叛的耶罗波安为王，于是以色列统一王国正式一分为二，北方10个支派归顺耶罗波安，史称以色列王国或北方王国；南方犹大和便雅悯两个支派仍忠于罗波安的统治，称犹大王国或南方王国。北方王国存在200多年，于公元前722年被亚述灭亡；南方王国存在350年左右，于公元前586年被新巴比伦灭亡。《圣经》与该时期相关的书卷是《撒母耳记》(上、下)、《列王纪》(上、下)、《历代志》(上、下)。

6. 被掳时期(The Exilic Period)

新巴比伦王国攻占犹大王国后，将其大批上层人士和知识分子掳到王国的其他地方，尤其是首都巴比伦，此事在以色列人历史上被称为"巴比伦之囚"。自此时起直到公元前538年，以色列人进入其历史上为期近半个世纪的被掳时期。从"巴比伦之囚"直到亚历山大征服时代,"以色列人"这一称呼逐渐被"犹太人"所取代。但此后的犹太人实际上是犹大王国子民的后代,因为北方王国的以色列人早已被异族同化。《圣经》中许多经卷与这段历史有关,如《耶利米哀歌》、《诗篇》、《但以理书》等。

7. 波斯时期(The Persian Period)

在该阶段,犹太人处于波斯帝国统治之下。新巴比伦对西亚的统治并没有维持很久。当它取代埃及占领西亚时,其西北米底王国境内爆发了由波斯人居鲁士领导的起义。居鲁士推翻了米底人的统治,建立了波斯帝国。公元前538年,波斯王居鲁士征服新巴比伦,此后直到公元前331年,犹太人便处于波斯统治之下。犹太人回到耶路撒冷后,很快投身于重建圣殿的工程,在公元前516年完工,历时20余年,史称第二圣殿。第二圣殿的建造过程本身,就是一个将犹太人逐渐凝聚在一起的过程。此外,圣殿的重建象征着遭受灭顶之灾的犹太人的重新崛起,是犹太民族不屈不挠的再生精神的具体体现。这一时期的犹太民族,政治上隶属波斯帝国,祭司和文士等宗教上层取代了王族和先知掌握着这个政教合一的联合体的领导权。《圣经》中的相关书卷是《以斯帖记》、《以斯拉书》、《尼希米书》。

8. 希腊时期(The Greek Period)

该阶段是犹太文化与希腊文化碰撞、融合的时期。亚历山大进入耶路撒冷的时间是公元前332年,犹太人的历史从此进入由希腊人统治的"希腊化时期"(公元前332年至前173年)。公元前334年,希腊马其顿国王亚历山大挺进西亚,希腊文化也随着他的铁骑大规模传入西亚,犹太人面临着又一次的考验。亚历山大立志把传播希腊思想和文化当作自己的天职,由此西亚各地进入"希腊化"时期,各民族大多被迫或自愿接受希腊文化。公元前330年,亚历山大灭波斯,巴勒斯坦成为亚历山大帝国的领土。公元前323年亚历山大死后,帝国领土顷刻间分崩离析,被他的几个将军分而占之。巴勒斯坦地区先后臣服于以埃及为中心的托勒密王朝和以叙利亚为中心的塞琉古王朝。托勒密王朝似乎比较宽容,没有采取强制性的措施迫使犹太人放弃自己的传统,因此希腊化运动对巴勒斯坦的犹太人影响不大,他们享有相当的宗教信仰自由。随着希腊化时代的开始,犹太教在外来文化和本民族传统撞击、融汇的大潮中,日趋分化成诸多派别,初期基督教即是其中之一。基督教诞生时,希腊化已经持续了300多年,希腊语成为当时地中海世界的通用语言。在这种背景下,希腊哲学难免在基督教神学里留下深深的痕迹,其中柏拉图主义和斯多葛主义的影响尤为明显。《圣经》与该时期相关的书卷是《传道书》、《约拿书》、《约伯记》等。

9. 罗马时期(The Roman Period)

基督教的诞生和传播就在该时期(右图为耶稣时代的巴勒斯坦)。约公元前67年,罗马派军队占领了巴勒斯

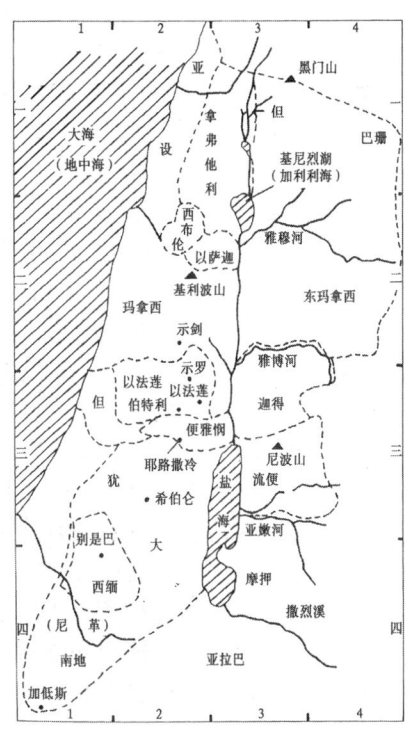

坦地区，犹太人从此又一次沦为异族臣民。犹太民族的历史进入了罗马统治时期。罗马人起初并不排斥当地的传统统治制度，只是要把占领地区划为行省，因此他们承认大祭司在犹太社会的司法管辖权。在公元前63年前后的20年间，以土买人安提帕德被罗马皇帝恺撒立为犹大区总督，并授予罗马公民的身份；他的儿子大希律被安东尼委派做犹大地区的王。希律死后犹大地区由罗马巡抚直接统治，完全成为罗马帝国的一个行省。相继到任的罗马巡抚有彼拉多、腓力斯和非斯都，前者见于福音书，后二者见于《使徒行传》，他们都以贪婪残忍著称。

自从希腊化后，犹太教文化与希腊文化不断碰撞，终于于公元1世纪在巴勒斯坦地区产生了一种新的宗教——基督教。《新约》就记载了基督教产生的过程以及耶稣及其门徒传教的过程，其中部分涉及保罗等使徒如何把基督教从巴勒斯坦传到罗马，又如何在罗马遭到迫害。《圣经》与该时期相关的书卷是《福音书》、《使徒行传》、《启示录》等。

走出《圣经》历史的犹太人的命运是怎样的呢？为反抗罗马的统治，犹太人进行过多次起义，尤其是公元70年和135年的最后两次大起义，历史上称为"犹太战争"。在这两次战争和历次的起义中，被屠杀的犹太人至少在一百五十万以上。剩余幸存的犹太人被迫逃出巴勒斯坦，向世界各地流散，从而进入长达近一千九百年的民族大流散时期(The Dispersion Period)。

四、《圣经》与西方文化

在向世界流散的过程中，犹太人一直把自己的宗教经典带在身边，因而《圣经》的影响波及很多民族。近代以来，基督教在世界范围内传播，也使《圣经》被翻译成多种民族语言，并在西方基督教民族和国家中得到广泛普及，不仅成为西方文学家和艺术家创作的灵感之源，而且渗透到人们的日常生活、行为规范、精神气质之中。歌德早就预言，世界可以按它的步伐飞速前进，人类的科学可以向着最高的阶段发展，但却没有任何东西可以取代《圣经》的地位。作为中国读者，我们肯定要问：《圣经》为什么具有如此大的影响力？作为一部书，《圣经》为什么能够从犹太教—基督教的宗教经典，成为西方文化的源泉，对西方文化乃至世界文化产生如此大的影响？这关键是由《圣经》文本自身决定的。《圣经》除了特有的意识形态色彩外，还具有"文化母本"的地位，而正是《圣经》作为文化母本的涵育作用，滋养和塑造了西方文化乃至世界文化。

在对《圣经》的传统解读中，《圣经》的宗教属性往往被视为其首要属性。而事实上，《圣经》还涵括了希伯来人早期生活中的各种世俗要素，其中既有具体的生活细节，也有各种观念情感。基于此，《圣经》已经被称为希伯来民族生活和思想的百科全书。作为犹太人的文化范本，《圣经》所浓缩的各种文化要素具有鲜明的恒定意义，诸如生活与生产、生与死、爱与恨、个人与世界、本族与异族、现在与未来、精神与物质、世俗与宗教等，这些都是人类生活的持久性内容和一般范畴。从这个意义上讲，《圣经》的意义和影响业已超越了犹太文化的范畴，它已经成为一部世界性文化经典，在文化多元的现代社会仍将发挥不可替代的作用。

作为文本的《圣经》并不是自足封闭的，而是开放的。《圣经》文本的开放性主要指：(1)《圣经》文本有很强的象征意义，这种象征意义与文字意义之间产生了巨大张力，从而导致《圣经》意义的多元化和文本阐释的开放性。(2)《圣经》文本的叙述中有很多空白点，对这些空白点的添补是开放性的。(3)诠释者的开放态度也赋予《圣经》文本更大的开放性。《圣经》文本的开放性不仅给西方艺术家提供了灵感的源泉，也可以使读者依照自己的兴趣和视角去"填充"《圣经》文本意义的"空缺"。需要强调的是，不同的读者根据不同的目的会对《圣经》作出不同的解读,但并非所有的解读都是基于对《圣经》的正确理解,如西方一些政治家不顾及《圣经》文本的语境,从中寻词摘句,对其政治目的加以"圣化",对此我们应仔细分辨。作为当代的中国大学生,我们的学习和研究的重心是《圣经》本身所蕴含的文化要素以及《圣经》对西方文化的影响,如对经济思想、教育理念、法律传统、文学艺术、建筑音乐等的影响。所以,我们希望同学们都能以开放的姿态和赏析的视角,通过主动的学习和积极的思考,正确认识西方文化中的《圣经》底蕴,正确识别西方文化中的基督教符号,以《圣经》为切入点,通识西方文化,培养自身的文化交流能力,为推动中西文化交流作出应有的贡献。

第一讲

希伯来神话故事：《创世记》（上）

The Hebrew Mythical Stories from *Genesis*

一、导读：希伯来主要神话及其特点

《创世记》(*Genesis*)是《旧约》的首卷，汇集了希伯来人的远古神话与传说，文学色彩浓重，可以说是圣经文学的开端。全卷计50章，为散文体。以第11章第9节为界，分为两部分：第一部分记述上帝创造万物和人类始祖的经过，包括"上帝六日创世"、"亚当夏娃在伊甸园"、"该隐、亚伯兄弟阋墙"、"挪亚方舟避洪水"、"人类建造巴别塔"等神话和传说。第二部分叙述希伯来族长亚伯拉罕及其子孙的生平传奇。这些神话、传说和传奇故事主要体现了古希伯来人对宇宙创始、人类起源、语言生成和民族来历等问题的思考，不仅在犹太教和基督教的神学领域中占有重要地位，而且在人类文化史上也颇具认识价值。

本讲选取《创世记》第一部分中五个神话故事和传说：
1. 创造世界：上帝在六日内创造了世界、万物和人类。
2. 伊甸园：亚当和夏娃在伊甸园未抵制住蛇的诱惑，偷吃"禁果"，被上帝逐出伊甸园。
3. 第一桩谋杀：亚当、夏娃的长子该隐因嫉妒杀死弟弟亚伯。
4. 挪亚方舟：挪亚建造巨大的方舟并带领全家和成对儿的动物躲避大洪水。
5. 巴别塔：人类企图建造高耸入云的巴别塔，结果被上帝变乱语言，流散各地。

二、选文及注释

Part 1

The Creation of the World

In the beginning God created the heaven and the earth. And the earth was without form, and void[1]; and darkness was upon the face of the deep[2]. And the Spirit of God[3] moved upon the face of the waters. And God said, "Let there be light": and there was light. And God saw the light, that it was good: and God divided the light from the darkness. And God called the light Day, and the darkness he called Night. And the evening and the morning[4] were the first day.

And God said, "Let there be a firmament[5] in the midst of the waters, and let it divide the waters from the waters." And God made the firmament, and divided the waters which

---

1. void /vɔɪd/ *adj.* empty; containing no matter 虚空的
2. the deep *n.* (黑暗所笼罩的)深渊。形容创世之前，上帝从虚无中创世，这是希腊化以后的玄学解释。
3. the Spirit of God 上帝的灵。希伯来原文中的"灵"还表示"风"。
4. the evening and the morning 此处将夜晚置于早晨之前，因为古希伯来人以黄昏为一天的开始。
5. firmament /ˈfɜːməmənt/ *n.* the heaven or sky 苍穹；天空。古希伯来人如我国古人认为天似穹窿。

were under the firmament from the waters which were above the firmament: and it was so. And God called the firmament Heaven. And the evening and the morning were the second day.

And God said, "Let the waters under the heaven be gathered together unto one place, and let the dry land appear": and it was so. And God called the dry land Earth; and the gathering together of the waters called he Seas: and God saw that it was good. And God said, "Let the earth bring forth grass, the herb yielding seed, and the fruit tree yielding fruit after his kind, whose seed is in itself, upon the earth": and it was so. And the earth brought forth grass, and herb yielding seed after his kind, and the tree yielding fruit, whose seed was in itself, after his kind: and God saw that it was good. And the evening and the morning were the third day.

And God said, "Let there be lights in the firmament of the heaven to divide the day from the night; and let them be for signs, and for seasons, and for days, and years[1]: and let them be for lights in the firmament of the heaven to give light upon the earth": and it was so.

And God made two great lights; the greater light to rule the day, and the lesser light to rule the night: he made the stars also. And God set them in the firmament of the heaven to give light upon the earth, and to rule over the day and over the night, and to divide the light from the darkness: and God saw that it was good. And the evening and the morning were the fourth day.

And God said, "Let the waters bring forth abundantly the moving creature that hath[2] life, and fowl that may fly above the earth in the open firmament of heaven." And God created great whales, and every living creature that moveth, which the waters brought forth abundantly, after their kind, and every winged fowl after his kind: and God saw that it was good. And God blessed them, saying, "Be fruitful, and multiply, and fill the waters in the seas, and let fowl multiply in the earth." And the evening and the morning were the fifth day.

And God said, "Let the earth bring forth the living creature after his kind, cattle, and creeping thing, and beast of the earth after his kind": and it was so. And God made the beast of the earth after his kind, and cattle after their kind, and every thing that creepeth upon the earth after his kind: and God saw that it was good.

And God said, "Let us make man in our image[3], after our likeness: and let them have dominion over[4] the fish of the sea, and over the fowl of the air and over the cattle, and over all the earth, and over every creeping thing that creepeth upon the earth." So God created man in his own image, in the image of God created he him; male and female created he them[5]. And God blessed them, and God said unto them, "Be fruitful, and multiply, and replenish the earth, and subdue it[6]: and have dominion over the fish of the sea, and over the fowl of the air, and over every living thing that moveth upon the earth." And God said, "Behold[7], I have given you every herb bearing seed, which is upon the face of all the earth, and every tree,

---

1. let them be for signs, and for seasons, and for days, and years 这些光体要作为记号, 定节令、日子和年岁。
2. hath *vt.*〈古〉have 的第三人称单数现在时用法, 同 has。下面出现的动词 creepeth、moveth 分别是 creep、move 的第三人称单数用法, 即 creeps、 moves。
3. in our image 按照我们的形象(上帝在和天使们说话)。此为《圣经》中一重要思想, 显示出上帝与人类有相同之处。
4. have dominion over 对……有控制权
5. in the image of God created he him; male and female created he them 这两句均是倒装句。正常语序应为: he created him (man) in the image of God, and he created them (male and female)。
6. replenish the earth, and subdue it (人类要)充满大地, 征服大地。replenish *vt.* to fill 充满; subdue *vt.* to conquer and subjugate; vanquish 征服; 使屈从。
7. behold (祈使语气)看哪!

in the which[1] is the fruit of a tree yielding seed; to you it shall be for meat. And to every beast of the earth, and to every fowl of the air, and to every thing that creepeth upon the earth, wherein[2] there is life, I have given every green herb for meat": and it was so. And God saw every thing that he had made, and, behold, it was very good. And the evening and the morning were the sixth day.

Thus the heavens and the earth were finished, and all the host[3] of them. And on the seventh day God ended his work which he had made; and he rested on the seventh day from all his work which he had made. And God blessed the seventh day, and sanctified[4] it: because that in it he had rested from all his work which God created and made. (1:1-23)

Part 2

The Garden of Eden[5]

In the day that the LORD God[6] made the earth and the heavens, and every plant of the field before it was in the earth, and every herb of the field before it grew: for the LORD God had not caused it to rain upon the earth, and there was not a man to till[7] the ground. But there went up a mist from the earth and watered the whole face of the ground. And the LORD God formed man of[8] the dust of the ground, and breathed into his nostrils the breath of life; and man became a living soul.

And the LORD God planted a garden eastward in Eden; and there he put the man whom he had formed. And out of the ground made the LORD God to grow every tree that is pleasant to the sight, and good for food; the tree of life[9] also in the midst of the garden, and the tree of knowledge of good and evil[10]. And a river went out of Eden to water the garden; and from thence[11] it was parted, and became into four heads. …

And the LORD God took the man, and put him into the garden of Eden to dress[12] it and to keep it. And the LORD God commanded the man, saying, "Of every tree of the garden thou mayest[13] freely eat: but of the tree of the knowledge of good and evil, thou shalt not eat of[14] it: for in the day that thou eatest thereof[15] thou shalt surely die."

---

1. in the which 非限制性定语从句，相当于 in which 或者 where
2. wherein *adv.* in which 在其中
3. host *n.* a great number 一大群；许多
4. sanctify /ˈsæŋktəfaɪ/ *vt.* to declare holy 使神圣
5. Eden /ˈiːdn/ 音译"伊甸"，意思是"丰美"。the garden of Eden 伊甸园，又称"地堂"，与"天堂"相对。意思同源自希腊语 paradeisos的 paradise（乐园）。
6. the LORD God 上帝耶和华。希伯来原文4个辅音字母 YHWH 首次出现在"伊甸园"故事中，读作 Yahweh /ˈjɑːweɪ/（德语为 Jahweh；中文音译"雅赫威"、"雅威"、"亚卫"），一般认为此名源于古希伯来语词根 hwh，意思是"在"、"是"、"生"。基督教新教将其翻译成英文时大部分译为 the Lord God, 有的英译本专门把 Lord 大写，用 the LORD God 或 the LORD 取代希伯来文 Yahweh 及其基督教读法 Jehovah /dʒɪˈhəʊvə/。
7. till *vt.* to prepare or cultivate (land) for crops 耕作；耕种
8. of *prep.* 相当于 by, 由；从中
9. the tree of life 生命树。吃了树上的果子可以长生不死。
10. the tree of knowledge of good and evil 辨善恶的智慧树。所结的果子被称为"禁果"（forbidden fruit）。
11. from thence 由此处。
12. dress *vt.* to cultivate (land or plants) 整治(土地)
13. thou mayest 〈古〉thou 是第二人称代词的古用法。第二人称单数的主格、宾格、所有格、所有格代词分别为: thou, thee, thy, thine; 第二人称复数主格、宾格、所有格、所有格代词分别为: you, ye, your, yours。情态动词和一般动词在第二人称单数现在时的情况下，通常词尾加上est, 如 may, eat 分别写作 mayest, eatest。
14. eat of "动词+of"是古英语动词用法，相对于及物动词 eat。下节的 brought of 同。
15. thereof *adv.* 将它

And the LORD God said, "It is not good that the man should be alone; I will make him an help meet for him[1]." And out of the ground the LORD God formed every beast of the field, and every fowl of the air; and brought them unto Adam[2] to see what he would call them: and whatsoever Adam called every living creature, that was the name thereof. And Adam gave names to all cattle, and to the fowl of the air, and to every beast of the field; but for Adam there was not found an help meet for him.

And the LORD God caused a deep sleep to fall upon Adam, and he slept: and he took one of his ribs, and closed up the flesh instead thereof; and the rib, which the LORD God had taken from man, made he a woman, and brought her unto the man.

And Adam said,

"This is now bone of my bones,
And flesh of my flesh:
She shall be called Woman,
Because she was taken out of Man."

Therefore shall a man leave his father and his mother, and shall cleave unto his wife: and they shall be one flesh. And they were both naked, the man and his wife, and were not ashàmed.

Now the serpent was more subtil[3] than any beast of the field which the LORD God had made.

And he said unto the woman, "Yea, hath God said, 'Ye shall not eat of every tree of the garden'?"

And the woman said unto the serpent, "We may eat of the fruit of the trees of the garden: but of the fruit of the tree which is in the midst of the garden, God hath said, 'Ye shall not eat of it, neither shall ye touch it, lest ye die.'"

And the serpent said unto the woman, "Ye shall not surely die: for God doth[4] know that in the day ye eat thereof, then your eyes shall be opened, and ye shall be as gods[5], knowing good and evil."

And when the woman saw that the tree was good for food, and that it was pleasant to the eyes, and a tree to be desired to make one wise, she took of the fruit thereof, and did eat, and gave also unto her husband with her[6]; and he did eat. And the eyes of them both were opened, and they knew that they were naked; and they sewed fig leaves[7] together, and made themselves aprons.

And they heard the voice of the LORD God walking in the garden in the cool of the day: and Adam and his wife hid themselves from the presence of the LORD God amongst the trees of the garden.

And the LORD God called unto Adam, and said unto him, "Where art thou?[8]"

---

1. an help meet for him 适合亚当的帮手 meet *adj.* fitting; proper 合适的; 般配的。
2. Adam /ˈædəm/ 音译"亚当", 意思是"人"。喻人类始祖。
3. subtil *adj.* 〈古〉crafty; cunning 阴险的; 狡猾的
4. doth 〈古〉do 的第三人称单数一般现在式
5. gods 指上帝身边的天使。通常上帝不直接和人类接触, 派天使与人交往。
6. her husband with her 和女人(夏娃)在一起的丈夫(亚当)。吃禁果时亚当和夏娃正在一起。
7. fig leaves 无花果树叶。
8. Where art thou? 〈古〉art 是系动词 be 的第二人称单数现在陈述语气。

And he said, "I heard thy voice in the garden, and I was afraid, because I was naked; and I hid myself."

And he said, "Who told thee that thou wast[1] naked? Hast thou eaten of the tree[2], whereof I commanded thee that thou shouldest not eat?"

And the man said, "The woman whom thou gavest to be with me, she gave me of the tree, and I did eat."

And the LORD God said unto the woman, "What is this that thou hast done?"

And the woman said, "The serpent beguiled[3] me, and I did eat."

And the LORD God said unto the serpent,

"Because thou hast done this,
   Thou art cursed above all cattle,
   And above every beast of the field;
   Upon thy belly shalt thou go,
   And dust shalt thou eat
   All the days of thy life:
   And I will put enmity[4] between thee and the woman,
   And between thy seed and her seed[5];
   It shall bruise thy head,
   And thou shalt bruise his heel."

Unto the woman he said,

   "I will greatly multiply thy sorrow and thy conception[6];
   In sorrow thou shalt bring forth children;
   And thy desire shall be to thy husband[7],
   And he shall rule over thee."

And unto Adam he said,
"Because thou hast hearkened[8] unto the voice of thy wife, and hast eaten of the tree, of which I commanded thee, saying, 'Thou shalt not eat of it':
   Cursed is the ground for thy sake;
   In sorrow shalt thou eat of it all the days of thy life;
   Thorns also and thistles[9] shall it bring forth to thee;
   And thou shalt eat the herb of the field;
   In the sweat of thy face[10] shalt thou eat bread,
   Till thou return unto the ground;
   For out of it wast thou taken:
   For dust thou art,
   And unto dust shalt thou return."

And Adam called his wife's name Eve[11]; because she was the mother of all living. Unto Adam also and to his wife did the LORD God make coats of skins, and clothed them.

And the LORD God said, "Behold, the man is become[12] as one of us, to know good and evil: and now, lest he put forth his hand, and take also of the tree of life, and eat, and

---

1. wast 〈古〉系动词 be 的过去式，用于第二人称单数
2. Hast thou eaten of the tree 你们吃了智慧树的果子了吗？下文有 she gave me of the tree 都省略了 the fruit (of the tree)。
3. beguile /bɪˈgaɪl/ vt. to deceive; delude 诓骗；诱惑
4. enmity n. deep-seated, often mutual hatred 敌意；憎恨
5. seed n. offspring 子孙；后代
6. conception n. (conceive 的名词形式)怀孕
7. thy desire shall be to thy husband 指妻子依恋丈夫。desire n. 渴望；情欲
8. hearken vi. to listen attentively 听；倾听
9. thistle n. 一种草本植物，长有刺状叶和由刺状苞片围绕的五颜六色的花头。这里泛指难以入口为食的荆棘杂草。
10. in the sweat of thy face 通过劳动和付出；必须汗流满面
11. Eve 音译"夏娃"或"厄娃"(见中国天主教"思高本")，意思是"活"、"生"。比喻"众生之母"，为人类女始祖。
12. is become 同 became。

live for ever": therefore the LORD God sent him forth from the garden of Eden, to till the ground from whence he was taken. So he drove out the man; and he placed at the east of the garden of Eden Cherubims[1], and a flaming sword which turned every way, to keep the way of the tree of life. (2:4–3:24 with 2:11–2:14 omitted)

Part 3

The First Murder

And Adam knew[2] Eve his wife; and she conceived, and bare Cain[3], and said, "I have gotten a man from the LORD." And she again bare his brother Abel[4]. And Abel was a keeper of sheep, but Cain was a tiller of the ground. And in process of time[5] it came to pass[6], that Cain brought of the fruit of the ground an offering[7] unto the LORD. And Abel, he also brought of the firstlings[8] of his flock and of the fat thereof. And the LORD had respect[9] unto Abel and to his offering: but unto Cain and to his offering he had not respect. And Cain was very wroth[10], and his countenance fell[11].

And the LORD said unto Cain, "Why art thou wroth? and why is thy countenance fallen? If thou doest well, shalt thou not be accepted? and if thou doest not well, sin lieth at the door. And unto thee shall be his desire, and thou shalt rule over him."

And Cain talked with Abel his brother: and it came to pass, when they were in the field, that Cain rose up against Abel his brother, and slew him.

And the LORD said unto Cain, "Where is Abel thy brother?"

And he said, "I know not: Am I my brother's keeper?"

And he said, "What hast thou done? the voice of thy brother's blood crieth unto me from the ground. And now art thou cursed from the earth, which hath opened her mouth to receive thy brother's blood from thy hand; when thou tillest the ground, it shall not henceforth[12] yield unto thee her strength; a fugitive[13] and a vagabond[14] shalt thou be in the earth."

And Cain said unto the LORD, "My punishment is greater than I can bear. Behold, thou hast driven me out this day from the face of the earth; and from thy face shall I be hid; and I shall be a fugitive and a vagabond in the earth; and it shall come to pass, that every one that findeth me shall slay me."

And the LORD said unto him, "Therefore whosoever slayeth Cain, vengeance[15] shall be taken on him sevenfold." And the LORD set a mark upon Cain, lest any finding him should kill him. And Cain went out from

---

1. Cherubim /ˈtʃerəbɪm/ 音译"基路伯"、"基路冰",有翅膀的小天使,源自巴比伦神话;意译"神丁"、"神兽"。
2. knew vt. 〈古〉know 的过去时,意思是"相认",婉言发生性关系,如汉语"同房"
3. Cain /keɪn/ 该隐,亚当和夏娃的长子,以农耕为生,他出于妒忌而谋杀了弟弟亚伯
4. Abel /ˈeɪbel/ 亚伯,亚当和夏娃的次子,以放牧为生
5. in process of time 随着时间推移。讲故事常用的词语,引出下一个故事情节。
6. it came to pass (或 it come to pass)表示讲述人稍作停顿,接着讲故事。
7. offering n. a contribution or gift, especially one made at a religious service 祭品
8. firstling n. the first born 头生仔
9. respect n. consideration or appreciation 喜欢; 纳悦
10. wroth adj. wrathful; angry 愤怒的; 生气的
11. his countenance fell (因怒气)一脸阴沉
12. henceforth adv. from this time forth; from now on 从此以后; 今后
13. fugitive n. 逃亡者
14. vagabond /ˈvæɡəbɒnd/ n. 流浪者
15. vengeance n. 复仇; 报仇

the presence of the LORD, and dwelt in the land of Nod[1], on the east of Eden. ...

And Adam knew his wife again; and she bare a son, and called his name Seth[2]: " For God," said she, "hath appointed[3] me another seed instead of Abel, whom Cain slew." And to Seth, to him also there was born a son; and he called his name Enos[4]: then began men to call upon the name of the LORD[5]. (4: 1–16; 4: 25–26)

Part 4

Noah's Ark[6]

Noah was a just man and perfect in his generations, and Noah walked with God. And Noah begat three sons, Shem, Ham, and Japheth.[7]

The earth also was corrupt before God, and the earth was filled with violence. And God looked upon the earth, and behold, it was corrupt; for all flesh had corrupted his way upon the earth.

And God said unto Noah, "The end of all flesh is come before me; for the earth is filled with violence through them; and, behold, I will destroy them with the earth. Make thee an ark of gopher wood[8]; rooms shalt thou make in the ark, and shalt pitch it within and without with pitch[9]. And this is the fashion which thou shalt make it of: The length of the ark shall be three hundred cubits[10], the breadth of it fifty cubits, and the height of it thirty cubits. A window shalt thou make to the ark, and in a cubit shalt thou finish it above; and the door of the ark shalt thou set in the side thereof; with lower, second, and third stories shalt thou make it. And, behold, I, even I, do bring a flood of waters upon the earth, to destroy all flesh, wherein is the breath of life, from under heaven; and every thing that is in the earth shall die. But with thee will I establish my covenant[11]; and thou shalt come into the ark, thou, and thy sons, and thy wife, and thy sons' wives with thee. And of every living thing of all flesh, two of every sort shalt thou bring into the ark, to keep them alive with thee; they shall be male and female. Of fowls after their kind, and of cattle after their kind, of every creeping thing of the earth after his kind, two of every sort shall come unto thee, to keep them alive. And take thou unto thee of all food that is eaten, and thou shalt gather it to thee; and it shall be for food for thee, and for them."

Thus did Noah; according to all that God commanded him, so did he. And the LORD said unto Noah, "Come thou and all thy house into the ark; for thee have I seen righteous before me in this generation. Of

---

1. the land of Nod 诺得之地。Nod 的意思是 "流荡"。
2. Seth 音译 "塞特",意思是 "恩赐",亚当和夏娃的第三个儿子
3. appoint vt. to grant or deign, especially by God (上帝)赐给
4. Enos /ˈiːnɒs/ 音译 "以诺士",意思是 "人类",塞特(Seth)的儿子
5. then began men to call upon the name of the LORD 自那时起人类开始呼唤耶和华的圣名,即向上帝祈祷、礼拜。
6. Noah /ˈnəʊə/ (人名)挪亚。挪亚是有名的义人,一家八口人得到上帝特别恩惠,乘坐方舟逃避了大洪水。Ark n. 本意是 "箱子",意译 "方舟"。汉语中的 "方舟" 指并在一起使用的双舟。
7. And Noah begat three sons, Shem, Ham, and Japheth. 挪亚有三个儿子:闪、含、雅弗。begat 是及物动词 beget 的过去时。beget vt. to father 专指父亲生儿女而言。
8. gopher wood 音译 "歌斐木",对其确指一直存在争议,但现代英文版《圣经》多将其译为 cypress,即柏树。
9. pitch it within and without with pitch 把方舟内外都涂上柏油。pitch v. 涂上树脂; n. 树脂;柏油。without adv. on the outside 在外面。
10. cubit n. (长度单位)腕尺;一肘,合45.7厘米。照此计算,方舟的体积大约为137×23×14米。
11. covenant n. an agreement which brings about a relationship of commitment between God and his people 上帝与其子民之间的约,是一种非平等主体间的约定。"约" 是《圣经》中一重要概念,此处首次出现,该希伯来词与 "责任" 概念密切相关。这里暗示上帝答应挪亚及其子孙(人类)的恩典。

every clean beast thou shalt take to thee by sevens, the male and his female; and of beasts that are not clean by two, the male and his female. Of fowls also of the air by sevens, the male and the female; to keep seed alive upon the face of all the earth. For yet seven days, and I will cause it to rain upon the earth forty days and forty nights; and every living substance[1] that I have made will I destroy from off the face of the earth."

And Noah did according unto all that the LORD commanded him. And Noah was six hundred years old when the flood of waters was upon the earth. And Noah went in, and his sons, and his wife, and his sons' wives with him, into the ark, because of the waters of the flood. Of clean beasts, and of beasts that are not clean, and of fowls, and of every thing that creepeth upon the earth, there went in two and two unto Noah into the ark, the male and the female, as God had commanded Noah. And it came to pass after seven days that the waters of the flood were upon the earth. In the six hundredth year of Noah's life, in the second month, the seventeenth day of the month, the same day were all the fountains of the great deep broken up, and the windows of heaven were opened. ... And the waters prevailed[2], and were increased greatly upon the earth; and the ark went upon the face of the waters. And the waters prevailed exceedingly upon the earth; and all the high hills, that were under the whole heaven, were covered. Fifteen cubits upward did the waters prevail; and the mountains were covered. And all flesh died that moved upon the earth, both of fowl, and of cattle, and of beast, and of every creeping thing that creepeth upon the earth, and every man: all in whose nostrils was the breath of life, of all that was in the dry land, died. And every living substance was destroyed which was upon the face of the ground, both man, and cattle, and the creeping things, and the fowl of the heaven; and they were destroyed from the earth: and Noah only remained alive, and they that were with him in the ark. And the waters prevailed upon the earth an hundred and fifty days.

And God remembered Noah, and every living thing, and all the cattle that was with him in the ark: and God made a wind to pass over the earth, and the water asswaged[3], the fountains also of the deep and the windows of heaven were stopped, and the rain from heaven was restrained; and the waters returned from off the earth continually: and after the end of the hundred and fifty days the waters were abated[4]. And the ark rested in the seventh month, on the seventeenth day of the month, upon the mountains of Ararat[5]. And the waters decreased continually until the tenth month: in the tenth month, on the first day of the month, were the tops of the mountains seen.

And it came to pass at the end of forty days, that Noah opened the window of the ark which he had made: and he sent forth a raven[6], which went forth to and fro[7], until the waters were dried up from off the earth. Also he sent forth a dove from him, to see if the waters were abated from off the face of the ground; but the dove found no rest for the sole of her foot, and she returned unto him into the ark, for the waters were on the face of the whole earth: then he put forth his hand, and took her, and pulled her in unto him into the ark. And he stayed yet other seven days; and again he sent forth the dove

---

1. substance *n*. living things (活的)灵，指生物
2. prevail *vi*. to be widespread in an area or at a particular time (雨水)泛滥
3. asswage *vt*. to recede; to pacify or calm (洪水)退却；回落
4. abate *vt*. to reduce in amount; to ebb (水势开始)回落
5. Ararat /ˈærəræt/ 音译"亚拉腊山"，在今土耳其东部。传说洪水之后挪亚方舟即停于此。
6. raven *n*. 乌鸦
7. to and fro back and forth 来回地。

out of the ark; and the dove came in to him in the evening; and, lo¹, in her mouth was an olive leaf pluckt off: so Noah knew that the waters were abated from off the earth. And he stayed yet other seven days; and sent forth the dove; which returned not again unto him any more. And it came to pass in the six hundredth and first year, in the first month, the first day of the month, the waters were dried up from off the earth: and Noah removed the covering of the ark, and looked, and, behold, the face of the ground was dry. And in the second month, on the seven and twentieth day of the month, was the earth dried.

And God spake unto Noah, saying, "Go forth of the ark, thou, and thy wife, and thy sons, and thy son's wives with thee. Bring forth with thee every living thing that is with thee, of all flesh, both of fowl, and of cattle, and of every creeping thing that creepeth upon the earth; that they may breed abundantly in the earth, and be fruitful, and multiply upon the earth.

And Noah went forth, and his sons, and his wife, and his sons' wives with him: every beast, every creeping thing, and every fowl, and whatsoever creepeth upon the earth, after their kinds, went forth out of the ark.

And Noah builded an altar unto the LORD; and took of every clean beast, and of every clean fowl, and offered burnt offerings² on the altar, and the LORD smelled a sweet savour; and the LORD said in his heart, "I will not again curse the ground any more for man's sake; for the imagination of man's heart is evil from his youth; neither will I again smite any more every thing living, as I have done. While the earth remaineth, seedtime and harvest, and cold and heat, and summer and winter, and day and night shall not cease."

And God blessed Noah and his sons, and said unto them, "Be fruitful, and multiply, and replenish the earth." (6: 9–7: 11; 7: 19–9: 1)

Part 5

The Tower of Babel³

And the whole earth was of one language, and of one speech. And it came to pass, as they journeyed from the east, that they found a plain in the land of Shinar⁴; and they dwelt there. And they said one to another,

"Go to, let us make brick, and burn them thoroughly." And they had brick for stone, and slime had they for morter⁵. And they said, "Go to, let us build us a city and a tower, whose top may reach unto heaven; and let us make us a name⁶, lest we be scattered abroad upon the face of the whole earth."

And the LORD came down to see the city and the tower, which the children of men builded. And the LORD said, "Behold, the people is one, and they have all one language; and this they begin to do: and now nothing will be restrained⁷ from them, which they have imagined to do. Go to, let us go down⁸, and there confound⁹ their language, that they may not understand one another's speech."

---

1. lo *int.* 瞧! 看!
2. burnt offerings 燔祭, 将牺牲剥皮斩碎, 烧化成烟的祭礼。
3. Tower of Babel /ˈbeɪbəl/ 音译 "巴别塔" (中国天主教 "思高本" 译作 "巴贝耳塔"; 又译 "巴比塔") 意译 "通天塔"。之所以得名 Babel (巴别), 是因为与 babal (搅乱) 谐音。
4. Shinar /ˈʃaɪnɑː/ *n.* (地名) 士拿平原。即幼发拉底河冲积平原上的巴比伦。
5. slime had they for morter 他们用粘土作灰泥。morter 即今之 mortar, 灰泥。
6. let us make us a name 替我们扬名。"名" 代表声誉和后代。
7. restrain (from) *vt.* to hold (a person) back to prevent 制止; 阻止
8. Go to, let us go down 让我们下去。文中反复出现 go to, 可理解为一种招呼语, 表示上帝在和天使们说话。
9. confound *vt.* to fail to distinguish; to mix up 使混淆

So the LORD scattered them abroad from thence upon the face of all the earth: and they left off[1] to build the city. Therefore is the name of it called Babel; because the LORD did there confound the language of all the earth: and from thence did the LORD scatter them abroad upon the face of all the earth. (11: 1–9)

三、圣经文化知识链接

1. 创世神话的对称性

《创世记》第一章讲述的是上帝在六日内创造宇宙万物的神话。19世纪末，美国圣经学者摩尔顿(R. G. Moulton)研究发现，上帝六日创世故事中的头3天和后3天的叙述存在惊人的平行(parallelism)，每节以"Let there be …"开始，以"And the evening and the morning were the … day"，句式的重复使得叙述具有诗节的匀称美(beauty in symmetry)，读起来富有节奏(cadence)，朗朗上口(rhythm)。请看下面的布局[2]：

单 日	双 日	说 明
1st day creation of light *God saw it was good*	4th day creation of lights *God saw it was good*	光→光体
2nd day creation of firmament dividing the waters *it was so*	5th day creation of life in waters and firmament *God saw it was good*	天→飞鸟 海→水族
3rd day creation of land *it was so* God saw it was good Creation of plants *it was so* God saw it was good	6th day creation of life on land *it was so* God saw it was good creation of human beings *it was so* God saw it was very good	陆地→植物、动物

前三天依次创造出光、天穹和海洋、陆地；后三天依次创造出光体、空中飞鸟和海里水族、陆地植物和动物；最后，在上帝完成创世工程后，用 it was *very* good 加以强调。这则创世神话表现出来的对称之美令人称奇。再进一步想，未出生的婴儿在母体子宫里的感觉是不是"空虚混沌、渊面黑暗"呢？而呱呱坠地之后，婴儿看到的第一种物质是不是"光"呢？由此看来，上帝六日创世的神话以简单的语言和朴素的思维表达了人类对自身来源的模糊记忆，也反映了人类逐渐摆脱混沌状态、寻找宇宙秩序的认识过程。

2. "该隐杀弟"与社会转型

该隐杀弟的重要起因，是因为上帝不悦纳该隐的供物田里的土产，而喜欢亚伯的供物头

---

1. leave off 停止（做某事）。
2. 郭秀梅著：《圣经浅析》(Siu May Kuo: *Venturing into the Bible*)，南京：南京大学出版社，1989年，第26页。

胎的羊羔。该隐耕地,成为农夫,亚伯放牧,做了牧人。两人从事的是农耕、畜牧两个不同"行业"。种植比畜牧更依赖土地,上帝却不保证年年丰收,似乎挑剔农夫的祭品,或者诅咒了土地。该隐和亚伯的劳动分工意味着人类早期的物质生产活动开始出现农业和畜牧业的分野,而上帝厚此薄彼暗示农业和畜牧业之间的矛盾,农业不如畜牧业受到人们的重视。考虑到古希伯来民族从游牧生活转入农耕社会的漫长过程,这个故事也能反映出古希伯来人(或者《创世记》的作者们)对游牧生活方式的怀旧和对农耕社会形式的排拒心理。

四、圣经文化专题

1. 希伯来神话的特质和魅力

首先,它用典型的神话思维应对和解说世界和人生的许多根本性问题。这种神话思维不以逻辑线性思考为特征,而是以形象的方法,通过对故事的叙述来完成。在这个意义上,神话具有一种特定的文学美感,而希伯来人的现世经验也从中得到了应有的昭示。譬如"该隐杀弟"的神话,实际上是通过故事的形式,把古代巴勒斯坦地区两个同宗不同族的部落之间的纷争表达出来。

其次,神话作为希伯来文化的一种"原初质料",不仅自身丰富、深厚,而且对后世希伯来文化的发展产生了重要影响。希伯来神话是希伯来民族生活经验的特定表征,体现了对世界、历史和现实的认知,这种认知可能对他们的未来生活发挥某种导引作用。而且,希伯来神话本身所包含的运思方式作为一种"原初质料",可能对希伯来文化产生更为久远的影响。

第三,希伯来神话有别于希腊神话故事。前者是独一上帝的王国,后者是众神家族的世界;前者只有神与人的双向关系,后者有诸神谱系间的纠葛。在希腊神话里,所谓的"神话"其实都是"人话",所谓的"神"几乎没有一个不是按照人的样子与人的意志打造出来的。天上的或人间的诸神所演绎出来的一幕幕可歌可泣的"神话故事"无一不打上人类社会的烙印。从内容上看,诸神之间有高低贵贱之分,有七情六欲,也有生死之恋;有复杂的感情纠葛,也有嫉妒或争风吃醋;有任人唯亲与打击报复,也有路见不平、拔刀相助。从故事场面来看,既有惊天地、泣鬼神的轰轰烈烈,又有说悄悄话或吹枕边风的细节描写。多个故事的主角往往是同一个神或人。因此,希腊神话故事彼此之间既有某种内在联系又有其相对的独立性。相比之下,希伯来神话的系统性十分鲜明,既有时间上的延续性,也有空间转换的秩序。具有绝对权威的耶和华神始终扮演着至关重要的角色,有时是绝对的主角,有时像导演一样隐藏在幕后。另外,希伯来神话呈现出作为"创造者"的神与作为"被造物"的人类之间的互动关系,这说明希伯来人已经意识到矛盾对立是历史前进的动力。

2.《创世记》的元典意义[1]

在跨文化的话语中,希伯来圣经显示的元典传承中的超神学意义十分明显。它是在综合了

---

1. 本项参考了刘洪一的文章"《圣经》的跨文化元典意义",载于《深圳大学学报》(人文社会科学版),2005年第4期,第61-66页;见第65页。

两河文化、乃至地中海和埃及文化的某些要素的基础上形成的，汇聚和呈现的是一系列既具新质意义又具初始性的文化意象和文化元素。这些文化意象和文化元素仿佛种子和基因，对后世西方文明、乃至世界文明产生启示性影响。以下是《创世记》中神话部分具有"起源"和"创始"意义的文化意象体系：

  时间与空间的起源(1:1)；
  物质宇宙的起源(1:1—25)；
  人类的起源(1:26—2:24)
  乌托邦的起源(2:8—17)；
  罪恶的起源(3:1—20)；
  理智与意识的起源(3:7—12)；
  救赎的起源(3:8—24)；
  家庭生活的起源(4:1—2)；
  争斗凶杀的起源(4:3—15)；
  城市生活的起源(4:18—22)；
  种族分类和国家的起源(10:1—32)；
  语言混乱的起源(11:1—9)。

  此外，各种观念学说，从律法、信仰、道德、伦理，到建筑、医学、教育、审美、艺术等文化事项，在希伯来圣经中都有"起始性"的集中呈现。更重要的是，希伯来圣经作为一种"起始性"的元典，在其传承过程中显示出明显的超神学意义。它虽以神学文本出现，然而它所承载的各种起始性文化元素却超越了神学的规限，不仅超越了犹太教的规限，也超越了基督教的规限，成为世俗性的文化要素，并对后世的文化成长产生了潜在而深刻的作用。

五、圣经典故集锦

1. **the creation**（创世）：典出《创世记》第1章1—31节上帝六天创世的神话，如第一句：In the beginning God created the heaven and the earth. *起初，神创造天地*。喻指"开天辟地，创造万物"。美国小说家、幽默大师马克·吐温(Mark Twain, 1835—1919)曾经借用该圣经典故嘲讽人类的自负：Man was made at the end of the week's work, when God was tired. 一位美国教师借用上帝创世和创造人类的大能来比喻教师职业之神圣：Being a teacher is being present at the creation, when the clay begins to breathe.

2. **Adam's ribs**（亚当的肋骨）：典出《创世记》第2章21—26节：And the LORD God caused a deep sleep to fall upon Adam, and he slept: and he took one of his ribs, and closed up the flesh instead thereof; And the rib, which the LORD God had taken from man, made he a woman, and brought her unto the man. *耶和华神使他沉睡，他就睡了。于是取下他的一条肋骨，又把肉合起来。耶和华神就用那人身上所取的肋骨，造成一个女人，领她到那人跟前。* 此典喻指女人。英国意识流小说家詹姆斯·乔伊斯的《尤利西斯》(James Joyce: *Ulysses*)中化用了这个典故：

  他（勃克·穆利根）若有所思地点点头，脱下长裤站起来，说了句老生常谈：

"红毛女人浪起来赛过山羊。"

　　他惊愕地住了口,并摸了摸随风呼啸着的衬衫里面的肋部。

　　"我的第十二根肋骨没有啦,"他大声说,"我是超人。没有牙齿的金赤和我都是超人。"
（《尤利西斯》上）

3. **Garden of Eden**（伊甸园）: 旧译"地堂",典出《创世记》第2章8—15节,亚当被造出后上帝给他的安身之所,指"乐园"、"人间天堂"。康熙皇帝在1693年为天主教"北堂"所作的律诗中有:"地堂久为初人闭,天路新凭圣子通。"鹿桥的《未央歌》第8章,伍宝笙发觉余孟勤和蔺燕梅的恋情后不无忧虑: 余孟勤这个人也怪。从前学校在北方时,在那种皇宫似的大学校里,人人都似伊甸园里的亚当和夏娃那样无忧无虑地过着天国的日子时,他便如挪亚预见了洪水似的,埋头准备他的方舟。

4. **Adam and Eve**（亚当和夏娃）: 喻指"人类始祖"、"恩爱情人",多喻指男女性关系。老舍的短篇小说《牺牲》中,"我"有意请毛博士吃饭借以试探他的脾性,毛博士果真推辞道:

　　"我们年轻的人应当省点钱,何必出去吃饭呢,我们将来必须有个小家庭,像美国那样的。钢丝床、澡盆、电炉,"说到这儿,他似乎看出一个理想的小乐园: 一对儿现代的亚当夏娃在电灯下低语。(《老舍文集》第8卷)

　　无名氏的小说《海艳》第九章"结合"中,印蒂和瞿萦在一个月夜划船,两人窃窃私语:

　　"那么,在这纯洁的月光下,我们该去掉那层不信赖的遮盖了。让我们真正全部浸浴在月光里吧! 让我们真正回到亚当夏娃吧!

　　……

　　三十分钟后,他们双斜躺在船舱里,绝对沉浴在月光里。

5. **bone of bones, flesh of flesh**（骨中骨,肉中肉）: 典出《创世记》第2章22—23节: And Adam said, This is now bone of my bones, and flesh of my flesh: she shall be called Woman, because she was taken out of Man. 那人说:"这是我骨中的骨,肉中的肉,可以称她为女人,因为她是从男人身上取出来的。"在英国女作家夏洛特·勃朗蒂的《简·爱》结尾,简在10年后谈及她和罗切斯特的婚姻:

I hold myself supremely blest — blest beyond what language can express; because I am my husband's life as fully as he is mine. No woman was ever nearer to her mate than I am: ever more absolutely bone of his bone and flesh of his flesh. 我认为自己极其幸福——幸福到言语都无法形容;因为我完全是我丈夫的生命,正如他完全是我的生命一样。没有一个女人比我更加同丈夫亲近,更加彻底地成为他的骨中骨,肉中肉。

6. **serpent**（蛇）: 典出《创世记》第3章1—5节: Now the serpent was more subtil than any beast of the field which the LORD God had made. And he said unto the woman, Yea, hath God said, Ye shall not eat of every tree of the garden? 蛇在伊甸园引诱夏娃偷吃"智慧树"的果子,使人类始祖犯下原罪。所以"蛇"一般指"魔鬼"、"引诱者"。无名氏的《海艳》第9章"结合"中描写了男女主人公的快乐心情:

　　在海滨,他们的灵魂像海一样赤裸,情绪像海一样明净。海就是他们的伊甸,唯一那条蛇是

"爱情"。这蛇在他们心里发声发音,叫他做这样、做那样。蛇是他们的上帝,他们从未拒绝过它的声音。

7. **forbidden fruit** (禁果):典出伊甸园中"知善恶果",即"智慧树"结的果子,人吃了能眼睛明亮、辨别善恶,但此果为上帝所禁。喻指不可触动的禁物,或因被禁止反而更想得到的东西。人们说"禁果好吃",或者认为"禁果"就是"苹果"(然而"禁果"或"苹果"并没有在《创世记》中出现过)。小说家无名氏的《海艳》第8章"炽恋"中,瞿萦终于在印蒂胸前道出了她欲罢不能的爱情:

当我才想用温情时,我全心的热烈到了脸上,却变成了一片冷静,到了嘴边,却是一些石子样的言语。越当我脸上对你最冰霜时,也就是我心里最桃李时。一个声音常在我耳边喊:"这个男人是一棵'禁树',他树上的禁果是吃不得的!"我永远用一种害怕的基本情绪接近你。

胡平的纪实文学《移民美国》写道:

虽人都是禁不住诱惑的亚当夏娃,但这诱惑也多半只在节假日时,才会变成一个红扑扑的苹果。

当代美国作家伊丽莎白 M·维兰(Elizabeth M·Whelan)在《禁酒的危险》(*Perils of Prohibition*)一文中把禁酒比作禁果:Banning drinking by young people makes badge of adulthood — a tantalizing forbidden fruit.[1]

8. **fig leaves** (无花果树叶):典出《创世记》第3章7节: And the eyes of them both were opened, and they knew that they were naked; and they sewed fig leaves together, and made themselves aprons. 他们二人的眼睛就明亮了,才知道自己是赤身露体,便拿无花果树的叶子,为自己编作裙子。比喻"遮羞包丑之物"。钱钟书在小说《围城》中引用了《创世记》、《出埃及记》、《马太福音》、《启示录》中的典故。如第一章里,把"留学文凭"比作遮挡亚当、夏娃下体的"无花果树叶":

方鸿渐受到两面夹攻,才知道留学文凭的重要。这一张文凭,仿佛有亚当、夏娃下身那片树叶的功用,可以遮羞包丑;小小一方纸能把一个人的空疏、寡陋、愚笨都掩盖起来。自己没有文凭,好像精神上赤条条的,没有包裹。(《围城》,人民文学出版社,1991年版第9页)

奇怪的是,在《围城》第201页,"亚当"还有另外一个名字:原人阿大(Adam)。冯骥才在日记体散文《末日夏娃》中写到,夏娃来到未来人类世界,第一次看到那些"矮小而古怪"的未来人类。她大吃一惊:

尽管如此,我的第一反应是害羞。下意识地把腿蜷缩起来,挡住下体,并闪电般地交叉双手捂住自己的双乳——因为他们正盯着我的身体看,而且看得目瞪口呆。我慌张的举动显然惊动了这些尖脸人。他们一溜烟似地跑得无影无踪。

我从树上取了一些无花果的枝叶,把自己的胸部和下体遮挡起来。当然我也注意到怎样把那些短裙编得更好看一些。翡翠一般的叶子和我羊脂一般雪白光亮的皮肤搭配起来,真是美丽又高贵。

9. **mark of Cain** (该隐的记号):典出《创世记》第4章9—15节: And the LORD set a mark upon

---

1. 该例句出自何其莘、童明(美)编著:《美国文化面面观》(*A Comprehensive Course Book for English Majors*)第2册,北京:外语教学与研究出版社,2005年,第158页。

Cain, lest any finding him should kill him. 耶和华给杀了弟弟的该隐立了一个记号，免得人遇见他就杀他。"该隐的记号"既是罪恶的记号，又是被保护的记号。美国小说家霍桑的《红字》第5章里对海丝特胸前佩戴的红字A作过这样的比喻：

In this manner, Hester came to have a part to perform in the world. With her native energy of character and rare capacity, it could not entirely cast her off, although it had set a mark upon her, more intolerable to a woman's heart than that which branded the brow of Cain. 就这样凭自己一双手，海丝特•白兰在众人面前活了下来。由于她生性倔强，手艺出众，要彻底摈弃她还不那么容易，尽管她佩戴的红字对女性来说是奇耻大辱，比在该隐额头烙上的印记还要难堪。

10. **olive branch**（橄榄枝）：典出《创世记》第8章6—12节：And the dove came in to him in the evening; and, lo, in her mouth was an olive leaf plucked off: so Noah knew that the waters were abated from off the earth. 挪亚在洪水消退后放出鸽子，鸽子飞回时嘴里叼着一片新拧下来的橄榄枝叶，挪亚就知道地上的水退了。此典泛指和平的象征。联合国会徽和美国国徽、总统徽章上都有橄榄枝图案。莎士比亚的戏剧《亨利六世》下篇第4幕第6场中，当克莱伦斯听到华列克不愿单独管理国政而举荐他时，他推辞道：

CLARENCE: No, Warwick, thou art worthy of the sway,/To whom the heavens in thy nativity/Adjudged an olive branch and laurel crown,/As likely to be blest in peace and war;/And therefore I yield thee my free consent.

克莱伦斯：不，华列克，你掌握政权可说是当之无愧。/当你诞生的时候，/上天已把橄榄枝和桂冠赋予你，/使你在和平和战争中都有福气。/因此，我对你是甘拜下风的。（《莎士比亚全集》第6卷）

六、课堂讨论题

1. 亚当和夏娃吃"禁果"前后人与上帝、亚当和夏娃、人与地、人与动物之间的关系有何变化？
2. 从创世神话到挪亚方舟故事，"上帝"形象有何变化？
3. 试比较《圣经》的造人神话和中国的造人神话。
4. 根据创世神话谈谈中西家庭观念的区别。

七、课后思考题

1. 你知道"原罪"说和中国古代关于人类本性的说法吗？
2. 你知道下面的文字来自哪里吗？是谁的手笔？

伊甸有树，一曰生命，一曰知识。神禁人勿食其实；魔乃侂蛇以诱夏娃，使食之，爰得生命知识。神怒，立逐人而诅蛇，蛇腹行而土食；人则劳其生，又得其死，罚且及于子孙，无不如是。亚当夏娃既去乐园，乃举二子，长曰亚伯，次曰凯因。亚伯牧羊，凯因耕植是事，尝出所有以献神。神喜脂膏而恶果实，斥凯因献不视；以是，凯因渐与亚伯争，终杀之。神则诅凯因，使不获地力，流于殊方。裴伦取其事作传奇，于神诘难。

3. 钱钟书的小说《围城》对古今中外典故的运用令人叫绝。除了"无花果树叶"之外，你知道《围城》里还有哪些圣经典故吗？

第二讲

希伯来族长故事:《创世记》(下)

Legends of the Hebrew Fathers from *Genesis*

一、导读: 希伯来族长时期

　　人类最早的文明出现在古代的中东地区,包括两河流域和尼罗河流域,也就是美索不达米亚和埃及。《创世记》第12—36章记载了希伯来族长时期(Patriarchal Period,公元前18至前16世纪)亚伯拉罕、其子以撒和其孙雅各三代族长在这片古老土地上的生活。亚伯拉罕通过献子之举经受住上帝的考验,以撒长大后育有双胞胎儿子,次子雅各为争夺长子权和父亲的临终祝福与哥哥以扫不和,远赴舅舅拉班家,以14年辛劳换来财富,娶了两表妹拉结和利亚,并将其侍女纳为妾,4个女人共为雅各生育12个儿子和1个女儿。在返回故乡途中,雅各与天使摔跤,被赐名"以色列",意思是"与天使摔跤并取胜"。《创世记》第37章、39—50章记载了雅各第11子约瑟及其兄弟们的故事。少年约瑟蔑视哥哥们遭到嫉妒,被贩卖到埃及,做了埃及法老护卫长的管家。护卫长夫人用美色引诱约瑟,约瑟不从,反被诬陷,投入监牢。后因给法老解梦有功擢升埃及宰相。雅各家族在迦南遇到饥荒,派遣10个儿子前往埃及籴粮。约瑟对昔日谋害自己的兄长们进行了考验,最终尽释前嫌,归于和好。约瑟将父亲及兄弟们接往埃及侨居,以色列十二支派逐渐形成。

　　本讲选取《创世记》5个部分:
1. 亚伯拉罕的服从: 亚伯拉罕得子、献子经受上帝的考验。
2. 雅各和以扫: 雅各用一碗红豆汤换取兄长以扫的长子权。
3. 雅各的家族: 雅各娶两表妹利亚和拉结,得十二子。
4. 犹大和他玛: 成了寡妇的他玛计诱公公犹大,为夫家生子延续香火。
5. 约瑟和他的兄弟们: 约瑟遭哥哥们陷害被贩卖到埃及,拒主人之妻诱惑被陷入狱。

二、选文及注释

Part 1

Abraham's Obedience

　　Now the LORD had said unto Abram[1], "Get thee out of thy country, and from thy kindred, and from thy father's house, unto a land that I will shew thee; and I will make of thee a great nation, and I will bless thee, and make thy name great; and thou shalt be a blessing: and I will bless them that

---

1. Abram /ˈeɪbrəm/ (人名)亚伯兰,是挪亚三子之一闪(Shem)的后代,为希伯来人(Hebrew)的第一代族人,被尊为希伯来人(今犹太人)的"始祖"。上帝为其改名叫 Abraham (亚伯拉罕),意思是"万国之父"、"万民之父"。

bless thee, and curse him that curseth thee: and in thee shall all families of the earth be blessed."

So Abram departed, as the LORD had spoken unto him; and Lot[1] went with him: and Abram was seventy and five years old when he departed out of Haran[2]. And Abram took Sarai[3] his wife, and Lot his brother's son, and all their substance[4] that they had gathered, and the souls that they had gotten in Haran; and they went forth to go into the land of Canaan[5]; and into the land of Canaan they came. (12: 1–5)

And when Abram was ninety years old and nine, the LORD appeared to Abram, and said unto him, "I am the Almighty God; walk before me, and be thou perfect. And I will make my covenant between me and thee, and will multiply thee exceedingly."

And Abram fell on his face[6]: and God talked with him, saying, "As for me, behold, my covenant is with thee, and thou shalt be a father of many nations. Neither shall thy name any more be called Abram, but thy name shall be Abraham; for a father of many nations have I made thee. ...

This is my covenant, which ye shall keep, between me and you and thy seed after thee; Every man child among you shall be circumcised[7]. And ye shall circumcise the flesh of your foreskin; and it shall be a token of the covenant betwixt[8] me and you. And he that is eight days old shall be circumcised among you, every man child in your generations, he that is born in the house, or bought with money of any stranger, which is not of thy seed. He that is born in thy house, and he that is bought with thy money, must needs[9] be circumcised: and my covenant shall be in your flesh for an everlasting covenant. And the uncircumcised man child whose flesh of his foreskin is not circumcised, that soul shall be cut off from his people; he hath broken my covenant."

And God said unto Abraham, "As for Sarai thy wife, thou shalt not call her name Sarai, but Sarah shall her name be." (17: 1–15 with 17:6–9 omitted)

And the LORD visited Sarah as he had said, and the LORD did unto Sarah as he had spoken. For Sarah conceived, and bare Abraham a son in his old age, at the set time of which God had spoken to him. And Abraham called the name of his son that was born unto him, whom Sarah bare to him, Isaac[10]. And Abraham circumcised his son Isaac being eight days old, as God had commanded him. And Abraham was an hundred years old, when his son Isaac was born unto him. (21: 1–5)

And it came to pass after these things that God did tempt[11] Abraham, and said unto

---

1. Lot (人名)罗得。亚伯兰的侄子，早年丧父，跟着亚伯兰一起生活。
2. Haran (地名)哈兰。亚伯兰带领家人离开家乡吾珥(Ur, 美索不达米亚南部最著名的城市)后，先来到哈兰居住，后从这里前往上帝应许之地迦南(Canaan)，哈兰正好是吾珥和迦南的中点。
3. Sarai /ˈsɛəraɪ/ (人名)撒拉，意思是"公主"。亚伯兰之妻，后上帝为其改名 Sarah /sɛərə/ (撒莱，意思也是"公主")。
4. substance n. material possessions; goods; wealth 财产
5. Canaan /ˈkeɪnən/ (地名)迦南，意思是"低地"。上帝赐给以色列圣祖的"应许之地"(the Land of Promise/ the Promised Land)，今巴勒斯坦一带。
6. fell on his face 俯伏在地，是敬拜的动作。
7. circumcise (the flesh of your foreskin) vt. 割掉阴茎的包皮，雅称"割礼"。原是部落的成人礼或订婚入籍的仪式。后文有 uncircumcised man child, 意思是"未行割礼的男婴"。
8. betwixt prep. 〈古〉between 在……之间
9. must needs 等于 must。第三人称单数做主语时一般现在时接 must needs。
10. Isaac /ˈaɪzək/ (人名)以撒，因为是亚伯拉罕和妻子撒莱所生之子，后文称其为"独生子"。实际上亚伯拉罕和撒莱的婢女夏甲所生之子以实玛利为长子，但因为出自婢女，因而地位低。Issac 意思是"笑"，源自上帝让撒莱发笑。
11. tempt vt. to entice sb. to do sth. that he does not know to be wrong or unwise 考验；试探

him, "Abraham": and he said, "Behold, here I am."

And he said, "Take now thy son, thine only son Isaac, whom thou lovest, and get thee into the land of Moriah[1] and offer him there for a burnt offering upon one of the mountains which I will tell thee of."

And Abraham rose up early in the morning, and saddled his ass[2], and took two of his young men with him, and Isaac his son, and clave[3] the wood for the burnt offering, and rose up, and went unto the place of which God had told him. Then on the third day Abraham lifted up his eyes, and saw the place afar off. And Abraham said unto his young men, "Abide ye here with the ass; and I and the lad will go yonder[4] and worship, and come again to you."

And Abraham took the wood of the burnt offering, and laid it upon Isaac his son; and he took the fire[5] in his hand, and a knife and they went both of them together. And Isaac spake unto Abraham his father, and said, "My father": and he said, "Here am I, my son." And he said, "Behold the fire and the wood: but where is the lamb for a burnt offering?" And Abraham said, "My son, God will provide himself a lamb for a burnt offering": so they went both of them together.

And they came to the place which God had told him of; and Abraham built an altar there, and laid the wood in order, and bound Isaac his son, and laid him on the altar upon the wood. And Abraham stretched forth his hand, and took the knife to slay his son.

And the angel of the LORD called unto him out of heaven, and said, "Abraham, Abraham": and he said, "Here am I."

And he said, "Lay not thine hand upon the lad, neither do thou any thing unto him: for now I know that thou fearest God, seeing thou hast not withheld[6] thy son, thine only son from me."

And Abraham lifted up his eyes, and looked, and behold behind him a ram caught in a thicket by his horns[7]: and Abraham went and took the ram, and offered him up for a burnt offering in the stead of his son. (22: 1–13)

Part 2

Jacob and Esau[8]

And Isaac was forty years old when he took Rebekah to wife, the daughter of Bethuel the Syrian of Padan-aram[9], the sister to Laban[10] the Syrian. And Isaac intreated[11] the LORD for his wife, because she was barren[12]: and the LORD was intreated of him[13], and Rebekah his wife conceived. And the children struggled together within her; and she said, "If it be so, why am I thus?[14]" And she went to inquire of the LORD. And the LORD said unto her,

---

1. Moriah n. (地名)摩利亚。就是后来所罗门建圣殿的地方。
2. saddled his ass 给毛驴放好鞍子(准备驮燔祭用的木柴)。saddle vt. 放鞍子。
3. clave ⟨古⟩ cleave to split with 劈开
4. go yonder 去那边。go yonder 比 go there 表示的距离更远。
5. fire n. 火石
6. withhold vt. to refuse to give (sth. that is due to or desired by another) 拒给；保留。这句话的意思是：你连自己的独生子也没有顾惜，奉献出来。
7. a ram caught in a thicket by his horns 犄角被灌木枝缠住的绵羊。thicket n. 灌木丛。
8. Jacob /ˈdʒeɪkəb/ and Esau /ˈiːsɔː/ (人名)雅各(意思是"抓住")和以扫(意思是"多毛")。两人是以撒和利百加(Rebekah /rɪˈbekə/)所生的双胞胎儿子。
9. the Syrian of Padan-aram 巴旦亚兰地的亚兰人。巴旦亚兰地即美索不达米亚。
10. Laban /ˈleɪbən/ (人名)拉班，利百加的哥哥，以撒之子雅各的妻子姐妹利亚(Leah)和拉结(Rachel)之父
11. intreat vt. to ask for earnestly 祈求
12. barren adj. ⟨古⟩(of a woman) infertile 不能生育的
13. the LORD was intreated of him 耶和华应允了以撒的祈求。
14. If it be so, why am I thus? 直译：若是这样，我为什么如此(命苦)呢？

"Two nations are in thy womb[1],

And two manner of people shall be separated from thy bowels[2];

And the one people shall be stronger than the other people;

And the elder shall serve the younger[3]."

And when her days to be delivered were fulfilled[4], behold, there were twins in her womb. And the first came out red, all over like an hairy garment; and they called his name Esau. And after that came his brother out, and his hand took hold on Esau's heel; and his name was called Jacob: and Isaac was threescore years old when she bare them. And the boys grew: and Esau was a cunning hunter, a man of the field[5]; and Jacob was a plain man[6], dwelling in tents. And Isaac loved Esau, because he did eat of his venison[7]: but Rebekah loved Jacob.

And Jacob sod[8] pottage; and Esau came from the field, and he was faint: and Esau said to Jacob, "Feed me, I pray thee, with that same red pottage[9]; for I am faint": therefore was his name called Edom[10].

And Jacob said, "Sell me this day thy birthright[11]."

And Esau said, "Behold, I am at the point to die: and what profit shall this birthright do to me?"

And Jacob said, "Swear to me this day!"

And he sware unto him: and he sold his birthright unto Jacob. Then Jacob gave Esau bread and pottage of lentils[12]; and he did eat and drink, and rose up, and went his way: thus Esau despised his birthright. (25: 20–34)

Part 3

Jacob's Family

Then Jacob went on his journey, and came into the land of the people of the east. And he looked, and behold a well in the field, and, lo, there were three flocks of sheep lying by it; for out of that well they watered the flocks: and a great stone was upon the well's mouth. And thither were all the flocks gathered: and they rolled the stone from the well's mouth, and watered the sheep, and put the stone again upon the well's mouth in his place.

And Jacob said unto them, "My brethren, whence be ye?" And they said, "Of Haran are we."

And he said unto them, "Know ye Laban the son of Nahor?" And they said, "We know him."

And he said unto them, "Is he well?" And they said, "He is well: and, behold, Rechel[13] his daughter cometh with the sheep."

And he said, "Lo, it is yet high day, neither is it time that the cattle should be gathered together: water ye the sheep, and go

---

1. thy womb 你的子宫，指利百加怀有身孕。
2. two manner of people shall be separated from thy bowels 两族要从你身上出来。manner *n.* kind; sort 种类；类别。thy bowel(你的肠)指代身体。
3. the elder shall serve the younger 两个婴儿乃代表两个国家，也是两个彼此敌对的民族，而大的要服侍小的。即先出生的以扫的后代服从于雅各的后代。
4. her days to be delivered were fulfilled 临盆。deliver *vt.* to give birth to a child 分娩。
5. a cunning hunter, a man of the field 以扫成为熟练的猎人，喜欢户外活动。
6. a plain man 指雅各好静。
7. venison *n.* the flesh of a game animal used as food 〈古〉野味
8. sod *vi.* 〈古〉seethe (煮沸)的过去时和过去分词
9. red pottage 红豆汤，用中东一种极其扁圆的扁豆和米混和煮成的红色稀粥。
10. Edom /'i:dəm/ (人名)以东，以扫的别名，意思是"红的"
11. birthright *n.* a special privilege accorded a first-born 长子权。长子权包括两种权利: 可得双倍遗产；可作一家之主。长子的名分是可以出卖的。
12. lentil *n.* 小扁豆
13. Rachel /'reɪtʃəl/ (人名)拉结，意思是"母羊"

and feed them." And they said, "We cannot, until all the flocks be gathered together, and till they roll the stone from the well's mouth; then we water the sheep."

And while he yet spake with them, Rachel came with her father's sheep: for she kept them. And it came to pass, when Jacob saw Rachel the daughter of Laban his mother's brother, and the sheep of Laban his mother's brother, that Jacob went near, and rolled the stone from the well's mouth, and watered the flock of Laban his mother's brother. And Jacob kissed Rachel, and lifted up his voice, and wept. And Jacob told Rachel that he was her father's brother[1], and that he was Rebekah's son: and she ran and told her father. And it came to pass, when Laban heard the tidings[2] of Jacob his sister's son, that he ran to meet him, and embraced him, and kissed him, and brought him to his house. And he told Laban all these things. And Laban said to him, "Surely thou art my bone and my flesh."[3] And he abode with him the space of a month[4].

And Laban said unto Jacob, "Because thou art my brother, shouldest thou therefore serve me for nought[5]? tell me, what shall thy wages be?"

And Laban had two daughters: the name of the elder was Leah[6], and the name of the younger was Rachel. Leah was tender eyed[7]; but Rachel was beautiful and well favoured. And Jacob loved Rachel; and said, "I will serve thee seven years for Rachel thy younger daughter."

And Laban said, "It is better that I give her to thee than that I should give her to another man: abide with me."

And Jacob served seven years for Rachel; and they seemed unto him but a few days, for the love he had to her. And Jacob said unto Laban, "Give me my wife, for my days are fulfilled, that I may go in unto her."

And Laban gathered together all the men of the place, and made a feast. And it came to pass in the evening that he took Leah his daughter, and brought her to him; and he went in unto her. And Laban gave unto his daughter Leah Zilpah[8] his maid for an handmaid.

And it came to pass, that in the morning, behold, it was Leah; and he said to Laban, "What is his thou hast done unto me? did not I serve with thee for Rachel? wherefore[9] then hast thou beguiled me?"

And Laban said, "It must not be so done in our country, to give the younger before the firstborn. Fulfill her week[10], and we will give thee this also for the service which thou shalt serve with me yet seven other years."

And Jacob did so, and fulfilled her week; he gave him Rachel his daughter to wife also. And Laban gave Rachel his daughter Bilhah[11] his handmaid to be her maid. And he went in also unto Rachel, and he loved also Rachel more than Leah, and served with him yet seven other years.

And when the LORD saw that Leah was hated, he opened her womb: but Rachel

---

1. (he was her father's) brother 兄弟，可以指普通的亲属，这里指"外甥"。
2. tidings *n.* news; information 音信；消息
3. Surely thou art my bone and my flesh. 你一定是我的骨肉。"骨肉"原文是"兄弟"。
4. he abode with him the space of a month 拉班留雅各在家里住了一个月。abode 是 abide（逗留）的过去式。
5. nought *n.* 〈古〉naught（零）的变体。拉班问外甥雅各能否为他白干。
6. Leah /lɪə/（人名）利亚，意思是"母牛"
7. tender eyed 眼睛温柔妩媚。根据上文，姐妹俩都可爱，雅各更爱拉结，原因是"利亚的眼睛虽然可爱，拉结却生得身材魅力，样貌娟秀"。
8. Zilpah /'zɪlpə/（人名）悉帕，利亚的使女，后成为雅各的妾
9. wherefore *adv.* why 为何
10. fulfill her week 指连续7天的婚庆结束。
11. Bilhah /'bɪlɑː/（人名）辟拉，拉结的使女，后成为雅各的妾

was barren. And Leah conceived, and bare a son, and she called his name Reuben[1]; for she said, "Surely the LORD hath looked upon my affliction; now therefore my husband will love me." And she conceived again, and bare a son; and said, "Because the LORD hath heard that I was hated, he hath therefore given me this son also": and she called his name Simeon. And she conceived again, and bare a son; and said, "Now this time will my husband be joined unto me[2], because I have born him three sons": therefore was his name called Levi. And she conceived again, and bare a son: she said, "Now will I praise the LORD"; therefore she called his name Judah; and left bearing[3]. (29)

And when Rachel saw that she bare Jacob no children, Rachel envied her sister; and said unto Jacob, "Give me children, or else I die."

And Jacob's anger was kindled[4] against Rachel: and he said, "Am I in God's stead[5], who hath withheld from thee the fruit of the womb[6]?"

And she said, "Behold my maid Bilhah, go in unto her; and she shall bear upon my knees, that I may also have children by her."

And she gave him Bilhah her hand maid to wife: and Jacob went in unto her. And Bilhah conceived, and bare Jacob a son. And Rachel said, "God hath judged me, and hath also heard my voice, and hath given me a son": therefore called she his name Dan[7]. And Bilhah Rachel's maid conceived again, and bare Jacob a second son. And Rachel said, "With great wrestlings have I wrestled with my sister, and I have prevailed[8]": and she called his named Naphtali.

When Leah saw that she had left bearing, she took Zilpah her maid, and gave her Jacob to wife. And Zilpah Leah's maid bare Jacob a son. And Leah said, "A troop cometh": and she called his name Gad[9]. And Zilpah Leah's maid bare Jacob a second son. And Leah said, "Happy am I, for the daughters will call me blessed": and she called his name Asher.

And Reuben went in the days of wheat harvest, and found mandrakes[10] in the field, and brought them unto his mother Leah. Then Rachel said to Leah, "Give me, I pray thee, of thy son's mandrakes."

And she said unto her, "Is it a small matter that thou hast taken my husband? and wouldest thou take away my son's mandrakes also?"

And Rachel said, "Therefore he shall lie with thee to night for thy son's mandrakes."

And Jacob came out of the field in the evening, and Leah went out to meet him, and said, "Thou must come in unto me; for surely I have hired thee with my son's mandrakes." And he lay with her that night.

And God hearkened unto Leah, and she conceived, and bare Jacob the fifth son. And Leah said, "God hath given me my hire, because I have given my maiden to my husband": and she called his name Issachar[11]. And Leah conceived again, and

---

1. Reuben /ˈruːbɪn/, Simeon /ˈsɪmɪən/, Levi /ˈliːvaɪ/, Judah /ˈdʒuːdə/（人名）雅各和利亚所生之子：吕便(旧译"流便"，意思是"有儿子"）、西缅(意思是"听见"）、利未(意思是"联合"）、犹大(意思是"赞美"）
2. be joined unto me 指丈夫与我同房。
3. left bearing 停止了生育。
4. kindle *vt.* to set fire; to ignite 点燃，指雅各对拉结发火
5. stead *n.* 替代。in God's stead: 雅各认为拉结是否生育在于上帝，自己作为丈夫也无奈。
6. withheld from thee the fruit of the womb 意思是上帝不赐给拉结生育能力。the fruit of the womb 是比喻法，指怀孕生子。
7. Dan /dæn/, Naphtali /ˈnæftəlaɪ/（人名）雅各和妾辟拉所生之子：但(意思是"伸冤"）和拿弗他利(意思是"相争"）
8. With great wrestlings have I wrestled with my sister, and I have prevailed 我和姐姐拼命斗到如今，我终于赢了。意思是拉结因使女辟拉为其生子，夺回了丈夫的宠爱
9. Gad /gæd/, Asher /ˈæʃə(r)/（人名）雅各和妾悉帕所生之子：迦得(意思是"万幸"）和亚设(意思是"有福"）
10. mandrake 风茄，又名"爱情果"。古人认为风茄的根和果实能催情怀孕。
11. Issachar /ˈɪsəkə(r)/, Zebulun /ˈzebjulən/, Dinah /ˈdaɪnə/（人名）雅各和利亚所生两个儿子以萨迦(意思是"报酬"）、西布伦(意思是"同住"）和一个女儿底拿(意思是"公道"）

bare Jacob the sixth son. And Leah said, "God hath endued me with a good dowry[1]; now will my husband dwell with me, because I have born him six sons": and she called his name Zebulun. And afterwards she bare a daughter, and called her name Dinah.

And God remembered Rachel, and God hearkened to her, and opened her womb. And she conceived, and bare a son; and said, "God hath taken away my reproach[2]": and she called his name Joseph[3]; and said, "The LORD shall add to me another son."

And it came to pass, when Rachel had born Joseph, that Jacob said unto Laban, "Send me away, that I may go unto mine own place, and to my country. Give me my wives and my children, for whom I have served thee, and let me go: for thou knowest my service which I have done thee." (30: 1–26)

Part 4

Judah and Tamar[4]

And it came to pass at that time, that Judah went down from his brethren, and turned in to a certain Adullamite[5], whose name was Hirah. And Judah saw there a daughter of a certain Canaanite[6], whose name was Shuah, and he took her, and went in unto her. And she conceived, and bare a son; and he called his name Er. And she conceived again, and bare a son; and she called his name Onan. And she yet again conceived, and bare a son; and called his name Shelah: and he was at Chezib, when she bare him[7].

And Judah took a wife for Er his firstborn, whose name was Tamar. And Er, Judah's firstborn, was wicked in the sight of the LORD[8]; and the LORD slew him. And Judah said unto Onan, "Go in unto thy brother's wife, and marry her, and raise up seed to thy brother[9]." And Onan knew that the seed should not be his; and it came to pass, when he went in unto his brother's wife, that he spilled it on the ground[10], lest that he should give seed to his brother. And the thing which he did displeased the LORD: wherefore he slew him also. Then said Judah to Tamar his daughter in law, "Remain a widow at thy father's house[11], till Shelah my son be grown": for he said, "Lest peradventure he die also, as his brethren did." And Tamar went and dwelt in her father's house.

And in process of time the daughter of Shuah Judah's wife died; and Judah was comforted[12], and went up unto his sheepshearers to Timnath, he and his friend Hirah the Adullamite. And it was told Tamar, saying, "Behold thy father in law goeth up to Timnath to shear his sheep." And she put her widow's garments off from her, and covered her with a vail[13], and wrapped herself, and sat in an open place,

---

1. God hath endued me with a good dowry 意思是上帝以厚礼赏赐我。endue (with) *vt.* to endow (with)赋予。dowry *n.* 嫁妆。
2. reproach *n.* disgrace 羞耻；耻辱。妇女不生育被视为耻辱。
3. Joseph /ˈdʒəʊzɪf/ (人名)约瑟(意思是"增添")，雅各和拉结所生之子。
4. Judah and Tamar /təˈmɑː/ 犹大和其儿媳他玛。
5. Adullamite *n.* 亚杜兰人。亚杜兰位于犹大的居住地希伯伦西北19公里。
6. Canaanite /ˈkeɪnənaɪt/ *n.* 迦南人。迦南的原住居民。犹大的三个儿子都受到迦南文化的感染。
7. he was at Chezib, when she bare him 妻子书亚生示拉的时候，犹大正在基悉。he指犹大；him 指儿子。
8. wicked in the sight of the LORD 意思是长子珥因作恶冒犯耶和华，耶和华取了他的性命。
9. raise up seed to thy brother (犹大劝次子俄南娶哥嫂)为兄续后。
10. he spilled it on the ground 俄南(在与寡嫂同房时)把精液溢在地上。
11. Remain a widow at thy father's house 回到你父家守寡去吧。
12. comfort *vt.* to relieve 缓解；减轻。犹大因居丧期满而痛苦缓解。
13. vail *n.* 是 veil 的变体，帕子；面纱。用帕子蒙住脸是当时妓女的打扮。harlot *n.* 妓女。他玛充当的是庙妓，比一般妓女(whore)社会地位高。

which is by the way to Timnath; for she saw that Shelah was grown, and she was not given unto him to wife. When Judah saw her, he thought her to be an harlot; because she had covered her face. And he turned unto her by the way, and said, "Go to, I pray thee, let me come in unto thee." (for he knew not that she was his daughter in law.) And she said, "What wilt thou give me, that thou mayest come in unto me?" And he said, "I will send thee a kid from the flock[1]." And she said, "Wilt thou give me a pledge[2], till thou send it?"

And he said, "What pledge shall I give thee?" And she said, "Thy signet[3], and thy bracelets[4], and thy staff[5] that is in thine hand." And he gave it her, and came in unto her, and she conceived by him. And she arose, and went away, and laid by her vail from her, and put on the garments of her widowhood. And Judah sent the kid by the hand of his friend the Adullamite, to receive his pledge from the woman's hand: but he found her not. Then he asked the men of that place, saying, "Where is the harlot, that was openly by the way side?" And they said, "There was no harlot in this place." And he returned to Judah, and said, "I cannot find her; and also the men of the place said, 'that there was no harlot in this place.'" And Judah said, "Let her take it to her, lest we be shamed: behold, I sent this kid, and thou hast not found her."

And it came to pass about three months after, that it was told Judah, saying, "Tamar thy daughter in law hath played the harlot; and also, behold, she is with child by whoredom[6]." And Judah said, "Bring her forth, and let her be burnt." When she was brought forth, she sent to her father in law, saying, "By the man, whose these are, am I with child," and she said, "Discern, I pray thee, whose are these, the signet, and bracelets, and staff." And Judah acknowledged them, and said, "She hath been more righteous than I; because that I gave her not to Shelah my son." And he knew her again no more[7].

And it came to pass in the time of her travail[8], that, behold, twins were in her womb. And it came to pass, when she travailed, that the one put out his hand: and the midwife took and bound upon his hand a scarlet thread, saying, "This came out first." And it came to pass, as he drew back his hand, that, behold, his brother came out: and she said, "How hast thou broken forth? this breach be upon thee[9]." Therefore his name was called Pharez. And afterward came out his brother, that had the scarlet thread upon his hand: and his name was called Zarah. (38)

---

1. a kid from the flock 羊群里的小山羊。
2. pledge *n.* 抵押品
3. signet *n.* 印；私人图章
4. bracelet *n.* 把私印缚在颈项上的绳子或链子
5. staff *n.* 象征家族权威的手杖
6. she is with child by whoredom 他玛做妓女怀上孩子。whoredom *n.* 卖淫。
7. he knew her again no more 犹大没再与他玛同房。犹大认儿媳为妻，他玛得了名分。
8. travail /trəˈveɪl/ *n.* 分娩
9. this breach be upon thee 你倒会钻空子。breach *n.* 裂口；空隙。

Part 5

Joseph and His Brothers

And Jacob dwelt in the land wherein his father was a stranger, in the land of Canaan. These are the generations of Jacob. Joseph, being seventeen years old, was feeding the flock with his brethren; and the lad was with the sons of Bilhah, and with the sons of Zilpah, his father's wives: and Joseph brought unto his father their evil report[1]. Now Israel loved Joseph more than all his children, because he was the son of his old age: and he made him a coat of many colours[2]. And when his brethren saw that their father loved him more than all his brethren, they hated him, and could not speak peaceably unto him[3]. And Joseph dreamed a dream, and he told it his brethren: and they hated him yet the more. And he said unto them,

"Hear, I pray you, this dream which I have dreamed: for, behold, we were binding sheaves[4] in the field, and, lo, my sheaf arose, and also stood upright; and, behold, your sheaves stood round about, and made obeisance[5] to my sheaf."

And his brethren said to him, "Shalt thou indeed reign over us? or shalt thou indeed have dominion over us?"

And they hated him yet the more for his dreams, and for his words. And he dreamed yet another dream, and told it his brethren, and said,

"Behold, I have dreamed a dream more, and, behold, the sun and the moon and the eleven stars[6] made obeisance to me."

And he told it to his father, and to his brethren: and his father rebuked[7] him, and said unto him, "What is this dream that thou hast dreamed? Shall I and thy mother and thy brethren indeed come to bow down ourselves to thee to the earth?" And his brethren envied him; but his father observed the saying[8]. (37: 1–11)

And it came to pass, when Joseph was come unto his brethren, that they stript Joseph out of his coat, his coat of many colours that was on him; and they took him, and cast him into a pit: and the pit was empty, there was no water in it. And they sat down to eat bread: and they lifted up their eyes and looked, and, behold, a company of Ishmeelites came from Gilead with their camels bearing spicery and balm and myrrh[9], going to carry it down to Egypt. And Judah said unto his brethren,

"What profit is it if we slay our brother, and conceal his blood? Come, and let us sell him to the Ishmeelites and let not our hand be upon him[10]; for he is our brother and our flesh."

And his brethren were content. Then there passed by Midianites merchantmen; and they drew and lifted up Joseph out of the pit and sold Joseph to the Ishmeelites for twenty pieces of silver: and they brought Joseph into Egypt. (37: 23–28)

And Joseph was brought down to Egypt;

---

1. Joseph brought unto his father their evil report 约瑟把哥哥们干的坏事向父亲讲了。
2. a coat of many colours 彩衣；一种色彩斑斓的长袍，长及手和脚踝。此处以体现约瑟与众兄弟的不同。是父亲宠爱约瑟的标志。
3. could not speak peaceably unto him 意思是哥哥们不说约瑟一句好话。
4. sheaf *n.* 麦捆
5. make obeisance /əʊˈbeɪsəns/ to sb. to bow to sb. 向某人鞠躬或致敬。
6. eleven stars 梦中11颗星星代表约瑟的11个兄弟，包括最小的弟弟便雅悯。太阳和月亮分别代表父亲和母亲。
7. rebuke *vt.* to criticize or reprove sharply 训斥
8. his father observed the saying 意思是做父亲的把这事存在心里。
9. spicery and balm and myrrh 香料、香脂、没药，是基列(Gilead)的名产。以实马利人(Ishmeelites)又称米甸人(Midianites)前往埃及贩卖这些特产，也把约瑟卖到了埃及。
10. lay hand upon sb. 意思是杀人。

and Potiphar[1], an officer of Pharaoh, captain of the guard, an Egyptian, bought him of the hands of the Ishmeelites, which had brought him down thither. And the LORD was with Joseph, and he was a prosperous man; and he was in the house of his master the Egyptian. And his master saw that the LORD was with him, and that the LORD made all that he did to prosper in his hand. And Joseph found grace in his sight, and he served him: and he made him overseer[2] over his house, and all that he had he put into his hand.

And it came to pass from the time that he had made him overseer in his house, and over all that he had, that the LORD blessed the Egyptian's house for Joseph's sake; and the blessing of the LORD was upon all that he had in the house, and in the field. And he left all that he had in Joseph's hand; and he knew not ought he had[3], save the bread which he did eat. And Joseph was a goodly person, and well favoured.

And it came to pass after these things, that his master's wife cast her eyes upon Joseph[4]; and she said, "Lie with me." But he refused, and said unto his master's wife, "Behold, my master wotteth[5] not what is with me in the house, and he hath committed all that he hath to my hand; there is none greater in this house than I; neither hath he kept back anything from me but thee, because thou art his wife: how then can I do this great wickedness, and sin against God?"

And it came to pass, as she spake to Joseph day by day, that he hearkened not unto her, to lie by her, or to be with her.

And it came to pass about this time, that Joseph went into the house to do his business; and there was none of the men of the house there within. And she caught him by his garment, saying, "Lie with me": and he left his garment in her hand, and fled, and got him out.

And it came to pass, when she saw that he had left his garment in her hand, and was fled forth, that she called unto the men of her house, and spake unto them, saying, "See, he hath brought in an Hebrew unto us to mock us; he came in unto me to lie with me, and I cried with a loud voice: and it came to pass, when he heard that I lifted up my voice and cried, that he left his garment with me, and fled, and got him out."

And she laid up his garment by her, until his lord came home. And she spake unto him according to these words, saying, "The Hebrew servant, which thou hast brought unto us, came in unto me to mock me: and it came to pass, as I lifted up my voice and cried, that he left his garment with me, and fled out."

And it came to pass, when his master heard the words of his wife, which she spake unto him, saying, "After this manner did thy servant to me"; that his wrath was kindled. And Joseph's master took him, and put him into the prison, a place where the king's prisoners were bound; and he was there in the prison.

But the LORD was with Joseph and shewed him mercy, and gave him favour in the sight of the keeper of the prison. And the keeper of the prison committed[6] to Joseph's hand all the prisoners that were in the prison; and whatsoever they did there, he was the doer of it. The keeper of the prison looked not to any thing that was under his hand; because the LORD was with him, and that which he did, the LORD made it to prosper. (39)

---

1. Potiphar /ˈpɒtɪfə/ (人名) 波提乏, 埃及法老的内臣兼侍卫长
2. overseer *n.* 管家
3. he knew not ought he had 主人不管家里的任何事。ought *n.* 同 *aught*, 任何事
4. cast her eyes upon Joseph 抛媚眼勾引约瑟。
5. wotteth 是古英语 *wit* (知道)的第三人称单数现在式
6. commit sth. to sb.'s hand 把某事托付给某人管理。

三、圣经文化知识链接

1.《创世记》里所叙述的历史和地理

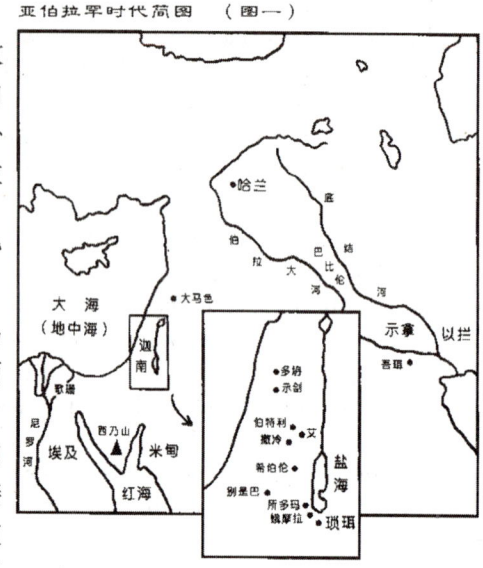

亚伯拉罕时代简图 （图一）

《圣经》里所涉及的历史约有数千年之久，除了上帝六日创世、亚当家族、挪亚家族的神话故事，希伯来远古族长们的传说大多发生在家庭内部，如亚伯拉罕之妻撒拉与其妾夏甲的纠纷、老仆人为以撒迎娶利百加、雅各与以扫之争、雅各在拉班家成家立业、约瑟与其兄弟们的悲欢离合等，基本上是"私人背景"(Private Settings)或家庭背景。从出埃及时代起，历经征服迦南、士师时代、王国时代、分国时代、波斯时代、希腊时代和罗马时代，以色列人经常处于各种民族纷争之中，与西亚、北非、南欧的古代大帝国埃及、亚述、巴比伦、波斯、希腊、罗马，以及巴勒斯坦内外的诸民族如迦南人、非利士人、摩押人、亚扪人、亚兰人等接连发生各种争端，加上以色列民族内部的宗教、道德、政治、经济等问题错综复杂，这些故事的展开更多是"公众背景"(Public Settings)[1]或社会背景。加拿大圣经学者诺思洛普·弗莱(Northrop Frye)则从宏观视野将《圣经》中的历史分为7个阶段：创世、变革、律法、智慧、预言、福音和启示[2]。

《圣经》里所包括的地域也非常广大，东起现今的伊朗，西抵西班牙，其间有中东、西亚、北非和南欧。近东文明发祥地形同"月湾"，因此被美国东方学者詹姆斯·亨利·布雷斯特德(James Henry Breasted)名之为"肥沃月湾"(Fertile Crescent)，其中心就是以色列，东部和中间是两河流域(底格里斯河、幼发拉底河)，即《圣经》中的美索不达米亚(Mesopotamia)，西端是现今的以色列，就是《旧约》中的迦南地(Canaan)。《旧约》中经常提到的另一个国家就是埃及，位于迦南地的西南方，只隔着西奈半岛的沙漠地带。一些《圣经》研究者指出，亚伯拉罕的迁徙从"月湾"的一端(迦勒底的吾珥)，经叙利亚、巴勒斯坦，走到另一端(埃及)。古希伯来人的生存发展与异族交往大致在此地带之内。(参见右上图)

2. 希伯来族长家谱

---

1. David Rhoads and Donald Michie. *Mark as Story: An Introduction to the Narrative of a Gospel*, p.67.
2. 弗莱著，郝振益等译：《伟大的代码——圣经与文学》，北京：北京大学出版社，1998年版，第111页。

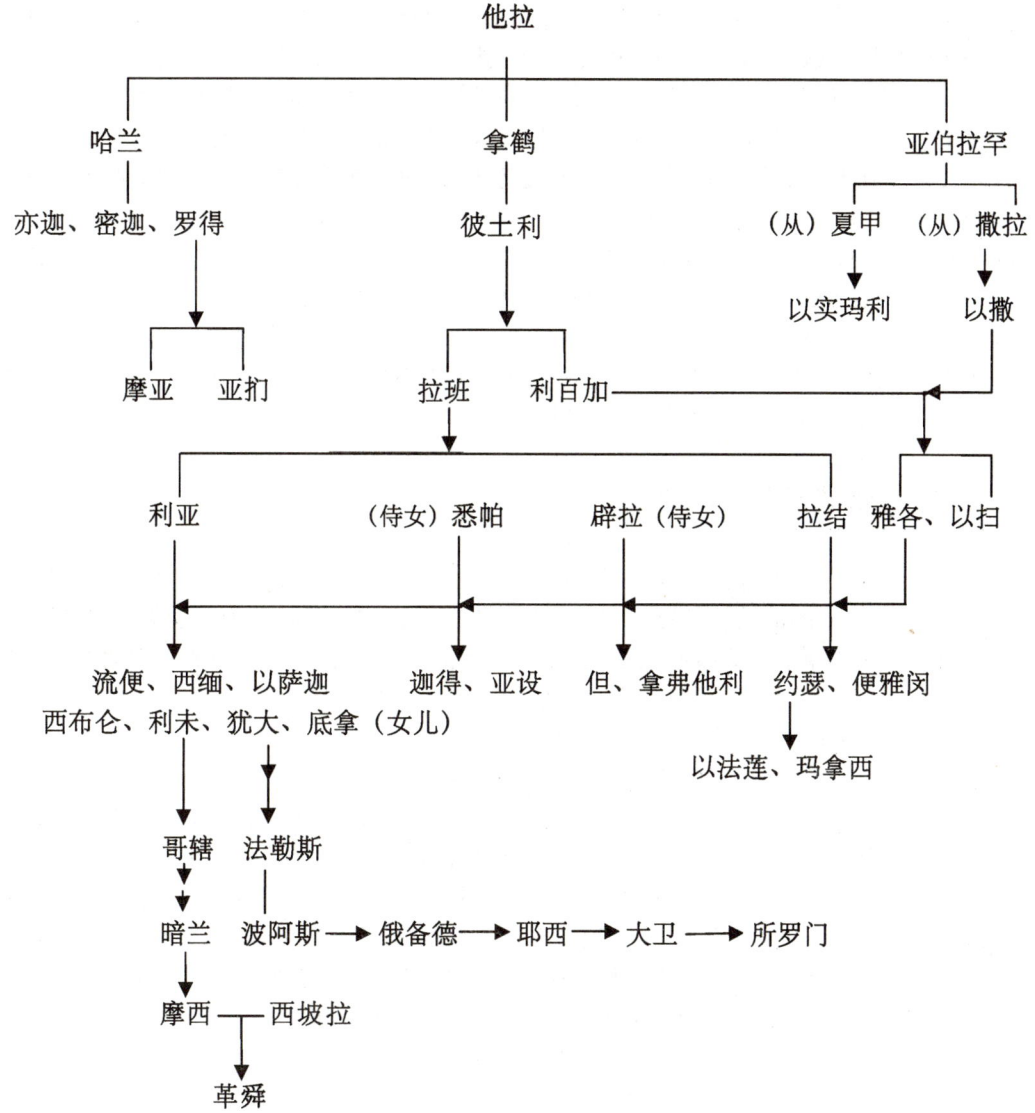

四、圣经文化专题

1. 约瑟的故事——成长小说的原型

"约瑟和他的兄弟们"是《旧约》里最精彩、最有戏剧性的故事之一。《古兰经》第12章也有约瑟(即"优素福")故事的记载。它首先是一个年轻人经受磨炼和成长的故事,从而奠定了西方"德育小说"(德语Bildungsroman)的传统。约瑟成长的历程可以概括为"得宠→蒙难→再得宠→再蒙难→最后成功"。约瑟从小被父亲偏爱,天真烂漫却因恃宠而傲视兄长,爱打小报告。被卖到埃及之后,他做过奴仆、受过冤枉、蹲过大狱,历尽艰辛。做了埃及宰相以后,约瑟的才干得到充分施展,全局观念和宏阔视野也逐步具备。见到曾经陷害他的哥哥们,约瑟能做到不计前嫌,以家族利益为重,并且十分谨慎、负责地考察了哥哥们。最后,解救了面临饥馑的以色列家族,终于成长为以色列民族的英雄人物。从约瑟的成长、挫折、成功故事,年轻人可以学到很多:一个人的成长过程不会一帆风顺、毫无波折;年少气盛、恃才恃宠会引起嫉妒、招致灾祸;忍耐、精明、担当、能干是实现自我的重要条件,然而,社会环境是复杂的,人际关系是微妙的,诱惑无处不在,必须小心谨慎、全面权衡;即使处于低潮、身陷困境也不能怨天尤人、自甘沉沦,而要励志自勉、等待转机;仁心和真诚乃做人之本,家庭和谐、人伦幸福更能促进事业的升腾。德国作家托马斯·曼(Thomas Mann, 1875—1955; 1944年入美国籍)因纳粹迫害而流亡期间,用10年时间(1933—1943)根据《创世记》关于约瑟的生平创作了系列长篇小说《约瑟和他的兄弟们》(*JOSEPH UND SEINE BRÜDER*),包括《雅各的故事》、《约瑟的青年时代》、《约瑟在埃及》和《赡养者约瑟》4部(*Joseph and His Brothers; Young Joseph; Joseph in Egypt; Joseph the Provider*)。约瑟的故事在《创世记》里只有14章,曼的小说长达一千页,可以想象作家增添了多少精彩的情节。小说颂扬了犹太人,给纳粹煽动的排犹反犹运动以有力的抨击。

2.《圣经》"契约"观的积极意义

"Covenant"一词专指《圣经》中记载的上帝与人类所立的"契约",简称"约"。契约观念(the idea of Covenant)是贯穿圣经的核心理念。《圣经》的作者们借契约观念描述了上帝对希伯来人的拣选以及希伯来人按照上帝的意愿构建全部律法的过程。虽然这种契约观念具有很浓的宗教色彩,但仔细分析,我们可以发现其中蕴含的诸多积极方面。

首先,契约关系有利于发挥人的主动性。从一定意义上讲,《圣经》中的"契约"理念是人类认识自己创造能力的一个里程碑。人类通过与上帝的亲缘关系、对上帝品性的分享,以及同上帝亲密而自愿的联系,确认了自己的自由意志和创造能力。人的自由意志有利于人发挥其主观能动性。这种互动虽然建立在神学框架之中,但在客观上起到发挥人的主体能动作用。

第二,契约关系有利于增强人的责任感。"契约"宣告人们出于对创造者的信仰而结成一族。契约观念中包含这样一种态度:即认为希伯来民族是一个道德实体,每个希伯来人都有责任和义务用自己的行为对上帝负责。同时,希伯来人彼此之间也应该相互负有责任,个体的行为代表着整个希伯来民族。因此,个人的一言一行都要体现出责任感。

第三,契约关系有利于推动整个社会的前进。上帝和希伯来人双方在这个契约关系中均是当事者。人作为立约的一方,便可以选择守约,也可以选择违约。在这种关系中,不只是人对上帝单方面、无限的尽忠尽职,而是强调上帝与人之间的交感互通,从而形成人与上帝之间的互动关系:人对上帝有践约的义务,上帝对人也要承担相应的义务,这种互动客观上推动了社会的前进。

五、圣经典故集锦

1. **Canaan**(迦南):典出《创世记》第12章1—9节: And the LORD appeared unto Abram, and said, Unto thy seed will I give this land. 上帝向亚伯拉罕显现说:"我要把这地赐给你的后裔。"这是"流着奶和蜜之地"。后指"应许之地"(the Land of Promise; the Promised Land)、"福地"、"乐土"。美国总统克林顿1997年连任的就职演说词中连续两次化用这一典故: Guided by the ancient vision of a promised land, let us set our sights upon a land of

new promise.

2. **Lot's wife** (罗得之妻): 典出《创世记》第18—19章, 罗得的妻子因好奇心切, 回头一望而遭到毁灭, 变成了一根盐柱。此典比喻好奇心切。英国小说家夏洛蒂·勃朗特的《简·爱》中化用了这个典故: 很好, 盼望你感觉到你说的那种满足。无论如何, 你自己的良知会告诉你, 现在, 就像罗得的妻子那样动摇害怕, 还为时过早。"(《简·爱》31章)

3. **circumcision** (割礼): 典出《创世记》第17章9—14节: This is my covenant, which ye shall keep, between me and you and thy seed after thee; Every man child among you shall be circumcised. 你们所有的男子, 都要受割礼, 这就是我与你, 并你的后裔所立的约, 是你们所当遵守的。此典本指上帝和亚伯拉罕之间的立约, 引申为犹太民族与上帝立约的标志。凡犹太民族的男子都要割去自己的阳皮, 只有受此割礼的男子才能算犹太民族的一员。"割礼"又衍生出"皈依教门"、"忠贞不渝"的意思。《尤利西斯》第9章里有这样一段:

他喋喋不休地讲下去:

"包皮的搜集者耶和华已经不在了。刚才我在博物馆里遇见过他。我到那儿去向海泡里诞生的阿佛洛狄特致意的。这位希腊女神从来没有歪起嘴来祷告过。

4. **dust and ashes** (灰尘): 典出《创世记》第2章7节: And the LORD God formed man of the dust of the ground, and breathed into his nostrils the breath of life; and man became a living soul. 耶和华神用地上的尘土造人, 将生气吹在他鼻孔里, 他就成了有灵的活人。在西方人的观念中, 人为尘土所造, 死后也归于尘土, 所以人在上帝面前是卑微的。《创世记》第18章27节载, 亚伯拉罕在上帝面前为所多玛求情时言道: Behold now, I have taken upon me to speak unto the Lord, which am but dust and ashes. 我虽然是灰尘, 还敢对主说话。说自己不过是"尘与灰"就是想表达自己的卑微。《约伯记》第42章6节, 约伯在上帝面前表达自己的卑微和无知时也说: Wherefore I abhor myself, and repent in dust and ashes. 我厌恶自己, 在尘土和炉灰中懊悔。托马斯·哈代的小说《德伯家的苔丝》(Thomas Hardy: Tess of the d'Urbervilles)第22章苔丝对德伯家的少爷 Alec 表示鄙视: Hate him she did not quite; but he was dust and ashes to her, and even for her name's sake she scarcely wished to marry him. 她倒不是十分怨恨他; 只是视他如尘土, 为自己的名声, 她也不愿嫁给他。又如美国犹太人联合会主席辛德勒(Alexander Schindler, 1925–2000)的美文 Two Truths to Live By 中有一句: Don't spend and waste your lives accumulating objects that will only turn to dust and ashes.

5. **burnt offering of Issac** (以撒的燔祭): 典出《创世记》第22章1—14节。上帝为考验亚伯拉罕的忠诚, 叫他杀爱子以撒献为燔祭, 亚伯拉罕遵命而行, 上帝遂派天使阻拦, 以一只公羊代替以撒作为燔祭。此典指"忍痛割爱, 以示诚心", "无保留的奉献"。

6. **a mess of pottage** (一碗红豆汤): 典出《创世记》第25章27—34节: And Jacob said, Swear to me this day; and he sware unto him: and he sold his birthright to Jacob. Then Jacob gave Esau bread and pottage of lantils ... 雅各说: "你今日对我起誓吧。"以扫就对他起了誓, 把长子的名分卖给雅各。于是雅各将饼和红豆汤给了以扫……按照古希伯来人的规矩, 父亲的遗

产绝大部分都归长子所有。以扫出于饥饿仅仅为了弟弟雅各给的一碗红豆汤就轻易放弃了长子的权利。该典故还可写作 sell one's birthright for a mess/bowl/plate of pottage/stew/lentil stew，意思是为眼前蝇头小利而出卖长远利益，或因小失大、见利忘义。马克思在《资本论》中借用该典故形象地说明了工人和资本家之间的阶级关系："自由"工人由于资本主义生产方式的发展，才自愿地，也就是说，才在社会条件的逼迫下，按照自己的日常生活资料的价格出卖自己一生的全部能动时间，出卖自己的劳动能力本身，为了一碗红豆汤出卖自己的长子继承权。(《马克思恩格斯全集》第23卷第301页)列宁在1902年写的《一封给地方自治人士的信》中说："实际生活已向我们充分证明投机取巧的策略是没有根基的和丧失理智的，这是为了'一碗红豆汤'而出卖了'长子权'；专制官僚起初攫取了长子权，现在又夺走了我们这碗'红豆汤'。"(《列宁全集》第6卷342页)中国抗日战争期间，汪精卫投靠日本人，于1940年3月30日在南京正式成立伪"中华民国国民政府"，以牺牲民族利益为代价换取个人的权力和荣耀，被宋庆龄斥为"为一碗红豆汤出卖长子权"。

7. **Jacob's Ladder** (雅各的天梯)：典出《创世记》第28章11—19节: And he dreamed, and behold a ladder set up on a certain place, and the top of it reached to heaven: and behold the angels of God ascending and descending on it. 雅各梦见一个梯子立在地上，梯子的头顶着天，有神的使者在梯子上，上去下来。此典引申为升天之路。安东尼·侯普在《增达的囚人》(Anthony Hope: *The Prisoner of Zenda*)中就借用了此典故:

管子装好了，国王问我的爵爷这是什么意思？"你问这管子是什么意思？"他回答："实话告诉你，它是改良的雅各的天梯。天梯，你读过《圣经》，是人从地上去天堂的路。我们认为陛下你如果去天堂，绝不能走平常人的路，所以我们就为你准备了一条与众不同的私人升天之路，俗人看不到你升天也打扰不了你。陛下，这就是这个管子的意思。"

8. **Joseph's coat of many colours** (约瑟的彩衣)：典出《创世记》第37章2—4节: Now Israel loved Joseph more than all his children, because he was the son of his old age; and he made him a coat of many colours. 以色列原来爱约瑟过于爱他的众子，因为约瑟是他年老生的，他给约瑟做了一件彩衣。约瑟被宠爱，穿上父亲为他特意做的彩衣，遭到哥哥们的嫉妒。这个典故喻指对别人炫耀、夸示自己的荣耀，也是被宠爱的象征。

9. **Joseph and Potiphar's wife** (约瑟和波提乏的妻子)：典出《创世记》第39章中俊美的约瑟拒绝主人妻子色诱的故事。美国作家爱默生在其《论自助》中写道: In your metaphysics you have denied personality to the Deity: yet when the devout motions of the soul come, yield to them heart and life, though they should clothe God with shape and color. Leave your theory as Joseph his coat in the hand of the harlot, and flee.[1] 在你的形而上学里，你已经拒绝给上帝赋予人格；然而当灵魂的种种虔诚意向到来之时，那就全心全意地服从它们好了，尽管它们竟然给上帝赋予了形体和色彩。就像约瑟把他的衣裳丢在淫妇手里那样，丢开你的理论逃跑吧。

---

1. Joel Porte. *Emerson's Prose and Poetry*, New York: W.W. Norton & Company, Inc. 2001, p.48.

10. **corn in Egypt**（埃及的粮食）：典出《创世记》第37章12节至41章49节，约瑟为埃及发展了农业，连续7个丰年后埃及的粮食多得"如同海边的沙"。此典比喻丰饶富足，供应充足，有备无患。

六、课堂讨论题

1. 谈谈神话与传说的区别。
2. 结合"亚伯拉罕献子"的故事说明圣经叙事"简约"、"含蓄"的特点。
3. 请从叙事学的角度解读"底拿受辱"的故事。
4. 谈谈"选民"观与美国政治的关系。

七、课后思考题

1. 《创世记》第24章记述，亚伯拉罕为儿子以撒择妻时，要求老仆人发誓务必要把未来的儿媳妇带回到迦南。试从意识形态的角度分析亚伯拉罕的想法。
2. 你知道《古兰经》对约瑟故事的叙述吗？
3. 你知道中国的"一赐乐业"教吗？

以色列民族的形成:《出埃及记》

Exodus, the Growth of Israel as a Nation

一、导读: 摩西与以色列民族的转折点

摩西是公元前13世纪以色列的民族英雄、宗教领袖、军事家和立法者。摩西一生的传奇故事记载于《出埃及记》(*Exodus*)、《利未记》(*Leviticus*)、《民数记》(*Numbers*)和《申命记》(*Deuteronomy*)四卷中。

希伯来族长雅各及其子孙移居埃及数百年后,人丁兴旺,发展成一个对埃及王朝有威胁力的民族。埃及的新王设法排挤他们,结果以色列人逐渐沦为受奴役的民族。埃及法老甚至下令让接生婆杀死新出生的希伯来男婴。摩西出生隐藏3个月后,父母无奈将其放进蒲草箱,蒲草箱顺尼罗河而下。摩西幸被法老的女儿救起并收养在宫中,受到良好教育。摩西长大后知道了自己的身世,一次为了保护同胞杀死了一个埃及人,被迫逃亡,来到米甸,成家立业。上帝从燃烧的荆棘丛中显现,晓谕摩西返回埃及解救同胞。摩西回到埃及后在法老面前展示了一系列惊人的奇迹,又借助神力给埃及地降下一连串的灾难。法老终于下令让以色列人离开埃及。摩西率领以色列人在沙漠流浪了40年,历经重重困难,过红海,在西奈山领受上帝颁布的"十诫"律法。摩西的继任者约书亚带领族人最终回到"应许之地"迦南,以色列民族逐渐形成。

本讲选取《出埃及记》中关于摩西的记载,分5部分:

1. 逃出埃及: 摩西出生后被法老的女儿收养,成年后因杀死埃及人逃出埃及。
2. 与法老斗争: 摩西返回埃及与法老斗法。
3. 第一个逾越节: 上帝杀死埃及人家的长子和头生家畜,却越过门口涂有羊血的以色列人家。
4. 摩西之歌: 庆祝以色列人胜利过红海、赞美上帝大能的颂歌。
5. 十诫: 摩西从西奈山上领受"十诫"法版,传达给以色列人。

二、选文及注释

Part 1

The Escape from Egypt

Now there rose up a new king over Egypt, which knew not Joseph. And he said unto his people, "Behold, the people of the children of Israel are more and mightier than we: Come on, let us deal wisely with them; lest they multiply, and it come to pass, that, when there falleth out any war, they join also unto our enemies, and fight against us, and so get them up out of the land."

Therefore they did set over them taskmasters to afflict them with their burdens.[1] And they build for Pharaoh treasure cities, Pithom and Rameses[2]. But the more they afflicted them, the more they multiplied and grew. And they were grieved because of the children of Israel. And the Egyptians made the children of Israel to serve with rigour[3]: and they made their lives bitter with hard bondage, in morter[4], and in brick, and in all manner of service in the field: all their service, wherein they made them serve, was with rigour.

And the king of Egypt spake to the Hebrew midwives, of which the name of the one was Shiphrah, and the name of the other Puah: and he said, "When ye do the office of a midwife[5] to the Hebrew women, and see them upon the stools[6]; if it be a son, then ye shall kill him: but if it be a daughter, then she shall live."

But the midwives feared God, and did not as the king of Egypt commanded them, but saved the men children alive.

And the king of Egypt called for the midwives, and said unto them, "Why have ye done this thing, and have saved the men children alive?"

And the midwives said unto Pharaoh, "Because the Hebrew women are not as the Egyptian women; for they are lively, and are delivered ere the midwives come in unto them[7]."

Therefore God dealt well with the midwives: and the people multiplied, and waxed very mighty. And it came to pass, because the midwives feared God, that he made them houses. And Pharaoh charged all his people, saying, "Every son that is born ye shall cast into the river, and every daughter ye shall save alive." (1: 8–22)

And there went a man of the house of Levi, and took to wife a daughter of Levi. And the woman conceived, and bare a son: and when she saw him that he was a goodly child, she hid him three months. And when she could not longer hide him, she took for him an ark of bulrushes, and daubed it with slime and with pitch[8], and put the child therein; and she laid it in the flags by the river's brink[9]. And his sister stood afar off, to wit[10] what would be done to him.

And the daughter of Pharaoh came down to wash herself at the river; and her maidens walked along by the river's side; and when she saw the ark among the flags, she sent her maid to fetch it. And when she had opened it, she saw the child: and, behold, the babe wept. And she had compassion on him, and said, "This is one of the Hebrews' children."

Then said his sister to Pharaoh's daughter, "Shall I go and call to thee a nurse of the Hebrew women, that she may nurse the child for thee?" And Pharaoh's daughter said to her, "Go."

And the maid went and called the child's mother.

And Pharaoh's daughter said unto her, "Take this child away, and nurse it for me, and I will give thee thy wages."

---

1. set over taskmasters to afflict them with their burdens 派监工用苦工折磨他们。afflict *vt.* to cause pain or trouble to sb. 使痛苦；折磨。名词形式为 affliction。
2. Pithom and Rameses (地名)法老仓库所在地比东和兰塞，位于尼罗河三角洲东北部。
3. (with) rigour *n.* severity or strictness 严格。指对以色列人严加管束。
4. morter *n.* 同 mortar, 灰泥
5. do the office of a midwife 为产妇接生。
6. upon the stools (婉言)临盆。
7. they are lively, and are delivered ere the midwives come in unto them 希伯来妇女身体健壮，不等接生婆到就分娩了。ere *prep.* before 〈古〉在……之前。
8. an ark of bulrushes, and daubed it with slime and with pitch 一个蒲草箱，把里面涂上防水的沥青和柏油。bulrush 蒲草，古代植物，遍布尼罗河下游。daub 涂抹。
9. the flags by the river's brink 尼罗河边的芦荻中。flag 生长在尼罗河畔的高大青草。
10. wit *vt.* to learn 〈古〉想知道

And the woman took the child, and nursed it. And the child grew, and she brought him unto Pharaoh's daughter, and he became her son. And she called his name Moses: and she said, "Because I drew him out of the water."

And it came to pass in those days, when Moses was grown, that he went out unto his brethren, and looked on their burdens: and he spied[1] an Egyptian smiting[2] an Hebrew, one of his brethren. And he looked this way and that way, and when he saw that there was no man, he slew the Egyptian, and hid him in the sand. And when he went out the second day, behold, two men of Hebrews strove together: and he said to him that did the wrong, "Wherefore smitest thou thy fellow?" And he said, "Who made thee a prince and a judge over us? intendest thou to kill me, as thou killedst the Egyptian?" And Moses feared, and said, "Surely this thing is known."

Now when Pharaoh heard this thing, he sought to slay Moses. But Moses fled from the face of Pharaoh, and dwelt in the land of Midian[3]; and he sat by a well.

Now the priest of Midian had seven daughters: and they came and drew water, and filled the troughs[4] to water their father's flock. And the shepherds came and drove them away: but Moses stood up and helped them, and watered their flock. And when they came to Reuel[5] their father, he said, "How is it that ye are come so soon to day?"

And they said, "An Egyptian delivered us out of the hand of the shepherds, and also drew water enough for us, and watered the flock."

And he said unto his daughters, "And where is he? why is it that ye have left the man? call him, that he may eat bread."

And Moses was content to dwell with the man: and he gave Moses Zipporah[6] his daughter. And he bare him a son, and he called his name Gershom[7]; for he said, "I have been a stranger in a strange land."

And it came to pass in process of time that the king of Egypt died: and the children of Israel sighed by reason of the bondage, and they cried, and their cry came up unto God by reason of[8] the bondage. And God heard their groaning, and God remembered his covenant with Abraham, with Issac, and with Jacob. And God looked upon the children of Israel, and God had respect unto them. (2)

Now Moses kept the flock of Jethro his father in law, the priest of Midian: and he led the flock to the backside of the desert, and came to the mountain of God, even to Horeb[9]. And the angel of the LORD appeared unto him in a flame of fire out of the midst of a bush: and he looked, and, behold, the bush burned with fire, and the bush was not consumed. And Moses said,

"I will now turn aside, and see this great sight, why the bush is not burnt."

And when the LORD saw that he turned aside to see, God called unto him out of the midst of the bush and said,

---

1. spy *vt.* to catch sight of 看见
2. smite *vt.* to strike 击打; 打架。过去式为 smote; 过去分词形式为 smitten。
3. Midian /ˈmɪdɪən/ (地名)米甸, 位于巴勒斯坦南部的旷野。亚伯拉罕与其妾基土拉所生的儿子中有一个叫 Midian。亚伯拉罕曾给他财物, 让他到东方居住, 他后来成为米甸人(Midianites)的始祖。米甸人为游牧民族, 与希伯来人有远亲关系。
4. trough *n.* 水槽
5. Reuel (人名)流珥, 米甸地的祭司, 摩西的岳父。第三章称摩西的岳父名叫 Jethro (叶忒罗)。
6. Zipporah /ˈzɪpərə/ (人名)西坡拉, 摩西的妻子。这个词的本义是"小鸟", 因此冯象在《摩西五经》中新译"雀娘"。
7. Gershom /ˈgɜːʃɒm/ (人名)革舜, 摩西的儿子。意思是"我是他乡之客"。
8. by reason of because of 因为; 由于。
9. Horeb /ˈhɔːreb/ (地名)和烈山, 即西奈山(Sinai /ˈsaɪnaɪ/), 位于西奈半岛, 确切位置不详

"Moses, Moses."

And he said, "Here am I."

And he said, "Draw not nigh hither[1]: put off thy shoes from off thy feet, for the place whereon thou standest is holy ground." Moreover he said, "I am the God of thy father, the God of Abraham, the God of Isaac, and the God of Jacob." And Moses hid his face; for he was afraid to look upon God.

And the LORD said, "I have surely seen the affliction of my people which are in Egypt, and have heard their cry by reason of their taskmasters; for I know their sorrows; and I am come down to deliver them out the hand of the Egyptians and to bring them up out of that land unto a good land and a large, unto a land flowing with milk and honey[2]; ... Now therefore, behold, the cry of the children of Israel is come unto me: and I have also seen the oppression wherewith the Egyptians oppress them. Come now therefore, and I will send thee unto Pharaoh, that thou mayest bring forth my people the children of Israel out of Egypt."

And Moses said unto God, "Who am I, that I should go unto Pharaoh, and that I should bring forth the children of Israel out of Egypt?"

And he said, "Certainly I will be with thee; and this shall be a token unto thee, that I have sent thee: When thou hast brought forth the people out of Egypt, ye shall serve God upon this mountain."

And Moses said unto God, "Behold, when I come unto the children of Israel, and shall say unto them, 'The God of your fathers hath sent me unto you'; and they shall say to me, 'What is his name?' what shall I say unto them?"

And God said unto Moses, "I AM THAT I AM[3]": and he said, "Thus shalt thou say unto the children of Israel. I AM hath sent me unto you." And God said moreover unto Moses, "Thus shalt thou say unto the children of Israel, 'The LORD God of your fathers, the God of Abraham, the God of Isaac, and the God of Jacob, hath sent me unto you,' ... And they shall hearken to thy voice: and thou shalt come, thou and the elders of Israel, unto the king of Egypt, and ye shall say unto him, "The LORD God of the Hebrews hath met with us: and now let us go, we beseech[4] thee, three days' journey into the wilderness, that we may sacrifice to the LORD our God.' And I am sure that the king of Egypt will not let you go, no, not by a mighty hand. And I will stretch out my hand, and smite Egypt with all my wonders which I will do in the midst thereof: and after that he will let you go. And I will give this people favour in the sight of the Egyptians: and it shall come to pass, that, when ye go, ye shall not go empty: but every woman shall borrow of her neighbour, and of her that sojourneth[5] in her house, jewels of silver, and jewels of gold, and raiment[6]: and ye shall put them upon your sons, and upon your daughters; and ye shall spoil the Egyptians." (3 with 3: 16–17 omitted)

Part 2

Struggle Against the Pharaoh

And afterward Moses and Aaron[7] went in, and told Pharaoh, "Thus saith the LORD God of Israel, 'Let my people go,

---

1. Draw not nigh hither 不要走近。nigh *adv.* near 〈古〉靠近; hither *adv.* toward to this place 到这。
2. a land flowing with milk and honey 流着奶与蜜之地, 形容那里物产丰富。
3. I AM THAT I AM 上帝这个答复在希伯来原文中是双关语, 大意是"我是我所是", 或"我将会是将来我所是"。中文译本一般译为"我是自有永有者"。上帝用这个名字来显示自己的绝对存在。
4. beseech *vt.* to request earnestly 恳求
5. sojourn *vi.* to reside temporarily 暂居; 逗留
6. raiment *n.* clothes; garment 〈古〉衣服
7. Aaron /ˈɛərən/ (人名)亚伦, 摩西的哥哥, 因为口才好被上帝指派协助摩西, 后成为犹太教的第一祭司长

that they may hold a feast[1] unto me in the wilderness.'"

And Pharaoh said, "Who is the LORD, that I should obey his voice to let Israel go? I know not the LORD, neither will I let Israel go."

And they said, "The God of the Hebrews hath met with us: let us go, we pray thee, three days' journey into the desert, and sacrifice unto the LORD our God; lest he fall upon us with pestilence[2], or with the sword."

And the king of Egypt said unto them, "Wherefore do ye, Moses and Aaron, let the people from their works? get you unto your burdens." ...

And Pharaoh commanded the same day the taskmasters of the people, and their officers, saying, "Ye shall no more give the people straw to make bricks, as heretofore: let them go and gather straw for themselves. And the tale[3] of the bricks, which they did make heretofore, ye shall lay upon them; ye shall not diminish[4] ought thereof: for they be idle[5]; therefore they cry, saying, 'Let us go and sacrifice to our God.' Let there more work be laid upon the men, that they may labour therein; and let them not regard vain words[6]."

And the taskmasters of the people went out, and their officers, and they spake to the people, saying, "Thus saith Pharaoh, 'I will not give you straw. Go ye, get you straw where ye can find it: yet not ought of your work shall be diminished[7].'"

So the people were scattered abroad throughout all the land of Egypt to gather stubble[8] instead of straw. And the taskmasters hasted[9] them, saying, "Fulfil your works, your daily tasks, as when there was straw."

And the officers of the children of Israel, which Pharaoh's taskmasters had set over them, were beaten, and demanded, "Wherefore have ye not fulfilled your task in making brick both yesterday and to day, as heretofore?"

Then the officers of the children of Israel came and cried unto Pharaoh, saying, "Wherefore dealest thou thus with thy servants? There is no straw given unto thy servants, and they say to us, 'Make brick': and, behold, thy servants are beaten; but the fault is in thine own people."

But he said, "Ye are idle, ye are idle: therefore ye say, 'Let us go and do sacrifice to the LORD.' Go therefore now, and work; for there shall no straw be given you, yet shall ye deliver the tale of bricks."

And the officers of the children of Israel did see that they were in evil case[10], after it was said, "Ye shall not minish[11] ought from your bricks of your daily task."

And they met Moses and Aaron, who stood in the way[12], as they came forth from Pharaoh: and they said unto them, "The LORD look upon you, and judge; because

---

1. hold a feast 守节。指给上帝献祭。
2. pestilence /ˈpestɪləns/ n. 瘟疫
3. tale n. a total 〈古〉总数
4. diminish vt. to reduce in number 减少；减量。注意 diminish 之后的 ought 是名词 aught (任何事；零)的变体，相当于 anything。
5. idle adj. lazy 懒惰的
6. regard vain words 听信虚谎的言语。指听信关于上帝要拯救以色列人的消息和传言。
7. yet not ought of your work shall be diminished 但是你们的劳动一点也不能减少。
8. stubble n. 碎秸，劣质的做砖原料
9. haste (即 hasten) vt. to urge sb. 催促；逼迫
10. in evil case 处境悲惨。evil adj. indicating future misfortune 不幸的
11. minish vt. 〈古〉减少
12. stand in the way 挡住路，意思是"正好碰上"。

ye have made our savour to be abhorred[1] in the eyes of Pharaoh, and in the eyes of his servants, to put a sword in their hand to slay us."

And Moses returned unto the LORD, and said, "Lord, wherefore hast thou so evil entreated[2] this people? why is it that thou hast sent me? For since I came to Pharaoh to speak in thy name, he hath done evil to this people; neither hast thou delivered thy people at all." (5)

And the LORD spake unto Moses and unto Aaron, saying, "When Pharaoh shall speak unto you, saying, 'Shew a miracle for you': then thou shall say unto Aaron, 'Take thy rod, and cast it before Pharaoh,' and it shall become a serpent."

And Moses and Aaron went in unto Pharaoh, and they did so as the LORD had commanded: and Aaron cast down his rod before Pharaoh, and before his servants, and it became a serpent. Then Pharaoh also called the wise men and the sorcerers[3]: now the magicians of Egypt, they also did in like manner with their enchantments[4]. For they cast down every man his rod, and they became serpents: but Aaron's rod swallowed up their rods. And he hardened[5] Pharaoh's heart, that he hearkened not unto them; as the LORD had said. (7: 8–13)

And Moses and Aaron did so, as the Lord commanded; and he lifted up the rod, and smote the waters that were in the river, in the sight of Pharaoh, and in the sight of his servants; and all the waters that were in the river were turned to blood. And the fish that was in the river died; and the river stank[6], and the Egyptians could not drink of the water of the river; and there was blood throughout all the land of Egypt. And the magicians of Egypt did so with their enchantments: and Pharaoh's heart was hardened, neither did he hearken unto them; as the LORD had said. And Pharaoh turned and went into his house, neither did he set his heart to this[7] also. And all the Egyptians digged round about the river for water to drink; for they could not drink of the water of the river. And seven days were fulfilled, after that the LORD had smitten the river[8]. (7: 20–25)

And the LORD spake unto Moses, "Say unto Aaron, 'Stretch forth thine hand with thy rod over the streams, over the rivers, and over the ponds, and cause frogs to come up upon the land of Egypt.'"

And Aaron stretched out his hand over the waters of Egypt: and the frogs came up, and covered the land of Egypt. And the magicians did so with their enchantments, and brought up frogs upon the land of Egypt.

The Pharaoh called for Moses and Aaron, and said, "Intreat[9] the LORD, that he may take away the frogs from me, and from my people; and I will let the people go, that they may do sacrifice unto the LORD."

And Moses said unto Pharaoh, "Glory over me: when shall I intreat for thee, and for thy servants, and for thy people, to destroy the frogs from thee and thy houses, that they may remain in the river only?"

And he said, "To morrow."

And he said, "Be it according to thy

---

1. savour to be abhorred 本意是"发出臭味"、"味道让人生厌",这里指以色列官长在埃及法老面前有了不好的印象。abhorred *adj.* disgusting, loathsome 让人憎恶的; 令人讨厌的
2. entreat *vt.* to treat 〈古〉对待
3. the wise men and the sorcerers 博士和术士。在埃及,宗教和法术是分不开的,学问高深者做祭司首领。
4. enchantment *n.* 魔法; 妖术
5. harden *vt.* to make unfeeling, unsympathetic, or callous 使(法老)心里刚硬或心意更加坚决。
6. stank 动词 stink 的过去式。stink *vt.* to emit a strong foul odor 发出恶臭。
7. set his heart to this 把这事放在心上。
8. the LORD had smitten the river 耶和华击打河水。指耶和华让尼罗河水变成血水,作为灾难降临埃及全境。
9. intreat *vt.* to make an earnest request 〈古〉entreat (恳求)的变体

word: that thou mayest know that there is none like unto the LORD our God. And the frogs shall depart from thee, and from thy houses, and from thy servants, and from thy people; they shall remain in the river only."

And Moses and Aaron went out from Pharaoh; and Moses cried unto the LORD because of the frogs which he had brought against Pharaoh. And the LORD did according to the word of Moses; and the frogs died out of the houses, out of the villages, and out of the fields. And they gathered them together upon heaps; and the land stank. But when Pharaoh saw that there was respite[1], he hardened his heart, and hearkened not unto them; as the LORD had said. (8: 5–15)

And the LORD said unto Moses, "Pharaoh shall not hearken unto you; that my wonders may be multiplied in the land of Egypt."

And Moses and Aaron did all these wonders before Pharaoh: and the LORD hardened Pharaoh's heart, so that he would not let the children of Israel go out of his land. (11: 9–10)

Part 3

The First Passover[2]

Moses called for all the elders of Israel, and said unto them, "Drew out and take you a lamb according to your families, and kill the passover. And ye shall take a bunch of hyssop[3], and dip it in the blood that is in the bason, and strike the lintel[4] and the two side posts with the blood that is in the bason; and none of you shall go out at the door of his house until the morning. For the LORD will pass through to smite the Egyptians; and when he seeth the blood upon the lintel, and on the two side posts, the LORD will pass over the door, and will not suffer the destroyer to come in unto your houses to smite you[5]. And ye shall observe[6] this thing for an ordinance[7] to thee and to thy sons for ever. And it shall come to pass, when ye be come to the land which the LORD will give you, according as he hath promised, that ye shall keep this service. And it shall come to pass, when your children shall say unto you, 'What mean ye by this service?' that ye shall say, "It is the sacrifice of the LORD's passover, who passed over the houses of the children of Israel in Egypt, when he smote the Egyptians, and delivered out houses."

And the people bowed the head and worshipped. And the children of Israel went away, and did as the LORD had commanded Moses and Aaron, so did they.

And it came to pass, that at midnight the LORD smote all the firstborn in the land of Egypt, from the firstborn of Pharaoh that sat on his throne unto the firstborn of the captive[8] that was in the dungeon[9]; and all the firstborn of cattle. And Pharaoh rose up in the night, he, and all his servants, and all the Egyptians; and there was a great cry in Egypt; for there was not a house where there was not one dead.

---

1. respite *n.* an interval of rest or relief 喘息；暂时的缓解。指蛙灾平息。
2. Passover *n.* 逾越节。第一句里 the passover 指逾越节献给上帝的羊羔。
3. a bunch of hyssop /ˈhɪsəp/ 一把牛膝草。牛膝草是一种唇形科植物，带有薄荷香味，常用来蘸洒祭牲之血。
4. lintel *n.* 门楣
5. the Lord will pass over the door, and will not suffer the destroyer to come in unto your house to smite you 上帝就会越过那门，不让灭命的(天使)进你们家，击杀你们。suffer *vt.* to permit; to allow 允许；容许。destroyer *n.* 指专司杀戮的天使。
6. observe *vt.* to adhere to; to abide by 遵守
7. ordinance *n.* a custom or practice established by long usage 礼俗
8. captive *n.* a prisoner of war 战俘；囚徒
9. dungeon *n.* an underground prion cell 监牢；地牢

And he called for Moses and Aaron by night, and said, "Rise up, and get you forth from among my people, both ye and the children of Israel; and go, serve the LORD, as ye have said. Also take your flocks and your herds, as ye have said, and be gone; and bless me also[1]."

And the Egyptians were urgent upon the people, that they might send them out of the land in haste; for they said, "We be all dead men.[2]"

And the people took their dough before it was leavened[3], their kneadingtroughs[4] being bound up in their clothes upon their shoulders. And the children of Israel did according to the word of Moses; and they borrowed of the Egyptians jewels of silver, and jewels of gold, and raiment: and the LORD gave the people favour in the sight of the Egyptians, so that they lent unto them such things as they required. And they spoiled the Egyptians[5]. And the children of Israel journeyed from Rameses to Succoth[6], about six hundred thousand on foot that were men, beside children. And a mixed multitude[7] went up also with them; and flocks, and herds, even very much cattle. And they baked unleavened cakes of the dough which they brought forth out of Egypt, for it was not leavened; because they were thrust out of Egypt, and could not tarry, neither had they prepared for themselves any victual[8]. (12: 21–39)

And it came to pass, when Pharaoh had let the people go, that God led them not through the way of the land of the Phillistines[9], although that was near; for God said, "Lest peradventure the people repent when they see war, and they return to Egypt": but God led the people about, through the way of the wilderness of the Red Sea[10]. And the children of Israel went up harnessed out of the land of Egypt[11]. And Moses took the bones of Joseph with him: for he had straitly sworn the children of Israel, saying, "God will surely visit you; and ye shall carry up my bones away hence with you."

And they took their journey from Succoth, and encamped in Etham[12], in the edge of the wilderness. And the LORD went before them by day in a pillar of a cloud, to lead them the way; and by night in a pillar of fire, to give them light; to go by day and night: He took not away the pillar of the cloud by day, nor the pillar of fire by night, from before the people. (13: 17–22)

And it was told the king of Egypt that the people fled: and the heart of Pharaoh and of his servants was turned against the people, and they said, "Why have we done this, that we have let Israel go from serving us?"

And he made ready his chariot, and took his people with him: And he took six

---

1. and bless me also 法老请求为他祝福，表示他已经完全屈服了。
2. We be all dead men. 我们都要死了。表示埃及人彻底害怕以色列人的上帝了。
3. dough before it was leavened 未经发酵的面。dough *n.* 生面团
4. kneadingtrough *n.* 和面用的盆。
5. they spoiled the Egyptians 以色列人把埃及人的财物夺去了。spoil *vt.* to rob (a person or a place) of goods or possessions by force or violence〈古〉抢夺
6. Succoth (地名)疏割，大约在兰塞东南80公里，是以色列人出埃及后第一个扎营的地方
7. a mixed multitude 闲杂人，大概是与以色列人通婚的埃及人或其他在埃及为奴的外族人，他们也乘机脱离法老的辖制。
8. victual *n.* food supplies; provision 食物；供给
9. the land of Phillistines 海上民族非利士人的土地，在地中海东岸。
10. the Red Sea 旧译"红海"，希伯来原文实际是"芦苇海"，指的是苏伊士湾及尼罗河三角洲东部的湖泽，与现在的红海无关。因此，冯象在《摩西五经》中新译"芦海"。
11. the children of Israel went up harnessed out of the land of Egypt 以色列人出埃及时随身带着兵器。harness *n.*〈古〉铠甲。这里用作动词，修饰主语。
12. Etham (地名)以倘。因为在旷野边缘，所以大概位于疏割以东。

hundred chosen chariots, and all the chariots of Egypt, and captains[1] over every one of them. And the LORD hardened the heart of Pharaoh king of Egypt, and he pursued after the children of Israel: and the children of Israel went out with an high hand[2]. But the Egyptians pursued after them, all the horses and chariots of Pharaoh, and his horsemen, and his army, and overtook them encamping by the sea, beside Pi-hahiroth, before Baal-zephon[3].

And when Pharaoh drew nigh, the children of Israel lifted up their eyes, and, behold, the Egyptians marched after them; and they were sore afraid: and the children of Israel cried out unto the LORD. And they said unto Moses, "Because there were no graves in Egypt, hast thou taken us away to die in the wilderness? Wherefore hast thou dealt thus with us, to carry us forth out of Egypt? Is not this the word that we did tell thee in Egypt, saying, 'Let us alone, that we may serve the Egyptians'? For it had been better for us to serve the Egyptians, than that we should die in the wilderness."

And Moses said unto the people, "Fear ye not, stand still, and see the salvation of the LORD[4], which he will shew to you to day: for the Egyptians whom ye have seen to day, ye shall see them again no more for ever. The LORD shall fight for you, and ye shall hold your peace[5]." (14: 5–14)

And the angel of God, which went before the camp of Israel, removed and went behind them; and the pillar of the cloud went from before their face, and stood behind them: And it came between the camp of the Egyptians and the camp of Israel; and it was a cloud and darkness to them, but it gave light by night to these: so that the one came not near the other all the night[6]. And Moses stretched out his hand over the sea; and the LORD caused the sea to go back by a strong east wind all that night, and made the sea dry land, and the waters were divided. And the children of Israel went into the midst of the sea upon the dry ground: and the waters were a wall unto them on their right hand, and on their left.

And the Egyptians pursued, and went in after them to the midst of the sea, even all Pharaoh's horses, his chariots, and his horsemen. And it came to pass, that in the morning watch[7] the LORD looked unto the host[8] of the Egyptians through the pillar of fire and of the cloud, and troubled the host of the Egyptians, and took off their chariot wheels, that they drave them heavily: so that the Egyptians said, "Let us flee from the face of Israel; for the LORD fighteth for them against the Egyptians."

And the LORD said unto Moses, "Stretch out thine hand over the sea, that the waters may come again upon the Egyptians, upon their chariots, and upon their horsemen."

And Moses stretched forth his hand over the sea, and the sea returned to his strength[9] when the morning appeared; and the Egyptians fled against it; and the LORD overthrew the Egyptians in the midst of the sea. And the waters returned, and covered the chariots, and the horsemen, and all the host of Pharaoh that came into the sea after them; there remained not so much as one of

---

1. captain *n.* (战车)兵长, 官阶名。原文为"第三人", 意思是每辆战车上除了驾驶者和一名战士外, 第三个人持盾牌协助保护战士。
2. with an high hand 指耶和华高举的手。此句的意思是以色列人出埃及靠的是耶和华的指引和拯救。
3. beside Pi-hahiroth, before Baal-zephon 靠近比哈希录, 对着巴力洗分。这两个地方都在疏割以北。
4. the salvation of the LORD 上帝对以色列人的拯救
5. hold one's peace 闭口; 保持缄默
6. the one came not near the other all the night (由于法老军队和以色列人被云柱隔开)双方一夜不得靠近。
7. morning watch 晨更。晚上分为三更, 每更约四小时, 因此晨更是凌晨2—6点间, 通常是突袭的好时机。
8. host *n.* an army 军队
9. the sea returned to his strength 海水又返回大海, 恢复原状。his 是拟人手法。

them.

But the children of Israel walked upon dry land in the midst of the sea; and the waters were a wall unto them on their right hand, and on their left. Thus the L<small>ORD</small> saved Israel that day out of the hand of the Egyptians; and Israel saw the Egyptians dead upon the sea shore. And Israel saw that great work which the L<small>ORD</small> did upon the Egyptians: and the people feared the L<small>ORD</small> and believed the L<small>ORD</small>, and his servant Moses. (14: 19–31)

Part 4

The Song of Moses

Then sang Moses and the children of Israel this song unto the L<small>ORD</small>, and spake, saying,

"I will sing unto the L<small>ORD</small>, for he hath triumphed gloriously:
The horse and his rider hath he thrown into the sea.
The L<small>ORD</small> is my strength and song,
And he is become my salvation:
He is my God, and I will prepare him an habitation[1];
My father's God, and I will exalt him.
The L<small>ORD</small> is a man of war[2]:
The L<small>ORD</small> is his name.
Pharaoh's chariots and his host hath he cast into the sea:
His chosen captains also are drowned in the Red sea.
The depths have covered them:
They sank into the bottom as a stone.
Thy right hand, O L<small>ORD</small>, is become glorious in power:
Thy right hand, O L<small>ORD</small>, hath dashed in pieces the enemy.
And in the greatness of thine excellency thou hast overthrown them that rose up against thee:
Thou sentest forth thy wrath, which consumed them as stubble.
And with the blast of thy nostrils[3] the waters were gathered together,
The floods stood upright as an heap,
And the depths were congealed in the heart of sea[4].
The enemy said,
'I will pursue, I will overtake, I will divide the spoil;
My lust shall be satisfied upon them;
I will draw my sword, my hand shall destroy them.'
Thou didst blow with thy wind, the sea covered them:
They sank as lead in the mighty waters.

Who is like unto thee, O L<small>ORD</small>, among the gods?
Who is like thee, glorious in holiness,
Fearful in praises, doing wonders?
Thou stretchedst out thy right hand,
The earth swallowed them.
Thou in thy mercy hast led forth the people which thou hast redeemed[5]:
Thou hast guided them in thy strength unto thy holy habitation[6].
The people shall hear, and be afraid:
Sorrow shall take hold on the inhabitants

---

1. habitation *n.* a place of abode; a residence 居所; 住处。摩西要设祭坛用于敬拜耶和华。
2. The L<small>ORD</small> is a man of war 耶和华是战士。意思是耶和华为了拯救选民而参与同埃及军队的战斗。
3. blast of thy nostrils 上帝鼻孔所吹之气。诗人用拟人手法(又如下文描写海水的力量)来形容上帝, 歌颂其大能。
4. the depths were congealed in the heart of sea 海中的深水凝结。congeal *vi.* to become semi-solid, especially on cooling 凝结
5. redeem *vt.* to save 救赎; 拯救。该词具有神学意义, 指从罪恶及其后果的状况中解救出来。
6. thy holy habitation 上帝的圣所。原意是牧羊之地, 广义上指整块应许之地。

of Palestina.[1]

Then the dukes of Edom[2] shall be amazed;

Thy mighty men of Moab[3], trembling shall take hold upon them;

All the inhabitants of Canaan shall melt away.[4]

Fear and dread shall fall upon them;

By the greatness of thine arm they shall be as still as a stone[5];

Till thy people pass over, O LORD,

Till the people pass over, which thou hast purchased.

Thou shalt bring them in, and plant them in the mountain of thine inheritance[6],

In the place, O LORD, which thou hast made for thee to dwell in,

In the Sanctuary, O Lord, which thy hands have established.

The LORD shall reign for ever and ever."

And Miriam[7] the prophetess, the sister of Aaron, took a timbrel[8] in her hand; and all the women went out after her with timbrels and with dances. And Miriam answered them,

"Sing ye to the LORD, for he hath triumphed gloriously;

The horse and his rider hath he thrown into the sea."(15: 1–21 with 15: 19 omitted)

Part 5

The Ten Commandments

So Moses brought Israel from the Red sea, and they went out into the wilderness of Shur[9]; and they went three days in the wilderness, and found no water. And when they came to Marah[10], they could not drink of waters of Marah, for they were bitter. And the people murmured against Moses, saying, "What shall we drink?"

And he cried unto the LORD; and the LORD shewed him a tree, which when he had cast into the waters, the waters were made sweet. (15: 22–25)

And the whole congregation[11] of the children of Israel murmured against Moses and Aaron in the wilderness: and the children of Israel said unto them, "Would to God we had died by the hand of the LORD in the land of Egypt, when we sat by the flesh pots, and when we did eat bread to the full; for ye have brought us forth into this wilderness, to kill this whole assembly[12] with hunger."

Then said the LORD unto Moses, "Behold, I will rain bread from heaven for you; and the people shall go out and gather a certain

---

1. Sorrow shall take hold on the inhabitants of Palestina. 恐惧笼罩非利士人。"巴勒斯坦的居民"指非利士人。
2. the dukes of Edom 以东的族长。雅各的长子以扫是以东人的始祖。
3. Thy mighty men of Moab 摩押的英雄。罗得和大女儿所生的儿子是摩押人之始祖。
4. All the inhabitants of Canaan shall melt away. 迦南的居民都胆战心寒。
5. as still as a stone 像石头一样呆然不动。形容吓得呆若木鸡。
6. plant them in the mountain of thine inheritance 直译：在你产业的山中培植他们。意思是上帝指引以色列人出埃及到达应许之地后将好好训导他们。此句简单总结出埃及的主要目标，即把神特别挑选的子民以色列人安顿在神居住的圣地上。"你产业的山上"是天与地在宇宙间的接触点，按照《圣经》后来的暗示，该处为锡安山。inheritance $n.$ 遗产；可供继承的产业。
7. Miriam /ˈmɪrɪəm/（人名）米利暗，摩西和亚伦的姐姐，是一个女先知。后因不服摩西为民众领袖，与亚伦口出怨言，遭上帝惩罚而患大麻风，摩西为她祈祷才得痊愈。冯象新译"米莲"。
8. timbrel $n.$ 小手鼓。以色列妇女和少女常常打起小手鼓载歌载舞欢庆胜利。
9. the wilderness of Shur 书珥的旷野。位于西奈半岛东北部。
10. Marah /ˈmeɪrə/（地名）玛拉，位于苏伊士湾北端南面80公里，那里的水富含矿盐，所以带苦涩味
11. congregation $n.$ the members of a specific religious group who regularly worship at a church or synagogue（犹太教）会众
12. assembly $n.$ a gathering 人群

rate¹ every day, that I may prove them, whether they will walk in my law, or no. And it shall come to pass, that on the sixth day they shall prepare that which they bring in; and it shall be twice as much as they gather daily." (16: 2–5)

And it came to pass, that at even the quails² came up, and covered the camp: and in the morning the dew lay round about the host. And when the dew that lay was gone up, behold, upon the face of the wilderness there lay a small round thing, as small as the hoar³ frost on the ground. And when the children of Israel saw it, they said one to another, "It is manna⁴": for they wist⁵ not what it was.

And Moses said unto them, "This is the bread which the LORD hath given you to eat. This is the thing which the LORD hath commanded, 'Gather of it every man according to his eating⁶, an omer for every man, according to the number of your persons; take ye every man for them which are in his tents.'"

And the children of Israel did so, and gathered, some more, some less. And when they did mete it with an omer⁷, he that gathered much had nothing over, and he that gathered little had no lack; they gathered every man according to his eating.

And Moses said, "Let no man leave of it till the morning."

Notwithstanding⁸ they hearkened not unto Moses; but some of them left of it until the morning, and it bred worms, and stank: and Moses was wroth with them. And they gathered it every morning, every man according to his eating: and when the sun waxed hot⁹, it melted.

And it came to pass, that on the sixth day they gathered twice as much bread, two omers for one man: and all the rulers of the congregation came and told Moses. And he said unto them, "This is that which the Lord hath said, 'To morrow is the rest of the holy sabbath¹⁰ unto the LORD: bake that which ye will bake to day, and seethe¹¹ that ye will seethe; and that which remaineth over lay up for you to be kept until the morning.'"

---

1. a certain rate 指每天搜集一份。rate *n.* a measure of sth. 份额
2. quail *n.* 鹌鹑。上帝连续赐下鹌鹑和吗哪, 满足以色列人的需要, 但如接下来所讲到的, 上帝是按着安息日的条例来供应食物的, 并借此试验以色列人是否忠于上帝的律法。
3. hoar *adj.* greyish white 灰白色的。hoar frost 白霜。
4. manna /ˈmænə/ *n.* (音译)吗哪。本意是: 这是什么? 后来摩西沿用此名, 称此种食物为"吗哪"。以色列人相信露水乃从天而降, 所以认为吗哪是和露水一起降落在地上的。
5. wist 古英语 wit (知道)的过去式
6. (his) eating 指一个人的口粮
7. mete it with an omer 用俄梅珥量一量(多收者不至多占, 少收者不至短缺)。mete *vt.* to measure 〈古〉测量; 称量。omer (音译)俄梅珥, 当时的容量单位, 约2.3公升, 是一个人一天的口粮。
8. notwithstanding *conj.* in spite of the fact that; although 虽然; 尽管
9. the sun waxed hot 太阳发热。意思是, 吗哪一经太阳照射就会溶化。wax. *vi.* to increase gradually in heat 变热
10. sabbath /ˈsæbəθ/ *n.* 安息日, 是犹太教的重要节日。又称 holy sabbath。
11. seethe *vt.* to come to a boil 〈古〉煮沸

And they laid it up till the morning, as Moses bade[1]: and it did not stink, neither was there any worm therein. And Moses said, "Eat that to day; for to day is a sabbath unto the LORD: to day ye shall not find it in the field. Six days ye shall gather it; but on the seventh day, which is the sabbath, in it there shall be none."

And it came to pass, that there went out some of the people on the seventh day for to gather, and they found none. (16: 13–27)

And the house of Israel called the name thereof Manna: and it was like coriander seed[2], white; and the taste of it was like wafers[3] made with honey.

And Moses said, "This is the thing which the LORD commandeth, 'Fill an omer of it to be kept for your generations; that they may see the bread wherewith I have fed you in the wilderness, when I brought you forth from the land of Egypt.'"

And Moses said unto Aaron, "Take a pot, and put an omer full of manna therein, and lay it up before the LORD, to be kept for your generations."

As the LORD commanded Moses, so Aaron laid it up before the Testimony[4], to be kept. And the children of Israel did eat manna forty years, until they came to a land inhabited; they did eat manna, until they came unto the borders of the land of Canaan. (16: 31–35)

In the third month, when the children of Israel were gone forth out of the land of Egypt, the same day came they into the wilderness of Sinai[5]. For they were departed from Rephidim[6], and were come to the desert of Sinai, and had pitched in the wilderness; and there Israel camped before the mount.

And Moses went up unto God, and the LORD called unto him out of the mountain, saying, "Thus shalt thou say to the house of Jacob, and tell the children of Israel: 'Ye have seen what I did unto the Egyptians, and how I bare you on eagles' wings[7], and brought you unto myself. Now therefore, if ye will obey my voice indeed, and keep my covenant, then ye shall be a peculiar treasure[8] unto me above all people: for all the earth is mine: and ye shall be unto me a kingdom of priests, and an holy nation[9]. These are the words which thou shalt speak unto the children of Israel.'" (19: 1–6)

And the LORD said unto Moses, "Go unto the people, and sanctify[10] them to day and to morrow, and let them wash their clothes, and be ready against the third day: for the third day the LORD will come down in the sight of all the people upon mount Sinai. And thou shalt set bounds unto the people round about, saying, 'Take heed to yourselves, that ye go not up into the mount, or touch the border of it: whosoever toucheth the mount shall be surely put to death.' There shall not an hand touch it, but

---

1. bade 动词 bid 的过去式。bid *vt.* to issue a command to; to direct 命令；吩咐
2. coriander seed 芫荽子，种子细小，呈灰白色，通常作熟菜的调味品。
3. wafer *n.* a thin, light, crisp biscuit 薄饼
4. the Testimony 法柜，也就是装着"十诫"法版的约柜。
5. the wilderness of Sinai /ˈsaɪnaɪ/ 西奈旷野，位于西奈半岛中部，又称"摩西山"(Mount Moses)，海拔2285米，后被尊为基督教的"神峰"(The Holy Peak)。
6. Rephidim (地名)利非订，在西奈山附近。此前这里发生过两件大事：摩西杖击磐石出水；以色列人与亚玛力人争战。
7. I bare you on eagles' wings 上帝像雄鹰一样把以色列人背在翅膀上。形容上帝对以色列人的特别保护。
8. peculiar treasure 珍贵的财宝。比喻上帝特选的子民以色列人。
9. ye shall be unto me a kingdom of priests, and an holy nation 你们要归我作祭司的国度，为圣洁的国民。
10. sanctify *vt.* 指洁净身体

he shall surely be stoned, or shot through; whether it be beast or man, it shall not live: when the trumpet soundeth long, they shall come up to the mount."

And Moses went down from the mount unto the people, and sanctified the people; and they washed their clothes. And he said unto the people, "Be ready against the third day; come not at your wives[1]."

And it came to pass on the third day in the morning, that there were thunders and lightnings, and a thick cloud upon the mount, and the voice of the trumpet exceeding loud; so that all the people that was in the camp trembled. And Moses brought forth the people out of the camp to meet with God; and they stood at the nether[2] part of the mount. (19: 10–17)

And God spake all these words, saying, "I am the LORD thy God, which have brought thee out of the land of Egypt, out of the house of bondage.

Thou shalt have no other gods before me.

Thou shalt not make unto thee any graven image[3], or any likeness of any thing that is in heaven above, or that is in the earth beneath, or that is in the water under the earth: Thou shalt not bow down thyself to them, nor serve them: for I the LORD thy God am a jealous God, visiting the iniquity of the fathers upon the children unto the third and fourth generation of them that hate me[4]; and shewing mercy unto thousands of them that love me, and keep my commandments.

Thou shalt not take the name of the LORD thy God in vain; for the LORD will not hold him guiltless that taketh his name in vain.

Remember the sabbath day, to keep it holy. Six days shalt thou labour, and do all thy work: but the seventh day is the sabbath of the LORD thy God: in it thou shalt not do any work, thou, nor thy son, nor thy daughter, thy manservant, nor thy maidservant, nor thy cattle, nor thy stranger that is within thy gates: for in six days the LORD made heaven and earth, the sea and all that in them is, and rested the seventh day: wherefore the LORD blessed the sabbath day, and hallowed[5] it.

Honour thy father and thy mother: that thy days[6] may be long upon the land which the LORD thy God giveth thee.

Thou shalt not kill.

Thou shalt not commit adultery[7].

Thou shalt not steal.

Thou shalt not bear false witness[8] against thy neighbour.

Thou shalt not covet[9] thy neighbour's house, thou shalt not covet thy neighbour's wife, nor his manservant, nor his maidservant, nor his ox, nor his ass, nor any thing that is thy neighbour's." (20: 1–17)

---

1. come not at your wives 不可与妻子同房。当时的风俗认为，刚和女人交合的男子暂时不宜参与圣职。
2. nether *adj.* lower 下面的
3. graven image 雕刻的偶像。graven 是 grave (雕刻)的过去分词形式。
4. a jealous God, visiting the iniquity of the fathers upon the children unto the third and fourth generation of them that hate me (我是)嫉恨邪神的上帝，恨我的，我必追讨他的罪，自父及子，直到三四代。visit *vt.* to afflict or assail 降临；攻击。iniquity *n.* wickedness 邪恶；罪恶。
5. hallow *vt.* to make as holy 使神圣
6. thy days 指人一生的时日，即寿命。第五诫意为"要孝敬你的父母，使你在耶和华你的神赐给你的地上得享长寿"。十诫由人敬畏神开始转向人际关系。
7. commit adultery 犯通奸罪。
8. bear false witness (against sb.) 作假证(陷害他人)。
9. covet *vt.* to desire for (that which is another's) 贪念；觊觎

三、圣经文化知识链接

1. 逾越节

逾越节(Passover)典出《出埃及记》第12章,为纪念耶和华救其子民出埃及时越过以色列人的家门而击杀埃及人家的长子这一历史事件,是犹太教的主要节日之一。此间,由家中长者讲述以色列的祖先摆脱埃及奴役、走向自由的故事,并制作烤鸡蛋作为节期食品,烤的时间越长,鸡蛋就越硬,越难破碎,以此象征以色列民族在长期的苦难中磨砺得更加顽强。一些学者考证,逾越节最初是牧民的节日,可一直追溯到希伯来人的游牧时代,也可能是闪族牧民共有的节日。只是希伯来人后来赋予了它特别的宗教意义。

《旧约》第3部书《利未记》集中记载了以色列的7大节日:逾越节、除酵节、初熟节、五旬节、吹角节、赎罪节和住棚节。住棚节(Festival of Booths; Festival of Tabernacle)专为纪念摩西带领以色列人出埃及,是以色列人一种"忆苦思甜"式的集体活动。"住棚节"在秋收后,从犹太历7月15日(公历10月中旬)开始,持续8天。前7天,人们住进帐篷或用树枝搭成的棚子,体验先祖的"住棚"生活,称"向主守住棚节"。第8天举行盛大集会,庆祝丰收,并向主献"燔祭"。

2. 以色列十二支派

《创世记》记载雅各与天使摔跤后改名为"以色列",因为他有12个儿子,以色列便派生出十二支,其雏形在《创世记》第49章雅各对12个儿子的临终祝福中已经显现。《出埃及记》开篇记载,雅各家族悉数迁至埃及后,繁衍生息,不断壮大。约400年后,他们不堪忍受埃及人的奴役,在摩西及其接班人约书亚的领导下,离开埃及到达迦南。期间,这些族人分为12个支派,各支派都取自雅各后代的名字。其中5个支派取名于雅各和第一个妻子利亚所生的6子中5人的名字:流便(Reuben)、西缅(Simeon)、犹大(Judah)、以萨迦(Issachar)、西布伦(Zebulun);2个支派取名于雅各和利亚的使女悉帕所生二子的名字:迦得(Gad)和亚设(Asher);2个支派取名于雅各和第二个妻子拉结的使女辟拉所生二子的名字:但(Dan)和拿弗他利(Naphtali);2个支派取名于雅各之子约瑟所生二子的名字,玛拿西(Manaseeh)和以法莲(Ephraim)(因为二人过继给雅各做儿子),1个支派取名于雅各和拉结所生次子的名字:便雅悯(Benjamin)。因利未人(Levites)被分散在12支派当中,所以不称其为独立支派。

摩西去世后,约书亚率领以色列人渡过约旦河,首先攻占了具有重要战略意义的耶利哥城。经过一些挫折,又攻占了伯特利东边的艾城,并在米伦湖一役击败夏琐王,完成了对迦南南北两部分的占领。以色列12支派以抽签方式分配了迦南的土地(《约书亚记》14:3—5; 12:1—42)。

四、圣经文化专题

1. "摩西十诫"及其社会意义

"十诫",来自希腊文Decalogue,原意是"十条指令"。"十诫"在《圣经》中出现了两次:《出埃及记》第20章和《申命记》第5章,两次的语句有差异,但基本内容还是一致的。它是以色列人一切立法的基础,也是西方文明核心的道德观。"十诫"借助上帝的名义为全人类规定了基本的道德标准,表达了圣经时代人们对个人和社会应尽义务的认识。[1]

第一诫要求以色列人绝对只信奉上帝,强调一神教信仰。

第二诫禁止任何形式的假神崇拜。以色列人不能建造任何上帝的偶像。以偶像形式将上帝固定在一个地方并加以控制,会毁掉上帝的权威。

第三诫禁止所有利用上帝名义的企图。古代近东人认为,人或物的名字是人或物能力与性格的延伸。上帝的名字只用来表明身份,以色列人从未对其作过完整的解释。

第四诫规定,在7天中留出一天休息,作为纪念上帝和对上帝的恩惠做出反省的日子。

第五诫提供了对家庭这个社会基本单位的维护法则。《旧约》对孝敬父母有着非常具体的说明,如不能打骂父母、不可悖逆父母,给父母丢脸意味着蔑视上帝的子民。

第六诫也是为了维护人类社会而定,其基本思想是,生命属于上帝,唯有上帝才有权主宰人的生命。因此上帝的子民不应该杀人或互相残杀。

第七诫保护婚姻的尊严,因为有了婚姻的纽带,丈夫和妻子已成为一体,而奸淫却违背丈夫与妻子间神圣的整体关系。

第八诫基于"财产乃拥有者其人的延续"的信仰,认为偷盗别人的财产是冒犯被盗者自身。

第九诫为维护社会的整体性而定。作假证不仅侵犯了受害人,而且使社会不能正常运转。

最后一诫不仅仅包含反对贪图他人之物的做法,还抨击了利用邻里的家庭或财富来满足私欲的德行。人决不能将自己的需求与快乐置于整个社会的需求之上。

摩西十诫作为犹太教的经典和希伯来国家的重要法律文献,是西方宗教中最早的宗教戒律之一,对犹太教、基督教教律的形成以及对其后的政治、法律都产生了巨大影响。从摩西十诫所反映的契约精神发展出了西方法律文明信守契约的精神,为西方后世契约型社会结构的形成奠定了基础。第八条关于个人财产神圣不可侵犯的观念成为西方《民商法》体系的基础,并为市场经济中以"契约"为纽带的商品交易奠定了基础。另外,通过十条戒律规定了人类的权利(受上帝保佑)和义务(十诫内容)和违约责任(受到惩罚),明确并统一了个人权利、义务和责任,这是《汉谟拉比法典》里面根本没有解决的。摩西十诫作为神学的戒律原则自然也会对作为世俗法律规则如部门法的形成和划分产生影响。路德派法学家就把各个部门法置于"十诫"的基础之上:依"不可杀人法"的诫命建立刑法,依"不可偷盗"的诫命建立财产法,依"不可奸淫"的诫命建立家庭法,依"不可作假见证"和"不可贪恋"的诫命建立契约法和有关私犯的法律。尽管十诫是以禁令的形式出现的,从语气上来看,是在约束人们的自由,而实际上,十诫为社会成员提供了最大尺度的自由。

2. "摩西十诫"与"五月花号公约"

"摩西十诫"具有丰富的社会意义。从一定程度上讲,我们可以把"十诫"看做对人的基本需要的部分论述,表达了人们对物质安全感的需要、对尊重他人的需要、对稳固的群体照顾的需要。这些思想在西方被逐渐演绎成对私有财产的保护,对人权的尊重和对政治的信赖。通

---

1. 帅培天等编:《圣经文学词典》,成都:四川人民出版社,1997年,第279-280页。

过立约的方式确立人与神的关系，人神关系被纳入了"法制"轨道，因为，既立了约，就必须践约，就必须用约中的条款约束自身。不仅人应如此，神也应如此。如果我们抛弃神学的外壳，用统治者，或国家来替代神的位置，这种立约关系则可视为"现代民主体制"的雏形。摩西与上帝立约的意义深远，它对资本主义制度产生了深刻影响。

1620年11月11日，经过66天的海上漂泊之后，"五月花"号帆船在现在的卡德角(Cape-God)外的普利茅斯港抛锚。在上岸之前，41名男乘客签订了一份公约，史称"五月花号公约"(*The Mayflower Compact*)。这份著名的文件也被人们称为"美国的出生证明"。1991年的《世界年鉴》评价该公约是"自动同意管理自己的一个协议，是美国的第一套成文法"，它预示了民主政治的许多理念。

In the name of God, Amen. We whose names are underwritten, the loyal subjects of our dread sovereign Lord, King James, by the grace of God, of Great Britain, France and Ireland king, defender of the faith, etc., having undertaken. For the glory of God, and advancement of the Christian faith, and honour of our king and country, a voyage to plant the first colony in the Northern parts of Virginia, do by these presents solemnly and mutually in the presence of God, and one of another, covenant and combine ourselves together into a civil body politic, for our better ordering and preservation and furtherance of the ends aforesaid and by virtue hereof to enact constitute, and frame such just and equal laws, ordinances, acts, constitutions, and offices, from time to time, as shall be thought most meet and convenient for the general good of the colony, unto which we promise all due submission and obedience. In witness whereof we have here under subscribed our names at Cape-Cod the 11th of November, in the year of the reign of our sovereign lord, King James, of England, France, and Ireland the eighteen, and of Scotland the fifty-fourth. Anno Domini 1620.[1]	以上帝的名义，阿门。 我等签约之人，信仰的捍卫者，蒙上帝保佑的大不列颠、法兰西和爱尔兰的国王詹姆士国王陛下的忠顺臣民。 为了上帝的荣耀，为了增进基督教信仰，为了我们国王和国家的荣誉，我们远涉重洋，在弗吉尼亚北部开拓第一块殖民地。我们在上帝面前一起庄严盟誓签约，自愿结成民众自治团体。为使上述目的得以顺利实施、维护和发展，也为将来能随时依此而制定和颁布有益于殖民地全体民众利益的公正与平等的法律、法规、法案、宪章和公职，我们全体都保证遵守和服从。 据此于公元1620年11月11日，于英格兰、法兰西、爱尔兰十八世国王暨苏格兰五十四世国王詹姆士陛下在位之年，我等在卡德角签署姓名如下。

在公约上签字的41名男乘客登陆后成为普利茅斯殖民地第一批拥有选举权的自由人，是殖民地政治的核心成员。"五月花号公约"的主要精神是要建立一个依照少数服从多数原则实行自治的共和政体，为每个成员提供平等、自由、选举等民主权利。"五月花号公约"被看做是美

---

1. 王波主编《美国重要历史文献导读——从殖民地时期到19世纪》，北京：北京大学出版社，2002年。

国历史上第一个政治契约文件。虽然公约上援引上帝旨意作为其存在的根据，但不难看出，清教徒更注重世俗政治实体的运作；上帝旨意高于一切作为一种不容怀疑的对全体清教徒的神圣约束，是世俗政府的法律基础。因此，"五月花号公约"又被认为是宗教契约转化为政治契约的最强有力的证据。通过公约，清教徒们相互认可了自己与上帝的特殊关系，并将这种关系转化为政治特权。自"五月花号公约"开始，殖民地形成了两条重要政治原则：一是成文法成为政府组织的基本法，二是政府和人民的关系被视为神圣的契约关系。这两条原则对后来制定美国宪法产生了深远的影响。

五、圣经典故集锦

1. **land flowing milk and honey** (流奶与蜜之地)：典出《出埃及记》第3章8节、第13章5节，指"丰饶之国"，"鱼米之乡"。上帝召唤摩西带领以色列人离开埃及，应许把他们带到"美好宽阔流奶与蜜之地"——迦南。
   英国浪漫主义诗人拜伦的《唐璜》第13章100节有诗句：
   Witness the lands which 'flow'd with milk and honey,'
   Held out unto the hungry Israelites;
   To this we have added since, the love of money,
   The only sort of pleasure which requites.
   Youth fades, and leaves our days no longer sunny;
   We tire of mistresses and parasites;
   But oh, ambrosial cash! Ah! who would lose thee?
   When we no more can use, or even abuse thee!

   请看那"流着奶与蜜之地"如何
   引诱饥饿的以色列人去到迦南
   以后我们又添上爱财，总起来
   就是唯一的乐趣给人以安慰。
   时光易逝！我们的日子不再明媚，
   情妇和食客也会使我们厌倦。
   可是，哎哟，芬芳的金钱！
   谁愿意，即使老得无法享用时，失去你？

   美国作家麦尔维尔的《白鲸》(*Moby Dick*)第6章《街道》，作者借叙述者以实玛利之口描写新贝德福，巧妙化用了这个典故：

   虽然就整个英格兰说来，这城市本身也许是个最适宜居住的可爱的地方。一点也不错，这是一个油水富足的地方，虽然不像迦南那样；却是一个遍地玉米美酒的地方。街上并不是遍地牛奶；春天也不是满街铺满鲜蛋。然而，人们走遍美洲，也找不到一个像新贝德福这样尽是贵族宅邸、华丽非凡的公园和花园的地方。

   英国意识流大师乔伊斯在《尤利西斯》中也化用这个典故：

   看啊，吾民，自何列市、尼波与比斯迦以及哈顿角峰，俯瞰那流淌奶与钱之地方。然而，汝供余饮者，苦奶也。(萧乾、文洁若译《尤利西斯》中)

2001年中国国家广播电台记者关娟娟新闻报道:
耶路撒冷什么都有，就是没有安全感。持续8个月的巴以冲突，已使这片被《圣经》誉为"流着奶和蜜的土地"再也找不到生活的安全感。

2. **Moses' hand** (摩西的手)：典出《出埃及记》第4章6节: And the LORD said furthermore unto him. Put now thine hand into thy bosom. And he put his hand into his bosom: and when he took it out, behold, his hand was leprous as snow. 摩西探问耶和华的权能时被告知："把手放在怀里。"他就把手放在怀里，及至抽出来，不料，"手长了大麻疯，有雪那样白"。奥马尔·哈雅姆(Omar Khayyam)的诗作《鲁拜集》开篇第4节写道：

新春苏活着旧时的希望，
使沉思的灵魂告了退藏，
退到那树枝上露出"摩西的白手"，
耶稣从地底叹息的地方。(郭沫若 译)

3. **Moses' rod** (摩西的杖)：典出《出埃及记》第4—10章，指"克敌制胜的法宝"、"神奇之物"。陈梦家的诗作《女人摩西的杖》中有反复的一句："女人，你好比古圣摩西的杖"。

4. **make bricks without straw** (作无草之砖)：指"强人所难"，类似中国的"巧妇难为无米之炊"。典出《出埃及记》第5章6—8节: And Pharaoh commanded the same day the taskmasters of the people, and their officers, saying, Ye shall no more give the people straw to make brick, as heretofore: let them go and gather straw for themselves. 当天法老吩咐督工的和官长说："你们不可照常把草给百姓做砖，叫他们自己去捡草。"埃及法老命令督工不给以色列人做砖用的草，还强迫他们按数交砖，作为对他们要求自由的惩罚。

5. **flesh-pot of Egypt** (埃及的肉锅)：指"往昔的苟安"、"对财富的贪恋"，也指"丰盛的筵席"、"罪恶的奢靡"。典出《出埃及记》第16章1—3节: And the whole congregation of the children of Israel murmured against Moses and Aaron in the wilderness: And the children of Israel said unto them, Would to God we had died by the hand of the LORD in the land of Egypt, when we sat by the flesh pots, and when we did eat bread to the full; for ye have brought us forth into this wilderness, to kill this whole assembly with hunger. 以色列全会众在旷野向摩西、亚伦发怨言，说："巴不得我们早死在埃及地耶和华的手下，那时我们坐在肉锅旁边，吃得饱足；你们将我们领出来，到这旷野，是要将这全会众都饿死啊。"指以色列人出埃及后因在旷野挨饿而怀恋过去在埃及时的饱足生活。詹姆斯·乔伊斯在《尤利西斯》(上)写道：哎，跟那些打饱嗝的出租马车车夫们挤挤碰碰在一块儿吃那廉价的炖牛杂碎，就像是吃埃及肉锅似的。

6. **Marah** (玛拉)：指"苦水"。典出《出埃及记》第15章23—25节: And when they came to Marah, they could not drink of the waters of Marah, for they were bitter: therefore the name of it was called Marah. 到了玛拉，不能喝那里的水；因为水苦，所以那地名叫玛拉。摩西率领以色列人过红海后来到书珥的旷野，三天找不到水喝。到了一个叫Marah的地方，却不能喝

那里的水，因为水苦。在耶和华的指示下，摩西把一棵树丢在水里，水就变甜了。美国诗人朗费罗在《新港的犹太人墓地》(The Jewish Cemetery at Newport)表达了对犹太人的同情：

他们总是吃着未发酵的面包，

忍受被放逐的恐惧和苦涩，

他们喂养着荒芜的心扉，

以含泪的玛拉解渴。

7. **Manna** (吗哪)：指"上帝赐的食物"。典出《出埃及记》第16章13—15节：And when the dew that lay was gone up, behold, upon the face of the wilderness there lay a small round thing, as small as the hoar frost on the ground. And when the children of Israel saw it, they said one to another: "It is manna?": for they wist not what it was. 露水上升之后，不料，野地面上有如白霜的小圆物，以色列人看见，不知道是什么，就彼此问："这是吗哪？"因为他们不知道是什么。以色列人连续吃"吗哪"40年，直到进入迦南。在莎士比亚的《威尼斯商人》最后一幕，富家女子鲍西亚及使女尼莉莎，同罗兰佐有如下对话：

(鲍西亚)喂，罗兰佐！我的书记也有一件好东西要给你哩。

(尼莉莎)是的，我可以送给他，不收一些费用。这儿是那犹太富翁亲笔签署的一张授赠产业的文契，声明他死了以后，全部资产都传给您和杰西卡，请你们收下吧。

(罗兰佐)两位好夫人，你们像是散布吗哪的天使，救济着饥饿的人们。(《莎士比亚全集》第3卷)

8. **sins of the fathers** (父辈的罪孽)：典出《出埃及记》第20章5节：Thou shalt not bow down thyself to them, nor serve them: for I the LORD thy God am a jealous God, visiting the iniquity of the fathers upon the children unto the third and fourth generation of them that hate me. 不可跪拜那些像，也不可侍奉它，因为我耶和华你的上帝，是忌邪的上帝。恨我的，我必追讨他的罪，自父及子，直到三四代。莎士比亚的《威尼斯商人》第3幕第5场一开始，小丑朗斯洛特对夏洛克的女儿杰西卡说："真的，不骗您，父亲的罪恶是要子女承当的，所以我倒真的在替您捏着一把汗呢。"

9. **eye for eye, tooth for tooth** (以眼还眼，以牙还牙)：指"针锋相对"、"以暴抗暴"，类似中国的"以其人之道还治其人之身"。典出《出埃及记》第21章23—25节：And if any mischief follow, then thou shalt give life for life, eye for eye, tooth for tooth, hand for hand, foot for foot, burning for burning, wound for wound, stripe for stripe. 若有别害，就要以命偿命，以眼还眼，以牙还牙，以手还手，以脚还脚，以烙还烙，以伤还伤，以打还打。这是以色列人的律法中的规定。巴金的散文集《电椅集》中的《罪与罚》开篇就直接引用了这个典故。(《巴金文集》第7卷)

10. **worship the golden calf** (拜金牛犊)：指"崇拜偶像"、"崇拜金钱"。典出《出埃及记》第32章1—29节。以色列人在摩西上西奈山之际逼其哥哥亚伦用金首饰为大家铸成一座金牛犊来顶礼膜拜。德国诗人海涅写有《金牛犊》一诗，生动再现了以色列人崇拜金牛犊的场景(见《海涅诗集》)。

六、课堂讨论题

1. "摩西十诫"和《五子之歌》所反映的文化差异。
2. "沙弥十戒"与"摩西十诫"有何区别?
3. "埃及十灾"反映了怎样的自然规律?

七、课后思考题

1. 你知道蝙蝠在中西文化中的不同内涵吗?
2. 有一部很好看的美国电影《十诫》,你知道吗?
3. 你知道哪些著名的摩西雕像和油画作品?
4. 世界卫生组织的会徽与摩西的"铜蛇杖"有何关系?

第四讲

以色列律法集萃:《利未记》、《民数记》和《申命记》
Leviticus, Numbers and Deuteronomy: Essence of Law

一、导读:律法书的特征

《圣经》作为犹太教—基督教的经典文本,蕴涵着丰富的法律资源。其中的"律法书"特指《旧约》卷首的5卷书——《创世记》、《出埃及记》、《利未记》(*Leviticus*)、《民数记》(*Numbers*)和《申命记》(*Deuteronomy*)。《利未记》大部分内容是有关犹太教礼仪的律法规定,间或述及以色列人在西奈旷野的经历;《民数记》叙述以色列人出埃及后在西奈旷野、巴兰旷野和摩押旷野的经历,涉及摩西核计民数、选立70长老等重大事件。《申命记》意为"律法重读"或"重申律法"。按照犹太传统,上帝在西奈山藉摩西颁布了一部律法和诫命,在摩押旷野又颁布了该律法的复制版,成为第二律法。尽管《圣经》中的律法表现出凌乱、严酷、唯心的特点,但整体来讲,其中蕴含的许多理念仍然具有现代意义。

这几部书兼有二重性质,它们既是远古历史或神人关系史的记录,又是以色列人的律法文献汇编。从部门法视角分析,包括宪法、民法、刑法和诉讼法。其主要特点体现在:形式上具有不集中性,内容上带有混杂性、世俗性、原始性。从整体来看,其内容、观念、用途都呈现出统一性特征。《出埃及记》是其中非常重要的一卷,但是后边的书卷——《利未记》、《民数记》、《申命记》涉及了律法的不同视角,蕴含了许多现代理念:如慈善思想、法律面前人人平等、注重教育、现代赔偿理念、珍爱动物和土地等;内容涉及所有权、债务、婚姻与家庭、财产继承、犯罪与刑法和司法制度等。这些律法折射出希伯来生活的时代特色及其蕴含的律法理念,对了解西方律法意义重大,同时我们还可以把这些理念与中国律法进行对比,挖掘其中的普世意义。基于以上特征,我们单辟一讲来集中学习这三卷书。

律法书涉及内容杂多,本讲主要选择以下6个主题,涉及《利未记》、《民数记》、《申命记》3部书卷:

1. 关于卫生和健康的条例。
2. 安息年和房地产的条例。
3. 关于六座"庇护城"的设立。
4. 关于"什一税"的条例。
5. 对国王资格的规定。
6. 关于男子参战的条例。

二、选文及注释

Part 1

On Sanitary and Health

"And for these ye shall be unclean: whosoever toucheth the carcase[1] of them shall be unclean until the even. And whosoever beareth ought of[2] the carcase of them shall wash his clothes, and be unclean until the even. The carcases of every beast which divideth the hoof, and is not clovenfooted[3], nor cheweth the cud[4], are unclean unto you: every one that toucheth them shall be unclean. And whatsoever goeth upon his paws among all manner[5] of beasts that go on all four, those are unclean unto you: whoso toucheth their carcase shall be unclean until the even. And he that beareth the carcase of them shall wash his clothes, and be unclean until the even: they are unclean unto you." (*Leviticus* 11: 24–28)

"And if any beast, of which ye may eat, die; he that toucheth the carcase thereof shall be unclean until the even. And he that eateth of the carcase of it shall wash his clothes, and be unclean until the even: he also that breareth the carcase of it shall wash his clothes, and be unclean until the even." (*Leviticus* 11: 39–40)

"And whatsoever man there be of the house of Israel, or of the strangers that sojourn among you, that eateth any manner of blood; I will even set my face against that soul that eateth blood, and will cut him off from among his people. For the life of the flesh is in the blood: and I have given it to you upon the altar to make an atonement[6] for your souls: for it is the blood that maketh an atonement for the soul. Therefore I said unto the children of Israel, 'No soul of you shall eat blood, neither shall any stranger that sojourneth among you eat blood.'"

"And whatsoever man there be of the children of Israel, or of the strangers that sojourn among you, which hunteth and catcheth any beast or fowl that may be eaten; he shall even pour out the blood thereof, and cover it with dust. For it is the life of all flesh; the blood of it is for the life thereof: therefore I said unto the children of Israel, 'Ye shall eat the blood of no manner of flesh: for the life of all flesh is the blood thereof: whosoever eateth it shall be cut off.'"

"And every soul that eateth that which died of itself, or that which was torn with beasts, whether it be one of your own country, or a stranger, he shall both wash his clothes, and bathe himself in water, and be unclean until the even; then shall he be clean.'" (*Leviticus* 17: 10–15)

Part 2

Sabbath and the Redemption of Land and Dwellings

And the LORD spake unto Moses in mount Sinai, saying, "Speak unto the children of Israel, and say unto them, 'When ye come into the land which I gave you, then shall the land keep a sabbath unto the LORD. Six years thou shalt sow thy field, and

---

1. carcase /ˈkɑːkəs/ *n.* the dead body of an animal (动物的)尸体
2. bear ought of 拿取。
3. clovenfooted *adj.* 有趾的 cloven *adj.* split or divided in two 劈开的，裂开的；分成两瓣的。
4. cud *n.* partly digested food returned from the first stomach of ruminants to the mouth for further chewing 反刍的食物
5. manner *n.* kind or sort 种类
6. atonement *n.* reparation or expiation for sin; the action of making amends for a wrong or injury 补偿，赎罪

Part 3

Appointment of Cities of Refuge[2]

When ye be come over Jordan into the land of Canaan; then ye shall appoint you cities to be cities of refuge for you; that the slayer[3] may flee thither, which killeth any person at unawares[4]. And they shall be unto you cities for refuge from the avenger[5]; that the manslayer die not, until he stand before the congregation in judgment. And of these cities which ye shall give six cities ye have for refuge. Ye shall give three cities on this side Jordan, and three cities shall ye give in the land of Canaan, which shall be cities of refuge. These six cities shall be a refuge, both for the children of Israel, and for the stranger, and for the sojourner among them: that every one that killeth any person unawares may flee thither.

And if he smite him with an instrument of iron, so that he die, he is a murderer: the murderer shall surely be put to death. And if he smite him with throwing a stone, wherewith he may die, and he die, he is a murderer: the murderer shall surely be put to death. Or if he smite him with an hand weapon of wood, wherewith he may die, and he die, he is a murderer: the murderer shall surly be put to death. The revenger of blood himself shall slay the murderer: when he meeteth him, he shall slay him. But if he thrust him of hatred[6], or hurl at him by laying of wait[7], that he die; or in enmity[8] smite him with his hand, that he die: he that smote him shall surely be put to death; for he is a murderer: the revenger of blood shall slay the murderer, when he meeteth him.

six years thou shalt prune thy vineyard, and gather in the fruit thereof; but in the seventh year shall be a sabbath of rest unto the land, a sabbath for the LORD: thou shalt neither sow thy field, nor prune thy vineyard. That which groweth of its own accord of thy harvest thou shalt not reap, neither gather the grapes of thy vine undressed: for it is a year of rest unto the land. And the sabbath of the land shall be meat for you; for thee, and for thy servant, and for thy maid, and for thy hired servant, and for thy stranger that sojourneth with thee, and for thy cattle, and for the beast that are in thy land, shall all the increase thereof be meat.'" (*Leviticus* 25: 1–7)

"The land shall not be sold for ever: for the land is mine, for ye are strangers and sojourners[1] with me. And in all the land of your possession ye shall grant a redemption for the land." (*Leviticus* 25: 23)

---

1. sojourner *n.* 寄居者
2. cities of refuge 庇护城。专门用作过失杀人犯庇护所的城市。
3. slayer *n.* 杀人者
4. unawares *adv.* without being aware of the situation 意外地
5. avenger *n.* 复仇者
6. he thrust him of hatred 因怀恨把人推倒。of 相当于 out of, 出于。
7. lay of wait 伏击；袭击。
8. enmity *n.* a state or feeling of active opposition or hostility 仇恨

But if he thrust him suddenly without enmity, or have cast upon him any thing without laying of wait, or with any stone, wherewith a man may die, seeing him not, and cast it upon him, that he die, and was not his enemy, neither sought his harm[1]: then the congregation shall judge between the slayer and the revenger of blood according to these judgments: and the congregation shall deliver the slayer out of the hand of the revenger of blood, and the congregation shall restore[2] him to the city of his refuge, whither he was fled: and he shall abide in it unto the death of the high priest, which was anointed with the holy oil. (*Numbers* 35: 10–25)

Part 4

On the Tithe

Thou shalt truly tithe[3] all the increase of thy seed[4], that the field bringeth forth year by year. And thou shalt eat before the LORD thy God, in the place which he shall choose to place his name there[5], the tithe of thy corn, of thy wine, and of thine oil, and the firstlings of thy herds and of thy flocks; that thou mayest learn to fear the LORD thy God always. And if the way be too long for thee, so that thou art not able to carry it; or if the place be too far from thee, which the LORD thy God shall choose to set his name there, when the LORD thy God hath blessed thee: then shalt thou turn it into money, and bind up the money in thine hand, and shalt go unto the place which the LORD thy God shall choose: and thou shalt bestow that money for whatsoever thy soul lusteth after[6], for oxen, or for sheep, or for wine, or for strong drink, or for whatsoever thy soul desireth: and thou shalt eat there before the LORD thy God, and thou shalt rejoice, thou, and thine household, and the Levite that is within thy gates; thou shalt not forsake him; for he hath no part nor inheritance[7] with thee.

At the end of three years thou shalt bring forth all the tithe of thine increase the same year, and shalt lay it up within thy gates: and the Levite, (because he hath no part nor inheritance with thee,) and the stranger, and the fatherless, and the widow, which are within thy gates, shall come, and shall eat and be satisfied; that the LORD thy God may bless thee in all the work of thine hand which thou doest. （*Deuteronomy* 14: 22–29）

At the end of every seven years thou shall make a release[8]. And this is the manner of the release: Every creditor[9] that lendeth ought unto his neighbor shall release it; he shall not exact[10] it of his neighbour, or of his brother; because it is called the LORD's release. Of a foreigner thou mayest exact it again: but that which is thine with thy brother thine hand shall release; Save when there shall be no poor among you; for the LORD shall greatly bless thee in the land which the LORD thy God giveth thee for an inheritance to possess it: Only if thou carefully hearken unto the voice of the LORD thy God, to observe to do all these commandments which I command thee this

---

1. seek his harm 加害他。
2. restore *vt.* to return sb. to a former place 遣送
3. tithe *vt.* 献出十分之一。什一奉献的规例早在亚伯拉罕时代已经出现，参见《创世记》第14章20节和第28章22节。该词当名词时指"十分之一"。
4. increase of thy seed 从种子所得，指收成。
5. place his name there 指神接受人们崇拜的地方。
6. lust after 随己心意。
7. no part nor inheritance （作为祭司族的利未人）既没地份也无产业。
8. release *n.* remit or discharge (a debt) 豁免，免债
9. creditor *n.* a person to whom money is owing 债主
10. exact *vt.* to demand and obtain (sth.) from sb. 索要；强求

day. (*Deuteronomy* 15: 1–5)

Part 5
Requirements of the King

When thou art come unto the land which the L<small>ORD</small> thy God giveth thee, and shalt possess it, and shalt dwell therein, and shalt say, "I will set a king over me, like as all the nations that are about me." Thou shalt in any wise[1] set him king over thee, whom the L<small>ORD</small> thy God shall choose: one from among thy brethren shalt thou set king over thee: thou mayest not set a stranger over thee, which is not thy brother. But he shall not multiply[2] horses to himself, nor cause the people to return to Egypt, to the end that he should multiply horses: forasmuch as the L<small>ORD</small> hath said unto you, Ye shall henceforth return no more that way. Neither shall he multiply wives[3] to himself, that his heart turn not away[4]: neither shall he greatly multiply to himself silver and gold. And it shall be, when he sitteth upon the throne of his kingdom, that he shall write him a copy of this law in a book out of that which is before the priests of the Levites: and it shall be with him, and he shall read therein all the days of his life: that he may learn to fear the L<small>ORD</small> his God, to keep all the words of this law and these statutes, to do them: that his heart be not lifted up above[5] his brethren, and that he turn not aside from the commandment, to the right hand, or to the left: to the end that he may prolong his days in his kingdom, he, and his children, in the midst of Israel. (*Deuteronomy* 17: 14–20)

Part 6
On Man Going to Battle

When thou goest out to battle against thine enemies, and seest horses, and chariots, and a people more than thou, be not afraid of them: for the L<small>ORD</small> thy God is with thee, which brought thee up out of the land of Egypt. And it shall be, when ye are come nigh unto the battle, that the priest shall approach and speak unto the people, and shall say unto them, "Hear, O Israel, ye approach this day unto battle against your enemies: let not your hearts faint, fear not, and do not tremble, neither be ye terrified because of them; for the L<small>ORD</small> your God is he that goeth with you, to fight for you against your enemies, to save you."

And the officers shall speak unto the people, saying, "What man is there that hath built a new house, and hath not dedicated it? let him go and return to his house, lest he die in the battle, and another man dedicate it. And what man is he that hath planted a vineyard, and hath not yet eaten of it? let him also go and return unto his house, lest he die in the battle, and another man eat of it. And what man is there that hath betrothed[6] a wife, and hath not taken her? let him go and return unto his house, lest he die in the battle, and another man take her."

And the officers shall speak further unto the people, and they shall say,

"What man is there that is fearful and faint hearted[7]? let him go and return unto his house, lest his brethren's heart faint as well as his heart."

And it shall be, when the officers have

---

1. in any wise 无论如何。
2. multiply *vt.* to increase or cause to increase greatly in number or quantity 增加；繁殖
3. wives 指嫔妃
4. his heart turn not away 他的心一点儿也不能偏离耶和华神。
5. life up above (心)变得高傲而瞧不起。
6. betroth *vt.* to formally engage (sb.) to be married 〈古〉订婚；男子答应娶某女子为妻
7. faint hearted lacking courage, timid 怯懦的；胆小的。

made an end of speaking unto the people, that they shall make captains of the armies to lead the people.

When thou comest nigh unto a city to fight against it, then proclaim peace[1] unto it. And it shall be, if it make thee answer of peace, and open unto thee, then it shall be, that all the people that is found therein shall be tributaries[2] unto thee, and they shall serve thee. And if it will make no peace with thee, but will make war against thee, then thou shalt besiege[3] it: and when the LORD thy God hath delivered it onto thine hands, thou shalt smite every male thereof with the edge of the sword: but the women, and the little ones, and the cattle, and all that in the city, even all the spoil[4] thereof, shalt thou take unto thyself; and thou shalt eat the spoil of thine enemies, which the LORD thy God hath given thee.

Thus shalt thou do unto all the cities which are very far off from thee, which are not of the cities of these nations. But of the cities of these people, which the LORD thy God doth give thee for an inheritance, thou shalt save alive nothing that breatheth: but thou shalt utterly destroy them; namely the Hittites, and the Amorites, the Canaanites, and the Perizzites, the Hivites, and the Jebusites[5]; as the LORD thy God hath commanded thee: that they teach you not to do after all their abominations[6], which they have done unto their gods; so should ye sin against the LORD your God. When thou shalt besiege a city a long time, in making war against it to take it, thou shalt not destroy the trees thereof by forcing an axe against them: for thou mayest eat of them, and thou shalt not cut them down (for the tree of the field is man's life) to employ them in the siege[7]: Only the trees which thou knowest that they be not trees for meat, thou shalt destroy and cut them down; and thou shalt build bulwarks[8] against the city that maketh war with thee, until it be subdued[9]. (*Deuteronomy* 20)

三、圣经文化知识链接

1. 什一税[10]

什一税(tithe)是欧洲中世纪时教会向全体基督徒征收的一种宗教捐税，用于维护教堂设施，供给主教、教士的圣俸及救济穷人。什一税的起源久远而复杂，《圣经》中对其有多处记载。什一税最早载于《利未记》，摩西向耶和华许愿："地上所有的，无论是地上的种子，树上的果子，十分之一是耶和华的，是归耶和华为圣的。……凡牛群羊群中，一切从杖下经过的，每第十只要归耶和华为圣。"(《利未记》27:30—33)在《申命记》中，摩西又重申了十分献一的条例："你要把撒种所产的，就是你田地每年所出的，十分取一分。又要把你的五谷、新酒和油的十分之一，

---

1. proclaim peace 提出议和。
2. tributary *n.* 附属国；臣民
3. besiege *vt.* to surround (a place) with armed forces in order to capture it or force its surrender 围攻
4. spoil *n.* goods taken forcibly from a person or a place 战利品
5. the Hittites, and the Amorites, the Canaanites, and the Perizzites, the Hivites, and the Jebusites 赫梯人、亚摩利人、迦南人、比利洗人、希未人、耶布斯人。都是已经生活在迦南地的民族。
6. abomination *n.* a thing that causes disgust or loathing 令人厌恶的事
7. siege *n.* 围城；包围
8. bulwark *n.* 用作围护的堡垒
9. subdue *vt.* to bring (a country or people) under control by force 制服；慑服
10. 本项参考了于平的文章《浅析中世纪英国什一税》，载于《首都师范大学学报》(社会科学版)，2007年增刊，第182-186页。

并牛群羊群中头生的,吃在耶和华你神面前……"(《申命记》14:22—23)于是,什一税成为犹太人宗教、经济生活的一部分。后来,基督教利用《圣经》中所称农产品的十分之一属于上帝的说法,要求信徒奉献什一税。

关于什一税的用途,《申命记》中规定:*"每逢三年的末一年,你要将本年的土产十分之一都取出来,积存在你的城中。在你城里无分无业的利末人,和你城里寄居的,并孤儿寡妇,都可以来,吃得饱足。这样,耶和华你的神必在你手里所办的一切事上赐福与你。"*(14:28—29)早期教会阶段,什一税是虔诚的基督徒自愿向教会捐赠的,教会用这些捐赠救助穷人。但到13世纪时,随着教会救济工作的弱化,什一税的救济功能大打折扣,其性质也随之改变,它不再是《圣经》中规定的慈善行为,转而开始具有国家征税的性质。应对不交纳什一税的措施引起了一些人的反感,有人甚至指出什一税制度阻碍了农业的发展,挫伤了农民的生产积极性,同时也阻碍了工商业的发展。人们对它的反抗情绪日益增长,这种反抗斗争也给教会敲响了警钟。

由此可见,后来的什一税更具世俗性。在某一历史阶段受到了教会的利用,成了教会腐败的工具。这一事实以及教会出售赎罪券等恶行,均体现了教会对《圣经》本意的偏离,宗教改革的最终爆发便顺理成章。但从整体来看,什一税规定本身并无可厚非,且蕴含慈善观念,它在历史上发挥的积极作用是不容抹杀的。

2."迦南"——流着奶和蜜的地方

迦南(今巴勒斯坦),位于地中海东岸、阿拉伯半岛西部,大致为东经34°34′至36°、北纬31°30′至33°30′之间的区域(见右图)。西部临海,南接埃及,东临约旦,北临黎巴嫩、叙利亚。这里面积狭小,计约一万平方英里。该地区虽然面积不大,但在希伯来历史上有着极其重要的地位,并被其经典文献称誉为"上帝应许之地"和"流奶与蜜之地"。

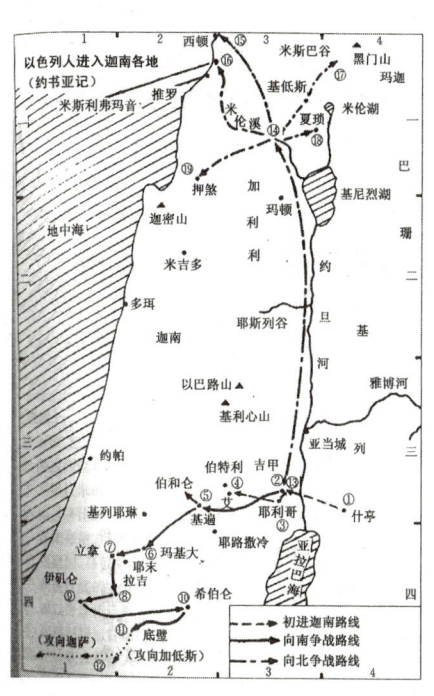

迦南地获此殊荣,并不是指迦南地理要素上的特征,而是指它的象征意义和文化意义。它表明迦南给希伯来人提供了无比丰富的文化资源,使得他们得以适应各种气候条件和人文条件,流浪、散居世界各地而自强不息。具体分析,"流奶与蜜之地"的称谓与以下几个因素相关:从自然地理要素来看,迦南虽并非得惠于大自然,资源丰富,但堪称"地球的模型",因为这里容纳了各种地理要素,这些要素构成了迦南地区自然地理景观上的综合性、模式性特征;从民族性意义来看,迦南对于犹太民族及其文化的生长无疑具有初始性的关键意义。公元前18世纪前后,希伯来人离开吾珥去迦南,离开迦南在埃及生息约400年,之后又返回迦南。这一历史本身有它的宗教和历史意义;从文化素质来看,迦南地处几大文明的中心,深受多边异质文化的影响,吸纳了异质文化的优秀元素,特别是南边的埃及文明与北边的美索不达米亚文化;从民族学来讲,因为迦南周围有众多部落,古希伯来人在这种部落冲突的夹缝中生存,才得以积累了宝贵的"思想资源"。

迦南是象征意义上"流着奶和蜜"的地方。这一隐喻贴切地揭示了这块土地所蕴藏和呈现的文化资源意义。迦南不仅浓缩了世界的多种主要地理特征,也滋生培养了丰富的文化要素,如复杂的种族关系等。因而可以说从该地流出的是"文化之奶",后世文化借助于这股富含文化意义的奶与蜜,得到进一步滋养。

四、圣经文化专题

1. "钦定本"法律英语的特点

圣经律法书蕴含着丰富的法律资源。钦定本《圣经》为英语学习者和爱好者提供了法律语言的范本。在阅读这些法律条例时,读者既能领略其法律本身的特色,还能领略钦定本《圣经》的精致美妙。作为法律英语的范本,钦定本的翻译在文字语言方面是经过反复推敲、千锤百炼而后产生的。它主要有以下特点:词汇术语化古语化;句子结构复杂化程式化;语言严谨、逻辑性强。这种例子随处可见,仅举数例。

(1) 多用结构复杂的长句。这样的长句大多由各种从句、分句、修饰结构构成,并且使用大量关联词,从而体现出思维视角的多层次性和逻辑的严密性。如,that … **But if a** man find a betrothed damsel in the field, and the man force her, and lie with her: **then** the man only that lay with her shall die: **but unto** the damsel thou shalt do nothing; there is in the damsel no sin worthy of death: **for as when** a man riseth against his neighbour, and slayeth him, **even so** is the matter: **for he** found her in the field, and the betrothed damsel cried, and there was none to save her. 从以上例句可以看出,句中出现了很多衔接词,从而在语篇结构上呈现出高度程式化的特征。在内容上,本法律条文把杀人的不同形式罗列得细致全面,几乎囊括了一切可能性,避免了歧义的产生。再如,本条例中也运用了大量衔接词语,以强化逻辑关系。从而使句法复杂但逻辑清晰,因果明确,与律法犯罪与惩罚之间的逻辑关系一致。并且从句式来讲,某些词语和结构的重复有利于形成铿锵点,从而给读者以节奏感。这样,读者记住的是带着节奏感的律法语言。

(2) 法律英语常用复合副词等专门法律词汇。如常以 here, there 和 where 等词在法律文件中当作词缀,与另一个或几个表示方位与原因指向的介词构成复合副词等专门法律词汇用语,以表示加强和确定之含义:hereafter (此后将来), herein (于此, 此中), hereinabove (在上文), hereinafter (在下文), here of (关于这个, 在本文件中), hereto (至此), wherefore (为什么), therein (在那个条款中)。此类古英语的使用使句子行文简练准确、逻辑严谨。另外,法律英语中多用同义词、多音节词,使句子读起来押韵、庄重、正式。如, **every one** that killeth **any** person unawares may flee thither. And if … **so that** he die, he is a murderer: the murderer shall surely be put to death. **And if he** smite him with throwing a stone, **wherewith** he may die, and he die, he is a murderer: the murderer **shall** surely be put to death. Or if he … **wherewith** he may die, and he die, (*Numbers* 35: 9–34)。

(3) 常使用标志性的法律英语。如带有指令性和强制性的词汇,充分表现了法律文件的权威性和约束性,使用情态动词shall表示"应当承担的责任与义务",而不用must,在法律文件中随处可见正式书面的词语，如《申命记》第16章6—22节、第18、19、20等章节。

从法律英语的表达方式，可以看出，法律英语要求内容必须准确、严密、客观和规范，以避免对法律条文的任意引申和推理。了解法律英语的这些特点，可以培养我们对法律英语的兴趣，提高语言鉴赏能力。

2. 希伯来律法对女性权益的保障

尽管希伯来人与世界上的许多民族一样有重男轻女的思想，但在摩西律法中，仍然在许多方面注重对女性权益的保障。

律法要求丈夫公正地对待妻子，不可胡乱加以诽谤：信口诋毁妻子的名誉和贞洁者，要罚银一百舍客勒，并终生不许休妻（《申命记》22:13—19）。以色列男子娶被掳女子为妻后，"若不喜悦她，就要由她随意出去，决不可为钱卖她，也不可当婢女待她。"（《申命记》21:14）虽然丈夫有权提出离婚，但不可随意休妻，必须要有正当的理由才能休妻。《旧约》中还有一些经文是保障寡妇及其他在社会上无法自力谋生的弱势人群的。对寡妇而言，官员有义务保护她免受债主欺负，免受掳掠者侵夺她的财物，在所有的民事案件中，要使她免受冤屈。《申命记》规定："每逢三年的末一年，你要将本年的出产十分之一都取出来，积存在你的城中。在你城里无分无业的利未人，和你城里寄居的，并孤儿寡妇，都可以来，吃得饱足。这样，耶和华你的神必在你手里所办的一切事上赐福与你。"（《申命记》14:28—29）又如："你在田间收割庄稼，若忘下一捆，不可回去再取，要留给寄居的与孤儿寡妇……你打橄榄树，枝上剩下的不可再打，要留给寄居的与孤儿寡妇。你摘葡萄园的葡萄，所剩下的不可再摘，要留给寄居的与孤儿寡妇。"（《申命记》24:19—21）在《申命记》中还要求邀请寡妇及其他处于社会弱势群体中的人，参加诸如七七节、住棚节之类节日的宴席（《申命记》16:9—11），使他们在神面前欢乐。耶和华许诺，凡济助寡妇的必得到赐福，凡欺压寡妇的必受惩罚。如："向寄居的和孤儿寡妇屈枉正直的，必受诅咒！"（《申命记》27: 19）再如："不可苦待寡妇和孤儿。若是苦待他们一点，他们向我哀求，我总要听他们的哀声，并要发烈怒，用刀杀你们，使你们的妻子为寡妇，儿女为孤儿。"（《出埃及记》22:22—24）"新娶妻之人，不可从军出征，也不可托他办理什么公事，……使妻快活。"（《申命记》24:5）

有关妇女利益的条例表明古犹太人对女性这一弱势社会群体的关注，体现出了《圣经》中保护妇女的意识。但这并不等于说《圣经》中主张男女平等，在圣经时代的男权社会，能够有这一意识，其积极意义是值得肯定的。

五、圣经典故集锦

1. **scapegoat**（替罪羊）：典出《利未记》第16章3—28节，大祭司亚伦将抽签抽出来的公羊作为本民族的替罪羊而放入旷野，让其带走本民族的一切罪过。此典比喻代人受过者。海涅的诗作《宗教辩论》中把耶稣比作一只替罪羊：我们的神，他就是爱，/他就像一只羔羊；/为了替我们赎罪，/他死在十字架上。胡平的纪实文学《移民美国》中有这样一则抗议公告：作为一个民选官员，哈里逊应该明白亚裔对法拉盛地区复苏的贡献。该区如今已成了纽约市的第四大商业区。她该努力在选区内提倡各种族之间的和谐。她没有这样做，相反她却挑拨新旧居民之间的团结，将亚裔移民当成代罪羔羊……

2. **yoke**（轭）：典出《利未记》第26章13节耶和华对摩西的晓谕：and I have broken the bands of your yoke, and made you go upright. 我也折断你们所负的轭，叫你们挺身而走。"轭"喻指套在身上的枷锁、受到的奴役和压迫。耶稣曾经教导门徒说：Take my yoke upon you, and learn of me: for I am meek and lowly in heart: and ye shall find rest unto your souls. For my yoke is easy, and my burden is light. "我心里柔和谦卑，你们当负我的轭，学我的样式；这样，你们心里就必得享安息。因为我的轭是容易的，我的担子是轻的。"(《马太福音》第11章29—30节)英国诗人弥尔顿的十四行诗《哀失明》(*On His Blindness*)中写道：

"Doth God exact day-labour, light denied?"
I fondly ask. But Patience, to prevent
That murmur, soon replies, "God doth not need
Either man's work or his own gifts. Who best
Bear his mild yoke, they serve him best . ...

"神要我白天做工，为何不给我光明？"
我喃喃自问。但"忍耐"立刻止住我，
不让抱怨："神并不需要人劳作，或还他礼物。
谁能承受他温和的轭，谁就奉献了最好的服务……

3. **Land of Promise**（应许之地）：又写作 the Promised Land；又称"流着奶与蜜之地"，典出《民数记》第10章29节。指迦南地(Canaan)，上帝许诺之处，喻指希望之乡、乐土。英国桂冠诗人丁尼生(Alfred Tennyson, 1809-1892)的诗作《爱情故事》(*The Lover's Tale*)描写一对恋人对美丽山景的赞叹：a land of promise, land of memory/a land of promise flowing with milk/and honey, of delicious memories.[1] 希望之地，承载美好记忆/希望之乡，流淌奶与蜜/爱情甜蜜的记忆。

4. **Aaron's Rod**（亚伦的杖）：典出《民数记》第17章1—13节。上帝让亚伦的杖发芽、开花、结熟杏，以证明他是被特选的大祭司。指蒙神拣选的标志，行使圣职的权利。劳伦斯在1922年发表了小说 *Aaron's Rod*（《亚伦的杖杆》），借用了"亚伦的黎杖"这一神话原型，以主人公亚伦手里神奇的长笛为对照隐喻，刻画了他从分裂走向再生的生命历程。美国盲人女作家 Helen Keller 的自传 *The Story of My Life* 中就引用了这个典故，盲少女从老师那里学会了很多词语，这些词语像"亚伦的黎杖开满鲜花"：words that were to make the world blossom for me, "like Aaron's rod, with flowers".

5. **covenant of salt**（盐约）：典出《民数记》第18章19节上帝与以色列人的立约：it is a covenant of salt for ever before the LORD unto thee and thy seed with thee. 这是给你和你的后裔在

---

1. 转引自 David Lyle Jeffrey. *A Dictionary of Biblical Tradition in English Literature*. Wm. B. Eerdmans Publishing Co. 1992. p434.

耶和华面前作为永远的盐约。在以色列人传统里,"盐"是"永不废弃"的象征,此典喻指不可背弃的盟约。在《历代记下》第13章5节亚比雅问:Ought ye not to know that the LORD God of Israel gave the kingdom over Israel to David for ever, even to him and his sons by a covenant of salt? (*II Chronicles* 13: 5)耶和华以色列的神曾立盐约,将以色列国永远赐给大卫和他的子孙,你们不知道吗?

6. **Balaam's ass**(巴兰的驴子):典出《民数记》第22章21—34节关于巴兰骑驴去见摩押王途中被天使阻拦、巴兰怒打驴子、驴子开口说话的故事。喻指俯首帖耳、言听计从者,也指平日驯顺、但突然反抗的人或物。英国浪漫主义诗人拜伦的长诗《唐璜》第12章26节中写道:
That even the purest people may mistake
Their way through virtue's primrose paths of snows;
And then men stare, as if a new ass spake
To Balaam, and from tongue to ear o'erflows
连最纯洁的人都不免
在"美德"的雪白的寻欢之途上
误入歧途。于是人们惊传相告,
好似巴兰的驴又说了话一样;
流言不胫而走。
劳伦斯在1922年1月26日给友人的一封信中提及Balaam's ass: 我把这部小说的底稿摆在了自己面前,力图做些修改,但它好像巴兰的驴子一样,无法改动,哪怕是微乎其微的改动。(见《劳伦斯书信选》,北方文艺出版社1988年版)

7. **city of refuge**(庇护城):典出《申命记》第4章41—43节,又见《约书亚记》第20章1—9节。指耶和华神晓谕摩西专为误杀人命的罪犯设立的避难之城。喻指逃避惩罚的安全之处,避难之地。美国作家爱默生在其《斯威登伯格》(*Swedenborg*, 1850)中说:"假如我们厌倦了圣人,那么,莎士比亚便是我们的逃城。"苏雪林在其著名论文《希伯来文化对中国之影响》中提到,《史记》中孟尝君"招致天下任侠奸人入薛中,盖六万余家矣。"(《孟尝君传》)他认为此举是受了希伯来圣经"六座庇护城"的影响。

8. **the apple of one's eye**(眼珠、瞳仁):典出《申命记》第32章10节:He led him in a desert land, and in the waste howling wilderness; he led him about, he instructed him, he kept him as the apple of his eye. 耶和华在旷野之地遇见了他,在荒凉之地和野兽吼叫的荒野,遇见了他,就环绕他,看顾他,保护他,好像保护自己眼中的瞳仁一样。在狄更斯的小说《老古玩店》中,矮子对狄克说:"my pet, my pupil, the apple of my eye, hey! Hey!"("我的宠物,我的徒弟,我的宝贝,嘿!嘿!")此处用来指矮子对狄克的爱惜之情。再如《简•爱》第38章中,简说:
Mr. Rochester continued blind the first two years of our union; perhaps it was that circumstance that drew us so very near — that knit us so very close; for I was then his vision, as I am still his right hand. Literally, I was (what he often called me) the apple of his

eye. 我们结婚以后头两年，罗切斯特先生的眼睛还一直是瞎的——也许正因为这种情况，我们才如此亲近——才如此紧密地联系在一起！因为在那个时候，我是他的视力，正像我还是他的右手一样。说实在的，我是他的瞳仁，他是这么叫我的。

9. **dew**（露水）：典出《申命记》第32章2节：My doctrine shall drop as the rain, my speech shall distil as the dew, as the small rain upon the tender herb, and as the showers upon the grass. 我的教训下降如雨，我的言语滴落如露，像细雨落在青草上，像甘霖降在蔬菜上。dew 有多种比喻意义，此处指培育。露水在巴勒斯坦居民的生活中占有非常重要的地位，可比喻"和平安宁"，如《诗篇》第133篇第3节写道：As the dew of Hermon, and as the dew that descended upon the mountains of Zion: for there the Lord commanded the blessing, even life for evermore. 又好比黑门的甘露，落在锡安的众山上，在那里有耶和华命定的福，就是永远的生命。又可比喻"君王之恩"，如《箴言》第19章第12节写道：The king's wrath is as the roaring of a lion; but his favour is as dew upon the grass. 王的愤怒，好像狮子的吼叫，他的恩宠，如同草上的朝露。

10. **vines of Sodom**（所多玛的葡萄）：典出《申命记》第32章32节摩西所言敌人的葡萄树：For their vine is of the vine of Sodom, and of the fields of Gomorrah: their grapes are grapes of gall, their clusters are bitter. 他们的葡萄树是所多玛的葡萄树，蛾摩拉田里所出产的，他们的葡萄是毒葡萄，整挂葡萄都是苦的。"所多玛"和"蛾摩拉"二城乃"罪恶之城"，与之相联系的词语均含贬义。"所多玛的葡萄"喻指"金玉其外、败絮其中"之人或物。与此典相联系的圣经典故还有两个：Dead Sea fruits 和 apple of Sodom，均指"华而不实"之人或事物。拜伦在其诗作《恰尔德·哈罗德游记》(*Childe Harold's Pilgrimage*) 中说：生活会使它/适应悲哀最苦涩的果实，/就像死海岸边的苹果，/多有的味道皆如同嚼蜡。特普罗(Trollop)在《弗阮莱的牧师之宅》(*Framley Parsonage*) 中写道："我不想说，婚姻的幸福就如同死海的苹果，当你咬下去后，在嘴里会变得苦涩无味。"有趣的是，apple of Sodom 似乎比 vine of Sodom 更常用。如：Nowadays few people believe in advertisements, which are almost regarded as a lure for people to buy some apple of Sodom. 眼下很少有人相信广告，因为广告简直就是诱惑人去买一些中看不中用的东西。

六、课堂讨论题

1. 阅读律法书的相关条例，对比中国人与犹太人的慈善观。
2. 谈谈律法书对饮食与卫生的规定。
3. 谈谈犹太教与养生保健。
4. "庇护城"专为杀人罪犯而设。你如何理解？

七、课后思考题

1. 从律法书看正义和公平的原则。
2. 从律法书看道德对社会文明的促进作用。
3. 谈谈赔偿条例的现代意义。
4. 律法书常用"寄居"一词描述犹太人与地球的关系,你知道其中的理念吗?

第五讲

时势造就的英雄：士师

Judges, "Heroes" in the Lawless Period

一、导读：士师秉政时期

《士师记》(*Judges*)在《旧约》里排在摩西五经、《约书亚记》(*Joshua*)之后。"士师"(Judge)在希伯来语中的意思是"审判者"，指以色列人建立国家之前各支派的临时首领。从约书亚去世至扫罗登位称王这段时间，称为士师秉政时期。摩西的继承者约书亚死后，以色列十二支派仅保持一个松散的联盟，没有任何中心权力机构，整个迦南也没有真正的统一。十二支派各自为政，生活混乱，道德堕落，经济贫困，常常遭受异族的侵犯，于是出现了热爱民族、以拯救同胞为己任、领导以色列人战胜仇敌、赢得独立的士师。《士师记》集中记载了12位士师的事迹。

《士师记》共21章，可分为3部分。第1部分记述当时以色列的政治、宗教状况。第2部分具体记述士师秉政的历史，包括以色列人六次背道、六次受压迫、六次蒙上帝拯救。第3部分是全书的附录，用事例说明以色列人宗教生活的混乱和道德的败坏：便雅悯人将利未人的妾奸污致死导致整个支派几乎被全歼。

本讲选取《士师记》中五位著名士师的故事：
1. 以笏的故事：左撇子英雄以笏假借献宝成功刺杀敌王。
2. 底波拉之歌：女士师底波拉为庆祝战役胜利作的赞歌。
3. 基甸的故事：农夫出身的基甸挑选精兵成功突袭敌军。
4. 耶弗他和他的女儿：耶弗他为取得胜利向耶和华许下诺言，不得不将独生女献给上帝。
5. 参孙与大利拉：大力士参孙经不住情人大利拉的诱惑说出自己力大无比的秘密，被腓力士人俘虏，受尽屈辱，最终杀敌数千并与敌人同归于尽。

二、选文及注释

Part 1

Ehud[1]

And the children of Israel did evil in the sight of the LORD, and served Baalim[2]: and they forsook[3] the LORD God of their fathers, which brought them out of the land of Egypt, and followed other gods, of the gods of the people that were round about them, and bowed themselves unto them, and

---

1. Ehud /ˈɪhuːd/（人名）以笏，是个左撇子
2. Baalim /ˈbeɪəlɪm/ *n.*（音译）巴力，古代迦南人信奉的司生生化育之神 Baal /ˈbeɪəl/ 的复数形式。喻指邪神或偶像。
3. forsook *vt.* forsake（抛弃；离弃）的过去式和过去分词

provoked the LORD to anger. (2: 11–12)

Nevertheless the LORD raised up judges, which delivered them out of the hand of those that spoiled them. And yet they would not hearken unto their judges, but they went a whoring[1] after other gods, and bowed themselves unto them: they turned quickly out of the way which their fathers walked in, obeying the commandments of the LORD; but they did not so. And when the LORD raised them up judges, then the LORD was with the judge, and delivered them out of the hand of their enemies all the days of the judge: for it repented the LORD because of their groanings by reason of[2] them that oppressed them and vexed[3] them. And it came to pass, when the judge was dead, that they returned, and corrupted themselves more than their fathers, in following other gods to serve them, and to bow down unto them; they ceased not from own doings, nor from their stubborn way. (2: 16–19)

And the children of Israel did evil again in the sight of the LORD: and the LORD strengthened Eglon the king of Moab[4] against Israel, because they had done evil in the sight of the LORD. And he gathered unto him the children of Ammon and Amalek[5], and went and smote Israel, and possessed the city of palm trees[6]. So the children of Israel served Eglon the king of Moab eighteen years.

But when the children of Israel cried unto the LORD, the LORD raised them up a deliverer, Ehud the Son of Gera, a Benjamite, a man lefthanded: and by him the children of Israel sent a present unto Eglon the king of Moab. But Ehud made him a dagger which had two edges, of a cubit length; and he did gird[7] it under his raiment upon his right thigh.

And he brought the present unto Eglon king of Moab: and Eglon was a very fat man. And when he had made an end to offer the present, he sent away the people that bare the present. But he himself turned again from the quarries that were by Gilgal[8], and said "I have a secret errand unto thee, O king": who said, "Keep silence."

And all that stood by him went out from him. And Ehud came unto him; and he was sitting in a summer parlour, which he had for himself alone. And Ehud said,

"I have a message from God unto thee."

And he arose out of his seat. And Ehud put forth his left hand, and took the dagger from his right thigh, and thrust it into his belly; and the haft[9] also went in after the blade; and the fat closed upon the blade, so that he could not draw the dagger out of his belly; and the dirt[10] came out. Then Ehud went forth through the porch, and shut the doors of the parlour upon him, and locked them. When he was gone out, his servants came; and when they saw that, behold, the doors of the parlour were locked, they said,

---

1. whore *vi.* to accept payment in exchange for sexual relations 卖淫。go a whoring 是比喻说法，指背离纯洁的信仰而叩拜其他神。
2. by reason of because of 因为；由于。以色列人受异族欺压和迫害，就哀哭叹气，这令耶和华感到后悔。第一个 them 指统治以色列民族的外族人。
3. vex *vt.* to cause sb. to suffer 使痛苦；遭受折磨
4. Eglon the king of Moab 摩押人的王伊矶伦。摩押是罗得(Lot)醉酒后和大女儿所生的儿子，是摩押人之始祖。
5. Ammon and Amalek 亚扪(人)和亚玛力(人)。亚扪：在摩押的东北；亚玛力：在犹大以南。两个民族都是以色列人出埃及前后生活在迦南附近的游牧部落。
6. the city of palm trees 棕树城耶利哥(Jericho)，约旦河西的重要城市，靠近死海。约书亚进攻迦南时率先攻陷此城(《约书亚记》2: 1—24)。士师时期，摩押王伊矶伦的军队以色列人，曾驻军于此。
7. gird *vt.* to encircle with 束缚；绑住
8. the quarries that were by Gilgal 靠近吉甲的雕石场。quarry *n.* 指开凿石像的地方，石像为偶像之类。
9. haft *n.*(短剑的)柄
10. the dirt 肚里的粪便。

"Surely he covereth his feet[1] in his summer chamber."

And they tarried till they were ashamed[2]: and, behold, he opened not the doors of the parlour; therefore they took a key, and opened them: and, behold, their lord was fallen down dead on the earth.

And Ehud escaped while they tarried, and passed beyond the quarries, and escaped unto Seirath[3]. And it came to pass, when he was come, that he blew a trumpet in the mountain of Ephraim[4], and the children of Israel went down with him from the mount, and he before them. And he said unto them, "Follow after me: for the LORD hath delivered your enemies the Moabites into your hand."

And they went down after him, and took the fords of Jordan[5] toward Moab, and suffered[6] not a man to pass over. And they slew of Moab at that time about ten thousand men, all lusty[7], and all men of valour[8]; and there escaped not a man. So Moab was subdued that day under the hand of Israel. And the land had rest fourscore years. (3: 12–30)

Part 2

The Song of Deborah

Then sang Deborah and Barak the son of Abinoam[9] on that day, saying,

"Praise ye the LORD for the avenging of Israel,

When the people willingly offered themselves.

Hear, O ye kings; give ear, O ye princes;

I, even I, will sing unto the LORD;

I will sing praise to the LORD God of Israel.

LORD, when thou wentest out of Seir[10],

When thou marchedst out of the field of Edom,

The earth trembled, and the heavens dropped,

The clouds also dropped water.

The mountains melted from before the LORD,

Even that Sinai from before the LORD God of Israel.

In the days of Shamgar the son of Anath[11],

In the days of Jael[12], the highways were unoccupied,

And the travellers walked through by-ways.

The inhabitants of the villages ceased, they ceased in Israel,

Until that I Deborah arose,

That I arose a mother in Israel.

They chose new gods;

Then was war in the gates:

---

1. covereth his feet (委婉语)解手。
2. they tarried till they were ashamed 仆人们等感到不对头。
3. Seirath (地名)西伊拉，地址不详
4. the mountain of Ephraim 以法莲山。
5. the fords of Jordan 约旦河的渡口。以色列人把守渡口，可以阻止驻守耶利哥的摩押兵逃走，又可以拦截从约旦河东岸来的增援部队。
6. suffer vt. to tolerate〈古〉容许
7. lusty adj. full of vigor or vitality; robust 健壮的；精壮的
8. valour n. great courage in the face of danger, especially in battle 勇猛；英勇
9. Deborah /ˈdebərə/ and Barak the son of Abinoam 女先知底波拉和亚比挪庵的儿子巴拉。巴拉是以色列人的军事将领。
10. Seir /sɪə/ (地名)西珥山，即下一行里的以东地(Edom)
11. In the days of Shamgar the son of Anath 亚拿之子珊迦。他虽然杀了600非利士人，但未能使百姓完全脱离异族的压制。
12. Jael /ˈdʒeɪəl/ (人名)雅亿，杀死来她家避难的敌将西西拉的以色列妇人

Was there a shield or spear seen
Among forty thousand in Israel?
My heart is toward the governors of Israel,
That offered themselves willingly among the people.
Bless ye the LORD.
Speak, ye that ride on white asses[1],
Ye that sit in judgment, and walk by the way.[2]
They that are delivered from the noise of archers
In the places of drawing water[3],
There shall they rehearse[4] the righteous acts of the LORD,
Even the righteous acts toward the inhabitants of his villages in Israel:
Then shall the people of the LORD go down to the gates.

Awake, awake, Deborah:
Awake, awake, utter a song:
Arise, Barak, and lead thy captivity captive[5], thou son of Abinoam.
Then he made him that remaineth have dominion over the nobles among the people:
The LORD made me have dominion over the mighty.

Out of Ephraim was there a root of them against Amalek;
After thee, Benjamin, among thy people;
Out of Machir came down governors,
And out of Zebulun they that handle the pen of the writer.
And the princes of Issachar were with Deborah;[6]
Even Issachar, and also Barak:
He was sent on foot into the valley.
For the divisions of Reuben[7]
There were great thoughts of heart.[8]
Why abodest[9] thou among the sheepfolds,
To hear the bleatings of the flocks[10]?
For the divisions of Reuben
There were great searchings of heart.
Gilead abode beyond Jordan:
And why did Dan remain in ships?
Asher continued on the sea shore,
And abode in his breaches.[11]
Zebulun and Naphtali[12] were a people that jeoparded their lives unto the death[13]
In the high places of the field.

The kings came and fought,
Then fought the kings of Canaan
In Taanach by the waters of Megiddo[14];
They took no gain of money.

---

1. ye that ride on white asses 骑白驴的人，指富人和统治阶层。
2. Ye that sit in judgment, and walk by the way. 等待纠纷处理结果的人和行路的人。前者指有财产、有纠纷的有钱人，后者指没有代步工具的穷人。底波拉邀请社会各阶层人士一同传扬耶和华的恩典。
3. They that are delivered from the noise of archers in the places of drawing water (直译)在打水的人中有弓箭手的说话声。意思是弓箭手从战车归来，恢复其平民身份，在打水处工作时述说耶和华的拯救。
4. rehearse *vt.* to repeat words of praise 颂扬
5. lead thy captivity captive 掳掠你的俘虏(敌人)。
6. Out of Machir came down governors, and out of Zebulun they that handle the pen of the writer. And the princes of Issachar were with Deborah 有官长从玛吉来了，有持着检点民数权杖的人从西布伦来了，以萨迦的首领和底波拉一同来了。底波拉称赞参与这次战役的以法莲、便雅悯、玛拿西、西布伦和以萨迦支派。
7. the divisions of Reuben 流便(地)的众溪水。注意：流便、基列、但和亚设没有参战，反映了没有法律，没有国王的时期以色列民族内部一片散沙、互相争斗的混乱状态。
8. There were great thoughts of heart. 有心怀大志的。
9. abodest 动词 abide (耐心等候)的过去式
10. the bleatings of the flocks 羊群的叫声。
11. Asher continued on the sea shore, and abode in his breaches. 亚设人在海口静坐，在港口安居。breach *n.* 裂口，指港口。
12. Naphtali 拿弗他利(人)
13. jeoparded their lives unto the death 拼命敢死。jeopard *vt.* 同jeopardized, to put (sb. or sth.) into a situation in which there is a danger or loss 冒着危险。
14. Then fought the kings of Canaan in Taanach by the waters of Megiddo 那时迦南诸王在米吉多水旁的他纳争战。

They fought from heaven;
The stars in their courses fought against Sisera.
The river of Kishon swept them away[1],
That ancient river, the river Kishon.
O my soul, thou hast trodden down strength.
Then were the horsehoofs[2] broken
By the means of pransings[3], the pransings of their mighty ones.

'Curse ye Meroz[4],' said the angel of the LORD,
'Curse ye bitterly the inhabitants thereof;
Because they came not to the help of the LORD,
To the help of the LORD against the mighty,'

Blessed above women shall Jael
The wife of Heber the Kenite[5] be,
Blessed shall she be above women in the tent.
He asked water, and she gave him milk;
She brought forth butter in a lordly[6] dish.
She put her hand to the nail,
And her right hand to the worksmen's hammer;
And with the hammer she smote Sisera[7], she smote off his head,
When she had pierced and stricken through his temples.
At her feet he bowed, he fell, he lay down:
At her feet he bowed, he fell:
Where he bowed, there he fell down dead.

The mother of Sisera looked out at a window,
And cried through the lattice[8],
'Why is his chariot so long in coming?
Why tarry the wheels of his chariots?'
Her wise ladies answered her,
Yea, she returned answer to herself,
'Have they not sped? have they not divided the prey;
To every man a damsel or two;
To Sisera a prey of divers colours,
A prey of divers colours of needlework,
Of divers colours of needlework on both sides, meet for the necks of them that take the spoil?'

So let all thine enemies perish, O LORD:
But let them that love him be as the sun when he goeth forth in his might." (5)

Part 3

Gideon[9]

And the children of Israel did evil in the sight of the LORD: and the LORD delivered them into the hand of Midian seven years. And the hand of Midian prevailed against Israel: and because of the Midianites the children of Israel made them the dens[10] which are in the mountains, and caves, and strong holds[11]. And so it was, when Israel had sown, that the Midianites came up, and

---

1. The river of Kishon swept them away 基顺古河把西西拉的军队冲没。
2. horsehoof *n.* 马蹄
3. pransing *n.* (of a horse) move with high springy steps (马蹄)腾跃
4. Meroz (地名)米罗斯。这里虽接近战场，但那里的村民畏缩不来参战。
5. Heber the Kenite (雅亿的丈夫)基尼人希百。
6. lordly *adj.* very dignified and noble 高贵的；珍贵的
7. Sisera /ˈsɪsərə/ (人名)西西拉，迦南王耶宾的大将
8. lattice *n.* 窗棂
9. Gideon /ˈɡɪdɪən/ (人名)基甸
10. den *n.* a wild mammals's hidden home 兽穴；洞穴
11. strong holds 堡垒；营寨。又可写作 stronghold。

the Amalekites, and the children of the east[1], even they came up against them; and they encamped[2] against them, and destroyed the increase of the earth[3], till thou come unto Gaza[4], and left no sustenance for Israel, neither sheep, nor ox, nor ass. For they came up with their cattle and their tents, and they came as grasshoppers for multitude; for both they and their camels were without number: and they entered into the land to destroy it. (6: 1–6)

And there came an angel of the LORD, and sat under an oak which was in Ophrah, that pertained unto Joash, the Abi-ezrite[5]: and his son Gideon threshed wheat by the winepress[6], to hide it from the Midianites. And the angel of the LORD appeared unto him, and said unto him, "The LORD is with thee, thou mighty man of valour."... (6: 11–12)

Then Jerubbal, who is Gideon, and all the people that were with him, rose up early, and pitched beside the well of Harod[7]: so that the host[8] of the Midianites were on the north side of them, by the hill of Moreh[9], in the valley. And the LORD said unto Gideon,

"The people that are with thee are too many for me to give the Midianites into their hands, lest Israel vaunt[10] themselves against me, saying, 'Mine own hand hath saved me.' Now therefore go to, proclaim in the ears of the people, saying, 'Whosoever is fearful and afraid, let him return and depart early from mount Gilead."

And there returned of the people twenty and two thousand; and there remained ten thousand. And the LORD said unto Gideon,

"The people are yet too many; bring them down unto the water, and I will try them for thee there: and it shall be, that of whom I say unto thee, 'This shall go with thee', the same shall go with thee; and of whomsoever I say unto thee, 'This shall not go with thee', the same shall not go[11]."

So he brought down the people unto the water: and the LORD said unto Gideon, "Every one that lappeth[12] of the water with his tongue, as a dog lappeth, him shalt thou set by himself; likewise every one that boweth down upon his knees to drink."

And the number of them that lapped, putting their hand to their mouth, were three hundred men: but all the rest of the people bowed down upon their knees to drink water. And the LORD said unto Gideon,

"By the three hundred men that lapped will I save you, and deliver the Midianites into thine hand: and let all the other people go every man unto his place."

So the people took victuals in their hand, and their trumpets: and he sent all the rest of Israel every man unto his tent, and retained those three hundred men: and the host of Midian was beneath him in the valley.

And it came to pass the same night, that

---

1. the children of the east 东方人，生活在叙利亚沙漠的民族，即今日的阿拉伯人。他们每年协助米甸人侵入以色列境内掠夺土产。
2. encamp *vi.* to settle in or to establish a camp 扎营
3. the increase of the earth 土地的产物。
4. Gaza /ˈɡɑːzə/ （地名）迦萨，是非利士五个主要城邑中最靠南的一个
5. an oak which was in Ophrah, that pertained unto Joash, the Abi-ezrite （天使坐在）俄弗拉地亚比以谢族人约阿施的橡树下。约阿施即基甸的父亲。pertain *vi.* to belong (to) or to be part of 属于。
6. threshed wheat by the winepress 挨着酒榨打麦子。酒榨用挖空的石块做成，凹处盛载葡萄，葡萄被凿踏后流出葡萄汁，汁沿着与凹处接驳的沟道往下流，滴进装葡萄汁的槽中。
7. the well of Harod 哈律泉。位于以萨迦境内基利波山向北山麓。
8. host *n.* an army 军队
9. the hill of Moreh 摩利冈。位于他泊山与基利波山之间。
10. vaunt (themselves) *vi.* to speak boastfully of 自夸
11. the same shall not go 意思是耶和华指着谁说"这个人不能去"，他就不能去。
12. lap (of) *vt.* to scoop (a liquid) into the mouth with the tongue 舔

the LORD said unto him, "Arise, get thee down unto the host; for I have delivered it into thine hand. But if thou fear to go down, go thou with Phurah[1] thy servant down to the host: and thou shalt hear what they say; and afterward shall thine hands be strengthened to go down unto the host."

Then went he down with Phurah his servant unto the outside of the armed that were in the host. And the Midianites and the Amalekites and all the children of the east lay along in the valley like grasshoppers for multitude; and their camels were without number, as the sand by the sea side for multitude. And when Gideon was come, behold, there was a man that told a dream unto his fellow, and said,

"Behold, I dreamed a dream, and, lo, a caked of barley bread tumbled into the host of Midian, and came unto a tent, and smote it that it fell and overturned it, that the tent lay along."

And his fellow answered and said,

"This is nothing else save the sword of Gideon the son of Joash, a man of Israel: for into his hand hath God delivered Midian, and all the host."

And it was so, when Gideon heard the telling of the dream, and the interpretation thereof, that he worshipped, and returned into the host of Israel, and said, "Arise; for the LORD hath delivered into your hand the host of Midian."

And he divided the three hundred men into three companies, and he put a trumpet in every man's hand, with empty pitchers[2], and lamps within the pitchers. And he said unto them, "Look on me, and do likewise: and, behold, when I come to the outside of the camp, it shall be that, as I do, so shall ye do. When I blow with a trumpet, I and all that are with me, then blow ye the trumpets also on every side of all the camp, and say, 'The sword of the LORD, and of Gideon.'"

So Gideon, and the hundred men that were with him, came unto the outside of the camp in the beginning of the middle watch[3]; and they had but newly set the watch: and they blew the trumpets, and brake the pitchers that were in their hands. And the three companies blew the trumpets, and brake the pitchers, and held the lamps in their left hands, and the trumpets in their right hands to blow withal[4]: and they cried, "The sword of the LORD, and of Gideon."

And they stood every man in his place round about the camp: and all the host ran, and cried, and fled. And the three hundred blew the trumpets, and the LORD set every man's sword against his fellow, even throughout all the host. (7: 1–22)

Part 4

Jephthah and His Daughter

Now Jephthah the Gileadite[5] was a mighty man of valour, and he was the son of an harlot: and Gilead begat Jephthah. And Gilead's wife bare him sons; and his wife's sons grew up, and they thrust out Jephthah, and said unto him, "Thou shalt not inherit in our father's house; for thou art the son of a strange woman[6]."

Then Jephthah fled from his brethren, and dwelt in the land of Tob[7]: and there were

---

1. Phurah (基甸的仆人)普拉
2. pitcher *n.* a large jug 陶瓶。基甸把三百人分成三队，把角和空瓶交在每个人手里，又把火把放在瓶里。瓶子里的火把是燃着的。
3. in the beginning of the middle watch 三更之初，约晚上10点钟。夜晚分作三更，每更约4个小时。middle watch 午夜(值勤)。
4. withal 等于 with，〈古〉用，用以。常用于宾语之后或句末。
5. Jephthah the Gileadite 基列人耶弗他。Gilead 是地名，耶弗他的父亲也叫此名。
6. a strange woman (婉言)妓女。
7. Tob (地名)陀伯

gathered vain men[1] to Jephthah, and went out with him.

And it came to pass in process of time, that the children of Ammon made war against Israel. And it was so, that when the children of Ammon made war against Israel, the elders of Gilead went to fetch Jephthah out of the land of Tob: and they said unto Jephthah, "Come and be our captain, that we may fight with the children of Ammon." (11: 1–6)

Then the Spirit of the LORD came upon Jephthah, and he passed over Gilead, and Manasseh[2], and passed over Mizpeh[3] of Gilead, and from Mizpeh of Gilead he passed over unto the children of Ammon. And Jephthah vowed a vow unto the LORD, and said,

"If thou shalt without fail deliver the children of Ammon into mine hands, then it shall be, that whatsoever cometh forth of the doors of my house to meet me, when I return in peace from the children of Ammon, shall surely be the LORD's, and I will offer it up for a burnt offering."

So Jephthah passed over unto the children of Ammon to fight against them; and the LORD delivered them into his hands. And he smote them from Aroer[4], even till thou come to Minnith[5], even twenty cities, and unto the plain of the vineyards, with a very great slaughter. Thus the children of Ammon were subdued before the children of Israel.

And Jephthah came to Mizpeh unto his house, and, behold, his daughter came out to meet him with timbrels and with dances: and she was his only child; beside her he had neither son nor daughter. And it came to pass, when he saw her, that he rent his clothes[6], and said,

"Alas, my daughter! thou hast brought me very low[7], and thou art one of them that trouble me: for I have opened my mouth unto the LORD, and I cannot go back."

And she said unto him, "My father, if thou hast opened thy mouth unto the LORD, do to me according to that which hath proceeded out of thy mouth; forasmuch as the LORD hath taken vengeance[8] for thee of thine enemies, even of the children of Ammon."

And she said unto her father,

"Let this thing be done for me: let me alone two months, that I may go up and down upon the mountains, and bewail[9] my virginity[10], I and my fellows."

And he said, "Go." And he sent her away for two months: and she went with her companions, and bewailed her virginity upon the mountains. And it came to pass at the end of two months, that she returned unto her father, who did with her according to his vow which he had vowed: and she knew no man. And it was a custom in Israel, that the daughters of Israel went yearly to lament[11] the daughter of Jephthah the Gileadite four days in a year. (11: 29–40)

---

1. vain men 匪徒，这里是褒义，指绿林好汉。耶弗他有领导才能，身边聚集了不少绿林好汉。异族亚扪人来犯之际，同胞赏识他的才干，请他回乡抗敌，做基列人的领袖。
2. Manasseh (地名)玛拿西
3. Mizpeh (地名)米斯巴
4. Aroer (地名)亚罗珥
5. Minnith (地名)米匿
6. rent his clothes 撕裂衣服。古以色列人感到痛苦、绝望时的举动。
7. bring sb. very low 让人愁苦、为难。耶弗他实在没有料到第一个出来迎接他的竟然是自己的独生女。
8. take vengeance 报仇；复仇。
9. bewail vt. to express great regret, sadness, or disappointment about sth. 哀哭
10. virginity n. the state of never having had sexual intercourse 处女之身
11. lament vt. to express passionate grief about 哀悼；悲泣。因为耶弗他女儿的事迹，以色列少女形成惯例，每年为她哀泣4天，怜惜她的悲苦遭遇。

Part 5

Samson and Delilah[1]

Then went Samson to Gaza, and saw there an harlot, and went in unto her. And it was told the Gazites[2], saying, "Samson is come hither." And they compassed[3] him in, and laid wait for[4] him all night in the gate of the city, and were quiet all the night, saying, "In the morning, when it is day, we shall kill him."

And Samson lay till midnight, and arose at midnight, and took the doors of the gate of the city, and the two posts, and went away with them, bar[5] and all, and put them upon his shoulders, and carried them up to the top of an hill that is before Hebron[6].

And it came to pass afterward, that he loved a woman in the valley of Sorek[7], whose name was Delilah. And the lords of the Philistines[8] came up unto her, and said unto her,

"Entice[9] him, and see wherein his great strength lieth, and by what means we may prevail against him, that we may bind him to afflict him: and we will give thee every one of us eleven hundred pieces of silver."

And Delilah said to Samson, "Tell me, I pray thee, wherein thy great strength lieth, and wherewith thou mightest be bound to afflict thee."

And Samson said unto her, "If they bind me with seven green withs[10] that were never dried, then shall I be weak, and be as another man."

Then the lords of the Philistines brought up to her seven green withs which had not been dried, and she bound him with them. Now there were men lying in wait, abiding[11] with her in the chamber. And she said unto him,

"The Philistines be upon thee, Samson." And he brake the withs, as a thread of tow[12] is broken when it toucheth the fire. So his strength was not known. And Delilah said unto Samson, "Behold, thou hast mocked me, and told me lies: now tell me, I pray thee, wherewith thou mightest be bound."

And he said unto her, "If they bind me with new ropes that never were occupied, then shall I be weak, and be as another man."

Delilah therefore took new ropes, and

---

1. Samson and Delilah /dɪˈlaɪlə/ (人名)参孙和大利拉。
2. Gazites 迦萨人
3. compass *vt.* to surround; to encircle 包围
4. laid wait for 等候。
5. bar *n.* 门闩
6. Hebron /ˈhiːbrən/ (地名)希伯仑。迦萨距希伯仑约38英里(61公里)。参孙将门扇、门柱和门闩一起拆下来，肩扛到位于山顶上的希伯仑。
7. the valley of Sorek (地名)梭烈谷
8. the lords of the Philistines 非利士人的首领。
9. entice *vt.* to tempt by offering pleasure or advantage 引诱；诱惑
10. green withs *n.* 用未干的藤条做成的绳子。with 同 withe 或 withy 柳条；藤条。
11. abide *vt.* to wait patiently for 耐心等候。指预先埋伏在内室。
12. a thread of tow 一条麻线。

bound him therewith, and said unto him, "The Philistines be upon thee, Samson." And there were liers[1] in wait abiding in the chamber. And he brake them from off his arms like a thread.

And Delilah said unto Samson, "Hitherto thou hast mocked me, and told me lies: tell me wherewith thou mightest be bound."

And he said unto her, "If thou weavest the seven locks of my head with the web[2]."

And she fastened it with the pin[3], and said unto him, "The Philistines be upon thee, Samson."

And he awaked out of his sleep, and went away with the pin of the beam[4], and with the web. And she said unto him,

"How canst thou say, I love thee, when thine heart is not with me? thou hast mocked me these three times, and hast not told me wherein thy great strength lieth."

And it came to pass, when she pressed him daily with her words, and urged him, so that his soul was vexed unto death; That he told her all his heart, and said unto her, "There hath not come a razor upon mine head; for I have been a Nazarite[5] unto God from my mother's womb: if I be shaven, then my strength will go from me, and I shall become weak, and be like any other man."

And when Delilah saw that he had told her all his heart, she sent and called for the lords of the Philistines, saying, "Come up this once, for he hath shewed me all his heart."

Then the lords of the Philistines came up unto her, and brought money in their hand. And she made him sleep upon her knees; and she called for a man, and she caused him to shave off the seven locks of his head; and she bagan to afflict him, and his strength went from him. And she said,

"The Philistines be upon thee, Samson." And he awoke out of his sleep, and said, "I will go out as at other times before, and shake myself." And he wist not that the LORD was departed from him.

But the Philistines took him, and put out his eyes, and brought him down to Gaza, and bound him with fetters of brass[6]; and he did grind[7] in the prison house. Howbeit[8] the hair of his head began to grow again after he was shaven.

Then the lords of the Philistines gathered them together for to offer a great sacrifice unto Dagon[9] their god, and to rejoice: for they said, "Our god hath delivered Samson our enemy into our hand."

And when the people saw him, they praised their god: for they said, "Our god hath delivered into our hands our enemy, and the destroyer of our country, which slew many of us."

And it came to pass, when their hearts were merry, that they said, "Call for Samson, that he may make us sport[10]."

---

1. lier *n.* 埋伏的人
2. If thou weavest the seven locks of my head with the web 你若将我头上的七条发绺与纬线同织就可以了。意思是把头发割下来当作经线配合纬线来织布。
3. pin *n.* 橛子
4. beam *n.* 织布机上的织轴
5. Nazarite /'næzəraɪt/ *n.* 音译"拿细耳",希伯来文的意思是"奉献者",指自愿奉献给上帝的人,无论男女都有此称
6. fetters of brass 铜链。fetter *n.* 脚镣。
7. grind *n.* 推磨(碾米)。推磨本是妇女干的活,非利士人让参孙推磨,让他受尽凌辱。
8. howbeit *adv.* nevertheless; however 〈古〉然而
9. Dagon *n.* 音译"大衮",非利士人的主神,其上半身是人,下半身是鱼。非利士人乃海上强族,故有此偶像,但被奉为农作物的神。大衮庙有前院和内室,非利士首领及其眷属大概坐在内院,观看参孙戏耍。内室有平顶伸出至前院,平顶用圆木砌成,上面拥挤者三千男女。平顶下面有上粗下细的木柱支撑。参孙大概请求引路的童子让他靠近这些立柱。
10. make us sport 让参孙表演武艺供非利士人取乐。make sport of sb. to make fun of 〈古〉取笑。

And they called for Samson out of the prison house; and he made them sport: and they set him between the pillars. And Samson said unto the lad that held him by the hand, "Suffer me that I may feel the pillars whereupon the house standeth, that I may lean upon them."

Now the house was full of men and women; and all the lords of the Philistines were there; and there were upon the roof about three thousand men and women, that beheld while Samson made sport. And Samson called unto the LORD, and said, "O Lord God, remember me, I pray thee, and strengthen me, I pray thee, only this once. O God, that I may be at once avenged of the Philistines for my two eyes."

And Samson took hold of the two middle pillars upon which the house stood, and on which it was borne up, of the one with his right hand, and of the other with his left. And Samson said, "Let me die with the Philistines."

And he bowed himself with all his might; and the house fell upon the lords, and upon all the people that were therein. So the dead which he slew at his death were more than they which he slew in his life. Then his brethren and all the house of his father came down, and took him, and brought him up, and buried him between Zorah and Eshtaol[1] in the buryingplace of Manoah his father[2]. And he judged Israel twenty years. (16)

三、圣经文化知识链接

1. 拿细耳

在读参孙的故事时我们知道参孙为拿细耳人(Nazarite)。"拿细耳"的意思是"归主"，该词最早出现在《民数记》第6章1—21节。耶和华对摩西说："你晓谕以色列人说：无路男女许了特别的愿，就是拿细耳人的愿，要离俗归耶和华。他要远离清酒、浓酒，也不可喝什么清酒、浓酒作的醋，不可喝什么葡萄汁，也不可吃鲜葡萄和干葡萄。在一切离俗的日子，凡葡萄树上结的，自核至皮所作的物，都不可吃。古希伯来人中有不少"拿细耳"，其生活严格遵守摩西律法的规定，如不饮酒、不剪发等。参孙一直留着长发，就是终身为"拿细耳"的标志，因此他说 I have been a Nazarite unto God from my mother's womb.（我在母胎中就是归神的拿细耳人）以色列的最后一位士师撒母耳(Samuel)和《新约》里的施洗约翰(John the Baptist)也都终身为"拿细耳"。

2. 非利士人与巴勒斯坦

《旧约》中多次提到的非利士人(Philistines)早已消失。非利士人很出名，这是因为他们是参孙、扫罗和大卫的故事里以色列人的对手。非利士人是居住在迦南南部海岸的古民族，其领土在后来的文献中被称为"非利士地"。根据《创世记》第10章6—14节说："含的儿子是古实、麦西、弗、迦南。……麦西生……迦斯路希人、迦斐托人；从迦斐托出来的有非利士人"(Casluhim (from which came the Philistines) and Caphtorim)。亚伯拉罕和以撒都曾经跟非利

---

1. Zorah and Eshtaol (地名)琐拉和以实陶
2. Manoah his father 参孙的父亲玛挪亚。

士人打过交道(《创世记》21:32、34; 26:1、18),但他们只是昙花一现,在迦南地并没有什么显著的地位。据《出埃及记》的记载,非利士人并不是迦南地的原住民。到了《士师记》,非利士人已经成为以色列人的死敌。他们征服了沿迦南西南部沿海带状地区的5座城市: 迦萨(Gasa)、迦特(Gath)、亚实基伦(Ashkelon)、亚实突(Ashdod)和以革伦(Ekron)。参孙跟非利士人的争战是很出名的。以后,他们一直都是以色列人的大敌。在非利士人最强之时,曾入侵到伯珊、基利波山、密抹等地。他们把迦南改名为"巴勒斯坦"(Palestine),这个名称确实起源于"非利士人"的希腊语和拉丁语形式。

四、圣经文化专题

1. 《士师记》展现的故事模式

在阅读《士师记》中主要士师的事迹过程中,细心的读者会留意到每个故事的开头基本相仿: 以色列人背弃他们的上帝耶和华,由于作恶招致外族的骚扰、欺凌和压制。然后他们呼求上帝的拯救,于是上帝"兴起"一位士师,救民众于水火,最后打败敌人,民族解放,安享太平若干年。士师们的故事重要情节一再重复: 以色列人作恶→上帝惩罚他们→他们求告耶和华→士师兴起拯救民族,如此构成一个"作恶→惩罚→呼救→解救"的模式(Evildoing → Punishment → Outcry → Deliverance)[1]。加拿大圣经学者弗莱指出,《士师记》实际上原本是部落首领的那些英雄们的故事集,被编辑成为一部联合起来的以色列人经历一系列危机的历史。以色列人始终带有叛逆精神,他们背弃上帝、遭受奴役、呼求上帝解放,然后一位士师被派来解救他们。这个叙述中有一系列不同的内容,而包装这些内容的则是不断重复的神话或叙述形式。由于作者的兴趣在于道德说教,在这种叙事结构中我们所读到的是不断重复的同一类故事。[2]

斯腾伯格指出,《旧约》叙事里存在着"犯罪→惩罚→呼救→拯救"这样一个反复出现的模式。大洪水灭世、罪恶之城所多玛和蛾摩拉被烧毁是大规模的灭绝,《约拿记》中的上帝威胁要毁灭尼尼微,《士师记》中上帝屡次把以色列人交在外族人手里,让他们受奴役,然后再拯救他们,等等,都符合这个模式。其实,整部《圣经》是一个更大的"犯罪→惩罚→呼救→拯救"模式或者框架。上帝曾奢望一劳永逸地消灭恶,但逐步认识到这是不可能的,从而承认了人类不完美,并与人类达成协议,即"约"。我们可以这样认为,《圣经》既是一部宗教文献,也是象征意义上的人类的善恶斗争史。

2. 从参孙的故事和耶弗他献女故事看古希伯来文学的悲喜剧性[3]

我们从"作恶→惩罚→呼救→解救"四部曲里发现,主宰一切的上帝无可动摇地位于神—人

---

1. Meir Sternberg: *The Poetics of Biblical Narrative: Ideological Literature and the Drama of Reading.* Bloomington: Indiana University Press, 1985, pp. 265–268.
2. 【加拿大】弗莱著,郝振益等译《伟大的代码——圣经与文学》,北京: 北京大学出版社,1998年版,第64页。
3. 本项参考杨建的文章"古代希伯来文学的悲喜剧性及民族意识",载于《外国文学研究》,2004年第6期,第103—111页。

关系的核心，以色列人永远置于悲喜剧主人公的地位。与此相一致的是，《圣经》中的故事既不是一个绝对感人的悲剧，也不是一种带有突转、玩笑色彩的喜剧，而是悲中有喜、喜中有悲的悲喜剧。

我们通过具体的故事看到，人的悔罪、得救既是喜剧，也是悲剧，因为尽管人的信仰恢复、灵魂得救，但人和神都付出了巨大的代价，如肉体毁灭、骨肉相残。反之，人的犯罪、受罚是悲剧，但人性不断觉醒、走向完善，从根本上来说也是喜剧。《士师记》中力士参孙的故事和耶弗他的女儿的故事就非常具有代表性。

力士参孙的故事是悲剧性的。一位士师——上帝的宠儿，因为好色、轻信、违背上帝的戒律（与外族通婚、吃不洁的食物）失掉了名节，失去了自由，饱受非利士人的凌辱与折磨，甚至失去了宝贵的生命，给本族百姓也造成了巨大损失。这是一出典型的英雄悲剧、性格悲剧，上帝也会为他的宠儿落泪。然而，参孙的故事又是喜剧性的，因为经过数次失败、受罚，参孙终于悔悟，坚定了信仰，接受了使命，重新回到上帝身边，重新获得上帝赐予的神力，最终与非利士人同归于尽，拯救了民族，也成全了自己——他在以色列民族史上留下了一世英名。

在耶弗他的女儿的故事中，我们首先读到的是凯旋者的欢呼，但与此同时，耶弗他的许愿应验在自己的女儿身上：载歌载舞、第一个跑出家门迎接他的生灵竟然是他的独生女。为了信守诺言，耶弗他必须把女儿献给神做牺牲，戏剧性的巧合和得胜者的喜悦顷刻变成了撕心裂肺的悲剧场面。耶弗他陷入了两难选择境地，悲、喜两种戏剧因素同时并存。出于坚定的信念，还是处女的女儿最终自觉地、义无反顾地走向死亡，只是在死之前，她恳求父亲*"容我去两个月，与同伴在山上，好哀哭我终为处女"*（《士师记》11:37）。在此，悲剧冲突是存在的，只是藏得较深，并非只有坚韧不拔的意志和义无反顾的奉献精神。希伯来民族善于化解高度的宗教理性和激越的生命意志之间的根本矛盾，消弭"以神为本"和"以人为本"之间的剧烈冲突，从而使希伯来文学显示出难得的悲喜剧性。

五、圣经典故集锦

1. **left-handed**（左撇子）：使用左手的人（便雅悯族后裔）。指反应敏捷的人。在以笏成功刺杀敌王时，他正是借助了左撇子的优势。

2. **Deborah**（底波拉）：典出《士师记》第4—5章女先知底波拉与巴拉将军一起率军与迦南人作战得胜的英勇故事，指女英雄。莎士比亚的剧本《亨利六世·上篇》第一幕第二场第104—105行，查理对贞德说*"你是一个女英雄，使起剑来赛过底波拉。"*

3. **Megiddo**（米吉多）：指"决战之地"、"最后的较量"。典出《士师记》第5章19—20节：The kings came and fought, then fought the kings of Canaan in Taanach by the waters of Megiddo; they took no gain of money. They fought from heaven; the stars in their courses fought against Sisera. *君王都来征战，那时迦南诸王在米吉多水旁的他纳征战，却未得掳掠钱财。星宿从天上征战，从其轨道攻击西西拉。*女士师底波拉助巴拉的大军在米吉多山与迦南王的大将西西拉决战，一举击溃敌人。《启示录》第16章16节：And he gathered them together into a place called in the Hebrew tongue Armageddon. *那三个魔鬼便叫众王聚集*

在一处，希伯来话叫作哈米吉多顿。论及善与恶最后的决战地点是Armageddon（哈米吉多顿），就是源于此典。

4. **Gideon** (基甸)：典出基甸率领300精兵成功突袭敌军的英雄故事，喻指出奇制胜之人、以少胜多的将领。基督教组织成立于1898年的一个出版、分发《圣经》的机构就取名 *The Gideons International* (国际基甸)。

5. **lap water to the mouth** (手舀水舔着喝)：典出《士师记》第7章4—8节基甸依据士兵喝水的姿态和方式挑选精兵的故事。用手舀水舔着喝说明其动作快、警惕高，而跪着喝水的士兵显得笨拙、拖沓。中世纪意大利诗人但丁在《神曲·炼狱篇》中述及此典时说："要记住那些希伯来人，他们跪着喝水时显得那么柔弱，因此基甸从山上去攻打米甸营时，没有带他们同去。"

6. **Jephthah's daughter** (耶弗他的女儿)：典出《士师记》第11章30—40节士师耶弗他献女的故事。莎士比亚的悲剧《哈姆雷特》第二幕第二场第403—412行，哈姆雷特对波洛涅斯说："以色列的士师耶弗他啊，你有一件怎样的宝贝！"波洛涅斯回答："要是您叫我耶弗他，陛下，那么我有一个爱如掌珠的娇女。"波洛涅斯所言"爱如掌珠的娇女"指他的女儿奥菲利娅。在《亨利六世·下篇》第五幕第一场第90—91行，克莱伦斯对华列克说："那种誓言，我如果认真遵守，就比那牺牲亲生女儿的耶弗他更加离经叛道。"此处的克莱伦斯认为，为了遵守誓言竟不惜牺牲亲生女儿，只是一种不合常理的离经叛道之事。

7. **Samson** (参孙)：指"大力士"，"与敌人同归于尽的壮士"。参孙有超人之力，曾徒手撕裂狮子、用驴腮骨杀死千敌，后中计被擒，在敌人欢庆胜利时用力弄断殿堂大柱柱而与敌人同归于尽。美国诗人朗费罗的《警告》一诗前部分叙述参孙的悲壮牺牲，后部分写道：

我们国土上也有个不幸的参孙，
膂力被剪除，戴上了铁锁钢镣；
在残忍的宴会上，他也会不顾身，
举起臂，把这个国家的支柱动摇，
一举把我们宽广的特权殿宇
变成一堆破碎的瓦砾和废墟！（《朗费罗诗选》）

美国作家麦尔维尔的长篇海上历险小说《白鲸》(*Moby Dick*)第132章"交响乐"中，作者对最后一次捕猎前的大海这样描写到：

天空晴朗，呈钢青色。在一片蔚蓝中，海空简直交融在一起；只是那显得焦虑的天际明朗得又清又滑，像个女人的脸，而那个粗犷、男人也似的海洋，却不住地起伏，有力而迟缓，像是熟睡的参孙的胸脯。

8. **Delilah** (大利拉)：指代"诱骗人的妖妇"，"美人计"、"色情间谍"。典出非利士女子大利拉利用美色探听参孙力量秘密的故事。Samson and Delilah (参孙与大利拉)则有"英雄难过美人关"之意。莎士比亚的喜剧《爱的徒劳》第一幕第二场第86—89行，亚马多说："绿色的确是情人们的颜色，可是我想参孙会爱一个绿皮肤的女人，却是不可思议的，他准是看中她有头脑。"毛子接着说:"不错,主人。头脑要绿,帽子也会绿的。"剧本借用此典,将绿色(代表恋情)和头脑(代表心计)巧妙联系起来。

9. **jawbone of an ass** (驴腮骨):典出《士师记》第15章15—17节: And he found a new jawbone of an ass, and put forth his hand, and took it, and slew a thousand men therewith. 参孙挣脱非利士人的捆绑后顺手捡起一块驴腮骨击杀一千敌人。弗雷(Christopher Fry)的小说《不能烧死的女人》(*The Lady's Not for Burning*)中,托马斯上吊的计划被詹尼特的昏厥破坏,为此他沮丧地说:"哦,不合时宜的女人,他怎么偏偏就被我的半块驴腮骨打折了呢。""驴腮骨"后来被引申为凶器。越南河内战争博物馆中,由美国战机残骸堆成的铁山就取名"腮骨山"。

10. **as one man** (如同一人):指万众一心,众志成城。典出《士师记》第20章1节: Then all the children of Israel went out, and the congregation was gathered together as one man, from Dan even to Beer-Sheba, with the land of Gilead, unto the LORD in Mizpeh. 于是以色列从但到别是巴,以及住基列地的众人都出来如同一人,聚集到米斯巴耶和华面前。此典令人想到中国的"军民团结如一人,试看天下谁能敌"。

六、课堂讨论题

1. 试比较"荆轲刺秦王"与"以笏行刺敌王"的异同。
2. 请以《底波拉之歌》为例分析圣经叙事抒情诗的特征。
3. 从耶弗他的女儿形象看希伯来民族精神。
4. 从参孙头发被剃、丧失神力看世界各国对头发的迷信。

七、课后思考题

1. 你知道作曲家怎样演绎"耶弗他的女儿"故事吗?
2. 《士师记》叙事的主线是杀戮,包含各种杀人故事。这些谋杀故事有什么特征?
3. 你看过美国电影 *Samson and Delilah* (《霸王妖姬》)吗?
4. 茅盾在抗日战争期间写过短篇小说《参孙的复仇》,你知道吗?

以色列统一王国：三代君王

Three Kings of the United Kingdom of Israel

一、导读：以色列王国时期

公元前11世纪，以色列最后一位士师撒母耳膏立扫罗为王，又经大卫王及其子所罗门，历时97年，这就是以色列统一王国时期。这四位以色列英雄人物的生平故事记录在《撒母耳记》上、下（1 Samuel, 2 Samuel），《列王纪》上、下（1 Kings, 2 Kings）四卷书里。

撒母耳应民众的呼吁，用抽签的方式公开选定扫罗为以色列第一任国王。牧羊出身的大卫少年时便因用机弦甩石的绝招击杀非利士巨人歌利亚而名声鹊起。他为扫罗王弹琴消遣，娶了王的女儿米甲，并与王的儿子约拿单结为挚友。百姓拥戴大卫，引起扫罗的嫉妒，遂千方百计除掉大卫。扫罗和三个儿子在一次惨烈战斗中壮烈捐躯，犹大部落在希伯仑拥立大卫为王，大卫不久就统一了南北，成为整个以色列的国王。大卫在位期间，以武力扩展疆土，并建立起一套典章制度，使以色列发展成一个真正的自主国家。其子所罗门继位后在京都耶路撒冷建成宏伟的耶和华圣殿和豪华的王宫。然而王室穷奢极侈，大卫执政期间争夺王权的斗争达到血腥的地步，所罗门执政时期人民负担沉重，异族宗教也传入以色列，如此种种，为统一王国的分裂埋下了祸根。

本讲选择《撒母耳记上》、《撒母耳记下》和《列王纪上》3卷书中5部分：

1. 撒母耳、扫罗和大卫：撒母耳公开选拔扫罗为王，大卫用甩石机杀死非利士巨人歌利亚，威望日隆，遭到扫罗王嫉妒。

2. 大卫和约拿单的友谊：扫罗之子约拿单与大卫结为生死之交，而扫罗欲将其除掉。大卫在约拿单的帮助下幸免遭害。

3. 大卫和拔示巴：大卫称王后居功自傲，霸占手下勇将乌利亚之妻——美貌的拔示巴，并用计杀害乌利亚。

4. 押沙龙为妹他玛复仇：大卫的长子暗嫩垂涎同父异母的妹妹他玛，将其奸污。他玛的亲兄押沙龙杀死暗嫩。

5. 所罗门王的智慧：大卫与拔示巴之子所罗门王以智慧著称，智断两妇夺一子案便为一例。

二、选文及注释

Part 1

Samuel, Saul and David

Then Samuel took a vial of oil, and poured it upon his head, and kissed him, and said, "*Is it* not because the LORD hath anointed[1] thee to be captain over his inheritance? …" (*1 Samuel* 10: 1)

---

1. anoint *vt.* to smear or rub with oil, typically as part of a religious ceremony 涂油(礼)，常常译为"膏立"为王

97

And Samuel called the people together unto the LORD to Mizpeh[1]; And said unto the children of Israel, "Thus saith the LORD God of Israel, I brought up Israel out of Egypt, and delivered you out of the hand of the Egyptians, and out of the hand of all kingdoms, and of them that oppressed you: And ye have this day rejected your God, who himself saved you out of all your adversities[2] and your tribulations[3]; and ye have said unto him, Nay, but set a king over us. Now therefore present yourselves before the LORD by[4] your tribes, and by your thousands." And when Samuel had caused all the tribes of Israel to come near, the tribe of Benjamin was taken[5]. When he had caused the tribe of Benjamin to come near by their families, the family of Matri was taken, and Saul the son of Kish was taken: and when they sought him, he could not be found. Therefore they enquired of the LORD further, if the man should yet come thither. And the LORD answered, "Behold, he hath hid himself among the stuff[6]." And they ran and fetched him thence: and when he stood among the people, he was higher than any of the people from his shoulders and upward. And Samuel said to all the people, "See ye him whom the LORD hath chosen, that there is none like him among all the people?" And all the people shouted, and said, "God save the king.[7]" Then Samuel told the people the manner of the kingdom[8], and wrote it in a book, and laid it up before the LORD. And Samuel sent all the people away, every man to his house. And Saul also went home to Gibeah[9]; and there went with him a band of men, whose hearts God had touched[10]. But the children of Belial[11] said, "How shall this man save us?" And they despised him, and brought him no presents. But he held his peace[12]. (*1 Samuel* 10: 17–27)

But the Spirit of the LORD departed from Saul, and an evil spirit from the LORD[13] troubled him. And Saul's servants said unto him, "Behold now, an evil spirit from God troubleth thee. Let our lord now command thy servants, which are before thee, to seek out a man, who is a cunning player on an harp: and it shall come to pass, when the evil spirit from God is upon thee, that he shall play with his hand, and thou shalt be well." And Saul said unto his servants, "Provide me now a man that can play well, and bring him to me." Then answered one of the servants, and said, "Behold, I have seen a son of Jesse the Beth-lehemite[14], that is cunning in playing, and a mighty valiant man, and a man of war, and prudent in matters, and a comely[15] person, and the LORD is with him." Wherefore Saul sent messengers unto Jesse, and said, "Send me David thy son, which is

---

1. Mizpeh (地名)米巴斯镇, 位于耶路撒冷以南。以色列诸侯在此会盟推举国王。
2. adversity *n*. a difficult and unpleasant situation 逆境；不幸
3. tribulation *n*. a cause of great trouble or suffering 苦难；磨难
4. by *prep*. 按照
5. taken (通过掣签)选中。掣签是当时人们寻求神旨意的方法。
6. stuff *n*. 指可以遮蔽的东西
7. God save the king. 意思是"愿王万岁！"
8. the manner of the kingdom 国法, 指对国王权力和责任的规定。
9. Gibeah (地名)基比亚, 位于耶路撒冷以北5公里
10. whose hearts God had touched 指顺从神的旨意认可扫罗为王的人。
11. Belial /ˈbiːliːəl/《圣经》特有的词语, 意思是"卑鄙"。在《新约》中指恶魔。children/men of Beliah 指匪徒或坏人。
12. hold one's peace 闭口不说话。扫罗对那些瞧不起他的人不予理睬。
13. evil spirit from the LORD 从耶和华那里来的恶魔或者惩罚, 指间歇性的精神困扰。
14. Jesse the Beth-lehemite 伯利恒人耶西, 大卫之父。
15. comely *adj*. pleasant to look at; attractive〈古〉英俊的；帅气的。这句话形容大卫的本领和仪表: 善于弹琴、勇猛善战、恭敬有礼、仪表堂堂。

with the sheep[1]." And Jesse took an ass laden with bread, and a bottle of wine, and a kid, and sent them by David his son unto Saul. And David came to Saul, and stood before him: and he loved him greatly; and he became his armourbearer[2]. And Saul sent to Jesse, saying, "Let David, I pray thee, stand before me; for he hath found favour in my sight." And it came to pass, when the evil spirit from God was upon Saul, that David took an harp, and played with his hand: so Saul was refreshed, and was well, and the evil spirit departed from him. (*1 Samuel* 16: 14–23)

And the Philistine[3] came on and drew near unto David; and the man that bare the shield went before him[4]. And when the Philistine looked about, and saw David, he disdained[5] him: for he was but a youth, and ruddy[6], and of a fair countenance[7]. And the Philistine said unto David, "Am I a dog, that thou comest to me with staves[8]?" And the Philistine cursed David by his gods[9]. And the Philistine said to David, "Come to me, and I will give thy flesh unto the fowls of the air, and to the beasts of the field." Then said David to the Philistine, "Thou comest to me with a sword, and with a spear, and with a shield: but I come to thee in the name of the LORD of hosts[10], the God of the armies of Israel, whom thou hast defied. This day will the LORD deliver thee into mine hand; and I will smite thee, and take thine head from thee; and I will give the carcases[11] of the host of the Philistines this day unto the fowls of the air, and to the wild beasts of the earth; that all the earth may know that there is a God in Israel. And all this assembly[12] shall know that the LORD saveth[13] not with sword and spear: for the battle is the LORD's, and he will give you into our hands." And it came to pass, when the Philistine arose, and came and drew nigh to meet David, that David hasted, and ran toward the army to meet the Philistine. And David put his hand in his bag, and took thence a stone, and slang it, and smote the Philistine in his forehead, that the stone sunk into his forehead; and he fell upon his face to the earth. So David prevailed over the Philistine with a sling[14] and with a stone, and smote the Philistine, and slew him; but there was no sword in the hand of David. Therefore David ran, and stood upon the Philistine, and took his sword, and drew it out of the sheath[15] thereof, and slew him, and cut off his head therewith. And when the Philistines saw their champion was dead, they fled. (*1 Samuel* 17: 41–51)

And it came to pass as they came, when David was returned from the slaughter[16] of the Philistine, that the women came out of all cities of Israel, singing and dancing, to meet king Saul, with tabrets[17], with joy,

---

1. with the sheep 指大卫的牧童出身。
2. armourbearer 给扫罗王拿兵器的人。意思是大卫成了王身边的护卫。
3. the Philistine 指非利士巨人歌利亚。
4. the man that bare the shield went before him 手持盾牌的兵士走在歌利亚前头作护卫。
5. disdain *vt.* to consider to be unworthy of one's consideration 藐视
6. ruddy *adj.* having a healthy, reddish color (面色)红润的
7. fair countenance 容貌俊美。
8. staves 名词 staff (棍子)的复数
9. by his gods 歌利亚指着自己的神诅咒大卫。
10. the LORD of hosts 万军之耶和华。比喻耶和华神的强大无比。下文还提到此战是神的战斗。
11. carcase *n.* the dead body of an animal (动物)尸体, 又可写作 carcass
12. all this assembly 在战场上的所有人。
13. the LORD saveth 神使人得胜。
14. sling *n.* a simple weapon in the form of a strap or loop, used to hurl stones or other small missiles 甩石机
15. sheath *n.* a close-fitting cover for the blade of a knife or sword 刀鞘
16. slaughter *n.* the killing of a large number of people or animals in a cruel or violent way 杀戮
17. tabret *n.* 小手鼓

and with instruments of musick. And the women answered *one another* as they played, and said, "Saul hath slain his thousands, and David his ten thousands." And Saul was very wroth, and the saying displeased him; and he said, "They have ascribed[1] unto David ten thousands, and to me they have ascribed but thousands: and what can he have more but the kingdom?" And Saul eyed[2] David from that day and forward.

And it came to pass on the morrow, that the evil spirit from God came upon Saul, and he prophesied[3] in the midst of the house: and David played with his hand, as at other times: and *there was* a javelin[4] in Saul's hand. And Saul cast the javelin; for he said, "I will smite David even to the wall *with it.*" And David avoided out of his presence[5] twice. And Saul was afraid of David, because the LORD was with him, and was departed from Saul. Therefore Saul removed him from him, and made him his captain over a thousand[6]; and he went out and came in before the people[7]. And David behaved himself wisely in all his ways; and the LORD was with him. Wherefore when Saul saw that he behaved himself very wisely, he was afraid of him. But all Israel and Judah loved David, because he went out and came in before them. (*1 Samuel* 18: 6–16)

Part 2

The Friendship of David and Jonathan

And Saul spake to Jonathan his son, and to all his servants, that they should kill David. But Jonathan Saul's son delighted much in David: and Jonathan told David, saying, "Saul my father seeketh to kill thee: now therefore, I pray thee, take heed to thyself[8] until the morning, and abide in a secret place, and hide thyself: and I will go out and stand beside my father in the field where thou art, and I will commune with my father of thee[9]; and what I see, that I will tell thee."

And Jonathan spake good of David unto Saul his father, and said unto him, "Let not the king sin against[10] his servant, against David; because he hath not sinned against thee, and because his works have been to thee-ward very good[11]: for he did put his life in his hand, and slew the Philistine, and the LORD wrought a great salvation for all Israel: thou sawest it, and didst rejoice: wherefore then wilt thou sin against innocent blood, to slay David without a cause?"

And Saul hearkened unto the voice of Jonathan: and Saul sware, "As the LORD liveth[12], he shall not be slain."

And Jonathan called David, and Jonathan shewed him all those things. And Jonathan brought David to Saul, and he was in his presence, as in times past[13].

---

1. ascribe sth. unto sb. 把……归功于(或推诿于)某人
2. eye *vt.* to look at closely 因嫉妒而怒视。
3. prophesy *vi.* to predict the future 说预言。这里指扫罗胡言乱语。
4. javelin *n.* a light spear thrown in a competitive sport or as a weapon 长矛, 扫罗的武器
5. his presence 扫罗用枪刺大卫的举动。
6. captain over a thousand 千夫长, 属于高级军事指挥官。
7. he went out and came in before the people 指大卫在作战中身先士卒。
8. take heed to thyself 你自己要小心。heed *n.* careful attention 小心; 留意。
9. commune with my father of thee 和父亲谈论你。commune *vi.* to share one's intimate thoughts or feelings (with sb.), especially on a spiritual level 与……谈心。
10. sin against sb. 得罪某人, 指杀死某人。
11. his works have been thee-ward very good 大卫的作为于你大有益处。thee-ward 为了你(扫罗)。
12. As the Lord liveth 起誓用语, 意思是对上帝起誓。
13. he was in his presence, as in times past 大卫又侍立在扫罗面前, 如同以前侍奉他一样。大卫此前曾在王宫里为扫罗弹琴驱病。

And there was war again: and David went out, and fought with the Philistines, and slew them with a great slaughter; and they fled from him. And the evil spirit from the LORD was upon Saul, as he sat in his house with his javelin in his hand: and David played with his hand. And Saul sought to smite David even to the wall with the javelin; but he slipped away out of Saul's presence, and he smote the javelin into the wall: and David fled, and escaped that night.

Saul also sent messengers unto David's house, to watch him, and to slay him in the morning: and Michal David's wife told him, saying, "If thou save not thy life to night, to morrow thou shalt be slain."

So Michal let David down through a window: and he went, and fled, and escaped. And Michal took an image[1], and laid it in the bed, and put a pillow of goats' *hair* for his bolster[2], and covered it with a cloth. And when Saul sent messengers to take David, she said, "He is sick."

And Saul sent the messengers again to see David, saying, "Bring him up to me in the bed, that I may slay him."

And when the messengers were come in, behold, there was an image in the bed, with a pillow of goats' *hair* for his bolster.

And Saul said unto Michal, "Why hast thou deceived me so, and sent away mine enemy, that he is escaped?"

And Michal answered Saul, "He said unto me, 'Let me go; why should I kill thee?'"

So David fled, and escaped, and came to Samuel to Ramah, and told him all that Saul had done to him. And he and Samuel went and dwelt in Naioth. (*1 Samuel* 19: 1–18)

And David fled from Naioth in Ramah, and came and said before Jonathan, "What have I done? what is mine iniquity? and what is my sin before thy father, that he seeketh my life?"

And he said unto him, "God forbid[3]; thou shalt not die: behold, my father will do nothing either great or small, but that he will shew it me: and why should my father hide this thing from me? it is not so."

And David sware moreover, and said, "Thy father certainly knoweth that I have found grace in thine eyes; and he saith, 'Let not Jonathan know this, lest he be grieved': but truly as the LORD liveth, and as thy soul liveth, there is but a step between me and death[4]." Then said Jonathan unto David, "Whatsoever thy soul desireth, I will even do it for thee."

And David said unto Jonathan, "Behold, to morrow is the new moon[5], and I should not fail to sit with the king at meat: but let me go, that I may hide myself in the field unto the third day at even. If thy father at all miss me[6], then say, 'David earnestly asked leave of me that he might run to Beth-lehem[7] his city: for *there is* a yearly sacrifice there for all the family.' If he say thus, 'It is well'; thy servant shall have peace: but if he be very wroth, then be sure that evil is determined by him[8]. Therefore thou shalt deal kindly with[9] thy servant; for thou hast brought thy servant into a covenant of the LORD with thee: notwithstanding, if there be in me iniquity, slay me thyself; for

---

1. an image 一尊神像。
2. a pillow of goat's hair for bolster 用羊毛充塞的枕头垫子。
3. God forbid （口语）苍天不容!意思是"但愿不会如此!"
4. a step between me and death 离死不过一步之遥。大卫知道自己的危险处境。
5. the new moon 初一，为扫罗王献祭和设筵的节日。
6. miss me 找我。
7. Beth-lehem /ˈbeθlɪhem/ （地名）伯利恒，耶路撒冷南部不远的小镇。耶稣就诞生于此。
8. evil is determined by him 意思是扫罗决意要杀大卫。
9. deal kindly with （约拿单忠于盟约而）善待大卫，即救大卫。

why shouldest thou bring me to thy father?" And Jonathan said, "Far be it from thee[1]: for if I knew certainly that evil were determined by my father to come upon thee, then would not I tell it thee?" Then said David to Jonathan, "Who shall tell me? or what *if* thy father answer thee roughly?"

And Jonathan said unto David, "Come, and let us go out into the field." And they went out both of them into the field. And Jonathan said unto David, "O LORD God of Israel, when I have sounded[2] my father about to morrow any time, *or* the third day, and, behold, if there be good toward David, and I then send not unto thee, and shew it thee; the LORD do so and much more to Jonathan: but if it please my father to do thee evil, then I will shew it thee, and send thee away, that thou mayest go in peace: and the LORD be with thee, as he hath been with my father. And thou shalt not only while yet I live shew me the kindness of the LORD, that I die not: but also thou shalt not cut off thy kindness from my house for ever: no, not when the LORD hath cut off the enemies of David every one from the face of earth."

So Jonathan made a covenant with the house of David, *saying*, "Let the LORD even require it at the hand of David's enemies." And Jonathan caused David to swear again, because he loved him: for he loved him as he loved his own soul.

Then Jonathan said to David, "To morrow is the new moon: and thou shalt be missed, because thy seat will be empty. And when thou hast stayed three days, then thou shalt go down quickly, and come to the place where thou didst hide thyself when the business was in hand[3], and shalt remain by the stone Ezel. And I will shoot three arrows on the side thereof, as though I shot at a mark[4]. And, behold, I will send a lad, *saying*, 'Go, find out the arrows.' If I expressly say unto the lad, "Behold, the arrows are on this side of thee, take them'; then come thou: for there is peace to thee, and no hurt; as the LORD liveth. But if I say thus unto the young man, 'Behold, the arrows are beyond thee'; go thy way: for the LORD hath sent thee away. And as touching the matter[5] which thou and I have spoken of, behold, the LORD be between thee and me for ever,"

So David hid himself in the field: and when the new moon was come, the king sat him down to eat meat. And the king sat upon his seat, as at other times, even upon a seat by the wall: and Jonathan arose, and Abner sat by Saul's side, and David's place was empty. Nevertheless Saul spake not any thing that day: for he thought, "Something hath befallen him, he is not clean[6]; surely he is not clean." And it came to pass on the morrow, which was the second day of the month, that David's place was empty: and Saul said unto Jonathan his son, "Wherefore cometh not the son of Jesse to meat, neither yesterday, nor to day?" And Jonathan answered Saul, "David earnestly asked leave of me to go to Beth-lehem: and he said, 'Let me go, I pray thee; for our family hath a sacrifice in the city; and my brother, he hath commanded me to be there: and now, if I have found favour in thine eyes, let me get away, I pray thee, and see my brethren.' Therefore he cometh not unto the king's table."

Then Saul's anger was kindled against Jonathan, and he said unto him, "Thou son of the perverse rebellious woman, do not I know that thou hast chosen the son

---

1. Far be it from thee 意思是断无此事。
2. sound *vt.* to measure the depth of 测探
3. the business was in hand 麻烦临头。
4. mark 箭靶
5. as touching the matter 至于今天两人所谈之事。touching *prep.* 相当于 concerning (关于)。
6. he is not clean 大卫偶染不洁。按法律要求,参加祭祀筵席的人必须洁净。染了不洁的人到晚上才可得洁净。大卫第二天应已洁净,却依然不出现在筵席上,这引起了扫罗的疑心。

of Jesse to thine own confusion[1], and unto the confusion of thy mother's nakedness? For as long as the son of Jesse liveth upon the ground, thou shalt not be established, nor thy kingdom[2]. Wherefore now send and fetch him unto me, for he shall surely die."

And Jonathan answered Saul his father, and said unto him, "Wherefore shall he be slain? what hath he done?" And Saul cast a javelin at him to smite him: whereby Jonathan knew that it was determined of his father to slay David. So Jonathan arose from the table in fierce anger, and did eat no meat the second day of the month: for he was grieved for David, because his father had done him shame.

And it came to pass in the morning, that Jonathan went out into the field at the time appointed with David, and a little lad with him. And he said unto his lad, "Run, find out now the arrows which I shoot."

And as the lad ran, he shot an arrow beyond him. And when the lad was come to the place of the arrow which Jonathan had shot, Jonathan cried after the lad, and said, "Is not the arrow beyond thee?" And Jonathan cried after the lad, "Make speed, haste, stay not."

And Jonathan's lad gathered up the arrows, and came to his master. But the lad knew not any thing: only Jonathan and David knew the matter. And Jonathan gave his artillery[3] unto his lad, and said unto him, "Go, carry them to the city." And as soon as the lad was gone, David arose out of a place toward the south, and fell on his face to the ground, and bowed himself three times: and they kissed one another, and wept one with another, until David exceeded. And Jonathan said to David, "Go in peace, forasmuch as we have sworn both of us in the name of the LORD, saying, 'The LORD be between me and thee, and between my seed and thy seed for ever." And he arose and departed: and Jonathan went into the city. (*1 Samuel* 20)

Part 3

David and Bath-sheba[4]

And it came to pass, after the year was expired[5], at the time when kings go forth to battle, that David sent Joab[6], and his servants

with him, and all Israel; and they destroyed the children of Ammon, and besieged Rabbah[7]. But David tarried still at Jerusalem.

And it came to pass in an eveningtide, that David arose from off his bed, and

---

1. confusion *n.* a mental state characterized by a lack of clear and orderly thought and behavior 失去分辨能力，这里是羞辱。unto the confusion of thy mother's nakedness 自取羞辱，也羞辱到你的母亲。扫罗盛怒之下说出了不得体的话，连儿子妈一起骂。
2. thou shalt not be established, nor thy kingdom 你和你的国必站立不住。扫罗想传位给儿子，认为只要大卫存活一天，自己的王国就不稳固。
3. artillery *n.* (约拿单的一套)弓箭
4. Bath-sheba /bæθˈʃiːbə/ (人名)拔示巴，乌利亚之妻，后嫁与大卫王，生下所罗门
5. expired *vt.* (of a period of time) to come to an end 期满 the year was expired 过了一年。
6. Joab (人名)约押，大卫的外甥，身居元帅之职
7. besiege *vt.* to surround (a place) with armed forces in order to capture it or force its surrender 包围；围困 Rabbah 拉巴城，亚扪的首都。

walked upon the roof of the king's house: and from the roof he saw a woman washing herself; and the woman was very beautiful to look upon. And David sent and enquired after the woman. And one said, "Is not this Bath-sheba, the daughter of Eliam, the wife of Uriah the Hittite[1]?"

And David sent messengers, and took her; and she came in unto him, and he lay with her; for she was purified from her uncleanness[2]: and she returned unto her house. And the woman conceived, and sent and told David, and said, "I am with child."

And David sent to Joab, saying, "Send me Uriah the Hittite." And Joab sent Uriah to David. And when Uriah was come unto him, David demanded of him how Joab did, and how the people did, and how the war prospered[3]. And David said to Uriah, "Go down to thy house, and wash thy feet." And Uriah departed out of the king's house, and there followed him a mess of meat[4] from the king. But Uriah slept at the door of the king's house with all the servants of his lord, and went not down to his house.

And when they had told David, saying, "Uriah went not down unto his house," David said unto Uriah, "Camest thou not from thy journey? why then didst thou not go down unto thine house?"

And Uriah said unto David, "The ark, and Israel, and Judah, abide in tents; and my lord Joab, and the servants of my lord, are encamped in the open fields; shall I then go into mine house, to eat and to drink, and to lie with my wife? as thou livest, and as thy soul liveth[5], I will not do this thing."

And David said to Uriah, "Tarry here to day also, and to morrow I will let thee depart."

So Uriah abode in Jerusalem that day, and the morrow. And when David had called him, he did eat and drink before him; and he made him drunk: and at even he went out to lie on his bed with the servants of his lord, but went not down to his house.

And it came to pass in the morning, that David wrote a letter to Joab, and sent it by the hand of Uriah. And he wrote in the letter, saying, "Set ye Uriah in the forefront of the hottest battle, and retire ye from him[6], that he may be smitten, and die."

And it came to pass, when Joab observed[7] the city, that he assigned Uriah unto a place where he knew that valiant men were. And the men of the city went out, and fought with Joab: and there fell some of the people of the servants of David; and Uriah the Hittite died also.

Then Joab sent and told David all the things concerning the war; and charged[8] the messenger, saying, "When thou hast made an end of telling the matters of the war unto the king, And if so be that the king's wrath arise, and he say unto thee, 'Wherefore approached ye so nigh unto the city when ye did fight? knew ye not that they would shoot from the wall? who smote Abimelech the son of Jerubbesheth? did not a woman cast a piece of millstone upon him from the wall, that he died in Thebez[9]? why went ye nigh the wall?' then say thou, 'Thy servant Uriah the Hittite is dead also.'"

So the messenger went, and came and

---

1. Uriah the Hittite 赫人乌利亚，意思是"耶和华之光"，拔示巴的丈夫，大卫的勇将。
2. purified from her uncleanness 拔示巴的月经刚洁净。uncleanness n. 不洁，指经期。
3. how the war prospered 战事进展如何。
4. a mess of meat 一份食物。
5. as thou livest, and as thy soul liveth 对你发誓。
6. retire ye from him 你们便后退，留下乌利亚。大卫的计谋是借刀杀人，让乌利亚陷入敌阵被杀。
7. observe vt. to surround and attack 围攻
8. charge vt. to entrust (sb.) with a task as a duty or responsibility 指示；吩咐
9. Abimelech the son of Jerubbesheth ... that he died in Thebez 据《士师记》第9章50—54节载，耶路比设（即"耶路巴力"，士师基甸的别名）的儿子亚比米勒攻打提备斯城时，城墙上有个妇人抛下一块磨石，正砸中他的头，亚米勒不治而亡。大卫借此说明近距离攻城的危险性。

shewed David all that Joab had sent him for. And the messenger said unto David, "Surely the men prevailed[1] against us, and came out unto us into the field, and we were upon them[2] even unto the entering of the gate. And the shooters shot from off the wall upon thy servants; and some of the king's servants be dead, and thy servant Uriah the Hittite is dead also."

Then David said unto the messenger, "Thus shalt thou say unto Joab, 'Let not this thing displease thee, for the sword devoureth one as well as another[3]: make thy battle more strong against the city, and overthrow it: and encourage thou him.'"

And when the wife of Uriah heard that Uriah her husband was dead, she mourned for her husband. And when the mourning was past, David sent and fetched her to his house, and she became his wife, and bare him a son. But the thing that David had done displeased the LORD. (*2 Samuel* 11)

Part 4

Absalom's Revenge of Amnon for Tamar[4]

And it came to pass after this, that Absalom the son of David had a fair sister, whose name was Tamar; and Amnon the son of David loved her. And Amnon was so vexed, that he fell sick for his sister Tamar[5]; for she was a virgin; and Amnon thought it hard for him to do any thing to her[6].

But Amnon had a friend, whose name was Jonadab, the son of Shimeah[7] David's brother: and Jonadab was a very subtil man. And he said unto him, "Why art thou, being a king's son, lean[8] from day to day? wilt thou not tell me?"

And Amnon said unto him, "I love Tamar, my brother Absalom's sister."

And Jonadab said unto him, "Lay thee down on thy bed, and make thyself sick: and when thy father cometh to see thee, say unto him, 'I pray thee, let my sister Tamar come, and give me meat, and dress the meat in my sight[9], that I may see it, and eat it at her hand.'"

So Amnon lay down, and made himself sick: and when the king was come to see him, Amnon said unto the king, "I pray thee, let Tamar my sister come, and make me a couple of cakes in my sight, that I may eat at her hand."

Then David sent home to Tamar, saying, "Go now to thy brother Amnon's house, and dress him meat."

So Tamar went to her brother Amnon's house; and he was laid down. And she took flour, and kneaded it, and made cakes in his sight, and did bake the cakes. And she took a pan, and poured them out before him; but he refused to eat. And Amnon said, "Have out all men from me." And they went out every man from him.

And Amnon said unto Tamar, "Bring the meat into the chamber, that I may eat of thine hand." And Tamar took the cakes which she had made, and brought them into the chamber to Amnon her brother. And when she had brought them unto him to eat,

---

1. prevail (against) *vi.* to prove more powerful or superior 占优势；强过
2. we were upon them 我们追杀他们。
3. the sword devoureth one as well as another 意思是刀剑不长眼，总会有人阵亡。devour *vt.* to destroy, consume, or waste 消灭；吞噬。
4. Absalom /ˈæbsələm/（人名）押沙龙，是大卫的三子。Amnon 暗嫩，大卫的长子。Tamar 他玛，大卫的女儿。
5. he fell sick for his sister Tamar 暗嫩对他玛相思成疾。
6. Amnon thought it hard for him to do any thing to her 因为他玛还是处女，身为公主，深居简出，不可随意走动，暗嫩难得见她一面。
7. Jonadab, the son of Shimeah 大卫兄长示米亚之子约拿达。
8. lean *adj.* (of a person or animal) thin; having no superfluous fat （日渐）消瘦的
9. dress the meat in my sight 当着我的面预备食物。

he took hold of her, and said unto her, "Come lie with me, my sister."

And she answered him, "Nay, my brother, do not force me; for no such thing ought to be done in Israel: do not thou this folly. And I, whither shall I cause my shame to go[1]? and as for thee, thou shalt be as one of the fools in Israel. Now therefore, I pray thee, speak unto the king; for he will not withhold me from thee[2]." Howbeit he would not hearken unto her voice: but, being stronger than she, forced her, and lay with her.

Then Amnon hated her exceedingly; so that the hatred wherewith he hated her was greater than the love wherewith he had loved her. And Amnon said unto her, "Arise, be gone."

And she said unto him, "There is no cause: this evil in sending me away is greater than the other that thou didst unto me."

But he would not hearken unto her. Then he called his servant that ministered[3] unto him, and said, "Put now this woman out from me, and bolt[4] the door after her." And she had a garment of divers colours[5] upon her: for with such robes were the king's daughters that were virgins apparelled[6]. Then his servant brought her out, and bolted the door after her.

And Tamar put ashes on her head[7]; and rent[8] her garment of divers colours that was on her, and laid her hand on her head, and went on crying. And Absalom her brother said unto her, "Hath Amnon thy brother been with thee? but hold now thy peace, my sister: he is thy brother; regard not this thing." So Tamar remained desolate in her brother Absalom's house.

But when King David heard of all these things, he was very wroth. And Absalom spake unto his brother Amnon neither good nor bad[9]: for Absalom hated Amnon, because he had forced his sister Tamar.

And it came to pass after two full years, that Absalom had sheepshearers in Baal-hazor[10], which is beside Ephraim: and Absalom invited all the king's sons. And Absalom came to the king, and said, "Behold now, thy servant hath sheepshearers; let the king, I beseech thee, and his servants go with thy servant."

And the king said to Absalom, "Nay, my son, let us not all now go, lest we be chargeable unto thee[11]." And he pressed[12] him: howbeit he would not go, but blessed him.

Then said Absalom, "If not, I pray thee, let my brother Amnon go with us."

And the king said unto him, "Why should he go with thee?"

But Absalom pressed him, that he let Amnon and all the king's sons go with him.

Now Absalom had commanded his servants, saying, "Mark ye now when Amnon's heart is merry with wine, and when I say unto you, 'Smite Amnon'; then kill him, fear not: have not I commanded you? be courageous, and be valiant."

And the servants of Absalom did unto

---

1. whither shall I cause my shame to go 我如何抹去我的耻辱呢?
2. he will not withhold me from thee 父王不会禁止让你拥有我。
3. minister *vi.* to attend to the needs of (sb.) 侍奉
4. bolt *vt.* to secure or lock with 插(门)
5. a garment of divers colours 彩衣，一种长袖长袍的外衣，是高贵身份的象征(百姓穿的是短袖衣服)。
6. apparel *vt.* to clothe (sb.) 〈古〉给某人穿上衣服
7. ashes on her head 他玛把灰尘撒在头上，表示极度伤心。
8. rent 动词 rend (撕裂)的过去式和过去分词
9. Absalom spake unto his brother Amnon neither good nor bad 押沙龙对暗嫩什么话都没说。
10. Baal-hazor (地名)以法莲边界的巴力夏琐，在耶路撒冷北面32公里处。
11. lest we be chargeable unto thee 免得我们让你耗费过多。chargeable *adj.* 昂贵的；难以负担的
12. press *vt.* to make strong efforts to persuade or force sb. to sth. 恳请。押沙龙再三请求大卫。

Amnon as Absalom had commanded: Then all the king's sons arose, and every man gat him up upon his mule, and fled. And it came to pass, while they were in the way, that tidings came to David, saying, "Absalom hath slain all the king's sons, and there is not of them left."

Then the king arose, and tare his garments, and lay on the earth; and all his servants stood by with their clothes rent. And Jonadab, the son of Shimeah David's brother, answered and said, "Let not my lord suppose that they have slain all the young men the king's sons; for Amnon only is dead: for by the appointment of Absalom this hath been determined from the day that he forced his sister Tamar. Now therefore let not my lord the king take the thing to his heart, to think that all the king's sons are dead: for Amnon only is dead.

But Absalom fled. And the young man that kept the watch lifted up his eyes, and looked, and, behold, there came much people by the way of the hill side behind him. And Jonadab said unto the king, "Behold, the king's sons come: as thy servant said, so it is."

And it came to pass, as soon as he had made an end of speaking, that, behold, the king's sons came, and lifted up their voice and wept: and the king also and all his servants wept very sore. But Absalom fled, and went to Talmai, the son of Ammihud, king of Geshur[1]. And David mourned for his son every day.

So Absalom fled, and went to Geshur, and was there three years. And the soul of King David longed to go forth unto Absalom: for he was comforted concerning Amnon[2], seeing he was dead. (*2 Samuel* 13)

Part 5

Solomon's Wisdom

Then came there two women, that were harlots, unto the king, and stood before him. And the one woman said, "O my lord, I and this woman dwell in one house; and I was delivered of[3] a child with her in the house. And it came to pass the third day after that I was delivered, that this woman was delivered also: and we were together; there was no stranger with us in the house, save we two in the house. And this woman's child died in the night; because she overlaid[4] it. And she arose at midnight, and took my son from beside me, while thine handmaid[5] slept, and laid it in her bosom, and laid her dead child in my bosom. And when I rose in the morning to give my child suck[6], behold, it was dead: but when I had considered it in the morning, behold, it was not my son, which I did bear." And the other woman said, "Nay; but the living is my son, and the dead is thy son." And this said, "No; but the dead is thy son, and the living is my son." Thus they spake before the king. Then said the king, "The one saith, 'This is my son that liveth, and thy son is the dead': and the other saith, 'Nay; but thy son is the dead, and my son is the living.'" And the king said, "Bring me a sword." And they brought a sword before the king. And king said, "Divide the living child in two, and give half to the one, and half to the other." Then spake the woman whose

---

1. Talmai, the son of Ammihud, king of Geshur 基述王亚米忽的儿子达买，是押沙龙的外祖父。基述属于亚兰人的小国。
2. he was comforted concerning Amnon 大卫的心不再怀恨押沙龙，对暗嫩的死也不再那么难过了。
3. was delivered of 生（孩子）。
4. overlaid *vt.* to overlade (cover the surface of sth. with a coating; to lie on top of 负压过重的过去时)，孩子被压致死。
5. thine handmaid 您的仆人。面对君王的谦称。
6. suck *n.* 喂奶

the living child was unto the king, for her bowels yearned upon her son[1], and she said, "O my lord, give her the living child, and in no wise slay it." But the other said, "Let it be neither mine nor thine, but divide it." Then the king answered and said, "Give her the living child, and in no wise[2] slay it: she is the mother thereof." And all Israel heard of the judgment which the king had judged; and they feared the king: for they saw that the wisdom of God was in him, to do judgment. (*1 Kings* 3: 16–28)

三、圣经文化知识链接

1. 犹太人的多种称谓

犹太人曾有希伯来人(Hebrew)、以色列人(Israel)、犹大人(Judah)、犹太人(Jew)等多种称谓。这些称谓的内涵复杂多解，可从其民族称谓的演变史上体现出来。

"希伯来"原意为"来自河那边的人"，是大约公元前18世纪至17世纪犹太人在其传说中的先祖亚伯拉罕带领下越过幼发拉底河、进入迦南(今巴勒斯坦)地区时，当地人对他们的称呼。据《创世记》(32:28)记载，亚伯拉罕之孙雅各曾与天使摔跤并获胜，此后雅各易名"以色列"，他的12个儿子的后裔便是以色列十二支派，"以色列"便成为希伯来的另一称谓。到了公元前11世纪，犹大部落首领大卫(约公元前1000—960年)兼并了北方的以色列，建立了统一王国。约公元前935年在国王罗波安统治时期，统一王国分裂，北部王国十个支派建立北朝以色列，南方两个支派立国为犹大。这样，希伯来人的部分后裔又有了"犹大"的称谓。北朝以色列在公元前722年为亚述帝国所灭，族人被俘虏，流散各地，终至不知去向。南国犹大亦劫运难逃，公元前586年新巴比伦攻陷圣城耶路撒冷，数万犹大精英和犹大民众被掳至巴比伦，即所谓"巴比伦之囚"。"犹太人"便是其时希腊、罗马人对沦陷后的犹大人的蔑称。公元2世纪后，"犹太人"一词的贬义逐渐淡化，成为希伯来人后裔的通常称谓。

严格地讲，"希伯来人"、"以色列人"、"犹大人"、"犹太人"既有一定的内在联系，又各有其特定的范畴意义，每一名称都写照了犹太人特定的历史文化。除"犹大"已较少使用外，"希伯来"、"以色列"和"犹太"是当今仍然流行的称谓。但在具体运用时一般又有约定俗成的侧重和习惯，如"希伯来语"、"犹太人"。"以色列"在今天又常常特指1948年后建立的"以色列国"，虽然从理论上讲所有具有以色列国籍的人均可被称为"以色列人"，但人们仍然把以色列国内的阿拉伯人与犹太人严格区分，很难将其混称为"以色列人"。可以说，犹太人在其早期历史中显现出的多样化称谓是"犹太人"复杂内涵的一种初始性的表征。

2. 大卫家族故事的一致性和完整性

《撒母耳记下》第11—20章中的叙事具有统一的"板块"性质。虽然每则叙事都包含一个独立的故事，专注于不同的事件和人物，但它们却被同一个整体情节维系在一起，有着相当紧

---

1. her bowels yearned upon her son (真为生母的)妇人可怜自己的孩子(欲放弃所有权)。bowels *n.* 〈古〉怜悯之心; 慈悲之心。yearn *vi.* to be filled with compassion 〈古〉怜悯。
2. in no wise in no way 绝不。

密的"因果结构"。故事以大卫和拔示巴通奸和谋杀乌利亚的罪过开始。大卫的罪过引发了拿单的谴责,之后,一系列灾难降临,作为对大卫的惩罚:

(1) 拔示巴与大卫所生的婴儿染病夭折;
(2) 女儿他玛被暗嫩强奸;
(3) 押沙龙杀死暗嫩;
(4) 押沙龙因反叛大卫而被杀。

这些叙事的主题结构彼此相仿:都是性犯罪导致了杀人:

大卫　　　+ 拔示巴　　　→乌利亚被杀
暗嫩　　　+ 他玛　　　　→暗嫩被杀
押沙龙　　+ 大卫的嫔妃　→押沙龙被杀

这种类似结构反映出蕴涵在故事中"一报还一报"的观点,通过这样的逻辑,这些小故事被统一到整个大卫故事的框架中。悲剧情节环环紧扣,呈现出"一报还一报"的因果逻辑,凸现了叙事的节奏感,进而体现了镶嵌在大卫家族悲剧中系列悲剧与整个悲剧的一致,强化了"一报还一报"的主题思想,最终体现出该家族故事的一致性和完整性的叙事美学视角。

四、圣经文化专题

1. 大卫:一个圆形人物[1]

英国小说美学家福斯特(E. M. Forster, 1879—1970)在1927年的著作《小说面面观》中提出"扁形人物"(a flat character)和"圆形人物"(a round character)的说法。[2]"扁形人物"指性格单一的人物,其性格稳定,行为模式固定,不受周围环境影响,在整部作品中无大变化。《旧约》里有许多角色属于"扁形人物"(《新约》里也有许多),有的在后世文化中甚至演变成某一概念的代言人,如该隐=杀人犯;亚伯=无辜受害者;挪亚=义人;大利拉=不忠的妻子。再如雅各的哥哥以扫为人厚道、诚朴易欺,这种性情贯其一生。士师耶弗他向上帝轻易许诺、也勇于承兑诺言,将独生女献为燔祭,显示出其性格的一致性。

"圆形人物"又可以理解为"浑圆人物",给人以立体感和丰厚感。他们处在复杂的人际关系之中和常有变化的环境之下,内在性情也有相应的发展历程,从而呈现出多侧面、多层次的复杂性格,甚至善、恶一体的多变人格。例如,大力士参孙的个性有多种特征:力大无穷,恃"力"不驯,独来独往;机智精明,有时言行幽默可笑;生性风流,贪恋女色。后世对参孙的理解也形形色色,印证了他作为"圆形人物"的复杂多面性。

《旧约》中刻画得最出色的"圆形人物"要属大卫。大卫的生平故事长达数万言,见于《撒母耳记》和《历代志》(上、下)。一个性格多重、血肉丰满的文学形象跃然纸上,成为具有极高审美价值的文学人物。我们看看大卫的不同表现:

---

1. 本项参考了梁工著:《圣经叙事艺术研究》,北京:商务印书馆,2006年,第89-101页。
2. 【英】E. M. 福斯特著,朱乃长译:《小说面面观》(英汉对照版),北京:中国对外翻译出版公司,2002年,第174页。

英勇善战，治国有方。此外，大卫还有杰出的文艺才华，喜爱音乐，会弹琴、舞蹈，相传还擅长做诗。

仁慈宽厚，以德报怨。面对扫罗这样一个褊狭暴虐的君王，大卫只是四处躲避，从不还击，甚至一再放弃轻取仇敌的机会。

虔敬上帝，以信立身。他以隆重的仪式将约柜迎入耶路撒冷，并着手规划圣殿，初步建立起政教合一的国家体制。

足智多谋，阴险狡诈。不屑说他为了霸占拔示巴设计谋杀乌利亚之残忍，单说大卫的外甥约押是个狠毒的小人，但大卫为了成就自己的王权霸业依然最大限度地利用他，让其多年身居元帅的要职，直到临终前才吩咐儿子所罗门务必处死他，铲除这颗国家的毒瘤。

真情毕备，亲切感人。大卫对扫罗父子的哀悼诗情真意切。大卫对儿子押沙龙反叛的矛盾心理更是作为国王和父亲的真情毕露："我儿押沙龙啊！我儿，我儿押沙龙啊！我恨不得替你死。押沙龙啊，我儿！我儿！"

无视戒律，变节投敌。在强娶拔示巴的故事中，大卫犯下"十诫"中的两条罪：不可奸淫；不可杀人。扫罗父子的战死其实也与大卫有一定干系，因为此间他与同扫罗军队争战的迦特王有联盟关系。

这些因素动人地组合在一起，构成一种多重矛盾交织错落的性格结构，使大卫成为一个令人回味不尽的"圆形人物"，彰显出具有深度的人性。

2. 扫罗和大卫王形象对西方自由观和权利观的影响[1]

目前西方自由社会通行的自由观和权利观在很大程度上是基督教影响的结果，而《圣经》中的扫罗和大卫两个国王形象可以佐证。

《圣经》对国王的个性给予了肯定与张扬，并赋予国王一系列高尚的品质和个性。如对扫罗王的记载："又健壮，又俊美，在以色列人中没有一个能比上他的；身体比众人高过一头"。(《撒母耳记上》9:2)

但是，国王又是人性弱点的体现者。我们可以发现，有作为的国王被作为民族英雄载入史册，然而，以色列人并不迷信国王，他们能以一种平常心去看待国王的功过是非，在充分肯定其作用、歌颂其美德的同时，并不刻意掩饰他们的弱点甚至罪过。扫罗王统一各部落，制服强敌，并捐躯疆场，表现出一代君王的威武与勇敢；但另一方面，他又嫉贤妒能，狭隘偏执，甚至不惜陷害忠良。大卫智能超人，才华横溢，作为国家的真正缔造者而名垂史册；但他又表现出许许多多的人性弱点，他曾卑劣地违背自己的诺言，并有过夺人之妻、残害无辜的可耻行为。

即便国王犯罪，也不免遭受到严厉的斥责和制裁，而履行"正义审判"的角色乃是先知。这可从(《撒母耳记下》12:7—14)先知拿单对大卫的抨击中看出。由此，我们可以看出"律法面前人人平等"的原则。国王犯罪，同样受到惩罚，国王必须在一个更高的基点上发挥作用，那就是摩西律法。《圣经》反复强调，上帝是基于完全平等的理念来塑造人、要求人。人与人之间虽然存在着种种差异，但人在本体上是平等的生灵，在法律面前没有人可以享受特权。《申命记》(17:14—20)中对君王资格和权力的限制有明确规定：君王不可为自己添加马匹、多积金银；也不可为自己多立嫔妃；必须遵守律法的规定，以免心高气傲，偏离诫命；登基时必须为自己抄录

---

1. 本项参考【美】施密特 (Alvin Schmidt) 著，汪晓丹等译：《基督教对文明的影响》，北京：北京大学出版社，2004年，第229页。

一本律法书,以备平时诵读。时至今日,欧美一些国家的总统就职仪式上仍有这方面的程序,总统宣誓时必须手按《圣经》。

五、圣经典故集锦

1. **dead dog**(死狗):指无用之人,废物。典出《撒母耳记上》第24章14节:After whom is the king of Israel come out? After whom dost thou pursue? After a dog, after a flea. 以色列王出来要寻找谁呢?追赶谁呢?不过是追赶一条死狗、一个蛇蚤就是了。这是大卫对追杀他的扫罗王所说的自贬之言。

2. **a man of Belial**(属彼列的人):指坏人,不义之徒。典出《撒母耳记上》第25章25节:Let not my lord, I pray thee, regard this man of Belial, even Nabal: for as his name is, so is he; Nabal is his name, and folly is with him: but I thine handmaid saw not the young men of my lord, whom thou didst send. 我主不要理这坏人拿八,他的性情与他的名相称;他名叫拿八(就是"愚顽"的意思),他为人果然愚顽。但我主打发的仆人、婢女并没有看见。"属彼列的人"是对辱骂大卫的富户拿八的称呼。

3. **David and Bath-sheba**(大卫和拔示巴):典出《撒母耳记下》第11章2—26节。引申为美男子和美女的关系。张资平的长篇小说《上帝的儿女们》第18章描写了一次聚会,余约瑟的儿子阿丙成了女孩子们的中心:
   外表的和内部的要素互成极端的正比例由亲体遗传下来了的余阿丙,他具有男性美的胴体,淡赤色的圆圆的脸儿,很像夺取了乌利亚(Uriah)的妻拔示巴(Bath-sheba)的大卫王,(撒母耳下第11章)能够使周围的一群女性在他的脚下俯伏跪拜。

4. **one's ewe lamb**(小母羊羔):典出《撒母耳记下》第12章2—3节:The rich man had exceeding many flocks and herds: But the poor man had nothing, save one little ewe lamb, which he had bought and nourished up: and it grew up together with him, and with his children; it did eat of his own meat, and drank of his own cup, and lay in his bosom, and was unto him as a daughter. 富户有许多牛群羊群;穷人除了所买来养活的一只小母羊羔之外,别无所有。羊羔在他家里和他儿女一同长大,吃他所吃的,喝他所喝的,睡在他怀中,在他看来如同女儿一样。这是先知拿单指责大卫强占乌利亚之妻时的比喻:一个牛羊成群的富人贪心不足,抢走一户穷人视为珍宝的唯一的小母羊羔。此典喻指"唯一的宝贝"、"独生孩子"、"仅有的财产"。

5. **Absalom's hair**(押沙龙的头发):典出《撒母耳记下》第14章25节—18章17节。押沙龙的头发又密又长,使其成为美男子;但这满头秀发却在他逃命时挂在树枝上,使他丢了性命。此典指"招致死命的美物"、"为保俊美而遭厄运"。

6. **Abishag**(亚比煞):指陪伴着老朽的美貌少女。典出《列王纪上》第1章1—4节:Now king

David was old and stricken in years; and they covered him with clothes, but he gat no heat. Wherefore his servants said unto him, Let there be sought for my lord the king a young virgin: and let her stand before the king, and let her cherish him, and let her lie in thy bosom, that my lord the king may get heat. So they sought for a fair damsel throughout all the coasts of Israel, and found Abishag a Shunammite, and brought her to the king. 大卫王年纪老迈，虽用被遮盖，仍不觉暖。所以臣仆对他说："不如为我主我王寻找一个处女，使她伺候王，奉养王，睡在王的怀中，好叫我主我王得暖。于是，在以色列全境寻找美貌的童女，寻得书念的一个童女亚比煞，就带到王那里。"墨西哥女作家伊内斯·阿莱唐多的小说取名《书念处女》(*Abishag the Shunammite*)描写少女露易莎被迫嫁给一个垂死的老人，受尽屈辱。[1]

7. **Elijah's mantle** (以利亚的外衣)：指师承、衣钵、传统、事业。典出《列王纪上》第19章19—21节：So he departed thence, and found Elisha the son of Shaphat, who was plowing with twelve yoke of oxen before him, and he with the twelfth: and Elisha passed by him, and cast his mantle upon him. And he left the oxen, and ran after Elisha, and said, Let me, I pray thee, kiss my father and my mother, and then I will follow thee. 于是，以利亚离开那里走了，遇见沙法的儿子以利沙耕地，在他前头有十二对牛，自己赶着第十二对。以利亚到他那里去，将自己的外衣搭在他身上。以利沙就离开牛跑到以利亚那里，说："求你容我先与父母吻别，然后我便跟随你。"先知以利亚将自己的外衣搭在以利沙身上，结果以利沙拜以利亚为师，跟随其云游四方。罗伯特·彭斯(Robert Burns)在其诗歌集第2版的献词中说："我的国家的诗歌天才发现了我，就像先知以利亚对耕地中的以利沙所做的，把他激情的外衣搭在我身上。"美国作家麦尔维尔在《比利·巴迪》(*Billy Budd*)中描写比利被吊起来的那天凌晨：就像赶着战车的先知消失在空中，把他的外衣丢给了以利亚，撒退的夜脱下它灰白的长袍给了缓缓浮现的白昼。

8. **Naboth's vineyard** (拿伯的葡萄园)：指令人垂涎的东西、梦寐以求之物，或者不择手段夺来的东西。典出《列王纪上》第21章1—16节亚哈王在王后耶洗别的怂恿下谋财害命，杀死平民拿伯，强夺其祖产葡萄园的故事。

9. **bruised reed** (压伤的芦苇)：指靠不住的盟友、不能依赖之物。典出《列王纪下》第18章21节：Now, behold, thou trustest upon the staff of this bruised reed, even upon Egypt, on which if a man lean, it will go into his hand, and pierce it: so is pharaoh king of Egypt unto all that trust on him. 看哪，你所倚靠的埃及，是那压伤的芦苇；人若靠这杖，就必刺透他的手。埃及法老向倚靠他的人也是这样。犹大国在面临亚述人围攻时想依靠埃及的支持，亚述大将拉伯沙基讽刺道：这等于依靠一根压伤的芦苇做的杖。《以赛亚书》第42章1—4节借耶和华之口说："看啊，我的仆人……压伤的芦苇，他不折断；将残的灯火，他不吹灭"(A bruised reed shall he not break, and the smoking flax shall he not quench: he shall bring forth judgment unto truth.)。这里的"芦苇"表示身处逆境仍然坚持。美国诗人朗费罗

---

[1]. 参见赵德明编拉美著名作家短篇小说选集《书念少女》(哈尔滨：黑龙江人民出版社，1983)。

(H. W. Longfellow, 1807—1882)的十四行诗《济慈》(Keats)后六行如下:
Lo! in the moonlight gleams a marble white,
On which I read: "Here lieth one whose name
Was writ in water." And was this the meed
Of his sweet singing? Rather let me write:
　"The smoking flax before it burst to flame
Was quenched by death, and broken the bruised reed."

看呵！月光下一方莹白的石碑，
碑上，我读到一句这样的铭言：
"名随逝水的一人，在此安歇。"
这就是对他妙曲仙喉的赞美？
不如让我写："压伤的芦苇已折断；
麻杆刚冒烟，没烧出旺火，便熄灭。"（《朗费罗诗选》）

中国青年作家余杰在北大读本科期间出版了随笔文集《压伤的芦苇》，书中有两处出现了"芦苇"：一处他说安徒生"是一棵受伤的芦苇，却永恒地挺立着。"另一处说"朋霍费尔的生命，就像是一棵压伤的芦苇。暴风雨终将过去，而这棵芦苇依然扎根在沙漠中。芦苇的存在证明了沙漠的无能，也启示着甘泉的降临。"

10. **Babylon**（巴比伦）：指邪恶之城、罪恶荒淫之地。典出《列王纪下》第24章1—20节。巴比伦在强盛时期曾派军队摧毁耶路撒冷城，把犹太人两次掳往巴比伦，引起犹太民族对巴比伦的深恶痛绝。在《启示录》第17章1—9节和第18章，"巴比伦"被比作"大淫妇"（Babylon as scarlet woman）。美国作家霍桑的《红字》中的女主人公海丝特在总督眼里是"巴比伦荡妇"；英国作家哈代的《德伯家的苔丝》中的女主人公苔丝在德伯眼里是"巴比伦女巫"。

六、课堂讨论题

1. 谈谈你对大卫悼念扫罗父子的诗《弓歌》的认识。
2. "二妇夺一子"的公案故事，除了《旧约》记载的所罗门断案故事，在古代印度、希腊、罗马也广为流传。你知道中国也有类似的故事吗？
3. 阅读"先知拿单谴责大卫"文本，谈谈《圣经》中英雄人物的塑造。

七、课后思考题

1. 庄严的力量与强烈的激情是崇力尚争精神在西方艺术中的反映。请以米开朗基罗的《大卫》雕像加以说明。
2. 谈谈"大卫星"与国际救援运动的标志"红色大卫盾"的关系。
3. 大卫和约拿单的友谊堪与"管鲍之交"相比。你知道这个中国历史故事吗？
4. 你知道"所罗门智娶示巴女王"的传说吗？

正义的呼告者：希伯来先知
The Hebrew Prophets, Spokesmen of Justice

一、导读：先知书概况

公元前8世纪，统一王国分裂为南、北两朝，这一时期不仅国内自相残杀，而且外患频繁。再加上社会贫富悬殊，道德沦丧，风气败坏，国家危在旦夕。于是出现了一批被称为上帝代言人的社会活动家——"先知"。他们从维护民族利益和被压迫人民的利益出发，不顾个人安危，为民请命，直言不讳地抨击统治者在政治、宗教、社会生活中的失误和罪恶，斥责、训诲、劝勉、惩罚背离耶和华的众百姓。他们在发表言论时经常使用"耶和华说"、"耶和华如此说"、"耶和华的话临到我说"、"这是耶和华说的"，这样做既增强了自己言论的权威性又保护了自己。一些先知把自己得到的"默示"记录下来，开创了以色列人的"先知文学"。

《旧约》的第四部分15卷以先知名字命名的"先知书"就是先知文学的代表作品。先知书的内容及形式并不固定，有些是借耶和华之名传讲预言，谈及未来；大部分则只是谈及当时的情形或责备以色列民的罪恶。按照篇幅的长短，先知书又被分成大先知书和小先知书两组。

本讲选取4部先知书里的内容：

1. 《以赛亚书》：描绘了未来弥赛亚时代的理想图景，含有"以色列的安慰书"，其中对乌托邦和大同社会的追求十分可贵。

2. 《耶利米书》：犹大即将被敌人围困，耶利米为同胞担忧和悲伤。先知忧国忧民意识和强烈的责任感由此可窥一斑。

3. 《以西结书》：以西结预见以色列的新生活，散居在异国的人民将归回故土，荒废之地将变成伊甸园。"枯骨复活"是该卷最著名的异象。

4. 《阿摩司书》：阿摩司呼吁以色列人悔改，呼吁公平和正义：let judgment run down as waters, and righteousness as a mighty stream（愿公平如浪涛滚滚，公义如江河滔滔）。这句话成为世界公义的响亮口号。

二、选文及注释

Part 1

Isaiah[1]

And there shall come forth a rod out of the stem of Jesse[2], and a Branch shall grow out of his roots: And the spirit of the L ORD shall rest upon him, the spirit of wisdom and understanding, the spirit of counsel

---

1. Isaiah /aɪˈzaɪə/ (人名)以赛亚。公元前8世纪的以色列先知、预言家。
2. a rod out of the stem of Jesse 耶西的树干必发出一枝。耶西是大卫之父，所以弥赛亚将出自大卫家族。

and might, the spirit of knowledge and of the fear of the LORD; And shall make him of quick understanding in the fear of the LORD: and he shall not judge after the sight of his eyes, neither reprove[1] after the hearing of his ears: But with righteousness shall he judge the poor, and reprove with equity for the meek of the earth[2]: and he shall smite the earth with the rod of his mouth[3], and with the breath of his lips shall he slay the wicked. And righteousness shall be the girdle of his loins, and faithfulness the girdle of his reins[4]. The wolf also shall dwell with the lamb, and the leopard shall lie down with the kid; and the calf and the young lion and the fatling[5] together; and a little child shall lead them. And the cow and the bear shall feed; their young ones shall lie down together: and the lion shall eat straw like the ox. And the sucking child shall play on the hole of the asp[6], and the weaned child[7] shall put his hand on the cockatrice's den[8]. They shall not hurt nor destroy in all my holy mountain: for the earth shall be full of the knowledge of the LORD[9], as the waters cover the sea. (11: 1–9)

"Comfort ye, comfort ye my people," saith your God. "Speak ye comfortably to Jerusalem, and cry unto her, that her warfare[10] is accomplished, that her iniquity is pardoned: for she hath received of the LORD's hand double for all her sins." The voice of him that crieth in the wilderness[11], "Prepare ye the way of the LORD, make straight in the desert a highway for our God. Every valley shall be exalted, and every mountain and hill shall be made low: and the crooked shall be made straight, and the rough places plain: And the glory of the LORD shall be revealed, and all flesh shall see it together: for the mouth of the LORD hath spoken it."

The voice said, "Cry." And he said, "What shall I cry?"

"All flesh is grass, and all the goodliness[12] thereof is as the flower of the field: the grass withereth, the flower fadeth: because the

---

1. reprove *vt.* to convey disapproval of 责备
2. the meek of the earth 世上的谦卑者。
3. smite the earth with the rod of his mouth 用口中杖击打世界。指弥赛亚的严正审判和惩罚。
4. righteousness shall be the girdle of his loins, and faithfulness the girdle of his reins 公义必作他的腰带；信实必作他的绳缠。比喻弥赛亚全然公义和信实。
5. fatling *n.* 肥壮的家畜
6. asp *n.* 小毒蛇；蝮蛇
7. the weaned child 刚断奶的孩童。wean *vt.* to be accustomed (often infant or other young mammal) to food other than its mother's milk 使断奶。
8. the cockatrice's den 毒蛇的洞穴上。
9. the earth shall be full of the knowledge of the LORD 遍地充满耶和华的知识。意思是人类都认识和信靠神。
10. warfare *n.* 争战。这里指百姓被掳的日子。
11. The voice of him that crieth in the wilderness 旷野的呼声，指公义的召唤。
12. goodliness *n.* physical attractiveness 美貌

spirit of the LORD bloweth upon it: surely the people is grass. The grass withereth, the flower fadeth: but the word of our God shall stand for ever." O Zion, that bringest good tidings, get thee up into the high mountain; O Jerusalem, that bringest good tidings, lift up thy voice with strength; lift it up, be not afraid; say unto the cities of Judah, "Behold your God!" Behold, the LORD God will come with strong hand, and his arm shall rule for him: behold, his reward is with him, and his work before him. He shall feed his flock like a shepherd: he shall gather the lambs with his arm, and carry them in his bosom, and shall gently lead those that are with young.

Who hath measured the waters in the hollow[1] of his hand, and meted out heaven with the span[2], and comprehended the dust of the earth in a measure[3], and weighed the mountains in scales, and the hills in a balance[4]? Who hath directed the Spirit of the LORD, or being his counseller[5] hath taught him? With whom took he counsel, and who instructed him, and taught him in the path of judgment, and taught him knowledge, and shewed to him the way of understanding? Behold, the nations are as a drop of a bucket, and are counted as the small dust of the balance: behold, he taketh up the isles as a very little thing. And Lebanon[6] is not sufficient to burn, nor the beasts thereof sufficient for a burnt offering. All nations before him are as nothing; and they are counted to him less than nothing, and vanity[7].

To whom then will ye liken[8] God? or what likeness will ye compare unto him? The workman melteth a graven image[9], and the goldsmith[10] spreadeth it over with gold, and casteth silver chains. He that is so impoverished[11] that he hath no oblation[12] chooseth a tree that will not rot; he seeketh unto him a cunning workman to prepare a graven image, that shall not be moved.

Have ye not known? have ye not heard? hath it not been told you from the beginning? have ye not understood from the foundations of the earth? It is he that sitteth upon the circle of the earth[13], and the inhabitants thereof are as grasshoppers[14]; that stretcheth out the heavens as a curtain, and spreadeth them out as a tent to dwell in: that bringeth the princes[15] to nothing; he maketh the judges of the earth as vanity. Yea, they shall not be planted; yea, they shall not be sown: yea, their stock[16] shall not take root in the earth: and he shall also blow upon them,

---

1. hollow *n.* (手)心
2. meted out heaven with the span 这句话的意思是人用手的虎口测量苍天，形容人的渺小。span *n.* 跨度，指拇指和食指张开时的跨距。mete out: to measure out 〈古〉测量。
3. comprehended the dust of the earth in a measure 这句话的意思是用升斗盛大地的尘土，不自量力。comprehend *vt.* to take in as a part; include 包含；包括。measure *n.* 一种器量，容量约1.1升(0.25加仑)。
4. balance *n.* 天平
5. counseller *n.* counsellor, a person who gives advice on a specified subject 谋士
6. Lebanon /ˈlebənən/ (地名)黎巴嫩。黎巴嫩多树木，这里指树木。
7. vanity *n.* 空虚
8. liken *vt.* to see, mention, or show as similar 把……比作
9. graven image 偶像；伪神。graven 是 grave (雕刻)的过去分词。
10. goldsmith *n.* 金匠
11. impoverish *vt.* to make poor 使贫穷；impoverished *adj.* poverty-stricken 贫穷的。
12. oblation *n.* 祭品
13. the circle of the earth 地球的外围，指苍穹。
14. the inhabitants thereof are as grasshoppers 地上的居民好像蝗虫。
15. prince *n.* 君王。神使君王归于虚无，意思是世上的王权盛衰操控在神的手中。
16. stock *n.* 树茎

and they shall wither, and the whirlwind[1] shall take them away as stubble[2].

"To whom then will ye liken me, or shall I be equal?" saith the Holy One[3]. "Lift up your eyes on high, and behold who hath created these things, that bringeth out their host[4] by number: he calleth them all by names by the greatness of his might, for that he is strong in power; not one faileth[5]."

Why sayest thou, O Jacob, and speakest, O Israel, "My way is hid from the LORD, and my judgment[6] is passed over from my God?" Hast thou not known? hast thou not heard, that the everlasting God, the LORD, the Creator of the ends of the earth, fainteth not, neither is weary? there is no searching of his understanding[7]. He giveth power to the faint; and to them that have no might he increaseth strength. Even the youths shall faint and be weary, and the young men shall utterly fall: but they that wait upon the LORD[8] shall renew their strength; they shall mount up[9] with wings as eagles; they shall run, and not be weary; and they shall walk, and not faint. (40)

Part 2

Jeremiah[10]

"Behold, he[11] shall come up as clouds, and his chariots shall be as a whirlwind: his horses are swifter than eagles." Woe unto us[12]! for we are spoiled. O Jerusalem, wash thine heart from wickedness, that thou mayest be saved. How long shall thy vain thoughts lodge[13] within thee? For a voice declareth from Dan[14], and publisheth affliction from mount Ephraim[15]. Make ye mention[16] to the nations; behold, publish against Jerusalem, that watchers come from a far country, and give out their voice against the cities of Judah. "As keepers of a field, are they against her[17] round about; because she hath been rebellious against me," saith the LORD. "Thy way and thy doings have procured[18] these things unto thee; this is thy wickedness, because it is bitter, because it reacheth unto thine heart.

My bowels, my bowels! I am pained at my very heart; my heart maketh a noise[19] in me; I cannot hold my peace, because thou

---

1. whirlwind *n.* 旋风
2. stubble *n.* (植物的)断秸秆；茬
3. Holy One 圣者，指以色列的圣者。
4. host *n.* 许多。指被造万物。造物主能数清万物，并给其一一命名。
5. not one faileth 一个都不缺。faileth 原形是 fail，是第三人称单数动词。
6. my judgment 意思是我的冤屈没有得到神的查问。
7. there is no searching of his understanding 造物主的智慧无法测度。
8. wait upon the LORD 等候神，意思是信赖神。
9. mount up 升腾；上升。
10. Jeremiah /ˈdʒerɪmaɪə/ （人名)耶利米。公元前7—6世纪的希伯来先知。
11. he 指即将围困犹大的仇敌
12. Woe unto us! (感叹句)我们有祸了!
13. lodge *vi.* to live in a place temporarily 居住
14. Dan (地名)但，位于以色列北部
15. publisheth affliction from mount Ephraim 从以法莲山报来祸患。以法莲山距耶路撒冷仅数公里之遥。
16. make mention 传达。
17. are they against her 敌人像看守田地的人一样围攻耶路撒冷。
18. procure *vt.* to cause (sth.) to happen 〈古〉招致
19. my heart maketh a noise 内心烦躁不安。

hast heard, O my soul, the sound of the trumpet, the alarm of war. Destruction upon destruction is cried[1]; for the whole land is spoiled[2]: suddenly are my tents spoiled, and my curtains in a moment. How long shall I see the standard[3], and hear the sound of the trumpet? "For my people is foolish, they have not known me; they are sottish[4] children, and they have none understanding: they are wise to do evil, but to do good they have no knowledge."

I beheld the earth, and, lo, it was without form, and void; and the heavens, and they had no light. I beheld the mountains, and, lo, they trembled, and all the hills moved lightly. I beheld, and, lo, there was no man, and all the birds of the heavens were fled. I beheld, and, lo, the fruitful place was a wilderness, and all the cities thereof were broken down at the presence of the LORD, and by his fierce anger.

For thus hath the LORD said, "The whole land shall be desolate; yet will I not make a full end. For this shall the earth mourn, and the heavens above be black: because I have spoken it, I have purposed[5] it, and will not repent, neither will I turn back[6] from it. The whole city shall flee for the noise of the horsemen and bowmen; they shall go into thickets[7], and climb up upon the rocks: every city shall be forsaken[8], and not a man dwell therein. And when thou art spoiled, what wilt thou do? Though thou clothest thyself with crimson[9], though thou deckest[10] thee with ornaments of gold, though thou rentest[11] thy face with painting, in vain shalt thou make thyself fair; thy lovers will despise thee, they will seek thy life[12]."

For I have heard a voice as of a woman in travail[13], and the anguish[14] as of her that bringeth forth her first child, the voice of the daughter of Zion, that bewaileth herself, that spreadeth her hands, saying, "Woe is me now! for my soul is wearied because of murderers." (4: 13–31)

Oh that my head were waters, and mine eyes a fountain of tears, that I might weep day and night for the slain of the daughter of my people! Oh that I had in the wilderness a lodging place of wayfaring[15] men; that I might leave my people, and go from them! for they be all adulterers[16], an assembly of treacherous men.

"And they bend their tongues like their bow for lies: but they are not valiant for the truth upon the earth; for they proceed from evil to evil[17], and they know not me," saith the LORD.

"Take ye heed every one of his neighbour, and trust ye not in any brother: for

---

1. Destruction upon destruction is cried 毁灭的消息频传。
2. spoil *vt.* to diminish or destroy 毁坏；摧毁
3. standard *n.* 旗；旗号
4. sottish *adj.* stupid and confused 迟钝的；愚蠢的
5. purpose *vt.* to have as one's intention or objective 打算；决心
6. turn back 改变主意。
7. thicket *n.* 灌木丛；密林
8. forsaken 动词 forsake（抛弃）的过去分词
9. crimson *n.* 深红色，指衣服
10. deck *vt.* to decorate or adorn brightly or festively 打扮
11. rent *vt.* 本意是"出租"，这里指给脸蛋涂脂抹粉
12. seek thy life 索命。
13. travail *n.* 分娩
14. anguish *n.* severe mental or physical pain or suffering 痛苦
15. wayfare *vi.* to travel on foot 旅行；步行
16. adulterer *n.* 犯通奸罪者
17. they are not valiant for the truth upon the earth; for they proceed from evil to evil 这两句话的意思是，犹大国实力变得强大却不追求真理，而是变本加厉作恶。

every brother will utterly supplant[1], and every neighbour will walk with slanders[2]. And they will deceive every one his neighbour, and will not speak the truth: they have taught their tongue to speak lies, and weary[3] themselves to commit iniquity. Thine habitation is in the midst of deceit;[4] through deceit they refuse to know me," saith the LORD:

Therefore thus saith the LORD of hosts, "Behold, I will melt them, and try them; for how shall I do for the daughter of my people? Their tongue is as an arrow shot out; it speaketh deceit: one speaketh peaceably[5] to his neighbour with his mouth, but in heart he layeth his wait[6]. Shall I not visit[7] them for these things?" saith the LORD:

"Shall not my soul be avenged on such a nation as this? For the mountains will I take up a weeping and wailing, and for the habitations of the wilderness a lamentation, because they are burned up, so that none can pass through them; neither can men hear the voice of the cattle; both the fowl of the heavens and the beast are fled; they are gone. And I will make Jerusalem heaps, and a den of dragons; and I will make the cities of Judah desolate, without an inhabitant." (9: 1–11)

Part 3

Ezekiel[8]

Moreover the word of the LORD came unto me, saying, "Son of man, when the house of Israel[9] dwelt in their own land, they defied it by their own way and by their doings: their way was before me as the uncleanness of a removed woman[10]. Wherefore I poured my fury upon them for the blood that they had shed upon the land, and for their idols wherewith they had polluted it: and I scattered them among the heathen, and they were dispersed through the countries: according to their way and according to their doings I judged them. And when they entered unto the heathen, whither they went, they profaned my holy name, when they said to them, 'These are the people of the LORD, and are gone forth out of his land.' But I had pity for mine holy name, which the house of Israel had profaned among the heathen, whither they went.

"Therefore say unto the house of Israel, 'Thus saith the Lord God; I do not this for your sakes, O house of Israel, but for mine holy name's sake, which ye have profaned among the heathen, whither ye went. And I will sanctify my great name, which was profaned among the heathen, which ye have profaned in the midst of them; and the heathen shall know that I am the LORD,' saith the Lord God, 'when I shall be sanctified in you before their eyes. For I will take you from among the heathen, and gather you out of all countries, and will bring you into your own land. Then will I sprinkle clean water upon you, and ye shall be clean: from all your filthiness, and from all your idols, will cleanse you. A new heart also will I give

---

1. supplant *vt.* to supersede and replace（以不正当手段）排挤
2. slander *n.* a false or damaging statement about sb. 诽谤
3. weary *vt.* to cause to become tired 使疲倦。形容人们尽想着作孽，不遗余力。
4. Thine habitation is in the midst of deceit 意思是你的住处在诡诈的人中，是比喻用法。
5. speaketh peaceably 说甜言蜜语。
6. lay one's wait 阴谋陷害（邻舍）。
7. visit *vt.* to punish (a person or wrongful act) 〈古〉惩罚；报复
8. Ezekiel /ɪˈziːkɪəl/（人名）以西结。公元前 6世纪的希伯来预言家，他号召犹太人走出巴比伦以回归敬神和信仰。
9. house of Israel 以色列之家。雅各更名为"以色列"后，他的家族和后代便称此名。
10. a removed woman （以色列人像）正在经期的妇女（一样污秽）。

you, and a new spirit will I put within you: and I will take away the stony heart out of your flesh, and I will give you an heart of flesh[1]. And I will put my spirit within you, and cause you to walk in my statutes[2], and ye shall keep my judgments, and do them. And ye shall dwell in the land that I gave to your fathers; and ye shall be my people, and I will be your God. I will also save you from all your uncleannesses: and I will call for the corn[3], and will increase it, and lay no famine upon you. And I will multiply the fruit of the tree, and the increase of the field, that ye shall receive no more reproach of famine among the heathen[4]. Then shall ye remember your own evil ways, and your doings that were not good, and shall lothe[5] yourselves in your own sight for your iniquities and for your abominations[6].

Not for your sakes do I this, saith the Lord God, be it known unto you: be ashamed and confounded[7] for your own ways, O house of Israel. Thus saith the Lord God; In the day that I shall have cleansed you from all your iniquities I will also cause you to dwell in the cities, and the wastes shall be builded. And the desolate land shall be tilled, whereas it lay desolate in the sight of all that passed by. And they shall say, 'This land that was desolate is become like the garden of Eden; and the waste and desolate and ruined cities are become fenced[8], and are inhabited.' Then the heathen that are left round about you shall know that I the LORD build the ruined places, and plant that that was desolate: I the LORD have spoken it, and I will do it.

Thus saith the Lord God; I will yet for this be enquired of by the house of Israel, to do it for them; I will increase them with men like a flock. As the holy flock[9], as the flock of Jerusalem in her solemn feasts; so shall the waste cities be filled with flocks of men: and they shall know that I am the LORD. (36: 16–38)

The hand of the LORD was upon me, and carried me out in the spirit of the LORD, and set me down in the midst of the valley which was full of bones, and caused me to pass by them round about: and, behold, there were very many in the open valley; and, lo, they were very dry. And he said unto me, "Son of man[10], can these bones live?" And I answered, "O Lord God, thou knowest[11]."

Again he said unto me, "Prophesy[12] upon these bones, and say unto them, 'O ye dry bones, hear the word of the LORD.'" Thus saith the Lord God unto theses bones, "Behold, I will cause breath to enter into you, and ye shall live: And I will lay sinews[13] upon you, and will bring up flesh upon you, and cover you with skin, and put breath in you, and ye shall live; and ye shall know that I am the LORD."

So I prophesied as I was commanded: and as I prophesied, there was a noise, and

---

1. an heart of flesh 肉心，喻指顺服神的心，与上句中 stony heart (喻指背逆的心)相对。
2. statute *n.* a law or decree made by a sovereign, or by God 〈古〉律例
3. call for the corn 神命令五谷丰登。
4. reproach of famine among the heathen 因饥荒受外邦人的讥诮。
5. lothe *vt.* 同 loathe, to feel intense dislike or disgust for 厌恶
6. abomination *n.* a thing that causes disgust or loathing 可憎恶的事
7. confound *vt.* to cause to be ashamed 〈古〉使羞愧；使不安；使狼狈
8. fence *vt.* to ward off 防护
9. holy flock 祭献用的羊群
10. son of man 人子。指以西结乃肉胎凡人。
11. thou knowest 直译"你是知道的"，这是以西结的慨叹：从人的角度看，久死枯干的人类尸骨绝对无法恢复生机，但是耶和华神无所不能。
12. prophesy *vt.* to say that (a specified thing) will happen in the future 预言
13. sinew *n.* 筋

behold a shaking[1], and the bones came together, bone to his bone. And when I beheld, lo, the sinews and the flesh came up upon them, and the skin covered them above: but there was no breath in them.

Then said he unto me, "Prophesy unto the wind, prophesy, son of man, and say to the wind," Thus saith the Lord God, "Come from the four winds[2], O breath, and breathe upon these slain, that they may live."

So I prophesied as he commanded me, and the breath came into them, and they lived, and stood up upon their feet, an exceeding great army[3].

Then he said unto me, "Son of man, these bones are the whole house of Israel: behold, they say, 'Our bones are dried, and our hope is lost: we are cut off for our parts[4].' Therefore prophesy and say unto them," Thus saith the Lord God, "Behold, O my people, I will open your graves, and cause you to come up out of your graves, and bring you into the land of Israel. And ye shall know that I am the LORD, when I have opened your graves, O my people, and brought you up out of your graves, and shall put my spirit in you, and ye shall live, and I shall place you in your own land: then shall ye know that I the LORD have spoken it, and performed it[5]," saith the LORD. (37: 1–14)

Part 4

Amos[6]

Hear ye this word which I take up against you, even a lamentation, O house of Israel. The virgin of Israel is fallen[7]; she shall no more rise: she is forsaken upon her land; there is none to raise her up.

For thus saith the Lord God, "The city that went out by a thousand shall leave an hundred, and that which went forth by an hundred shall leave ten, to the house of Israel."

For thus saith the LORD unto the house of Israel, "Seek ye me, and ye shall live: but seek not Beth-el, nor enter into Gilgal, and pass not to Beer-sheba[8]: for Gilgal shall surely go into captivity, and Beth-el shall come to nought."

Seek the LORD, and ye shall live; lest he break out like fire in the house of Joseph, and devour[9] it, and there be none to quench[10] it in Beth-el. Ye who turn judgment to wormwood[11], and leave off righteousness in the earth, Seek him that maketh the seven stars and Orion[12], and turneth the shadow of death into the morning, and maketh the day dark with night: that calleth for the waters of the sea, and poureth them out upon the face of the earth: The LORD is his name: That strengtheneth the spoiled against the

---

1. shaking *n.* 指骸骨移动并相连结时的声响, 如地震一般
2. four winds 指来自四方的气息。
3. an exceeding great army 数目庞大的军队。
4. we are cut off for our parts 我们已灭绝尽净。
5. performed it 意思是耶和华的所有预言完全实现。
6. Amos /ˈeɪmɒs/ (人名) 阿摩司。公元前8世纪的希伯来先知。
7. fall *vi.* 跌倒, 喻指灭亡。这里把以色列民比作未出嫁就死去的处女, 令人惋惜。
8. Beth-el, Gigal, Beer-sheba 三个地名: 伯特利、吉甲、别是巴。据《创世记》(26:23–25; 28:10–22; 46:1–4)记载, 上帝曾在这三个地方向列祖显现, 百姓以为到这些圣地去献祭便是寻求上帝。
9. devour *vt.* to eat (food or prey) hungrily or quickly 吞吃
10. quench *vt.* to extinguish (a fire) 熄灭
11. turn judgment to wormwood 使公平变为苦艾。
12. that maketh the seven stars and Orion 那造出昴星和参星的, 即上帝。Orion *n.* 猎户座。

strong, so that the spoiled shall come against the fortress. They hate him that rebuketh in the gate, and they abhor[1] him that speaketh uprightly.

Forasmuch[2] therefore as your treading[3] is upon the poor, and ye take from him burdens of wheat[4]: ye have built houses of hewn[5] stone, but ye shall not dwell in them; ye have planted pleasant vineyards, but ye shall not drink wine of them. For I know your manifold transgressions[6] and your mighty sins: they afflict the just[7], they take a bribe[8], and they turn aside[9] the poor in the gate from their right. Therefore the prudent[10] shall keep silence in that time; for it is an evil time.

Seek good, and not evil, that ye may live: and so the LORD, the God of hosts, shall be with you, as ye have spoken. Hate the evil, and love the good, and establish judgment[11] in the gate: it may be that the LORD God of hosts will be gracious unto the remnant of Joseph[12].

Therefore the LORD, the God of hosts, the Lord, saith thus; "Wailing shall be in all streets; and they shall say in all the highways[13], 'Alas[14]! alas!' and they shall call the husbandman[15] to mourning, and such as are skilful of lamentation to wailing. And in all vineyards shall be wailing: for I will pass through thee," saith the LORD.

Woe unto you that desire the day of the LORD! to what end is it for you? the day of the LORD is darkness, and not light. As if a man did flee from a lion, and a bear met him; or went into the house, and leaned his hand on the wall, and a serpent bit him. Shall not the day of the LORD be darkness, and not light? even very dark, and no brightness in it?

I hate, I despise your feast days, and I will not smell in your solemn assemblies[16]. Though ye offer me burnt offerings and your meat offerings, I will not accept them: neither will I regard the peace offerings[17] of your fat beasts. Take thou away from me the noise of thy songs; for I will not hear the melody of thy viols[18]. But let judgment run down as waters, and righteousness as a mighty stream. (5: 1–24)

"Behold, the eyes of the Lord God are upon the sinful kingdom[19], and I will destroy it from off the face of the earth; saving that I will not utterly destroy the house of Jacob," saith the LORD.

"For, lo, I will command, and I will sift[20] the house of Israel among all nations, like as corn is sifted in a sieve[21], yet shall not the

---

1. abhor *vt.* to regard with disgust and hatred 憎恶; 痛恨
2. Forasmuch *conj.* 由于; 鉴于
3. tread *vt.* 踩踏; 指压迫(穷人)。
4. burdens of wheat 大量的麦子。
5. hewn 动词 hew (砍伐)的过去分词。hew *vt.* to chop or cut 砍伐。
6. manifold transgressions 各种各样的犯罪。
7. afflict the just 折磨义人。
8. take a bribe 收受贿赂。
9. turn aside 屈枉。
10. the prudent 聪明人。
11. establish judgment 伸张正义。
12. gracious unto the remnant of Joseph 向约瑟的余民施恩。意思是百姓不会全部灭绝。
13. highways 街市
14. alas *int.* 哀哉!
15. husbandman *n.* 农夫
16. not smell in your solemn assemblies 对隆重的聚会不喜欢。
17. peace offering 平安祭。
18. viol *n.* 一种古琴
19. the sinful kingdom 有罪的国, 指以色列。
20. sift *vt.* to put (a fine or loose substance) through a sieve so as to remove lumps or larger particles 筛撒。上帝要毁灭以色列国, 将其人民分散在列国之中, 做重新拣选。
21. sieve *n.* 筛子

least grain fall upon the earth. All the sinners of my people shall die by the sword, which say, 'The evil shall not overtake nor prevent us.' In that day will I raise up the tabernacle of David[1] that is fallen, and close up the breaches[2] thereof; and I will raise up his ruins, and I will build it as in the days of old: that they may possess the remnant of Edom, and of all the heathen[3], which are called by my name," saith the LORD that doeth this.

"Behold, the days come," saith the LORD, "that the plowman shall overtake the reaper, and the treader of grapes him that soweth seed[4]; and the mountains shall drop sweet wine, and all the hills shall melt[5]. And I will bring again the captivity of my people of Israel, and they shall build the waste cities, and inhabit them; and they shall plant vineyards, and drink the wine thereof; they shall also make gardens, and eat the fruit of them. And I will plant them upon their land, and they shall no more be pulled up out of their land which I have given them," saith the LORD thy God. (9: 8–15)

三、圣经文化知识链接

1. 先知文学的异象手法

在先知文学作品中，作者有时泼墨挥毫，直抒胸臆；有时峰回路转，通过一段故事、一个画面，甚至一个异象，暗示自己的思想意图。其中先知们常用的异象手法可视为希伯来人一大遗产。它不以具体的现实生活为摹写对象，而着意刻画某个含意晦涩的幻觉或梦境，再由耶和华、天使或先知对其加以解释。如"神的宝座"、"枯骨复活"（《以赛亚书》1; 37:1—14）、"金台的异象"、"飞卷的异象"、"马车的异象"（《撒迦利亚书》4:1—14; 5:1—4; 6:1—8）等。异象手法的特色可从"飞卷的异象"略见一斑：

> 我又举目观看，见有一飞行的书卷。他问我说："你看见什么？"我回答说："我看见飞行的书卷，长二十肘，宽十肘。"他对我说："这是发出行在遍地上的咒诅。凡偷窃的，必按卷上这面的话除灭；凡起假誓的，必按卷上那面的话除灭。万军之耶和华说，我必使这书卷出去，进入偷窃人的家和指我名起假誓人的家。必常在他家里，连房屋带木石都毁灭了。"

这个异象由两个部分组成：先知看到含义不明的书卷；天使揭开其中之谜：耶和华用这飞卷咒诅盗贼和发假誓者。这些异象类似于梦境、幻觉。在现代哲学家和心理学家看来，先知置身于异象中的所见与所闻，实际上就是人类欲望和梦想的一种超自然的存在，一个建立在幻觉的、超验的层面上的意愿的喷发。用费尔巴哈的话来说，这是"人类的精神之梦"，在人认为是上帝的，其实就是人自己的精神、灵魂，而人的精神、灵魂和心其实就是他的上帝，上帝是人之公开的内心，是人之坦白的自我；宗教是对人的隐秘宝藏的庄严的揭幕，是人最内在的思想的

---

1. tabernacle of David 大卫的帐幕，喻指大卫王朝。
2. breach *n*. 裂口
3. heathen *n*. a person who is not a believer in Christianity as regarded by those who do 不信上帝的人
4. the plowman shall overtake the reaper, and the treader of grapes him that soweth seed 这句话的意思是耕田的人必紧接着收割的人，踹葡萄的人必紧接着撒种的。形容农活不断的丰收景象。
5. melt *vt*. to make or become liquefied by heating 使融化。"小山必融化"形容因葡萄丰收而酒香遍野。

自白,甚至是对自己的爱情秘密的公开供认。

2. 先知书与浪漫主义[1]

先知文学在形式上蕴含着浪漫主义的要素,主要表现是:在严峻的现实面前和对理想的描述之中给人们带来希望和快乐,强调对理想的追求,并借此超越变幻无常、难以驾驭的现实生活;追求感情的天然流露和思绪的超然无羁,体现为奇异的想象力、神秘的氛围描写和对无限的渴求等。

首先,先知书充满对无限的追求。浪漫主义的典型特征是感受和渴求无限。[2]现实的苦难促使先知们去思考,渴求理想的社会。在先知的世界里,上帝是世界的道德之神,是人类望尘莫及的正义与不朽的化身。因此,对万能上帝之律法的遵守和对公义与至善的永恒追求,成了先知们的理想追求。这些追求主要体现为他们的乌托邦思想(《阿摩司书》7:12;《以赛亚书》32:16—18)和大同思想(《以赛亚书》2:2—4)。

其次,先知书具有浓重的神话和象征意蕴,具体表现为寓言或异象,即通过一个场面或一件器具曲折地表达某种寓意。这样的段落十分常见,如《以西结书》描绘的"枯骨复活"场面:先知奉耶和华之命让干枯的尸骨复活,果然听见了"瑟瑟的声音(noise)";"骚动(shaking)"之间,骨头彼此连接起来;枯骨开始生筋长肉,裹上皮肤;生命之气进入躯体,躯体就活了,站立起来;他们数目多得足够编成"军队(army)"。这个带有现代科幻色彩、令人不可思议的场面象征并预示沦落异邦、仰人鼻息的希伯来人必将重归故乡,再度强盛。

最后,先知书还充满热情、浪漫和幻想。先知们目光敏锐,有先知先觉的才能,带有诗人的气质。可以说,先知书基本上是诗,是富于热情和幻想的诗。马克思曾说克伦威尔领导的资产阶级革命借用了"《旧约全书》中的语言、热情和幻想[3]",指的就是先知书所具有的诗的激情、革命勇气和战斗精神。

四、圣经文化专题

1. 先知的身份及其思想特征

先知主要指公元前8世纪到公元前5世纪这段时间被称为"正典先知"的人。这一时期,希伯来民族内忧外患。民族的盛世已经过去,国势渐衰,国内政治分裂,社会贫富悬殊,道德沦丧,社会风气日下;国外强邻压境。先知正是在这种严酷的社会背景下登上历史舞台的。就《圣经》本意而言,"先知"一般指接受上帝委派,听取上帝启示并向民众传达上帝旨意的人。实质上他们是当时社会的批评家、政治改革的倡导者和民族的精神导师。先知是希伯来文明发展过程中的一个特殊群体,他们一直被视为希伯来思想的代表人物。先知思想是希伯来文明中的一

---

1. 本项参考胡经之主编《西方文艺理论名著教程》(上卷)第二版,北京:北京大学出版社,2003年,第474页;
   【美】威尔肯斯(Wilkens)、帕杰特(Padgett)著:《基督教与西方思想》(卷二),北京:北京大学出版社,2005年,第11页。
2. 同上,第12页。
3. 马克思著:《路易·波拿巴的雾月十八日》,载于《马克思恩格斯全集》第一卷,第604-605页。

个独特组成部分,具有以下特征:

第一、强烈的现实性。先知常对未来做出预言,但实际上他们所关心的主要是现实现世的社会状况。对现实的关注,使他们深切地认识到社会的种种弊端甚至罪恶,认识到社会的不公、道德的堕落,并置身度外、愤言时弊。先知揭示社会道德沦丧、奢侈、骄横、压迫穷人、贿赂及诬告陷害等丑恶现象,继而猛烈地对此展开批判。与先知对现实罪恶的批判相辅相成的是他们对以色列人的劝诫,目的是让人民清楚自己的错误,同时又看到未来是光明的,从而推动社会思想、道德的进步。

第二、先知书的进步思想如主持正义、爱国主义、理想主义等,其内核裹上了宗教神学的外衣,因而表现出种种局限。他们在谴责社会罪恶时要求人们皈依上帝,改邪归正,这种说教在严酷现实面前难免显得苍白无力。他们是热忱的爱国主义者,但是他们对本民族深沉的爱往往与对四邻敌族的仇恨交织在一起。在对待外族异邦的态度上,多数先知都表现出比较狭隘的民族主义观念,只是一味地痛加咒骂。比如他们声言耶和华要对侵犯过以色列、犹大的国家和民族如埃及、亚述、巴比伦、叙利亚等国施行无情审判,烧毁他们的宫殿,掳走他们的国民,杀戮他们的首领,把他们国王的骸骨"焚成灰烬"。他们在面临外敌入侵时主张乞灵于上帝的庇护而反对与邻族结盟(《以赛亚书》30:1—2;《何西阿书》5:13),就显得荒唐、幼稚。

第三、先知们固然描绘了理想世界,却寄希望于上帝恩赐的乌托邦,他们虽给苦难同胞某种精神慰藉,但从一定程度上来讲,可以说是一副自我安慰的麻醉剂。在人神关系认识上,先知的思想中更多地体现出上帝的相对性、可变性的人格特征。先知书中的上帝并非律法书、历史书那般绝对、威严、冷漠、缺少变化、毫无生气,相反,显示出既疾恶如仇又感情充沛,且威严中不乏慈爱,表现出充满激情的人格特征。这些描述体现出先知丰富强烈的情感色彩和独特的感染力、对善与恶和社会现实的深刻认识以及对人民的强烈责任感。

2. 先知书多样化的艺术表现手法[1]

先知书不仅蕴含着丰富的思想,而且呈现出高度的艺术技巧。先知书的表达方式多种多样,有诗歌、演说、散文,还有"启示体"。先知文学风格也千姿百态,各有千秋,主要体现在善用重叠、夸张、比喻、拟人、反讽等几个方面。

首先,天启式的叙述模式。先知书是署有先知姓名的一种显示出独特人格特征的自我表述,这使得每一部先知书都有自己的特色;但是共同的民族血脉、共同的命运和历史、共同的思想与使命又使得他们在叙述模式上不约而同地呈现出明显的共性。这种共性最显著的表征就是:"天启式"体裁。如耶和华说:"虽然如此,你们仍应禁食、哭泣、悲哀,一心归向我。"(《约珥书》2:12)不可否认的是,先知们所言及的内容具有现实主义的真实性,启示体裁使先知的语言平添了神秘主义色彩,从而更具威力。

第二,诗体与散文穿插糅合的文体。在先知书中,叙事或描写时一般用散文,抒发情感时则转而为诗。先知书(尤其三大先知书)的基本部分是散文体的记叙、描写或议论。其中除大量劝善之辞外,还有不少文学色彩很浓的小故事,以及散见各处的历史纪事、先知行传等。如《耶利米书》较详尽地记载了先和耶利米一生的种种遭遇——他因刚直不阿、敢讲真话而遭到祭司和上层社会众人的围攻咒骂;他的书稿被国王约雅敬用刀割碎,"扔到火盆中,直到全卷化为

---

1. 本项参考朱维之主编:《古希伯来文学史》,北京:高等教育出版社,2001年,第110页。

灰烬"；他还惨遭便雅悯首领的毒打与监禁，在狱中被囚多日。当散文叙事难尽心曲时，先知们便挥舞诗笔，引吭高歌起来。

第三，独特的诗体文学。除诗文相间的文体外，有些先知书卷几乎全部用诗歌写成，其显著特点是善用重叠法，即同一个单词、同一句式或有关句子反复使用，以使作品布局工整、铿锵有力、富有节奏感，如《俄巴底亚书》、《约珥书》、《那鸿书》。因此有学者早就发现：先知即诗人。先知们的诗笔描绘过繁华的耶路撒冷街市、凄冷的巴比伦河畔、刀光剑影的战场和优美恬静的葡萄园……先知们诗意焕发的语言总能把读者带进一个奇异的艺术境界，使之受到诗人情绪的浓重感染。例如，当阿摩司痛感以色列人罪大恶极，已沦落到非毁灭不可的地步时，曾以有力的诗句传达神谕，言说先知的职责：

以色列人啊，你们全家是我从埃及地领上来的，
当听耶和华攻击你们的话。
在地上万族中，我只认识你们；
因此，我必追讨你们的一切罪孽。
二人若不同心，岂能同行呢？
狮子若非抓食，岂能在林中咆哮呢？
少壮狮子若无所得，岂能从洞中发声呢？
若没有机槛，雀鸟岂能陷在罗网里呢？
罗网若无所得，岂能从地上翻起呢？
城中若吹角，百姓岂不惊恐呢？
灾祸若临到一城，岂非耶和华所降的吗？
主耶和华若不将奥秘指示给他的仆人——众先知，
就一无所行。
狮子吼叫，谁不惧怕呢？
主耶和华发命，谁能不说预言呢？（《阿摩司书》，3:1—8）

该预言以诗歌的形式表明先知没有回避上帝与以色列的特殊关系，而是直切主题，讲述了上帝为什么要追讨以色列人的罪恶，以上帝的口吻直言不讳而又语重心长。其推理逻辑如下：若以色列人没有犯罪，上帝怎能讨伐以色列呢？如上帝不是和以色列有特殊关系，又怎能讨伐以色列呢？灾难将降临到这个城市，不是我先知本人编出来的，没有上帝的指示，我怎能编出呢？上帝已经发出指示，让我作为先知传出神谕，我又怎么能不说呢？

这一逻辑缜密的诗文既是先知对下文言及惩罚前的一个自我表白，也是对缺乏忧患意识人们的一种唤醒。

第四，独特的异象手法。先知们用异象表达各种情感，如阿摩司对富人欺压穷人的现象心怀不满。他用异象给压迫者判罪：

"我要击打柱顶，锤击圣殿的栋梁，使整个屋宇倒塌下来，打碎每个人的头。我要用刀剑杀死其余的人，一个也不能避免，一个也逃不掉。哪怕他们挖了地洞，钻进阴间，我也要把他们抓出来！哪怕他们爬上了天，也要把他们拉下来！哪怕他们逃到迦密山顶，我也要去搜索，把他们找出来！哪怕他们藏在海底，我也要叫海怪吞吃他们！哪怕他们被俘虏了，我也要

叫敌人处死他们！我已经决定要消灭他们，决不可怜他们[1]。"（《阿摩司书》9：1—4）

这段话入木三分地道出先知对以色列已危在旦夕的深刻认识和悲切体验。

先知书多样化的艺术表现手法体现出高亢有力的言语风格、激愤昂扬的情调特质、火热的激情和感人肺腑的力量，因而具有恒久不衰的艺术魅力和感染力。

五、圣经典故集锦

1. **beat swords into plowshares, and spears into pruninghooks**（铸剑为犁、制枪为镰）：指化干戈为玉帛、变战争为和平。典出《以赛亚书》第2章4节：And he shall judge among the nations, and shall rebuke many people: and they shall beat their swords into plowshares, and their spears into pruninghooks: nation shall not lift up sword against nation, neither shall they learn war any more. 他们要将刀打成犁头，把枪打成镰刀。这国不举刀攻击那国，他们也不再学习战事。这是以赛亚对未来太平盛世的憧憬。

2. **the women of Zion**（锡安的女子）：指风骚娘们、轻佻女子、浪荡女郎，或因妖艳轻浮而招致灾祸的女子。典出《以赛亚书》第3章16—24节：Moreover the LORD saith, Because the daughters of Zion are haughty, and walk with stretched forth necks and wanton eyes, walking and mincing as they go, and making a tinkling with their feet: Therefore the Lord will smite with a scab the crown of the head of the daughters of Zion, and the LORD will discover their secret parts. 因为锡安的女子狂傲，行走挺项，卖弄眼目，俏步徐行，脚下玎珰，所以主必使锡安的女子头长秃疮，耶和华又使她们赤露下体。此处锡安女子喻指以色列。先知通过这种比喻教训以色列人。

3. **the Prince of Peace**（和平之君）：指救主、明君。典出《以赛亚书》第9章6节：For unto us a child is born, unto us a son is given: and the government shall be upon his shoulder: and his name shall be called Wonderful, Counsellor, The mighty God, The everlasting Father, The Prince of Peace. 因有一婴孩为我们而生，有一子赐给我们，政权必担在他的肩上，他名称为奇妙、策士、全能的神、永恒的父、和平的君。这是以赛亚的预言，是对耶稣基督的预表。2003年美国太子行总裁杨应瑞先生在天津建立了取名"和平之君儿童福利院"。2006年8月31日在香港文化中心音乐厅举行了"和平之君慈善音乐夜(Prince of Peace Charity Concert Night)"。

4. **Leviathan**（利维坦）：喻指强大的国家、世俗政权。典出《以赛亚书》第27章1节：In that day the LORD with his sore and great and strong sword shall punish leviathan the piercing serpent; even leviathan the crooked serpent; and he shall slay the dragon that is in the sea. 到那日，耶和华必用他刚硬有力的大刀，刑罚鳄鱼，就是那快行的蛇；刑罚鳄鱼，就是那曲行的

---

[1] 为体现译文的文学性，此处未采用和合本译文，而采用了朱维之著《圣经文学十二讲》第245页译文。

蛇，并杀海中的大龙。利维坦是一种力大无穷的海怪，通常被描述为鲸鱼、海豚或鳄鱼的形状。人们为了抵御各种外来的风险，自己创造了一个能让自己有归属感的庞然大物——政府，但政府这个"利维坦"有双面的性格。它由人组成，也由人来运作，因此也就具有了人性的那种半神半兽的品质；它在保护人的同时，又在吃人。所以，有这样一种说法：人类社会的最高理想就是把利维坦关进笼子里。英国资产阶级革命时期的政治思想家托马斯·霍布斯(Thomas Hobbes, 1588—1679)的代表作《利维坦》(*Leviathan*, 1651)，借用这个意象来论证君权至上，反对君权神授。

5. **the potter and the clay** (窑匠和器皿)：指上下有别、主仆有等，比喻受造者不可能违反造物主的旨意。《以赛亚书》第45章9节载：Shall the clay say to him that fashioneth it, What makest thou? 泥土岂可对抟弄他的说，你作什么呢? 第64章8节又载：But now, O, LORD, thou art our father; we are the clay, and thou our potter; and we all are the work of thy hand. 耶和华啊，现在你仍是我们的父！我们是泥，你是窑匠，我们都是你手的工作。《耶利米书》第18章4节载：And the vessel that he made of clay was marred in the hand of the potter: so he made it again another vessel, as seemed good to the potter to make it. 窑匠用泥做的器皿，在他手中做坏了，他又用这泥另做别的器皿。窑匠看怎样好，就怎样做。《罗马书》第9章21节载：Hath not the potter power over the clay, of the same lump to make one vessel unto honour, and another unto dishonour? 窑匠难道没有权柄从一团泥里拿一块做成贵重的器皿，又拿一块做成卑贱的器皿吗? 因此基督教徒认为，万能的神是窑匠，自己是他手中的陶泥。"泥土音乐"One Day专辑中有一首曲子取名《泥土的祷告》(*Potter & Clay*)。

6. **can the leopard change his spots** (豹岂能改变斑点)：指本性难移、恶习难改。典出《耶利米书》第13章23节：Can the Ethiopian change his skin, or the leopard his spots? Then may ye also do good, that are accustomed to do evil. 古实人岂能改变皮肤呢? 豹岂能改变斑点呢? 若能，你们这习惯行恶的，便能行善了。

7. **the cords and bars of a yoke** (绳索与轭)：指奴役与压迫、高压统治。典出《耶利米书》第27章2—8节："你做绳索与轭，加在自己的颈项上。"

8. **a wall of a plumb-line** (准绳之墙)：指量罪罚恶之处、正义的审判。典出《阿摩司书》第7章7—9节：And the LORD unto me, Amos, what seest thou? And I said, A plumbline. Then said the LORD, Behold, I will set a plumbline in the midst of my people Israel: I will not again pass by them any more. 耶和华对我说："阿摩司啊，你看见什么?"我说："看见准绳。"主说："我要吊起准绳在我民以色列中，我必不再宽恕他们。"

9. **Jonah's voyage** (约拿的旅程)：指不幸的航程、失败的计划。典出《约拿书》第1章4节至第2章10节，约拿违抗神命乘船远逃，海上遇到暴风雨被吞入鱼腹三日，又被吐出。

10. **Jonah's gourd** (约拿的蓖麻)：喻指生命短暂却让人留恋之物、瞬息即逝的幸福。典出《约拿书》第4章6—11节，上帝安排一株蓖麻为烈日下的约拿遮阴，次日清晨又让虫子咬死蓖麻，使约拿饱受灼晒之苦。

六、课堂讨论题

1. 比较希伯来先知与儒家圣人。
2. 阅读先知书中对植物的描写，分析其中折射出的希伯来人的环保意识。
3. 讨论《先知书》以植物为载体的思维模式。
4. 谈谈先知书的批判性。

七、课后思考题

1. 《耶利米书》中出现了"公马鸣牝"的比喻，这一比喻与中国的哪种表述相似？
2. 谈谈马丁·路德·金在其演说词中对《圣经》的引用。
3. 你知道李登辉如何利用《圣经》为其政治服务吗？

人生苦难的思索：《约伯记》

Job, Probing into Bitterness of Life

一、导读: 希伯来戏剧的雏形

英语习语 *as poor as Job* 就是源于《约伯记》，意思是穷得像约伯，约伯则是《约伯记》里的主人公。《约伯记》是虚构的故事，采用了类似剧本的文体: 开始有"序幕"，结尾有"尾声"，均为散文体; 中间的独白和对话皆为诗体。这种散文体叙事与长篇诗体交相融合的形式在古代近东文学中非常独特。

有7子3女的富人约伯虔诚信仰耶和华，在言行上无可指责。上帝在天庭中与神子撒旦针对"约伯敬畏上帝是否无缘无故"发生了争论。于是上帝允许撒旦让约伯遭受突如其来的考验，蒙受一系列沉重打击，先后失去他的财富、仆人、子女以及健康、尊荣和社会地位。起初约伯因冲动抱怨自己的不幸，诅咒自己的生日。来探望约伯的三个朋友轮流发表言论，对他的处境加以评论，谴责多于同情。约伯分别予以回答，为自己无罪却遭受如此天谴进行辩护，控诉上帝的不义和对自己的敌视。上帝从旋风中亲自回答约伯，陈述其创造世界和维护世界的种种威力。约伯被深深折服，承认自己的无知妄言。于是上帝补偿给他加倍的财富。

《约伯记》气势磅礴，又不失简洁文雅; 体裁变化多端，有独白、对话，也有祈祷、颂赞; 修辞手段多变、高超，拟人生动、壮观。《约伯记》不愧是希伯来智慧文学的巅峰之作，又堪称世界文学中具有代表性的杰作之一，与但丁的《神曲》和歌德的《浮士德》并列为人类探索自身与宇宙奥秘的三部曲。

本讲选取《约伯记》中4个片段:

1. 约伯的独白: 约伯通过诅咒自己的生日来表达内心的绝望: Why died I not from the womb? (我为何不出母胎就死去?)。

2. 约伯答复朋友: 约伯慨叹人生: My days are swifter than a weaver's shuttle, and are spent without hope. (日子比织梭还快，都消耗在无望之中)。

3. 约伯质问上帝: 约伯追问上帝为何对他如此残酷: Remember, I beseech thee, that thou hast made me as the clay; And wilt thou bring me into dust again? (求你记念，制造我如砖泥一般; 你还要使我归于尘土吗?)。

4. 上帝答复约伯: 约伯听完上帝的陈述，终于降服: Wherefore I abhor myself, and repent in dust and ashes. (因此我厌恶自己，在尘土和炉灰中懊悔。)

二、选文及注释

Part 1

Job's Monologues

Let the day perish wherein I was born,
And the night[1] in which it was said, "There is a man child conceived."
Let that day be darkness;
Let not God regard it from above[2],
Neither let the light shine upon it.
Let darkness and the shadow of death stain[3] it;
Let a cloud dwell upon it;
Let the blackness of the day[4] terrify it.
As for that night, let darkness seize upon it;
Let it not be joined unto the days of the year,
Let it not come into the number of the months.[5]
Lo, let that night be solitary[6],
Let no joyful voice come therein.
Let them curse it that curse the day[7],
Who are ready to raise up their mourning[8].
Let the stars of the twilight thereof be dark;
Let it look for light, but have none;
Neither let it see the dawning of the day:
Because it shut not up the doors of my mother's womb,
Nor hid sorrow from mine eyes.
Why died I not from the womb?
Why did I not give up the ghost[9] when I came out of the belly?
Why did the knees[10] prevent me?
Or why the breasts that I should suck?
For now should I have lain still and been quiet,
I should have slept: then had I been at rest,
With kings and counsellors[11] of the earth,
Which built desolate places for themselves;
Or with princes that had gold,
Who filled their houses with silver:
Or as an hidden untimely birth[12] I had not been;
As infants which never saw light[13].
There the wicked cease from troubling;
And there the weary be at rest.
There the prisoners rest together;
They hear not the voice of the oppressor.
The small and great[14] are there;
And the servant is free from his master.

---

1. Let the day ... And the night ...: 约伯诅咒的"日"和"夜"同指他出生的那一天。
2. Let not God regard it from above 愿上帝不从上面寻找它。"它"指约伯的生日。时令为上帝所设定,所以约伯希望上帝没有设定他出生的那日。
3. stain *vt.* 弄脏; 玷污。意思是把(自己的生日)涂抹掉。
4. the blackness of the day 指日食。
5. Let it not come into the number of the months. 生日的那一天不入月中的数目,意思是根本没有他生日的那一天。
6. let that night be solitary 愿那夜没有生育能力。拟人的说法。
7. Let them curse it that curse the day that 句和下句的 Who 都是 them 的定语。
8. raise up their mourning 惹动海怪们的叫声。their 指海怪。
9. give up the ghost 放弃灵魂,指气绝而死。
10. the knees "膝" 指父亲的膝, 表示父亲接纳新生孩婴。
11. counsellor *n.* 谋士
12. an hidden untimely birth 指小产的胎儿。
13. infants which never saw light 指死婴。
14. the small and great (死人)无论贵贱。

Wherefore is light given[1] to him that is in misery,
And life unto the bitter in soul;
Which long for death, but it cometh not;
And dig for it more than for hid treasures[2];
Which rejoice exceedingly,
And are glad, when they can find the grave?
Why is light given to a man whose way is hid[3],
And whom God hath hedged in[4]?
For my sighing cometh before I eat,
And my roarings are poured out like the waters[5].
For the thing which I greatly feared[6] is come upon me,
And that which I was afraid of is come unto me.
I was not in safety, neither had I rest, neither was I quiet;
Yet trouble came. (3: 3–26)

Part 2

Job's Answer to His Friend

But Job answered and said,
"O that my grief were throughly weighed,
And my calamity laid in the balances together!
For now it would be heavier than the sand of the sea:
Therefore my words are swallowed up[7].
For the arrows of the Almighty[8] are within me,
The poison whereof drinketh up my spirit:
The terrors of God do set themselves in array[9] against me.
Doth the wild ass bray[10] when he hath grass?
Or loweth[11] the ox over his fodder[12]?
Can that which is unsavoury[13] be eaten without salt?
Or is there any taste in the white[14] of an egg?
The things that my soul refused to touch are as my sorrowful meat.
Oh that I might have my request[15];
And that God would grant me the thing that I long for!
Even that it would please God to destroy me;
That he would let loose his hand, and cut me off!
Then should I yet have comfort;
Yea, I would harden[16] myself in sorrow:
Let him not spare;

---

1. is light given "有光" 指有生命。为何把生命赐给患难之人。
2. dig for it more than for hid treasures 寻求死胜过寻找财宝。
3. whose way is hid 人的道路被遮蔽, 形容人生艰难。
4. God hath hedged in 上帝(把他)四面围住。形容人生困苦。
5. my roarings are poured out like the waters 愁烦如水涌出。形容没有止境。
6. the thing which I greatly feared 我害怕的事, 指人生的苦短和煎熬。
7. swallow up 吞没。这里指约伯发言冒失。
8. the arrows of the Almighty 全能者的(毒)箭。指神对约伯身心的考验。
9. in array 呈列队状。
10. bray *vi.* 驴叫声, 指哀声。
11. low *vi.* 牛叫声。
12. fodder *n.* 饲料; 草料。
13. unsavoury *adj.* disagreeable to taste 难吃的。
14. the white (鸡蛋的)蛋清。希伯来原文的意思很难确定, 大概指一种无味的食物。
15. Oh that I might have my request 但愿我得着所求的, 指立即死去, 摆脱眼前的切身痛苦。下一句 the thing that I long for 我所切望的, 也是此意。
16. harden *vt.* to enable to withstand physical or mental hardship 使(自己)经得起考验

For I have not concealed[1] the words of the Holy One.

What is my strength, that I should hope?

And what is mine end[2], that I should prolong my life?

Is my strength the strength of stones?

Or is my flesh of brass[3]?

Is not my help in me?

And is wisdom driven quite[4] from me?

To him that is afflicted[5] pity should be shewed from his friend;

But he forsaketh[6] the fear of the Almighty.

My brethren have dealt deceitfully as a brook[7],

And as the stream of brooks they pass away;

Which are blackish by reason of the ice[8],

And wherein the snow is hid:

What time they wax[9] warm, they vanish:

When it is hot, they are consumed out of their place.

The paths of their way are turned aside;

They go to nothing, and perish.

The troops of Tema[10] looked,

The companies of Sheba waited for them.

They were confounded[11] because they had hoped[12];

They came thither, and were ashamed.

For now ye are no thing;

Ye see my casting down[13], and are afraid.

Did I say, 'Bring unto me?'

Or, 'Give a reward for me of[14] your substance?'

Or, 'Deliver me from the enemy's hand?'

Or, 'Redeem me from the hand of the mighty?'

Teach me, and I will hold my tongue:

And cause me to understand wherein I have erred[15].

How forcible are right words!

But what doth your arguing reprove?

Do ye imagine to reprove words,

And the speeches of one that is desperate,

Which are as wind?

Yea, ye overwhelm the fatherless[16],

And ye dig a pit for your friend.

Now therefore be content[17], look upon me;

For it is evident unto you if I lie.

Return, I pray you, let it not be iniquity;

Yea, return again, my righteousness is in it.

Is there iniquity in my tongue?

Cannot my taste discern perverse[18] things? (6)

Is there not an appointed time[19] to man

---

1. conceal *vt.* to hide; to prevent from being known 遮蔽，引申为背弃
2. mine end 我的结局。
3. brass *n.* 铜
4. driven quite (智慧被)赶出殆尽。quite *adv.* absolutely or completely 彻底地。
5. him that is afflicted 受痛苦煎熬的人。
6. forsake *vt.* to abandon or leave 抛弃；离弃
7. dealt deceitfully as a brook 诡诈像弯曲的溪流。
8. blackish by reason of the ice 因结冰而发黑。
9. wax *vi.* to increase in heat 变暖和
10. Tema (种族)提玛。在红海阿卡巴湾东部。
11. confound *vt.* to cause to be ashamed 使窘迫；使羞愧
12. they had hoped 满怀希望却落空。
13. casting down 打倒，引申为"灾难"。
14. of 相当于from
15. err *vi.* to make a mistake 犯错；犯罪
16. overwhelm the fatherless 制服孤儿。希伯来原文的意思是通过抓阄得到孤儿。
17. content *adj.* satisfied 满意的
18. perverse *adj.* contrary to the accepted or expected standard or practice 不正当的。这句话的意思是：我的口岂不能辨别不义的事情吗？
19. an appointed time 被指定的时间，引申为"劳役"。

upon earth?

Are not his days also like the days of an hireling[1]?

As a servant earnestly desireth the shadow[2],

And as an hireling looketh for the reward of his work:

So am I made to possess months of vanity[3],

And wearisome nights are appointed to me.

When I lie down, I say,

'When shall I arise, and the night be gone?'

And I am full of tossings[4] to and fro unto the dawning of the day.

My flesh is clothed with worms and clods of dust[5];

My skin is broken, and become loathsome[6].

My days are swifter than a weaver's shuttle, and are spent without hope.

O remember that my life is wind:

Mine eye shall no more see good.

The eye of him that hath seen me shall see me no more:

Thine eyes are upon me, and I am not[7].

As the cloud is consumed and vanisheth away:

So he that goeth down to the grave shall come up no more.

He shall return no more to his house,

Neither shall his place[8] know him any more.

Therefore I will not refrain my mouth[9];

I will speak in the anguish of my spirit;

I will complain in the bitterness of my soul.

Am I a sea, or a whale, that thou settest a watch[10] over me?

When I say, 'My bed shall comfort me, my couch shall ease my complaint.'

Then thou scarest me with dreams, and terrifiest me through visions[11]:

So that my soul chooseth strangling[12], and death rather than my life.

I loathe it; I would not live alway[13]:

Let me alone; for my days are vanity.

What is man, that thou shouldest magnify[14] him?

And that thou shouldest set thine heart upon him?

And that thou shouldest visit[15] him every morning,

And try[16] him every moment?

How long wilt thou not depart from me,

Nor let me alone till I swallow down my spittle[17]?

I have sinned;

What shall I do unto thee, O thou

---

1. hireling *n.* 雇工，尤其指为了金钱而承担卑下的或令人不快的工作的人
2. shadow *n.* 暮影，指日落后歇工
3. months of vanity 空虚的岁月。
4. tossing *n.* the state of moving from side to side or back and force 辗转反侧，指彻夜难眠
5. clothed with worms and clods of dust 以虫子和尘土为衣。
6. loathsome *adj.* arousing loathing; abhorrent 可恶的；讨厌的
7. I am not 我却不在世上了。
8. his place 他的故乡。
9. refrain my mouth 禁止我的口(说话)。
10. set a watch (over sb.) 防备。
11. vision *n.* a mental image of what the future will or could be like 异象，这里指可怕的梦境
12. strangling 动词 strangle (窒息；扼死)的名词形式
13. alway *adv.* 等于 always
14. magnify *vt.* 本意为放大，意思是看重(人类)
15. visit *vt.* to inspect 察看；监察
16. try *vt.* to test 考验；试炼
17. spittle *n.* 唾沫

preserver of men[1]?

Why hast thou set me as a mark[2] against thee,

So that I am a burden to myself[3]?

And why dost thou not pardon my transgression[4],

And take away mine iniquity?

For now shall I sleep in the dust;

And thou shalt seek me in the morning, but I shall not be[5]."(7)

Part 3

Job's Questions at God

"My soul is weary[6] of my life;

I will leave my complaint upon myself[7];

I will speak in the bitterness of my soul.

I will say unto God,

Do not condemn[8] me;

Shew me wherefore thou contendest[9] with me.

Is it good unto thee that thou shouldest oppress,

That thou shouldest despise the work of thine hands,

And shine upon the counsel of the wicked[10]?

Hast thou eyes of flesh? or seest thou as man seeth?

Are thy days as the days of man? are thy years as man's days,

That thou enquirest after mine iniquity[11], and searchest after my sin?

Thou knowest that I am not wicked;

And there is none that can deliver out of thine hand.[12]

Thine hands have made me and fashioned[13] me together round about;

Yet thou dost destroy me.

Remember, I beseech thee, that thou hast made me as the clay;

And wilt thou bring me into dust again?

Hast thou not poured me out as milk, and curdled[14] me like cheese?

Thou hast clothed me with skin and flesh,

And hast fenced me with bones and sinews.

Thou hast granted me life and favour,

---

1. preserver of men 监察世人的主。
2. mark *n.* (射箭的)靶子
3. a burden to myself 成为自己的重担,意思是厌弃自己的性命。
4. transgression *n.* violation of moral or social boundaries 犯罪
5. I shall not be 我将不在人世。
6. weary *adj.* 厌烦的
7. leave ... upon myself 由着自己(去做)。
8. condemn *vt.* to sentence (sb.) to a particular punishment, especially death 判刑;定罪
9. contend *v.* to assert sth. as a position in an argument 辩争;争论
10. the counsel of the wicked 恶人的计谋。
11. enquirest after mine iniquity 追问我的罪孽。
12. And there is none that can deliver out of thine hand. 这句话的意思是: 你知道没有什么可以救我脱离你的手。
13. fashion *vt.* to make into a particular form 造就;塑造成
14. curdle *vt.* to become congealed 使变成凝乳;凝结

And thy visitation[1] hath preserved my spirit.

And these things hast thou hid in thine heart:

I know that this is with thee.

If I sin, then thou markest[2] me,

And thou wilt not acquit[3] me from mine iniquity.

If I be wicked, woe unto[4] me;

And if I be righteous, yet will I not lift up my head.

I am full of confusion;

Therefore see thou mine affliction;

For it increaseth.

Thou huntest me as a fierce lion:

And again thou shewest thyself marvellous upon me[5].

Thou renewest thy witnesses against me[6],

And increasest thine indignation[7] upon me;

Changes and war are against me.[8]

Wherefore then hast thou brought me forth out of the womb?

Oh that I had given up the ghost, and no eye had seen me!

I should have been as though I had not been;

I should have been carried from the womb to the grave.

Are not my days few? cease then[9], and let me alone,

That I may take comfort a little,

Before I go whence I shall not return,

Even to the land of darkness and the shadow of death;

A land of darkness, as darkness itself;

And of the shadow of death, without any order[10],

And where the light is as darkness." (10)

Part 4

God's Answer to Job

Then the LORD answered Job out of the whirlwind, and said,

"Who is this that darkeneth counsel[11] by words without knowledge?

Gird up now thy loins[12] like a man;

For I will demand of thee, and answer thou me.

Where wast thou when I laid the foundations of the earth?

Declare, if thou hast understanding.

Who hath laid the measures thereof, if thou knowest?

Or who hath stretched the line[13] upon it?

Whereupon are the foundations thereof fastened?

Or who laid the corner stone thereof;

When the morning stars sang together,

And all the sons of God shouted for joy?

Or who shut up the sea with doors,

When it brake[14] forth, as if it had issued[15] out of the womb?

When I made the cloud the garment

---

1. visitation *n.* 巡视；眷顾
2. mark *vt.* to make a visible trace or impression on 打分；做标记
3. acquit *vt.* to free (sb.) from a criminal charge by a verdict of not guilty 赦免
4. woe unto sb. 愿某人遭殃!
5. thou shewest thyself marvellous upon me 你在我身上彰显你的奇能。
6. renewest thy witnesses against me 重立见证(攻击我)。指约伯接二连三遭受的苦楚。
7. indignation *n.* anger or annoyance provoked by what is perceived as unfair treatment 愤怒；愤慨
8. Changes and war are against me. 如派兵轮番发动攻击。
9. cease then 求神住手吧。意思是不要再给我生的时日，让我赶紧死去。
10. without any order 毫无秩序。
11. darkeneth counsel (用无知的言语)使神的旨意暧昧不明。
12. gird up one's loins 本义是"束起腰布"，引申义"准备好行动"。这里指准备好与神答辩。
13. line *n.* 准绳
14. brake *vt.* 〈古〉break 的过去时
15. issue *vi.* to flow out 流出

thereof,

And thick darkness a swaddlingband[1] for it,

And brake up for it my decreed place, and set bars and doors,

And said, 'Hitherto shalt thou come, but no further:

And here shall thy proud waves be stayed?'

Hast thou commanded the morning since thy days[2];

And caused the dayspring[3] to know his place;

That it might take hold of[4] the ends of the earth,

That the wicked might be shaken out of it[5]?

It is turned as clay to the seal[6];

And they[7] stand as a garment.

And from the wicked their light is withholden[8],

And the high arm[9] shall be broken.

Hast thou entered into the springs of the sea?

Or hast thou walked in the search of the depth[10]?

Have the gates of death been opened unto thee?

Or hast thou seen the doors of the shadow of death?

Hast thou perceived the breadth of the earth?

Declare if thou knowest it all.

Where is the way where light dwelleth?

And as for darkness, where is the place thereof,

That thou shouldest take it to the bound[11] thereof,

And that thou shouldest know the paths to the house thereof?

Knowest thou it, because thou wast then born?[12]

Or because the number of thy days is great?

Hast thou entered into the treasures[13] of the snow?

Or hast thou seen the treasures of the hail,

Which I have reserved[14] against the time of trouble, against the day of battle and war?

By what way is the light parted,

Which scattereth the east wind upon the earth?

Who hath divided a watercourse for the overflowing of waters,

Or a way for the lightning of thunder;

To cause it to rain on the earth, where no man is;

On the wilderness, wherein there is no man;

To satisfy the desolate and waste ground;

And to cause the bud of the tender herb to spring forth[15]?

Hath the rain a father?

Or who hath begotten the drops of dew?

Out of whose womb came the ice?

---

1. swaddlingband 包裹布；襁褓
2. since thy days 自从你出生以来。
3. dayspring *n.* 黎明；拂晓
4. take hold of (晨光)照亮。
5. be shaken out it (恶人)被晨光从地极抖掉。
6. It is turned as clay to the seal (有了晨光)地面改变像地上盖上了印戳。
7. they 指地上万象
8. withhold *vt.* to refuse to give (sth. that is due to or is desired by another) 制止；不给。
9. high arm 高举的臂膀，喻指傲慢的人。
10. in the search of the depth 寻找大海的深渊。
11. take it to the bound 把黑暗带回它的本位。bound *n.* 边界。
12. Knowest thou it, because thou wast then born? 你是知道的，因为你已经出生。
13. treasure *n.* 仓库；宝库
14. Which I have reserved 冰和雹乃神的储备，意思是神掌管一切自然力量。
15. spring forth 抽芽；生长。

And the hoary[1] frost of heaven,
Who hath gendered[2] it?
The waters are hid as with a stone[3],
And the face of the deep is frozen …" (38: 1–30)

…

Then Job answered the LORD, and said,
"I know that thou canst do every thing,
And that no thought can be withholden from thee.
Who is he that hideth counsel without knowledge?
Therefore have I uttered that I understood not;
Things too wonderful for me, which I knew not.
Hear, I beseech thee, and I will speak:
I will demand of[4] thee, and declare thou unto me[5].
I have heard of thee by the hearing of the ear:
But now mine eye seeth thee.
Wherefore I abhor myself, and repent in dust and ashes." (42: 1–6)

三、圣经文化知识链接

1. 《约伯记》的哲学思考

一般认为，《约伯记》关注的是"人生受苦的问题"。实际上，作者通过约伯的经历还要探讨一些更深刻、更广阔的议题：上帝的性质、人的性质以及上帝与人的关系。占本书多半篇幅的对话并非学究式的讨论，而是更具高度论辩色彩、探讨人类生存问题的诗体哲学论文。"好人为什么受苦？"这一问题不仅为教内人士所关注，也为历代思想家所瞩目。如瑞士著名心理学家荣格写有《回答约伯》(*Answer to Job*)，从心理学角度试图给予解答；美国知名哲学家乔赛亚·罗伊斯(Josiah Royce, 1855—1916)写了《约伯的问题》(*The Problem of Job*)，力图从自己的哲学立场回答约伯的难题。奥地利现代主义作家卡夫卡不仅身上流淌着希伯来人的血液，他的意识里也汹涌着希伯来圣经中《约伯记》的思想感情。著名圣经学者弗莱(Northrop Frye)评价卡夫卡(Franz Kafka, 1883—1924)时指出，他的全部作品就是对《约伯记》的注解[6]。

2. 从宗教角度看"智慧"

对人生和智慧的探讨，是宗教与哲学的叠合之处，犹如通过两条途径探询同一个问题，但结论不同。从宗教角度来讲，超绝的智慧惟上帝才拥有，而从哲学角度来讲，会得出相反的结论。 这是因为，在历史发展的历程中，当人类对很多自然规律和宇宙奥秘疑惑不解时，就全部将它们归为"上天的奥秘"，也就是《圣经》中所谈到的上帝的智慧。之所以得出这种结论，是与历史发展的阶段和人的认知水平分不开的。总体来讲，这反映了人们对于世界的探讨和认知过

---

1. hoary *adj.* gray or white 灰白色的
2. gender *vt.* to engender 酿成
3. The waters are hid as with a stone 诸水坚硬如石头。指河水冰冻。
4. demand of sb. 提问。
5. declare thou unto me 求你指示我。
6. Frye, Northrop. *Anatomy of Criticism*. Princeton: Princeton University Press, 1957, p.42.

程,体现了先人对智慧的强烈渴望和神化。

《约伯记》第28章13—21节这样论及智慧:"智慧的价值无人能知,在有人之地无处可寻。深渊说,不在我内;沧海说,不在我中。"

智慧从何处来呢?
聪明在哪里呢?
她向一切有生命的眼目隐藏,
也对空中的飞鸟掩蔽。

古希伯来诗人认为,人的智慧无论先天带来还是后天经验中得来,都是上帝恩赐的礼物,因为只有上帝向人启示智慧时,人才能领略她。《约伯记》还论及智慧与上帝的关系:"神明白智慧的道路,晓得智慧的所在。因他监察直到地极,遍观普天之下。……他对人说:'敬畏主就是智慧,远离恶就是聪明。'"这里就涉及智慧的宗教特质方面。

《圣经》中有不少章节论及智慧的宗教特质,认为人的智慧是有限的,因而是不完备的,惟独上帝的智慧是无穷尽的,所以是完全的。上帝的智慧不但彰显于他对世界各个范围的全备认识,而且表现为他必能成就自己的意愿。宇宙万物和人类都是运用智慧的成果,自然界和历史均由他藉智慧来管理。这种智慧既包括分辨善恶的本领,也包括赏善罚恶的能力。"神义论",或叫"业报观"认为,好人肯定得到上帝的恩赐,恶人肯定遭到上帝的惩罚。《约伯记》正是对这种思想提出了质疑。可以说,到了约伯记时期,这种思想受到了挑战,约伯的诘问就是其中的例子。尽管约伯最后归顺上帝,没有动摇神义论,但却对其进行了冲击,对神义论的质疑在《传道书》中又得到了进一步深化。

四、圣经文化专题

1.《约伯记》的戏剧性

戏剧性常常与偶然性、巧合、骤变等现象相联系。虽说《圣经》不是为了搬上舞台而创作的,但《圣经》中处处都充满着戏剧性的冲突。我们在读《圣经》的时候,甚至很容易就可以想象出各个人物说话的抑扬顿挫。这种圣经话语给人们带来的想象往往富有强烈的戏剧性。《圣经》自始至终是一部充满着戏剧性的作品,其中接近于一部舞台剧本的是《约伯记》。约伯记的戏剧性主要体现在以下几点:

第一、《约伯记》中的戏剧性体现在其冲突性上。所谓"没有冲突就没有戏",就是这种观点的通俗表述。本卷书的主题是好人为什么受苦。真正的论证焦点集中在人物性格的冲突之上。其中的辩论给人留下深刻的印象。其中的人物相互影响、相互较量,故事中的戏剧性对话与人物性格冲突十分引人注目。故事更接近舞台上发生的一切。我们甚至可以想象他们辩论时都想说服对方、战胜对方的神态。

第二、《约伯记》的戏剧性体现在骤变上。约伯本来很富有,但祸从天降,体现出一种突发性。另外,本来读者以为约伯胆敢挑战上帝,说自己没有犯罪,上帝肯定会大大惩罚这种胆敢向上帝权威质疑的人。出乎意料的结果是约伯被上帝悦纳且得到赏赐。

第三、从结构上来讲，全书的构思十分精巧，属典范的戏剧体结构。其中的故事缘起是戏剧的开端，约伯和友人的三轮论辩以及以利户的插话是戏剧的发展，上帝和约伯的对话是戏剧的高潮，最后结局是戏剧的尾声，起承转合，脉络分明。

第四、从该卷书的语言来看，论辩部分多因篇幅过长而不宜搬上舞台，但在开端和结局，某些段落极富戏剧语言的特色，如第一章13至19节：这个场面先写四位报信人接连上报凶信，每人都先讲灾情，再说"惟有我一人逃脱，来报信给你"；传报的内容由牲畜、仆人到约伯的儿女，逐层递进。《约伯记》的语言辞藻华丽，句法多变，极富艺术表现力。文中用了夸张的手法，比如，约伯的羊群数量，极富戏剧效果。

就戏剧场面而论，《约伯记》如同经典的古希腊悲剧，场景极其壮阔：上至天上上帝与撒旦的对话，下及人间约伯和朋友们的论辩；故事缘起时，天上密谋和人间灾难两度交替出现，高潮时，上帝和约伯又两次直接交谈，它们都将天与地、神与人连成一个混容的整体。以上帝从旋风中对约伯的答复为例，上帝从旋风中出现，这个场景本身就极具戏剧性，形象生动、逼真。另外，上帝的口气咄咄逼人，使人顿感一种居高临下的威慑力量。读者可以想象到声音的严厉和辩论的铿锵。接着上帝又连发炮似地发出一系列提问，以层出不穷的自然之谜质问得约伯张口结舌，无言以对。

最后，从整体来看，场景的转换从天庭到人间，从人间到天庭，对话的宏大、争辩的激烈及上帝威严的声音效果，富于动感，加之丰富的想象力，所有这些因素都使得《约伯记》具有戏剧性特色和极强的文学价值，同时有力地强化了主题。

2. 从《约伯记》看希伯来人的求索精神

犹太人自古推崇智慧，尊重智者，乐于探索为人处世之道、自然规律和宇宙奥秘。《约伯记》透露出的锲而不舍的探索精神，可以说是犹太民族探索精神的一个缩影。

首先，从叙事结构上来讲，作者不只是进行封闭式的叙述，而是引入一种截然不同的文体形态——智慧对话。智慧对话创造了真理的另外一种表达方式，即真理并不是在一个人的头脑中产生和形成的，它产生于共同寻求真理的群体之间。它只是单单地将所有的声音并置对举，要求读者自己来判断各个声音的有效性。从对话中，我们看到，以利法起码是按理演绎，他的人生观建立在经验之上；比勒达则是基于传统。以利法之人生观是以观察为基础，比勒达之人生观是以传统为基础，而琐法的则是以假设为基础。他们三人的推理方式不同，但是，他们是在进行推理，进行探索。从他们三人与约伯的辩论来看，颇有一种百家争鸣的味道。可以说，以利法代表的是哲学之声，比勒达代表的是历史之声，而琐法代表的则是正统之声。从这个意义上来讲，《圣经》采用他们彼此之间的辩论方式，反映出了当时社会的几种不同思潮的斗争。

其次，《圣经》中善恶报应的伦理原则和上帝的公义形象，在《约伯记》中遇到了有力的挑战。约伯是一个正直虔诚的义人，但在一个极短的时期内，连续遇到巨大的灾难，在丧失全部的家产后，自己也"从脚掌到头顶"受到毒疮、恶疾的折磨与摧残。由此引发的问题是，像约伯这样的义人，为什么会无辜受苦？更进一层，便上升到这样一种思考：即上帝是否是公义的？是否惩恶扬善？于是，约伯向上帝进行了发问：好人为什么受苦？他还明确表示，上帝与人疏远、隔膜和对立，甚至代表人的利益疾呼："愿人得与上帝辩白，如同人与朋友辩白一样。"（约16:21）这些诗行显示出一个无畏的精神探索者形象。为了寻求正义和真理，他不怕皮肉之苦、心灵之痛、亲人疏远、朋友围攻，乃至"至高者"敌视，表现出不屈不挠、孜孜求索的可贵精神，这种发问本身就是求索精神的体现。约伯不再满足于被动地认为上帝的一切言语和行为都是不可置疑的。

另外，从探索的结果来看，《圣经》是承认求索的价值的。因为敢于说实话，富有求索精神，约伯得到了上帝的喜悦。最后约伯在上帝面前驯服了。这个结果在一些人看来可能是生硬而不合逻辑的，但是就希伯来历史文化传统的逻辑来说，这却是完全可以理解的。

再次，从约伯本人来看，他可谓古犹太英勇无畏的精神探索者的典型，其性格特征是勇于探求和敢于反抗。他无视传统，怀疑权威，在寻求正义和维护人权的曲径上艰难行进，纵有皮肉之苦、心灵之痛甚至死亡的威胁，都毫不退缩；即使亲人疏远、朋友围攻乃至"至高者"敌视，也坚持争辩。在当时这种探索精神本身就是极其珍贵的。

《约伯记》中的探索给我们的启示是：宇宙自身的固有本质和人类的存在之间有一种矛盾。不管我们承认与否，这种矛盾是客观存在的，也是无法回避的，二者共同造成了人类存在意义上的悲剧性。在探讨这种矛盾的过程中，人会迷茫、迟疑，甚至误入歧途，但这是通往真理的必经之路。

五、圣经典故集锦

1. **Job's news**（报给约伯的消息）：指"凶讯"、"噩耗"。典出第1章13—19节，约伯家遭难，接二连三报来凶讯。

2. **Job's patience**（约伯的忍耐）：指"极度的忍耐"、"非常克制"。典出第1章20—22节，约伯虽遭受磨难仍克制自己，一如既往地敬神行义。

3. **Naked I came, naked I shall return**（赤身而来、赤身而归）：指"赤条条来去无牵挂"、"身外之物生时带不来、死时带不走"。典出第1章21节，约伯丧失了财产和儿女却泰然处之，对上帝说：Naked came I out of my mother's womb, and naked shall I return thither: the Lord gave, and the Lord hath taken away; blessed be the name of the Lord. 我赤身出于母胎，也必赤身归回。赏赐的是耶和华，收取的也是耶和华。

4. **seek death more eagerly than hidden treasure**（求死胜于求隐藏的珍宝）：指"万念俱灰、只求一死"，"求生不得、求死不成"、"好死胜于赖活着"。典出第3章21节，约伯认为活着受难还不如死：Which long for death, but it cometh not; and dig for it more than for hid treasures. (他们)切望死，却不得死；求死胜于求隐藏的珍宝。

5. **make all my bones to shake, the hair stand on end**（百骨打战、毫毛直立）：指"毛骨悚然"。典出第4章14—15节：Fear came upon me, and trembling, which made all my bones to shake. Then a spirit passed before my face; the hair of my flesh stood up. 恐惧战兢临到我身，使我百骨打战。有灵从我面前经过，我身上的毫毛直立。这是以利法劝约伯之言。

6. **as the sparks fly upward** （如同火星飞腾）：指"在劫难逃"、"不可避免"、"像自然规律那样丝毫不爽"。典出第5章7节，以利法劝约伯之言：Yet man is born unto trouble, as the sparks fly upwards. 人生在世必遇患难，如同火星飞腾。

7. **like the swiftest boat, as fast as an eagle swooping down on a rabbit** （如快船，如急落抓食的鹰）：指"人生如过隙白驹、过眼烟云"，"时如流水、光阴易逝"。典出第9章25至26节：Now my days are swifter than a post: they flee away, they see no good. They are passed away as the swift ships: as the eagle that hasteth to the prey. 这是约伯对人生的感叹："我的日子比跑信的更快，急速过去，不见福乐。我的日子过去如快船，如急落抓食的鹰。"

8. **escape by the skin of one's teeth** （只剩牙皮逃脱了）：指"死里逃生、幸免于难"、"侥幸而逃"。典出第19章20节：My bone cleaveth to my skin and to my flesh, and I am escaped with the skin of my teeth. 我的皮肉紧贴骨头，我只剩牙皮逃脱了。这是约伯在描述自己遭受种种灾难后又身患毒疮这种险恶处境时所说的话。

9. **kiss my own hand** （亲吻己手）：指"自我为大"、"尊重自己"。典出第31章26至28节：If I beheld the sun when it shined, or the moon walking in brightness; And my heart hath been secretly enticed, or my mouth hath kissed my hand. This also were an iniquity to be punished by the judge: for I should have denied the God that is above. 我若见太阳发光，明月行在空中，心就暗暗被引诱，口便亲手。这也是审判官当罚的罪孽，又是我背弃在上的神。这是约伯自责之言。

10. **Job's Leviathan** （约伯的海怪）：典出第41章1—2节：Canst thou draw out leviathan an hook or his tongue with a cord which thou lettest down? Canst thou put an hook into his nose? Or bore his jaw through with a thorn? "你能以鱼钩钓上鳄鱼？以绳索捆住它的舌头？你岂能以鼻圈穿过它的鼻子，以钩子刺透它的腮骨？《简·爱》第15章中就用了这个典故："I will like it," said I, dare like it, and (he subjoined moodily) I will keep my word; I will break obstacles to happiness, to goodness — Yes, goodness; I wish to be a better man than I have been; than I am — as Job's Leviathan broke the spear the dart and the habergeon; hindrances which others count as iron and brass, I will esteem but straw and rotten wood."[1]

六、课堂讨论题

1. 《约伯记》与屈原的《天问》好有一比。你是怎么理解的？
2. 从约伯与上帝争辩中，你体会到了什么样的人文内涵？

---

1. *Jane Eyre*. Airmont Publishing Company, Inc., 1963: 135.

七、课后思考题

1. 传统的叙事性作品常有完整的情节,包括起、承、转、合(或开端、发展、高潮、结局)等部分,有的还有序幕和尾声。请以《约伯记》为例说明这一叙事特征。
2. 许多人认为希伯来文化和希腊罗马文化是西方文化的两大源头,你能从《约伯记》和《圣经》其他章节中解读出来吗?
3. 从比较的视角谈谈圣经悲剧与希腊悲剧。

第九讲 田园牧歌:《路得记》

Ruth, an Idyllic Story

一、导读:《路得记》的舞台剧效果

《路得记》是一部优美的短篇小说。美丽善良的路得本是摩押女子,嫁给了寄居在摩押地的一家犹大人,但不久成了寡妇。婆婆拿俄米返回故乡伯利恒之际,劝路得改嫁,路得却坚持跟随婆婆,赡养其生。在伯利恒,路得靠拾麦穗维持婆媳俩人的生活,遇见麦田的主人、善良的财主波阿斯。波阿斯嘉许路得的美德,给予保护和款待。路得听从婆婆的劝告,按习俗请求波阿斯纳她为妻,为婆婆家续立后嗣。波阿斯接受了请求,与路得喜结良缘。路得婚后生子,成为大卫的曾祖母,被列入犹太人的族谱。《路得记》中最著名的一句话,是路得对婆婆劝自己改嫁时的答复: thy people shall be my people, and thy God my God(你的国就是我的国,你的神就是我的神)。这句话也是《路得记》唯一提到"神"的地方。

《路得记》属于"圣著"类,但具有很强的政治思想倾向。其写作时间是公元前3世纪,而当时写成的两卷书《以斯拉记》(*Ezra*)和《尼西米记》(*Nehemiah*)都宣扬狭隘的民族主义思想,即为了维护血统和宗教信仰的"纯洁"而禁止与外族通婚。《路得记》的作者显然反对这种做法,其写作主旨就是通过路得两次与犹大族人结婚的情节,反对禁止异族通婚的狭隘民族主义,宣扬各民族间的团结。

《路得记》是古希伯来人的一篇田园牧歌,更是一件完整的艺术品,被认为是西方文学短篇小说之祖。它不但有相当的长度("钦定本"英文只有3,000余单词)、相对的独立性、完整的故事情节和情节的起伏发展,而且具备小说体裁的生动人物塑造和复杂人物关系,路得、拿俄米、波阿斯三个主要人物形象鲜明,人物对话在语气和用字上恰如其人身份。全书四章分为四个场景:"婆媳分别"、"路得初遇波阿斯"、"打麦场上"、"城门议亲",颇具舞台艺术效果。《路得记》中有收割庄稼的场景描写,所以这卷书在犹太人的节期中占有特殊地位,每逢"五旬节"(即收割节)要在会堂朗读。

本讲选取《路得记》4个场景:
1. 路得跟随婆婆拿俄米返故乡。
2. 路得在麦田遇见波阿斯。
3. 路得在打麦场向波阿斯求婚。
4. 波阿斯在城门议亲,迎娶路得。

二、选文及注释

Part 1

Ruth Following Naomi[1]

Now it came to pass in the days when the judges ruled, that there was a famine[2] in the land. And a certain of Beth-lehem-judah went to sojourn in the country of Moab[3], he, and his wife, and his two sons. And the name of the man was Elimelech, and the name of his wife Naomi, and the name of his two sons Mahlon and Chilion[4], Ephrathites of Beth-lehem-judah. And they came into the country of Moab, and continued there. And Elimelech Naomi's husband died; and she was left, and her two sons. And they took them wives of the women of Moab; the name of the one was Orpah, and the name of the other Ruth: and they dwelled there about ten years. And Mahlon and Chilion died also both of them; and the woman was left of her two sons and her husband[5].

Then she arose with her daughters in law, that she might return from the country of Moab: for she had heard in the country of Moab how that the LORD had visited his people in giving them bread. Wherefore she went forth out of the place where she was, and her two daughters in law with her; and they went on the way to return unto the land of Judah.

And Naomi said unto her two daughters in law, "Go, return each to her mother's house: the LORD deal kindly with you, as ye have dealt with the dead, and with me. The LORD grant you that ye may find rest, each of you in the house of her husband.[6]"

Then she kissed them; and they lifted up their voice, and wept. And they said unto her, "Surely we will return with thee unto thy people."

And Naomi said, "Turn again, my daughters: why will ye go with me? are there yet any more sons in my womb, that they may be your husbands? Turn again, my daughters, go your way; for I am too old to have an husband. If I should say, I have hope, if I should have an husband also to night, and should also bear sons; would ye tarry for them till they were grown? would ye stay for them from having husbands? nay, my daughters; for it grieveth me for your sakes that the hand of the LORD is gone out against me[7]."

And they lifted up their voice, and wept again: and Orpah kissed her mother in law; but Ruth clave unto her. And she said, "Behold, thy sister in law is gone back unto her people, and unto her gods: return thou after thy sister in law."

And Ruth said, "Intreat me not to leave thee, or to return from following after thee:

---

1. Ruth /ruːθ/(人名)路得，意思是"美丽"。注意：本卷书人物的名字有暗示作用。Naomi /ˈneɪəmɪ/（人名）拿俄米，意思是"甜美"。以利米勒(Elimelech, 意思是"神是王")之妻。
2. famine *n.* extreme scarcity of food 饥荒
3. a certain of Beth-lehem-judah went to sojourn in the country of Moab 一家伯利恒的犹大人寄居在摩押地。摩押地指约旦河东亚嫩河以北的肥沃高原。
4. Mahlon and Chilion 拿俄米两个儿子的名字，"玛伦"是路得的丈夫，名字的意思是"羸弱"；"基连"，意思是"憔悴"。
5. the woman was left of her two sons and her husband 剩下拿俄米没有儿子也没有丈夫。
6. The LORD grant you that ye may find rest, each of you in the house of her husband. 意思是愿耶和华让你们找到新丈夫，过上安定生活。
7. it grieveth me for your sakes that the hand of the LORD is gone out against me 有你们我才愁苦，因为耶和华伸手攻击我。

for whither thou goest, I will go; and where thou lodgest, I will lodge: thy people shall be my people, and thy God my God: where thou diest, will I die, and there will I be buried: the LORD do so to me, and more also, if ought but death part thee and me."

When she saw that she was stedfastly minded to go with her, then she left speaking unto her.

So they two went until they came to Beth-lehem. And it came to pass, when they were come to Beth-lehem, that all the city was moved about them, and they said, "Is this Naomi?"

And she said unto them, "Call me not Naomi, call me Mara¹: for the Almighty² hath dealt very bitterly with me. I went out full, and the LORD hath brought me home again empty³: why then call ye me Naomi, seeing the LORD hath testified against me⁴, and the Almighty hath afflicted⁵ me?"

So Naomi returned, and Ruth the Moabitess, her daughter in law, with her, which returned out of the country of Moab: and they came to Beth-lehem in the beginning of barley harvest. (1)

Part 2

Ruth Encountering Boaz⁶

And Naomi had a kinsman of her husband's, a mighty man of wealth, of the family of Elimelech; and his name was Boaz. And Ruth the Moabitess said unto Naomi, "Let me now go to the field, and glean ears of corn after him in whose sight I shall find grace⁷." And she said unto her, "Go, my daughter." And she went, and came, and gleaned in the field after the reapers: and her hap was to light on a part of the field belonging unto Boaz⁸, who was of the kindred of Elimelech.

And, behold, Boaz came from Beth-lehem, and said unto the reapers, "The LORD be with you." And they answered him, "The LORD bless thee."

Then said Boaz unto his servant that was set over the reapers, "Whose damsel⁹ is this?"

And the servant that was set over the reapers answered and said, "It is the

---

1. Call me not Naomi, call me Mara 不要叫我拿俄米，叫我玛拉吧。"拿俄米"本意是"甜"，而"玛拉"的意思是"苦"。
2. the Almighty 全能者，指上帝。这个名称常见于《约伯记》，意为上帝万能，可降灾惩罚人，而人类无力阻拦。
3. I went out full, and the LORD hath brought me home again empty 意思是我离开家乡时有丈夫和儿子，返回时却孤苦伶仃。
4. seeing the LORD hath testified against me 耶和华降祸于我。seeing conj. 因为；鉴于。testify against 作不利于某人的证明。
5. afflict vt. to cause pain or trouble to 折磨；打击
6. Boaz /ˈbəuæz/ (人名)波阿斯，伯利恒的财主。
7. glean ears of corn after him in whose sight I shall find grace 我蒙谁的恩就在谁身后拾麦穗。按照当时以色列的法律，路得这样的穷人可以在田地里拾取遗留的麦穗。
8. her hap was to light on a part of the field belonging unto Boaz 她碰巧来到波阿斯的一块田里。hap n. 运气；偶然。
9. damsel n. a young unmarried woman ⟨古⟩少女；姑娘

Moabitish damsel that came back with Naomi out of the country of Moab: and she said, 'I pray you, let me glean and gather after the reapers among the sheaves': so she came, and hath continued even from the morning until now, that she tarried a little in the house."

Then said Boaz unto Ruth, "Hearest thou not, my daughter? Go not to glean in another field, neither go from hence, but abide here fast by my maidens: let thine eyes be on the field that they do reap, and go thou after them: have I not charged the young men that they shall not touch thee? and when thou art athirst[1], go unto the vessels, and drink of that which the young men have drawn."

Then she fell on her face, and bowed herself to the ground, and said unto him, "Why have I found grace in thine eyes, that thou shouldest take knowledge of me[2], seeing I am a stranger?"

And Boaz answered and said unto her, "It hath fully been shewed me all that thou hast done unto thy mother in law since the death of thine husband: and how thou hast left thy father and thy mother, and the land of thy nativity, and art come unto a people which thou knewest not heretofore. The LORD recompense[3] thy work, and a full reward be given thee of the LORD God of Israel, under whose wings thou art come to trust."

Then she said, "Let me find favour in thy sight, my Lord; for that thou hast comforted me, and for that thou hast spoken friendly unto thine handmaid, though I be not like unto one of thine handmaidens."

And Boaz said unto her, "At mealtime come thou hither, and eat of the bread, and dip thy morsel in the vinegar[4]."

And she sat beside the reapers: and he reached her parched corn[5], and she did eat, and was sufficed[6], and left. And when she was risen up to glean, Boaz commanded his young men, saying, "Let her glean even among the sheaves, and reproach her not: And let fall also some of the handfuls of purpose for her, and leave them, that she may glean them, and rebuke her not."

So she gleaned in the field until even, and beat out that she had gleaned: and it was about an ephah of barley[7]. And she took it up, and went into the city: and her mother in law saw what she had gleaned: and she brought forth, and gave to her that she had reserved after she was sufficed.

And her mother in law said unto her, "Where hast thou gleaned to day? and where wroughtest[8] thou? blessed be he that did take knowledge of thee."

And she shewed her mother in law with whom she had wrought, and said, "The man's name with whom I wrought to day is Boaz."

And Naomi said unto her daughter in law, "Blessed be he of the LORD, who hath not left off his kindness to the living and to the dead."

And Naomi said unto her, "The man is near of kin unto us, one of our next kinsmen."

And Ruth the Moabitess said, "He said unto me also, 'Thou shalt keep fast by my young men, until they have ended all my harvest.' "

And Naomi said unto Ruth her daughter

---

1. athirst *adj.* thirsty 〈古〉口渴的
2. take knowledge of me 意思是顾恤路得。
3. recompense *vt.* to reward 补偿
4. dip thy morsel in the vinegar 饼蘸醋吃。morsel *n.* a small piece of food 一小块食物。
5. he reached her parched corn 波阿斯递给路得烤麦穗吃。
6. was sufficed 还有剩余。路得把剩下的烤麦穗带回家给了婆婆吃。
7. an ephah of barley 1伊法大麦, 合36公斤。
8. wrought(est) 动词 work 的过去式

in law, "It is good, my daughter, that thou go out with his maidens, that they meet thee not in any other field."

So she kept fast by the maidens of Boaz to glean unto the end of barley harvest and of wheat harvest; and dwelt with her mother in law. (2)

Part 3

Ruth Courting to Boaz

Then Naomi her mother in law said unto her, "My daughter, shall I not seek rest for thee, that it may be well with thee[1]? And now is not Boaz of our kindred[2], with whose maidens thou wast? Behold, he winnoweth[3] barley to night in the threshingfloor. Wash thyself therefore, and anoint thee, and put thy raiment upon thee, and get thee down to the floor: but make not thyself known unto the man, until he shalt have done eating and drinking. And it shall be, when he lieth down, that thou shalt mark the place where he shall lie, and thou shalt go in, and uncover his feet[4], and lay thee down; and he will tell thee what thou shalt do."

And she said unto her, "All that thou sayest unto me I will do."

And she went down unto the floor, and did according to all that her mother in law bade her. And when Boaz had eaten and drunk, and his heart was merry, he went to lie down at the end of the heap of corn: and she came softly, and uncovered his feet, and laid her down. And it came to pass at midnight, that the man was afraid, and turned himself: and, behold, a woman lay at his feet.

And he said, "Who art thou?"

And she answered, "I am Ruth thine handmaid: spread therefore thy skirt over thine handmaid; for thou art a near kinsman."

And he said, "Blessed be thou of the LORD, my daughter: for thou hast shewed more kindness in the latter end than at the beginning, inasmuch as thou followedst not young men, whether poor or rich. And now, my daughter, fear not: I will do to thee all that thou requirest: for all the city of my people doth know that thou art a virtuous woman. And now it is true that I am thy near kinsman: howbeit there is a kinsman nearer than I. Tarry this night, and it shall be in the morning, that if he will perform unto thee the part of a kinsman[5], well; let him do the kinsman's part; but if he will not do the part of a kinsman to thee, then will I do the part of a kinsman to thee, as the LORD liveth: lie down until the morning."

And she lay at his feet until the morning: and she rose up before one could know another[6].

And he said, "Let it not be known that a woman came into the floor." Also he said, "Bring the veil[7] that thou hast upon thee, and hold it."

And when she held it, he measured six measures of barley[8] and laid it on her: and she went into the city. And when she came to her mother in law, she said, "Who art thou, my daughter?"

And she told her all that the man had

---

1. seek rest for thee, that it may be well with thee 为你找个安身之处, 让你享福。拿俄米打算让路得嫁给波阿斯。
2. And now is not Boaz of our kindred 波阿斯不是我们的近亲吗？
3. winnow /ˈwɪnəʊ/ vt. to remove (chaff) from grain 簸；扬(谷)。波阿斯今晚在打谷场上簸大麦。
4. uncover his feet 拿俄米让路得躺在波阿斯的脚旁, 表示路得身份卑微。这可能是当时求婚的习俗。
5. if he will perform unto thee the part of a kinsman 看那人是否愿意履行近亲的义务, 即娶近亲兄弟的遗孀为妻, 为兄弟延续香火。
6. before one could know another 彼此不能辨认的时候, 意思是不到天亮。
7. the veil 指路得的外罩衣。
8. six measures of barley 约24升大麦。

done to her. And she said, "These six measures of barley gave he me; for he said to me, 'Go not empty unto thy mother in law.'"

Then said she, "Sit still, my daughter, until thou know how the matter will fall: for the man will not be in rest, until he have finished the thing this day." (3)

Part 4

Boaz Marrying to Ruth

Then went Boaz up to the gate, and sat him down there: and, behold, the kinsman of whom Boaz spake came by: unto whom he said, "Ho, such a one![1] turn aside, sit down here."

And he turned aside, and sat down. And he took ten men of the elders of the city, and said, "Sit ye down here." And they sat down.

And he said unto the kinsman, "Naomi, that is come again out of the country of Moab, selleth a parcel of land, which was our brother Elimelech's: and I thought to advertise[2] thee, saying, 'Buy it before the inhabitants, and before the elders of my people. If thou wilt redeem it, redeem it[3]': but if thou wilt not redeem it, then tell me, that I may know: for there is none to redeem it beside thee; and I am after thee."

And he said, "I will redeem it."

Then said Boaz, "What day thou buyest the field of the hand of Naomi, thou must buy it also if Ruth the Moabitess, the wife of the dead, to raise up the name of the dead upon his inheritance[4]."

And the kinsman said, "I cannot redeem it for myself, lest I mar[5] mine own inheritance: redeem thou my right to thyself; for I cannot redeem it."

Now this was the manner in former time in Israel concerning redeeming and concerning changing, for to confirm all things; a man plucked off his shoe, and gave it to his neighbour[6]: and this was a testimony in Israel. Therefore the kinsman said unto Boaz, "Buy it for thee." So he drew off his shoe.

And Boaz said unto the elders, and unto all the people, "Ye are witnesses this day, that I have bought all that was Elimelech's, and all that was Chilion's and Mahlon's, of the hand of Naomi. Moreover Ruth the Moabitess, the wife of Mahlon, have I purchased to be my wife, to raise up the name of the dead upon his inheritance, that the name of the dead be not cut off from among his brethren, and from the gate of his place: ye are witnesses this day."

And all the people that were in the gate, and the elders, said, "We are witnesses. The LORD make the woman that is come into thine house like Rachel and like Leah[7], which two did build the house of Israel: and do thou worthily in Ephratah, and be famous in Beth-lehem: and let thy house be like the house of Pharez, whom Tarmar bare unto Judah[8], of the seed which the LORD shall give thee of this young woman."

So Boaz took Ruth, and she was his wife: and when he went in unto her, the LORD gave her conception, and she bare a son.

---

1. Ho, such a one! 作者不愿指出这个人的名字，因此让波阿斯称呼他"某人"。
2. advertise *vt.* to notify (sb.) of sth. 〈古〉告知；提醒
3. redeem it 赎回那块土地。谁要对拿俄米一家尽近亲的义务，就需要赎回她家的田产。
4. raise up the name of the dead upon his inheritance 使死者在产业上留存他的名。注意：要尽作为近亲的义务，不仅要用自家的钱买已死兄弟的田产，还要供养所娶的寡妇和日后共同生育的孩子，而所生孩子和所赎田产都不归在尽义务者名下。所以，尽这样的义务需要无私的精神。
5. mar *vt.* to impair the quality or appearance of; to spoil 毁坏，损坏
6. a man plucked off his shoe, and gave it to his neighbour 意思是脱鞋者自愿放弃优先选择权，转交给别人。
7. like Rachel and like Leah 拉结、利亚姐妹俩是雅各（又称"以色列"）的妻子。
8. the house of Pharez, whom Tarmar bare unto Judah 据《创世记》第38章载，法勒斯是犹大和他玛所生的孪生子之一，后壮大为法勒斯族。大卫和耶稣都是其后裔。

And the women said unto Naomi, "Blessed be the LORD, which hath not left thee this day without a kinsman, that his name may be famous in Israel. And he shall be unto thee a restorer of thy life, and a nourisher of thine old age[1]: for thy daughter in law, which loveth thee, which is better to thee than seven sons, hath born him."

And Naomi took the child, and laid it in her bosom, and became nurse unto it. And the women her neighbours gave it a name, saying, "There is a son born to Naomi." And they called his name Obed: he is the father of Jesse, the father of David[2]." (4)

三、圣经文化知识链接

1. "寡妇内嫁制"与《路得记》

"摩西五经"的末卷《申命记》第24章19节明确了一条关于拾麦穗的"律法"："你们在田里收割谷物后，如果遗下一些在田里，就不要回头去拿来，要留给外族人和孤儿寡妇拾取，好叫上帝使你们凡事蒙福。"路得具有"外族人"和"寡妇"的双重身份，这就为《路得记》的问世埋下了伏笔。《申命记》第25章5—6节的规定："兄弟同居，若死了一个没有儿子，死人的妻子不可出嫁外人，他丈夫的兄弟当尽弟兄的本分娶她为妻，与她同房。妇人生的长子必归死兄的名下，免得他的名字在以色列中涂抹了。"这就是"寡妇内嫁制"，它是远古父系氏族社会流传下来的风俗，对于古代希伯来民族具有特殊的意义。

希伯来人是闪族的一支，自公元前两千年由两河流域迁到迦南地区。在之后的千百年间，他们始终处在异族包围之中，屡遭动荡、迁徙、征服、驱逐，经历了无数次大大小小的民族危机而幸存下来。因此，保持氏族传统和民族的独立性对希伯来人来说始终是性命攸关的问题。"寡妇内嫁制"就这样从氏族时代一直保持下来，甚至具有法定的性质。在《路得记》中，拿俄米和路得都是寡妇。按照这个规矩，波阿斯该娶的是拿俄米，而不是路得。但是，拿俄米已经不能生育了，所以她周围的人，包括那些长老们，都默认了波阿斯和路得在辈分上的替换。路得和波阿斯生的头一个男孩俄备得，一出生就被拿俄米认为养子。

不过，波阿斯在城门议亲时用"买"(buy)字来谈买地，也用"买"字来谈"娶"路得。由此可见，古代以色列女人不仅被当作传宗接代的工具，而且是男人的财产。

"寡妇内嫁制"并非希伯来律法所独有。今日非洲霍屯督人实行的"兄终弟及制"、印度洋安达曼岛民的"妻死娶小姨、夫死嫁小叔"、中国的彝族所谓的"小叔填房式的转房制"等，都是这种氏族社会遗风的反映。

2. 《路得记》的男权意识

《路得记》歌颂了路得和拿俄米的自主性，可谓为妇女的自主行为唱了赞歌。但是，仔细分析整部小说文本，我们还是可以发现其男权意识形态的渗透。先看路得采取自主行为的背景。

---

1. a restorer of thy life, and a nourisher of thine old age 孩子必使你生活充实，必为你养老。nourisher *n.* 养育者。
2. Obed: he is the father of Jesse, the father of David （路得和波阿斯所生的儿子）俄备得，是耶西的父亲。耶西乃是大卫之父。

路得主动接近波阿斯,并与之结为夫妻,为自己的前途作了选择。但这一选择是在她没有了公公、丈夫,同时也没有小叔子的情况下发生的。再看路得采取自主性行为的合法性。路得是通过维护与己有关的男性的利益,来维护自己的权利的。她同波阿斯结婚是为了给自己的先夫留名,她与波阿斯所生的孩子是要继承先夫的姓氏,这样就可以实现为先夫家族传宗接代的目的——而在当时男权制度下妇女的价值主要是通过为男性家族传宗接代而体现的。再从路得自主行为的方式看,她在采取行动时是以合作者的身份出现的。路得追随婆婆,在拾麦穗时与波阿斯相识后,她听从了婆婆的劝告和鼓励才做出主动的求婚行为,委婉的求婚方式也是婆婆教给的。不仅如此,路得还要听从波阿斯的解释,耐心等待一场命运的抉择——波阿斯与她先夫家血缘更近的另一名男性至亲之间。另外,路得的婚姻权利并非攥在自己手中,而是取决于两个男性的最终决定。可见,路得在获得婚姻的过程中,采取的是与相关人员(婆婆、波阿斯、另一个男性)合作的方式,这样,由于男权意识的写作背景,路得的自主行为性质就被淡化了。

四、圣经文化专题

1.《路得记》的意识形态文本性质

《路得记》是一曲超越自我和民族的颂歌,充满人类仁慈、忠诚和爱,又是一部关于妇女的书。拿俄米仁慈、通达、幽默;路得忠贞、贤惠、孝敬;婆媳之间互敬互爱,亲情感人,成为圣经人物廊里两个令人难忘的女性形象。婆媳俩在困境中积极主动,召唤以色列男人承担责任。在故事结尾,是伯利恒的妇女而不是波阿斯或其他男性为路得的儿子命名"俄备得",并解释其出生的意义。这种以真诚为贵的主张与当时占绝对上风的父权制故事形成鲜明的对照。

《路得记》的意识形态文本特征也是很明显的。从《创世记》所开列的族谱来看,摩押人和以色列人本属同一民族血统,摩押人的始祖是罗得被亲生女儿灌醉后乱伦所生的儿子"摩押"。摩押的后代后来定居死海东岸的外约旦平原,建立了自己的国家,崇奉本族的保护神巴力昆珥和基抹,因而被耶和华的子民以色列人视为寇仇,从摩西时代双方就开始对立和冲突。《路得记》中明显提到路得在宗教信仰上的"改宗"。路得坚决地对婆婆拿俄米说:thy people shall be my people, and thy God my God(你的国就是我的国,你的上帝就是我的上帝)。而路得在波阿斯那里听到了安慰的话:The Lord recompense thy work, and a full reward be given thee of the Lord of Israel, under whose wings thou art come to trust(愿上帝报答你,你来投以色列的上帝,在他的翅膀下必得庇佑,愿你得他的赏赐)。这句话可以被看做以色列人对一切其他民族的告白,也是《路得记》文本的意识形态本质:一切外族,甚至以色列人的敌人,只要不崇拜邪神和偶像,改信以色列人的上帝,就能得到耶和华的庇护,就能得到幸福的回报。

2. 结合《路得记》和《圣经》其他章节,谈谈婚姻的神圣性

《圣经》中的爱情观,可以用两个字来表达:一个是"悦"——两情相悦之"悦";另一个是"许"——生死相许之"许"。前者更类似于"欲爱",后者类似于"挚爱"。[1]《雅歌》中更多地

---

1. 参见齐宏伟著:《心有灵犀:欧美文学与信仰传统》,北京:北京大学出版社,2006年,第169页。

表现了两情相悦,对纯真爱情的歌颂、期望和追求。《圣经》其他书卷里也有对夫妻"欲爱"的赞同。如《传道书》(9:9)谈及丈夫当与妻子享受婚姻的快乐:在你一生虚空的年日,就是上帝赐你在日光之下虚空的年日,当同你所爱的妻快活度日,因为那是你生前在日光之下劳碌的事上所得的份。

《路得记》给我们很多启示,婚姻具有神圣性,可谓其中之一。《路得记》歌颂了家庭的价值,故事贯穿始终的主题是寻求一个家,更强调夫妻的"生死相许",歌颂的是婚姻的责任和神圣。在希伯来人看来,婚姻是上帝为人所设立的。正是因为亚当"独居不好",上帝才为他造了伴侣"夏娃"。《圣经》认为婚姻的纽带比父母与子女的关系更为牢固,所以,"人要离开父母,与妻子连合,二人成为一体"(《创世记》2:24—25)。从"二人成为一体"的表述可以看出,男女双方相互委身是婚姻中庄严的承诺。夫妻不再是两个分开的人,而是"合二为一";他们要共同分享生命旅程中所有的幸福与快乐,也要共同承担生命旅程中所有的苦难与悲伤。所以希伯来人对于婚姻持一种欣然接受的态度。在他们看来,没有结婚的人无论男女都不是完整意义上的人。这样,《士师记》耶弗他的女儿,因父亲对上帝发誓的缘故,终生不得婚嫁,"为她终为处女哀哭"达两个月之久(《士师记》11:30—40),就不难理解了。在《以赛亚书》书中,先知以赛亚在论及耶和华的惩罚时说:"你的男丁必倒在刀下;你的勇士必死在阵上……在那日,七个女人必拉住一个男人说:'我们吃自己的食物,穿自己的衣服,但求你许我们归你名下,求你除掉我们的羞耻。'"(《以赛亚书》3:25—4:1)从这段话中可见,没有婚嫁的女人会蒙羞耻。总而言之,希伯来人强调婚姻的重要性,赞美婚姻带来的各种幸福。

在《路得记》中,路得和丈夫可谓生死相许。在丈夫离世后,她把这种对丈夫的责任转移到婆婆的身上。因为路得的丈夫没有弟弟,另外,婆婆拿俄米也不可能再生儿子作为路得未来的丈夫。那么,路得弃婆婆而留在自己的本土和国家,于情于理都无可厚非,但是她毅然选择了陪同婆婆,这也从另一个层面说明了她对婚姻的珍视。

《路得记》所反映的希伯来人对婚姻神圣性的态度,被基督教所继承。这可以在基督教国家教堂婚礼的誓言中体现出来。许多人在教堂举行婚礼,体现出婚礼的神圣性。人们从影视上看到教堂婚礼的场面,不由得产生向往之情。证婚牧师与新人的对话更是令人神往:

I, ××× take thee ×××, to my wedded husband, to have and to hold from this day forward, for better or worse, for richer or poorer, in sickness, and in health, to love, cherish, and to obey, till death us do part, according to God's holy ordinance; and thereto I give thee my troth. 我,某某,以你,某某,为缔婚的丈夫,从今天起,无论顺境或逆境,无论丰裕或饥馑,无论健康或疾病,我都爱恋你、珍惜你、服从你,只有死才将我们分离,按照上帝的仪式,我把忠诚交给你。

新娘发誓结束,男子重说一遍誓词,只是在念到 to obey 时改为 I plight thee my troth (我发誓对你忠诚),然后互戴戒指,新人要说:With this ring I thee wed, with my body I thee worship, and with all my worldly goods I thee endow. 随着这枚戒指我与你结婚,我用我的身体来崇拜你,我把我世上所有的财产都给予你。

基督教认为,婚姻是上帝赐给人类的神圣礼物。新人在教堂庄严、肃穆的气氛中缔结婚姻,面对上帝的代言人牧师宣告自己的婚姻誓言,体现了他们对"一夫一妻"婚姻观念的坚守和对家庭义务的重视。近年来在中国,新人到民政部门登记结婚时,登记员模仿教堂婚礼中牧师的角色,向新郎和新娘提出相关问题(无神论的问题)。新人在郑重回答这些问题时,想必能感受到婚姻的神圣。

五、圣经典故集锦

1. **Mara** (玛拉):指"苦命之人"。典出《路得记》第1章20—21节: And she said unto them, Call me not Naomi, call me Mara: for the Almighty hath dealt very bitterly with me." "满载而出, 空空而归",拿俄米回到故乡时不让乡亲们称她寓意"甜"的Naomi,而让大家叫她 Mara, 意思是"苦",因为此时她已经失去丈夫和两个儿子。"玛拉"指"苦命之人"。

2. **put off his sandal and give it to the other party** (脱鞋给人):指"自动弃权,义无反悔","拍板定夺"、"一锤定音"。典出《路得记》第4章7—8节: Now this was the manner in former time in Israel concerning redeeming and concerning changing, for to confirm all things; a man plucked off his shoe, and gave it to his neighbour: and this was a testimony in Israel. 从前,在以色列中要定夺什么事,或赎回,或交易,这人就脱鞋给那人。以色列人都以此为证据。按照古以色列对财产赎回或交易事项的习俗,放弃者应该脱下鞋子交给承担者,作为凭证。

3. *文学家和诗人对《路得记》的引用*:法国文豪雨果在其诗作 *Booz Endormi* 描写了波阿斯和路得的爱情故事。雨果一改波阿斯有恩于路得的传统认识,认为路得有恩于波阿斯。雨果以浪漫主义笔触写出路得的天真、单纯和童趣。在草影迷蒙的麦场上,波阿斯早已进入梦乡,路得却在沉思。群星闪烁,点缀着漫无边际的夜空,一钩明亮的新月高挂于西天,这时的路得:

> 透过面纱,半张着眼,在仰望重霄,
> 哪个神?哪个农夫?在此永恒的夏天,
> 收获后,马而虎之,回家时,心不在焉,
> 在星星的麦田里丢下金色的镰刀?[1]

英国浪漫主义诗人济慈(John Keats, 1795—1821)在抒情诗 *Ode to a Nightingale* (《夜莺颂》)第7节写道:

> Perhaps the self-same song that found a path
> Through the sad heart of Ruth, when sick for home,
> She stood in tears amid the alien corn;

诗人从自己听到的夜莺之歌联想到在异乡麦田上拾麦穗的路得:她情系故土,心中忧

---

[1] 参见梁工的文章"古犹太民族的和谐社会理想——以《路得记》为例",载于《世界宗教文化》,2008年第2期,第12页。

伤，默默流泪，仿佛听到了同样令人惆怅的夜莺之歌。

英国浪漫主义诗人拜伦在《唐璜》第13章96节把追求真理比作路得拾麦穗：

> But from being farmers, we turn gleaners, gleaning
> The scanty but right-well thresh'd ears of truth;
> And, gentle reader! when you gather meaning,
> You may be Boaz, and I — modest Ruth
>
> 但我们从农夫变为拾麦穗的了，
> 只要见到真理的谷粒就捡拾。
> 亲爱的读者！我这样东拾西捡，
> 真像可怜的露斯[1]，而您是波阿斯。

六、课堂讨论题

1. 《路得记》被人称为"史诗体牧歌"，你认同吗？
2. 谈谈《路得记》在整部《圣经》结构编排中的美学意义。
3. 分析《路得记》的叙事美学特征。

七、思考题

1. 结合亚伯拉罕的故事谈谈路得的冒险精神。
2. 中外民俗和文学中都有"鞋子"的隐语，暗喻男女两性间的情事。试举例说明。
3. 赏析海耶兹的油画《路得拾穗》。

---

1. 即路得——编者注。

第十讲 宫廷小说：《以斯帖记》

Esther, a Court Story

一、导读

《以斯帖记》(*Esther*)是希伯来圣经中唯一没有提及"上帝"的一卷书。"以斯帖"('ester)原文为波斯文，意思是"星"，喻指众女子之中的明星。本书的写作主旨是介绍犹太人"普珥节"(Purim)的来历。

以斯帖的故事发生在约公元前470年左右的以斯拉时代，正值波斯帝国鼎盛之际，其王为薛西斯一世(Xerxes I)，在《以斯帖记》中被称为"亚哈随鲁"(Ahasuerus)。亚哈随鲁王下诏在全国挑选美女为后，犹太美貌女子以斯帖当选入宫，并被册立为后。以斯帖的养父末底改因拒不跪拜，得罪了权臣哈曼。哈曼怀恨在心，阴谋灭绝国内所有的犹太人。以斯帖得知严重的事态，违反禁例而求见亚哈随鲁王。以斯帖在招待王的宴会上揭露哈曼的阴谋，哈曼自食其果，被送上自己本来为末底改准备的绞架上，末底改擢升宰相之职，犹太人杀戮仇敌，定立"普珥日"，以纪念本民族躲过劫难。后世犹太人于"普珥节"在会堂朗读《以斯帖记》。

《以斯帖记》是一部以宫廷生活为背景的斗智小说，情节曲折，人物生动。以斯帖容貌端丽，遇事明断，镇静自若，舍己救人，被誉为古今女子的模范。"需要我死，就让我死吧"(if I perish, I perish)是以斯帖的名言。

《以斯帖记》共10章。选文从第2章开始，选取5部分：
1. 以斯帖被立为王后。
2. 哈曼计谋除灭犹太人。
3. 以斯帖决定冒死见王。
4. 以斯帖智胜哈曼。
5. "普珥节"的设立。

二、选文及注释

Part 1

Esther Becoming the Queen

After these things, when the wrath of King Ahasuerus[1] was appeased[2], he remembered Vashti[3], and what she had done, and what was decreed against her.[4]

Then said the king's servants that mini-

---

1. Ahasuerus /əˌhæzjuˈərəs/（人名）亚哈随鲁，波斯国王，以斯帖的故事发生在他继位的第3年
2. appease *vt.* to bring calm to; to soothe 平息
3. Vashti /ˈvæʃtaɪ/（人名）瓦实提，波斯王后
4. what was decreed against her 王降旨废去瓦实提的王后之位。decree *vt.* 颁令；*n.* 法令；判决。尤指国家最高领导人颁布的法令

stered unto him, "Let there be fair young virgins sought for the king: and let the king appoint officers in all the provinces of his kingdom[1], that they may gather all the fair young virgins unto Shushan[2] the palace, to the house of the women, unto the custody of Hege the king's chamberlain, keeper of the women[3]; and let their things for purification[4] be given them, and let the maiden which pleaseth the king be queen instead of Vashti."

And the thing pleased the king; and he did so.

Now in Shushan the palace there was a certain Jew, whose name was Mordecai[5], the son of Jair, the son of Shimei, the son of Kish, a Benjamite; who had been carried away from Jerusalem with the captivity which had been carried away with Jeconiah king of Judah, whom Nebuchadnezzar the king of Babylon had carried away[6]. And he brought up Hadassah, that is, Esther[7], his uncle's daughter: for she had neither father nor mother, and the maid was fair and beautiful; whom Mordecai, when her father and mother were dead, took for his own daughter.

So it came to pass, when the king's commandment and his decree was heard, and when many maidens were gathered unto Shushan the palace, to the custody of Hegai, that Esther was brought also unto the king's house, to the custody of Hegai, keeper of the women.

And the maiden pleased him, and she obtained kindness of him; and he speedily gave her her things for purification, with such things as belonged to her, and seven maidens, which were meet to be given her, out of the king's house: and he preferred her and her maids unto the best place of the house of the women. Esther had not showed her people nor her kindred[8]: for Mordecai had charged her that she should not shew it. And Mordecai walked every day before the court of the women's house, to know how Esther did, and what should become of her.

---

1. all the provinces of his kingdom 波斯王朝的疆域广大，东至印度西北的印度河，西至古实，即北苏丹。共127个"省"，但各"省"可能是按种族居住地划分的。
2. Shushan /ˈʃuːʃæn/ （地名）书珊，波斯王朝的都城，位于波斯西南，距波斯湾约240公里
3. custody of Hege the king's chamberlain, keeper of the women 王的太监希该（下文写作 Hegai），掌管内宫女眷。custody n. 监管；保管。chamberlain n. （国王的）侍从。
4. purification n. the state of being clean and purified 洁净。下文谈及，入选的美女必须用香料洁身，并进行美容按摩才得见国王，从这些描写可以看出当时的美容发展水平和对美容的注重。
5. Mordecai /ˈmɔːdəkaɪ/ 末底改，便雅悯人基士的曾孙、示每的孙子、睚珥的儿子（the son of Jair, the son of Shimei, the son of Kish, a Benjamite）。可能的情况是，末底改的曾祖父那代人被掳至巴比伦。
6. who had been carried away from Jerusalem with the captivity which had been carried away with Jeconiah king of Judah, whom Nebuchadnezzar the king of Babylon had carried away 巴比伦王尼布甲撒将犹大王耶哥尼雅和百姓从耶路撒冷掳走时，末底改也在其中。
7. Hadassah /həˈdɑːsə/, that is, Esther /ˈestə/ 以斯帖的希伯来名字"哈大沙"，为希伯来一种植物的名字。
8. Esther had not showed her people nor her kindred 以斯帖没有显露自己的籍贯和宗族。

Now when every maid's turn was come to go in to King Ahasuerus, after that she had been twelve months, according to the manner of the women (for so were the days of their purifications accomplished, to wit[1], six months with oil of myrrh, and six months with sweet odours, and with other things for the purifying of the women); then thus came every maiden unto the king; whatsoever she desired was given her to go with her out of the house of the women unto the king's house. In the evening she went, and on the morrow she returned into the second house of the women[2], to the custody of Shaashgaz, the king's chamberlain, which kept the concubines: she came in unto the king no more, except the king delighted in her, and that she were called by name.

Now when the turn of Esther, the daughter of Abihail the uncle of Mordecai, who had taken her for his daughter, was come to go in unto the king, she required nothing but what Hegai the king's chamberlain, the keeper of the women, appointed. And Esther obtained favour in the sight of all them that looked upon her. So Esther was taken unto King Ahasuerus into his house royal in the tenth month, which is the month Tebeth[3], in the seventh year of his reign.

And the king loved Esther above all the women, and she obtained grace and favour in his sight more than all the virgins; so that he set the royal crown upon her head, and made her queen instead of Vashti. Then the king made a great feast unto all his princes[4] and his servants, even Esther's feast; and he made a release to the provinces[5], and gave gifts, according to the state of the king. And when the virgins were gathered together the second time, then Mordecai sat in the king's gate. Esther had not yet shewed her kindred nor her people; as Mordecai had charged her: for Esther did the commandment of Mordecai, like as when she was brought up with him.

In those days, while Mordecai sat in the king's gate, two of the king's chamberlains, Bigthan and Teresh, of those which kept the door, were wroth, and sought to lay hand on the king Ahasuerus. And the thing was known to Mordecai, who told it unto Esther the queen; and Esther certified the king thereof in Mordecai's name. And when inquisition was made of the matter[6], it was found out; therefore they were both hanged on a tree: and it was written in the book of the chronicles[7] before the king. (2)

Part 2

Haman[8]'s Plot for Killing the Jews

After these things did King Ahasuerus promote Haman the son of Hammedatha the Agagite, and advanced[9] him, and set his seat above all the princes that were with him. And all the king's servants, that were in the king's gate, bowed, and reverenced[10] Haman: for the king had so commanded

---

1. **to wit** that is to say; namely 也就是说。
2. **the second house of the women** 第二院，可能是内宫的一部分，王的嫔妃的居所。
3. **Tebeth** (犹太历) 提别月
4. **his princes** 国王的亲贵。
5. **made a release to the provinces** 免去各省的赋税。
6. **inquisition was made of the matter** 正常语序为: inquisition of the matter was made 事情被调查清楚。
7. **the book of the chronicles** 国史书。
8. **Haman** /ˈheɪmæn/ the son of Hammedatha the Agagite 王抬举亚甲族哈米大他的儿子哈曼。亚甲族是亚玛力王亚甲的后裔，而亚玛力人是犹太人的仇敌，是受诅咒的民族。这似乎可以解释末底改不肯给哈曼跪拜的原因。另外，末底改不下跪的原因还在于犹太教信仰。不能敬拜偶像，不能敬拜任何人。下跪是敬拜的一种表示。
9. **advance** *vt.* to promote to a higher rank 提升；使升级
10. **reverence** *vt.* to show respect to 致敬；*n.* an act showing respect, especially a bow or curtsy 尊敬。该词是正式用语。

concerning him. But Mordecai bowed not, nor did him reverence. Then the king's servants, which were in the king's gate, said unto Mordecai, "Why transgressest[1] thou the king's commandment?"

Now it came to pass, when they spoke daily unto him, and he hearkened not unto them, that they had told Haman, to see whether Mordecai's matters would stand: for he had told them that he was a Jew. And when Haman saw that Mordecai bowed not, nor did him reverence, then was Haman full of wrath. And he thought scorn to lay hands on Mordecai alone; for they had shewed him the people of Mordecai: wherefore Haman sought to destroy all the Jews that were throughout the whole kingdom of Ahasuerus, even the people of Mordecai.

In the first month, that is, the month Nisan, in the twelfth year of king Ahasuerus, they cast Pur, that is, the lot, before Haman from day to day, and from month to month, to the twelfth month, that is the month Adar[2]. And Haman said unto King Ahasuerus, "There is a certain people scattered abroad and dispersed[3] among the people in all the provinces of thy kingdom; and their laws are diverse from all people; neither keep they the king's laws: therefore it is not for the king's profit to suffer them[4]. If it please the king, let it be written that they may be destroyed: and I will pay ten thousand talents of silver[5] to the hands of those that have the charge of the business, to bring it into the king's treasuries."

And the king took his ring from his hand, and gave it unto Haman[6] the son of Hammedatha the Agagite, the Jews' enemy. And the king said unto Haman, "The silver is given to thee, the people also, to do with them as it seemeth good to thee."

Then were the king's scribes[7] called on the thirteenth day of the first month, and there was written according to all that Haman had commanded unto the king's lieutenants[8], and to the governors that were over every province, and to the rulers of every people of every province according to the writing thereof, and to every people after their language; in the name of King Ahasuerus was it written, and sealed with the king's ring.

And the letters were sent by posts into all the king's provinces, to destroy, to kill, and to cause to perish[9], all Jews, both young and old, little children and women, in one day, even upon the thirteenth day of the twelfth month, which is the month Adar, and to take the spoil of them for a prey[10]. The copy of the writing for a commandment to be given in every province was published unto all people, that they should be ready against that day[11]. The posts went out, being hastened by the king's commandment, and the decree

---

1. transgress *vt.* to commit an offense by violating a law or command 违反。常用于违反宗教律例等。
2. the month Adar /ˈeɪdɑː/ 犹太历第12个月份"亚达月"，在公历2、3月间，共29或30天。
3. disperse *vt.* to scatter 分散
4. it is not for the king's profit to suffer them 容留他们于王无益。suffer *vt.* to tolerate 〈古〉容许；容留。
5. ten thousand talents of silver 1万他连得银子。talent *n.*(计量单位)他连得，使用于古代希腊、罗马和中东的一种重量和货币单位。作重量单位时，1他连得约36公斤。因此1万他连得时值不菲，约当时波斯王朝1年税收的三分之二。根据故事猜测，这个数目大概是哈曼的财产，也可能是哈曼预计可以从消灭的犹太人那里捞回的财产数量。
6. the king took his ring from his hand, and gave it unto Haman 王把戒指给了哈曼使用。王的戒指有类似玉玺的作用，盖有王戒图案的文书代表王命。所以王把戒指给哈曼，是一种象征，象征着王给哈曼权力。
7. king's scribes 王宫的书记员。
8. king's lieutenants 王的总督。
9. perish *vt.* to destroy 灭绝；毁灭。该词比 destroy 更富诗意。从这些词语的选择和用法，我们可以看出钦定本英语的诗意。
10. take the spoil of them for a prey 掠夺犹太人的财物。spoil *n.* 〈古〉掠夺之物。prey *n.* 掠夺。
11. published unto all people, that they should be ready against that day 宣告给各族，让他们到那日有所准备。

was given in Shushan the palace. And the king and Haman sat down to drink; but the city Shushan was perplexed[1]. (3)

Part 3

Esther's Decision

When Mordecai perceived all that was done, Mordecai rent his clothes, and put on sackcloth with ashes[2], and went out into the midst of the city, and cried with a loud and a bitter cry; and came even before the king's gate; for none might enter into the king's gate clothed with sackcloth. And in every province, whithersoever the king's commandment and his decree came, there was great mourning among the Jews, and fasting, and weeping, and wailing; many lay in sackcloth and ashes.

So Esther's maids and her chamberlains came and told it her. Then was the queen exceedingly grieved; and she sent raiment to clothe Mordecai, and to take away his sackcloth from him: but he received it not.

Then called Esther for Hatach, one of the king's chamberlains, whom he had appointed to attend upon her, and gave him a commandment to Mordecai, to know what it was, and why it was. So Hatach went forth to Mordecai unto the street of the city, which was before the king's gate. And Mordecai told him of all that had happened unto him, and of the sum of the money that Haman had promised to pay to the king's treasuries for the Jews, to destroy them. Also he gave him the copy of the writing of the decree that was given at Shushan to destroy them, to shew it unto Esther, and to declare it unto her, and to charge her that she should go in unto the king, to make supplication[3] unto him, and to make request before him for her people. And Hatach came and told Esther the words of Mordecai.

Again Esther spake unto Hatach, and gave him commandment unto Mordecai; "All the king's servants, and the people of the king's provinces, do know, that whosoever, whether man or woman, shall come unto the king into the inner court, who is not called, there is one law of his to put him to death, except such to whom the king shall hold out the golden sceptre[4], that he may live: but I have not been called to come in unto the king these thirty days." And they told to Mordecai Esther's words.

Then Mordecai commanded to answer Esther, "Think not with thyself that thou shalt escape in the king's house, more than all the Jews. For if thou altogether holdest thy peace at this time, then shall there enlargement and deliverance arise to the Jews from another place[5]; but thou and thy father's house shall be destroyed: and who knoweth whether thou art come to the kingdom for such a time as this?[6]"

Then Esther bade them return Mordecai this answer, "Go, gather together all the Jews that are present in Shushan, and fast ye for me, and neither eat nor drink three days,

---

1. perplexed *adj.* baffled or confused 混乱的。注意此处上下文的讽刺意味，犹太人都痛哭，而王和哈曼却高兴得饮酒。这些铺垫，对以后事态的逆向发展尤其重要。
2. rent his clothes, and put on sackcloth with ashes 撕裂衣服，穿麻衣，蒙灰尘。古时表示极度哀伤和受耻辱的举动。
3. supplication *n.* begging or asking for sth. earnestly or humbly 恳求
4. golden sceptre 国王的权杖、金杖，象征王权。
5. shall there enlargement and deliverance arise to the Jews from another place （此刻你保持沉默）犹太人必从别处获得解脱和拯救。在这关键时刻，如果以斯帖不敢冒险求王以救民命，也许犹太人从别处获得拯救。有学者认为，从别处得到拯救可能暗指上帝庇佑。注意这句话中的威胁语气和言外之意。其言外之意是你现在什么都不需要考虑，马上行动。
6. who knoweth whether thou art come to the kingdom for such a time as this? 岂知你得了王后的名分不是为了眼下的危难吗？意思是以斯帖贵为王后的最终使命是在危难时刻解救整个民族。

night or day: I also and my maidens will fast likewise; and so will I go in unto the king, which is not according to the law: and if I perish, I perish."

So Mordecai went his way, and did according to all that Esther had commanded him. (4)

Now it came to pass on the third day, that Esther put on her royal apparel, and stood in the inner court of the king's house, over against the king's house: and the king sat upon his royal throne in the royal house, over against the gate of the house. And it was so, when the king saw Esther the queen standing in the court, that she obtained favour in his sight: and the king held out to Esther the golden sceptre that was in his hand. So Esther drew near, and touched the top of the sceptre.

Then said the king unto her, "What wilt thou, queen Esther? and what is thy request? it shall be even given thee to the half of the kingdom."

And Esther answered, "If it seem good unto the king, let the king and Haman come this day unto the banquet that I have prepared for him."

Then the king said, "Cause Haman to make haste, that he may do as Esther hath said."

So the king and Haman came to the banquet that Esther had prepared.

And the king said unto Esther at the banquet of wine, "What is thy petition? and it shall be granted thee: and what is thy request? even to the half of the kingdom it shall be performed."

Then answered Esther, and said, "My petition and my request is: If I have found favour in the sight of the king, and if it please the king to grant my petition, and to perform my request, let the king and Haman come to the banquet that I shall prepare for them, and I will do to morrow as the king hath said."

Then went Haman forth that day joyful and with a glad heart: but when Haman saw Mordecai in the king's gate, that he stood not up, nor moved for him, he was full of indignation against Mordecai. Nevertheless Haman refrained himself: and when he came home, he sent and called for his friends, and Zeresh his wife. And Haman told them of the glory of his riches, and the multitude of his children, and all the things wherein the king had promoted him, and how he had advanced him above the princes and servants of the king.

Haman said moreover, "Yea, Esther the queen did let no man come in with the king unto the banquet that she had prepared but myself; and to morrow am I invited unto her also with the king. Yet all this availeth[1] me nothing, so long as I see Mordecai the Jew sitting at the king's gate."

Then said Zeresh his wife and all his friends unto him, "Let a gallows be made of fifty cubits high[2], and to morrow speak thou unto the king that Mordecai may be hanged thereon: then go thou in merrily with the king unto the banquet."

And the thing pleased Haman; and he caused the gallows to be made. (5)

Part 4

Esther's Victory Over Haman

On that night could not the king sleep, and he commanded to bring the book of records of the chronicles; and they were read before the king. And it was found written, that Mordecai had told of Bigthana and Teresh, two of the king's chamberlains, the

---

1. avail *vt.* to help or benefit 有益于。哈曼一看见末底改坐在朝门(不敬服他)，一切的荣耀也不令他感到高兴。
2. gallows be made of fifty cubits high 23米高的木绞架，相当于当时城墙的高度，约相当于现在八层楼的高度。注意这里的夸张用法。《以斯帖记》中有很多夸张的用法，如第一章关于宫殿和宴会的描写。cubit *n.* 肘尺。一种古代长度单位，自肘至中指端，长约18至22英寸。

keepers of the door, who sought to lay hand on the king Ahasuerus.

And the king said, "What honour and dignity hath been done to Mordecai for this?"

Then said the king's servants that ministered unto him, "There is nothing done for him."

And the king said, "Who is in the court?"

Now Haman was come into the outward court of the king's house, to speak unto the king to hang Mordecai on the gallows that he had prepared for him. and the king's servants said unto him, "Behold, Haman standeth in the court."

And the king said, "Let him come in."

So Haman came in. and the king said unto him, "What shall be done unto the man whom the king delighteth to honour?"

Now Haman thought in his heart, "To whom would the king delight to do honour more than to myself?" And Haman answered the king, "For the man whom the king delighteth to honour, let the royal apparel be brought which the king useth to wear, and the horse that the king rideth upon, and the crown royal which is set upon his head; and let this apparel and horse be delivered to the hand of one of the king's most noble princes, that they may array the man withal whom the king delighteth to honour[1], and bring him on horseback through the street of the city, and proclaim before him, 'Thus shall it be done to the man whom the king delighteth to honour.'"

Then the king said to Haman, "Make haste, and take the apparel and the horse, as thou hast said, and do even so to Mordecai the Jew, that sitteth at the king's gate. Let nothing fail of all that thou hast spoken.[2]"

Then took Haman the apparel and the horse, and arrayed Mordecai, and brought him on horseback through the street of the city, and proclaimed before him, "Thus shall it be done unto the man whom the king delighteth to honour."

And Mordecai came again to the king's gate. But Haman hasted to his house mourning, and having his head covered. And Haman told Zeresh his wife and all his friends every thing that had befallen him.

Then said his wise men and Zeresh his wife unto him, "If Mordecai be of the seed of the Jews, before whom thou hast begun to fall, thou shalt not prevail against him, but shalt surely fall before him.[3]"

And while they were yet talking with him, came the king's chamberlains, and hasted to bring Haman unto the banquet that Esther had prepared. (6)

So the king and Haman came to banquet with Esther the queen. And the king said again unto Esther on the second day at the banquet of wine, "What is thy petition, queen Esther? and it shall be granted thee: and what is thy request? and it shall be performed, even to the half of the kingdom."

Then Esther the queen answered and said, "If I have found favour in thy sight, O king, and if it please the king, let my life be given me at my petition, and my people at my request[4]: for we are sold, I and my people, to be destroyed, to be slain, and to perish. But if we had been sold for bondmen and bondwomen, I had held my tongue, although the enemy could not countervail

---

1. array the man withal whom the king delighteth to honour 给王喜悦的这个人穿上王常穿的朝服作为赏赐。withal (whom) *prep.* 相当于 with。
2. Let nothing fail of all that thou hast spoken. 凡你所说的一样也不要缺。动词 fail 前置是为了句子的平衡。fail *vt.* to leave (sth.) undone; to neglect 疏忽；忘记。
3. If Mordecai ... fall before him. 这句话的意思是，因为末底改是犹太人，哈曼则会败给他。小说中没有交代其中的逻辑。我们认为这种逻辑可能有两种：一是犹太人很聪明，所以与其为敌，必败无疑；二是他们对犹太人的上帝有所了解，也说明犹太人的上帝威名四海，无所不能，与其子民斗法必败无疑。
4. let my life be given me at my petition, and my people at my request 我所求的是愿王保全我的性命，我所愿的是王保全我的族人。

the king's damage[1]".

The the king Ahasuerus answered and said unto Esther the queen, "Who is he, and where is he, that durst[2] presume in his heart to do so?"

And Esther said, "The adversary[3] and enemy is this wicked Haman." Then Haman was afraid before the king and the queen.

And the king arising from the banquet of wine in his wrath went into the palace garden: and Haman stood up to make request for his life to Esther the queen; for he saw that there was evil determined against him by the king[4].

Then the king returned out of the palace garden into the place of the banquet of wine; and Haman was fallen upon the bed whereon Esther was. Then said the king, "Will he force the queen also before me in the house?"

As the word went out of the king's mouth, they covered Haman's face. And Harbonah, one of the chamberlains, said before the king, "Behold also, the gallows fifty cubits high, which Haman had made for Mordecai, who had spoken good for the king, standeth in the house of Haman."

Then the king said, "Hang him thereon."

So they hanged Haman on the gallows that he had prepared for Mordecai. Then was the king's wrath pacified. (7)

Part 5

Observing the Purim[5]

Now in the twelfth month, that is, the month Adar, on the thirteenth day of the same when the king's commandment and his decree drew near to be put in execution[6], in the day that the enemies of the Jews hoped to have power over them, (though it was turned to the contrary, that the Jews had rule over them that hated them;) the Jews gathered themselves together in their cities throughout all the provinces of the king Ahasuerus, to lay hand on such as sought their hurt[7]: and no man could withstand[8] them; for the fear of them fell upon all people. And all the rulers of the provinces, and the lieutenants[9], and the deputies[10], and officers of the king, helped the Jews; because the fear of Mordecai fell upon them. For Mordecai was great in the king's house, and his fame went out throughout all the provinces: for this man Mordecai waxed[11] greater and greater. And the Jews smote all their enemies with the stroke of the sword, and slaughter, and destruction, and did what they would unto those that hated them. And in Shushan the palace the Jews slew and destroyed five hundred men. (9: 1–6)

And Mordecai wrote these things, and sent letters unto all the Jews that were in all the provinces of the king Ahasuerus, both nigh and far, to stablish[12] this among them, that they should keep the fourteenth day of the month Adar, and the fifteenth day of the same, yearly, as the days wherein the Jews rested[13] from their enemies, and the month which was turned unto them from sorrow to joy, and from mourning into a good day:

---

1. countervail the king's damage 补偿王的损失。意思是，若我和我的族人被灭绝，对王来说也是巨大损失。
2. durst 〈古〉动词 dare (敢)的过去式和过去分词。
3. adversary *n.* an enemy 敌人
4. that there was evil determined against him by the king 王定意要加罪于他。
5. Purim /ˈpjuərɪm/ *n.* (犹太教节日)普珥日，又称"掣签节"
6. put in execution 颁布施行。
7. such as sought their hurt 那些想加害于他们的敌人。
8. withsatnd *vt.* to resist 〈古〉反抗
9. lieutenant *n.* 指总督
10. deputy *n.* 省长
11. wax *vi.* to become larger and stronger (文学用法)名声日隆
12. stablish *vt.* to establish 〈古〉使坚固
13. rest *vt.* 指得救；得平安

that they should make them days of feasting and joy, and of sending portions[1] one to another, and gifts to the poor. (9: 20–22)

三、圣经文化知识链接

1. "普珥节"

Purim 原为波斯文，意思是"掣签"，源自《以斯帖记》中记载的哈曼"掣签"而决定在亚达月(12月)13日诛灭波斯全境的犹太人。以斯帖和末底改经过努力，反败为胜，借助王除掉了哈曼，并于亚达月13、14两日剪除哈曼死党和犹太人所有仇敌，从此，把亚达月14、15两日定为"普珥节"，以庆祝犹太人取得这次决定其民族命运的胜利。犹太人每年在亚达月13日先禁食一天，称为"以斯帖斋"。到了夜晚，所有的人都去会堂参加集会。14、15日，人们再度集聚会堂，诵读、聆听《以斯帖记》。节日期间，人们互赠礼物，大摆宴席，开怀畅饮。"普珥节"(Festival of Purim)后来成了以色列人的狂欢节。

2. 希伯来小说的主题特色

一般认为，希伯来小说包含以下作品：《旧约》里歌颂民族团结的《路得记》、《约拿书》，反对异族压迫、宣扬爱国主义的《以斯帖记》、《次经》里的《犹滴传》，以及《次经》中歌颂正义、反对邪恶的《苏撒拿传》、《彼勒与大龙》和《多比传》。这些作品均为短篇，数量不多，但主题很宏大，或追求正义，或赞美和谐，或歌颂爱国行为。可谓多彩多姿，各具特色。希伯来小说的正面主人公大都显示出强大的精神和道德力量。他们不是为了狭隘的私欲四处奔走，而是超越自我，为了他人，为了民众，乃至为了全民族的利益而英勇斗争，表现出强烈的正义感、坚定的信念和勇于牺牲的献身精神。例如，以斯帖敢于冒死闯宫见王，犹滴敢于只身入敌营杀敌帅，但以理则在险恶的环境中力胜顽敌。他们不以体力取胜，而是以精神、道义的巨大力量压倒敌人或对手，使读者为之惊叹、振奋。这样的主题有利于激发人民的斗志、增强民族凝聚力。小说在涉及这些主题时呈现出显著的民族审美特色和独特的叙事美感。比如《路得记》在倡导民族团结、赞美和谐社会的同时，呈现出田园牧歌的动态美、自然美和艺术美。

四、圣经文化专题

1. 希伯来小说的叙事美学特征

《圣经》中有各种文体，其中有诗歌、散文、演讲、小说等等。从《创世记》关于亚伯拉罕、雅各、约瑟等始祖的叙述，我们可以看出希伯来小说的雏形。到《路得记》、《以斯帖记》时期，小说已经趋向成熟，其叙事完整、主题明确，并且呈现出叙事美学的特征。其叙事美学特征可

---

1. portion *n.* a part of sth. divided between people; a share 一份，这里指礼物

简单总结如下:

第一、情节多变,跌宕起伏,具有一种动态美。小说素材往往来自历史轶事或民间传说,故事性较强,有较大的吸引力和感染力。例如,以斯帖的故事迂回多变,矛盾冲突十分激烈,情节也错综复杂。动态美还表现为作者不注重人物的静态描写和心理刻画,而注重通过复杂的矛盾冲突揭示主人公的独特性格。如为挽救族人,以斯帖与国王和哈曼斗智斗勇;她的胆略和机智,是通过她在民族危亡关头的英雄行为展现出来的。

第二、结构工整,具有一种对称美。《以斯帖记》中的人物明显具有对称性,以斯帖与瓦实提两后对称,末底改与哈曼两相交锋,国王亚哈随鲁则居于中心,把4个人物连接起来。另外,故事中还常常出现对称性情节,如宰相哈曼派人做了一个大木架,准备用来吊死末底改,可结果自己反被吊死在上面;在《路得记》中,路得和嫂子、路得的丈夫和哥哥、年老的拿俄米和年轻的路得、波阿斯和那位至亲等人物都构成叙事的对称美。

第三、写实主义与浪漫主义并存,表现出朴素美、真挚美和幻想美。比如,《路得记》是一篇写实主义小说,读者从中可看到两千年前希伯来农村的生活风貌,体会到希伯来人对于纯朴生活的热爱。路得忠诚、善良、勤劳,以其真挚、美好的感情为故事赋予了很强的艺术感染力。另一方面,希伯来民族富于宗教感情,这种感情激发了他们丰富的想象力,从而形成小说离奇的情节,富于浪漫主义色调和乐观主义的结尾。如约拿在鱼腹三天三夜的情节,《路得记》"有情人终成眷属"和《以斯帖记》大败敌人的结尾。

2. 希伯来圣经中的男权话语

希伯来圣经中存在大量歧视、虐待女性并将女性置于从属、次等地位视为财产的记述。希伯来律法对女性的从属地位有详尽的阐述和规定。如《出埃及记》第20章17节、《申命记》第5章21节都规定,女人是男人的财产,女人无权控制自己的身体。男人都愿意娶一个处女为妻,但对于他的贞操及忠诚与否并没有任何限定。《申命记》第24章1—4节还规定女人没有离婚和拥有自己财产的权利。《利未记》第15章不仅将女人排斥于圣职以外,而且与男人相比,她是不洁的,月经期间要受到严格的隔离和控制。《利未记》第27章1—7节甚至规定女人的身价也低得多。这种观点使古以色列人认为,献祭时雄性动物是上帝喜悦的祭品。

古代以色列妇女的生活苦境可以从以下事例中体现出来:《创世记》第19章8节记载,罗得为了保护两位房客(其实是天使),宁可把两个还是处女的女儿交给所多玛人,任凭他们为所欲为。而他的这一举动却被认为是忠义的。雅各为拉班劳动14年,所得的"酬劳"是他的两个女儿。《士师记》第11章29—40节中耶弗他为了一个荒唐的许诺,将独生女献了燔祭。《撒母耳记下》第6章14—23节,贵为公主的米甲,先是被父亲扫罗赐给大卫,又被父亲另嫁他人,大卫作王后才把米甲接回,米甲的丈夫哭泣着追赶。此处说明米甲是扫罗和大卫政治斗争的牺牲品,没有决定自己婚姻大事的自主权(《撒母耳记下》3:14—16)。在《撒母耳记下》第13章,大卫不惜采用卑鄙的谋杀手段,霸占乌利亚的貌美妻子拔示巴。《传道书》对妇女的态度总体上是歧视性的。如第7章26—28节说:"我得知有这样的妇人,比死还苦;她的心是网罗,手是锁链。凡蒙神喜悦的人,必能躲避她;有罪的人,却被她缠住了。"传道者说:"看哪,一千个男子中,我找到一个正直人;但众女子中,没有找到一个。"

需要强调的是，这仅仅是《圣经》对妇女态度的一个侧面。《圣经》对妇女的态度有它自身的时代局限性，受到了时代和经济发展水平的制约。(《圣经》其他章节又体现了对女性权益的保障。如《申命记》22: 13—19节、14: 28—29节、24: 19—21节。)

五、圣经典故集锦

1. **Queen Vashti** (王后瓦实提)：源自第1章9—22节。指"因高傲而失宠的女人"、"因为美貌而忘乎所以的女子"、"蔑视丈夫的妻子"。以美貌出名、却任性执拗的波斯王后瓦实提，违抗王旨而不愿露面见客，终被国王废除其王后之位。

2. **in sackcloth and ashes** (披麻蒙灰)：源自第4章1—3节。指"悲痛欲绝"、"痛切哀悼"、"深深忏悔"。末底改听到哈曼怂恿国王准备杀绝犹太人的不幸消息后，撕裂衣服，披麻衣蒙灰尘，在城中痛苦哀号。

3. **stretch out the golden sceptre** (伸出金杖)：源自第4章11节至第5章2节波斯国的一个定例。任何人如果没有得到王的召令而擅入内院都会被置以死罪，除非国王向此人伸出金杖才能赦免其死。

4. **Haman's gallows** (哈曼的木绞架)：源自第5章9节至第7章10节。哈曼设立高高的木绞架本来想绞死末底改，不料阴谋未遂，自己反被绞死在这个木绞架上。此典指"请君入瓮"、"以其人之道还治其人之身"。

5. **Ahasuerus's half kingdom** (亚哈随鲁的半个王国)：源自第5章3节亚哈随鲁王对以斯帖的许诺，比喻慷慨大方的许诺赠予。《简·爱》第24章里有这样一段：
"Utter it, Jane; but I wish that instead of mere inquiry into, perhaps, a secret, it was a wish for half my estate." "Now, King Ahasuerus! What do I want with half your estate? Do you think I am a Jew — Usurer, seeking good investment in land? I would much rather have all your confidence. You will not exclude me from your confidence, if you admit me to your heart?" "说吧，简；不过但愿你希望的不只是打听一下——也许是打听一个秘密吧——而是希望得到我的一半田产。" "啊，亚哈随鲁王！我要你的一半田产有什么用呢？你以为我是个放高利贷的犹太人，想在田地上找个好的投资吗？我宁可要你完全跟我推心置腹。既然你让我进入你的心，那你就不会把心里话瞒着我吧？"

六、课堂讨论题

1. 《以斯帖记》在刻画人物形象时用了反衬的手法，你发现了吗？
2. 结合以前所学章节，谈谈犹太民族的装饰艺术。

3. 请赏析法国著名画家泰奥多尔·沙塞里奥的油画《梳妆中的以斯帖》。

七、课后思考题

1. 有一部美国电影《与王共一夜》(One Night with the King)。你看过吗？
2. 《以斯帖记》交代历史背景时提到了"米底亚"(Media)这个词。而传说中的巴比伦"空中花园"就是专给米底亚公主建造的。你知道这个传说吗？
3. 谈谈《以斯帖记》对欧洲戏剧的影响。

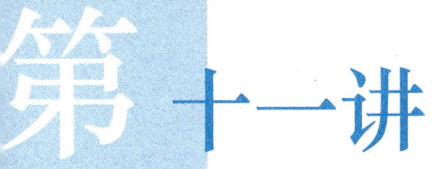

第十一讲 希伯来诗歌荟萃：《诗篇》

Psalms, an Anthology of Hebrew Poems and Songs

一、导读：主题及文体特色

《诗篇》是《圣经》中最大的诗歌汇集，共有150首，各长短不一，长者达176节（如第119首），短者仅两行（第117首）。希伯来人称之为 Tehillim（音译"德锡灵"），意思是"赞美之歌"。整卷的基本精神是对耶和华的崇拜和赞美，是一部宗教意味很浓的抒情诗集。《诗篇》历经数代文人学士的多次锤炼才得以定型，大约在公元前300年汇集成目前的全集。可分为9类：赞美诗、忏悔诗、祈祷诗、诅咒诗、咏史诗、智慧诗、自然诗、弥赛亚诗和个别特殊诗。《诗篇》与其他经卷之间存在着各种互涉现象，是其他经卷的折射和概括，素有"小圣经"之称。

《诗篇》的艺术特色有三。首先是语言的简洁性，希伯来诗句通常很少超过3个词；其次是常用"平行体"；第三是丰富的文学意象。此外，重叠、字母序诗也是《诗篇》多处采用的手法。

本讲把所选的诗篇分为4部分：

第1部分：第1首是代序的诗篇，统领全卷，属于智慧诗。"溪边之树"（a tree planted by the rivers of water）和"风中秕糠"（the chaff which the wind driveth away）是著名的比喻，分别指代义人和恶人。第19篇是一篇想象丰富、修辞独到的赞美诗，歌颂上帝的造化之功。第23首是最出名的赞美诗。"耶和华是我的牧者，我必不致缺乏"（The LORD is my shepherd; I shall not want）一句闻名遐迩。

第2部分：第104首为较长的自然诗，是对《创世记》第1章的诗体注释，诗人借景抒情，情寓景中，抒发对上帝的无限敬畏之情，不禁发出由衷的赞叹：I will sing unto the LORD as long as I live（只要我活着就要赞美上帝）。

第3部分：第131首是简短的祈祷诗，诗人把自己比作"断奶的孩子"（a weaned child），把上帝比作母亲，隐喻独特。第137首是被掳掠者的哀歌，抒写被囚于巴比伦的犹太人对故园的思念和眷恋，表达他们对仇敌的刻骨仇恨。该诗开头 By the rivers of Babylon 被经常引用和化用。

第4部分：第147首是赞美诗，诗人呼吁同胞颂赞耶和华，因他的智慧无法测度，怜悯以色列人。第150首属于"大哈利路亚颂诗"（Halleluiah）意思是"赞美上帝"，常用于欢庆重大节日的歌舞和咏诵活动。诗中提到不少古代乐器，形象地再现了人们歌咏时的具体情景。该篇连用11个 Praise，渲染了整卷《诗篇》的主旨。

二、选文及注释

Part 1

Psalm 1

Blessed is the man that walketh not in the counsel of the ungodly[1],

Nor standeth in the way of sinners,

Nor sitteth in the seat of the scornful.

But his delight is in the law of the LORD;

And in his law doth he meditate day and night[2].

And he shall be like a tree planted by the rivers of water,

That bringeth forth his fruit in his season:

His leaf also shall not wither;

And whatsoever he doeth shall prosper.

The ungodly are not so:

But are like the chaff[3] which the wind driveth away.

Therefore the ungodly shall not stand in the judgment,

Nor sinners in the congregation of the righteous[4].

For the LORD knoweth the way of the righteous:

But the way of the ungodly shall perish.

Psalm 19

The heavens declare the glory of God;

And the firmament sheweth his handywork.

Day unto day uttereth speech,

And night unto night sheweth knowledge.

There is no speech nor language,

Where their voice is not heard.

Their line is gone out through all the earth[5],

And their words to the end of the world.

In them hath he set a tabernacle for the sun[6],

Which is as a bridegroom coming out of his chamber,

And rejoiceth as a strong man to run a race.

His going forth is from the end of the heaven,

And his circuit unto the ends of it[7]:

And there is nothing hid from the heat thereof.

The law of the LORD is perfect, converting[8] the soul:

The testimony of the LORD is sure, making wise the simple[9].

The statutes of the LORD are right, rejoicing the heart:

The commandment of the LORD is pure, enlightening the eyes.

The fear of the LORD is clean, enduring for ever[10]:

The judgments of the LORD are true and righteous altogether.

---

1. walketh not in the counsel of the ungodly 不跟从恶人的计谋。counsel *n.* advice 指计策。
2. in his law doth he meditate day and night 义人日夜思量耶和华的律法。
3. chaff *n.* 秕糠
4. Nor sinners in the congregation of the righteous 罪人不能在义人的聚会中站立。
5. Their line is gone out through all the earth 智慧的音讯传遍人间。line 希伯来原文意思是"绳索"。
6. a tabernacle for the sun 太阳的帐幕,指天空。
7. his circuit unto the ends of it 它(太阳)的行程遍布四极。circuit *n.* 周游;行程。
8. convert *vt.* to change the form, character, or function of sth. 更新;转变
9. The testimony of the Lord is sure, making wise the simple. 上帝的法度可靠,让愚昧人得到智慧。
10. The fear of the Lord (敬畏上帝)是希伯来文的直译。The fear of the Lord is clean, enduring for ever 意译为:上帝的规范纯真,永远存留。

More to be desired are they than gold, yea, than much fine gold:

Sweeter also than honey and the honeycomb.

Moreover by them is thy servant warned:

And in keeping of them there is great reward.[1]

Who can understand his errors?

Cleanse thou me from secret faults.

Keep back thy servant also from presumptuous[2] sins;

Let them not have dominion over me: then shall I be upright,

And I shall be innocent[3] from the great transgression.

Let the words of my mouth, and the meditation of my heart, be acceptable in thy sight,

O LORD, my strength, and my redeemer[4].

Psalm 23

The LORD is my shepherd; I shall not want[5],

He maketh me to lie down in green pastures:

He leadeth me beside the still waters.

He restoreth[6] my soul;

He leadeth me in the paths of righteousness for his name's sake.

Yea, though I walk through the valley of the shadow of death,

I will fear no evil: for thou art with me;

Thy rod and thy staff they comfort me.[7]

Thou preparest a table before me in the presence of mine enemies:

Thou anointed my head with oil; my cup runneth over.[8]

Surely goodness and mercy shall follow me all the days of my life:

And I will dwell in the house of the LORD for ever.

Part 2

Psalm 104

Bless the LORD, O my soul.

O LORD my God, thou art very great;

Thou art clothed with honour and majesty.

Who coverest thyself with light as with a garment:

Who stretchest out the heavens like a curtain:

Who layeth the beams of his chambers in the waters[9]:

Who maketh the clouds his chariot:

Who walketh upon the wings of the wind:

Who maketh his angels spirits;

His ministers[10] a flaming fire:

Who laid the foundations of the earth,

That it should not be removed for ever.

Thou coveredst it with the deep as with a garment:

The waters stood above the mountains.

At thy rebuke they fled[11];

At the voice of thy thunder they hasted away.

---

1. Sweeter also ... great reward. 这三句的意思是：它们比金子值得恭慕，胜过纯金；/它们比蜜甘甜，胜过蜂蜜；/你的仆人尚且得到提醒，谨守诫命，便受益无穷。
2. presumptuous *adj.* going beyond what is right or proper; excessively forward 专横的；放肆的
3. innocent *adj.* free from moral wrong; not sinful 无罪的；免于犯罪的
4. redeemer *n.* 赎身者；救主
5. want *vt.* to be destitute or needy 缺乏
6. restore *vt.* to return sb. to a former condition or position 使苏醒
7. Thy rod and thy staff they comfort me. (上帝被比作牧羊人)你的杖、你的竿都安慰我。
8. Thou anointed my head with oil; my cup runneth over. 你用油膏我的头，使我的福杯满溢。"福"(杯)是后人的加译。君王加冕时被膏立(经常在事前)，但宴会嘉宾也会以油膏头。
9. his chambers in the waters 上帝在水中建造住所。犹太人认为宇宙像一幢房子，下屋是阴间，中屋是地面，地面上有苍穹，而苍穹以上就是诸水，也是耶和华的居所。
10. minister *n.* 仆人。火焰喻指上帝的仆人。
11. At thy rebuke they fled 你一声斥责，水就奔逃。

They go up by the mountains; they go down by the valleys

Unto the place which thou hast founded for them.

Thou hast set a bound that they may not pass over;

That they turn not again to cover the earth.

He sendeth the springs into the valleys,

Which run among the hills.

They give drink to every beast of the field:

The wild asses quench[1] their thirst.

By them shall the fowls of the heaven have their habitation,

Which sing among the branches.

He watereth the hills from his chambers:

The earth is satisfied with the fruit of thy works.

He causeth the grass to grow for the cattle,

And herb for the service of man:

That he may bring forth food out of the earth;

And wine that maketh glad the heart of man,

And oil to make his face to shine,

And bread which strengtheneth man's heart.

The trees of the LORD are full of sap[2];

The cedars[3] of Lebanon, which he hath planted;

Where the birds make their nests:

As for the stork[4], the fir trees are her house.

The high hills are a refuge for the wild goats;

And the rocks for the conies[5].

He appointed the moon for seasons:

The sun knoweth his going down.

Thou makest darkness, and it is night:

Wherein all the beasts of the forest do creep forth.

The young lions roar after their prey,

And seek their meat from God[6].

The sun ariseth, they gather themselves together,

And lay them down in their dens.

Man goeth forth unto his work

And to his labour until the evening.

O LORD, how manifold are thy works![7] In wisdom hast thou made them all:

The earth is full of thy riches.[8]

So is this great and wide sea,

Wherein are things creeping innumerable,

Both small and great beasts.

There go the ships:

There is that leviathan[9], whom thou hast made to play therein.

These wait all upon thee;

That thou mayest give them their meat in due season.

That thou givest them they gather:

Thou openest thine hand, they are filled with good.[10]

Thou hidest thy face[11], they are troubled:

Thou takest away their breath, they die,

---

1. quench *vt.* to satisfy 满足
2. full of sap 指得到雨水的充分滋润, sap *n.* 树汁。
3. cedar *n.* 香柏
4. stork *n.* 鹳
5. cony *n.* (coney 的变体)穴兔; 石獾
6. seek their meat from God 寻找上帝所赐的食物。
7. O Lord, how manifold are thy works! 上帝啊, 你的创造何其繁多!
8. The earth is full of thy riches. 地上充满你的创造之物。
9. leviathan *n.* 音译"利维坦", 指鲸鱼之类的海中巨兽
10. These wait all upon thee ... Thou openest thine hand, they are filled with good. 它们都仰赖你。你按时令给它们食物。你赐给食物, 它们便吃。你慷慨给予, 它们便得饱足。
11. Thou hidest thy face 上帝掩面, 指上帝不再施恩于万物。

And return to their dust.

Thou sendest forth thy spirit, they are created:

And thou renewset the face of the earth.

The glory of the LORD shall endure for ever:

The LORD shall rejoice in his works.

He looketh on the earth, and it trembleth:

He toucheth the hills, and they smoke.

I will sing unto the LORD as long as I live:

I will sing praise to my God while I have my being.

My meditation[1] of him shall be sweet:

I will be glad in the LORD.

Let the sinners be consumed[2] out of the earth,

And let the wicked be no more.

Bless thou the LORD, O my soul.

Praise ye the LORD.

Part 3

Psalm 131

LORD, my heart is not haughty[3],
Nor mine eyes lofty[4]:
Neither do I exercise myself in great matters[5],
Or in things too high for me.

Surely I have behaved and quieted myself[6],
As a child that is weaned of his mother:
My soul is even as a weaned child.
Let Israel hope in the LORD
From henceforth and for ever.

Psalm 137

By the rivers of Babylon,
There we sat down, yea, we wept,
When we remembered Zion[7].
We hanged our harps
Upon the willows in the midst thereof.
For there they that carried us away captive[8] required of us a song;
And they that wasted us required of us mirth[9], saying,
"Sing us one of the songs of Zion."
How shall we sing the LORD's song
In a strange land[10]?
If I forget thee, O Jerusalem,
Let my right hand forget her cunning.[11]
If I do not remember thee,
Let my tongue cleave to the roof of my mouth[12];
If I prefer not Jerusalem above my chief joy[13].
Remember, O LORD, the children of Edom[14] in the day of Jerusalem;
Who said, "Raise it, raise it, even to the

---

1. meditation *n.* a written discourse expressing considered thoughts on God 沉思。指这首赞美上帝的诗歌。
2. consume *vt.* to completely destroy 消灭；毁灭
3. haughty *adj.* scornfully and condescendingly proud 傲慢的
4. lofty *adj.* arrogant; haughty 高傲的
5. exercise myself in great matters 做重大而测不透的事。
6. behaved and quieted myself 行为检点，心中安静。
7. Zion /ˈzaɪən/（又写作 Sion, 地名）锡安，耶路撒冷建有圣殿的一座山，是以色列的圣地。广义上耶路撒冷和全以色列都称为"锡安"。犹太复国主义称为 Zionism。
8. they that carried us away captive 掳掠我们的人。captive *adj.* taken and held prisoner, as in war 被俘的，作宾语补足语。
9. they that wasted us required of us mirth 折磨我们的人要我们娱乐他们。waste *vt.* to make progressively weaker and more emaciated〈古〉折磨。mirth *n.* amusement, especially as expressed in laughter 欢笑。
10. strange land 异国他乡。指敌人的土地。
11. Let my right hand forget her cunning. 让我的右手忘记弹奏乐器的技巧。比喻让手枯萎。
12. Let my tongue cleave to the roof of my mouth 让我的舌头紧贴上腭。意思是不能放声歌唱。
13. prefer not Jerusalem above my chief joy 不是以耶路撒冷为我最大的喜乐。
14. the children of Edom 以东人，帮助巴比伦人毁灭耶路撒冷的帮凶。

foundation thereof[1]."

O daughter of Babylon, who art to be destroyed;
Happy shall he be that rewardeth thee as thou hast served us.[2]
Happy shall he be, that taketh and dasheth thy little ones[3] against the stones.

Part 4

Psalm 147

Praise ye the LORD:
For it is good to sing praises unto our God;
For it is pleasant; *and* praise is comely[4].
The LORD doth build up Jerusalem:
He gathereth together the outcasts of Israel[5].
He healeth the broken in heart,
And bindeth up their wounds.
He telleth the number of the stars;
He calleth them all by *their* names.
Great is our Lord, and of great power:
His understanding *is* infinite.[6]
The LORD lifteth up the meek:
He casteth the wicked down to the ground.
Sing unto the LORD with thanksgiving;
Sing praise upon the harp unto our God:
Who covereth the heaven with clouds,
Who prepareth rain for the earth,
Who maketh grass to grow upon the mountains.

He giveth to the beast his food,
And to the young ravens[7] which cry.
He delighteth not in the strength of the horse[8]:
He taketh not pleasure in the legs of a man[9].
The LORD taketh pleasure in them that fear him,
In those that hope in his mercy.
Praise the LORD, O Jerusalem;
Praise thy God, O Zion.
For he hath strengthened the bars of thy gates;
He hath blessed thy children within thee.
He maketh peace in thy borders,
And filleth thee with the finest of the wheat.
He sendeth forth his commandment upon earth:
His word runneth very swiftly.
He giveth snow like wool:
He scattereth the hoarfrost[10] like ashes.
He casteth forth his ice like morsels[11]:
Who can stand before his cold[12]?
He sendeth out his word, and melteth them:
He causeth his wind to blow, and the waters flow.
He sheweth his word unto Jacob,
His statutes and his judgments[13] unto Israel.
He hath not dealt so with any nation:
And as for his judgments, they have not known them.

---

1. rase it, even to the foundation thereof 拆毁耶路撒冷的根基。意思是将其夷为平地。
2. Happy shall he be that rewardeth thee as thou hast served us. 照着你加给我们的残暴来报复你的人，他是多么有福啊！诗人祈求上帝以严厉的手段惩罚帮凶以东人。
3. dasheth thy little ones 把婴孩摔死(在石头上)。
4. comely *adj.* suitable 适时的
5. the outcasts of Israel 失去家园的以色列人。
6. His understanding *is* infinite. 耶和华的智慧无法测度。
7. raven *n.* 乌鸦；渡鸦
8. the strength of the horse 马的力气。
9. the legs of a man 人的快腿。比喻人类的自负。
10. hoarfrost *n.* 白霜
11. morsel *n.* 冰雹
12. before his cold 在耶和华命令的寒冷中人不能站立。形容神的力量之大，人类无法抵抗。
13. His statutes and his judgments 耶和华的律例和典章。

Praise ye the LORD.

Psalm 150

Praise ye the LORD.
Praise God in his sanctuary[1]:
Praise him in the firmament of his power[2].
Praise him for his mighty acts:
Praise him according to his excellent greatness.
Praise him with the sound of the trumpet:
Praise him with the psaltery[3] and harp.
Praise him with the timbrel and dance:
Praise him with stringed instruments and organs[4].
Praise him upon the loud cymbals[5]:
Praise him upon the high sounding cymbals.
Let every thing that hath breath praise the LORD.
Praise ye the LORD.

三、圣经文化知识链接

1. 咏史诗与以色列民族凝聚力

"咏史诗"是以重大历史事件为题材的希伯来圣诗。《诗篇》第78、105、106、114等篇章是这类诗歌的名作。诗章从耶和华与早期希伯来族长立约写起，而后是耶和华赐予迦南之地，约瑟被卖为奴，以色列人在埃及遭受奴役，摩西带领民众出埃及、穿红海、越旷野，最后写到大卫以色列的王。

古希伯来人的历史交织着各种艰难困苦的经历，回顾并咏颂这些经历，是他们增强民族凝聚力的重要手段。可以设想，每当以色列人回忆起这些历史的奇迹，他们会重温祖先那种逃离苦海后扬眉吐气的快乐。快乐之余，他们也会悟出先辈们成功的背后上帝的神力。科学地讲，先辈们的英雄业绩是靠信心、意志和智慧创造出来的，这无疑是令他们引以为豪的历史，也成了后辈对自己民族自信的依据。由此，他们会产生这样的信念：我们既然是希伯来人的后代，既然是摩西的后代，也当然是"上帝的选民"，上帝眷顾我们的祖先，并且与祖先立下了世代相传的"约"，那么我们肯定也可以像祖先那样创造奇迹。对这种历史事件的追忆，无疑可以成为应对前进道路上任何困难和逆境的信心之泉、力量之源。正是"上帝选民→创造奇迹→民族自信→追忆历史→强化自信→前进动力……"这样一个良性循环，使得以色列民族曾经获得、并将继续获得无穷的力量。

2. "锡安山"(Zion)与"犹太复国主义"(Zionism)

山脉之所以有宗教意义，主要因为它们可以给人安全感，同时象征着肥沃多产。山脉是上帝所造世界秩序性和稳定性的见证，象征着上帝的力量和永恒。锡安山与西奈山一样，在犹太

---

1. sanctuary *n.* a sacred place, such as a church 圣所
2. the firmament of his power 直译"耶和华显示伟力的苍穹"。
3. psaltery *n.* 索尔特里琴，一种拨弦乐器
4. organ *n.* 风琴
5. cymbal *n.* 钹，一种打击乐器

教历史上具有划时代的意义。[1]

锡安(Zion)是巴勒斯坦耶路撒冷的一座山名,传说是大卫建王宫和所罗门建圣殿的坐落处,但具体位置说法不一。依照古代基督教东、西教会的传说,锡安山位于耶路撒冷城西南,近世考证家多数认为是城东的山脊,犹太教则以"锡安"指耶路撒冷城。

锡安在《诗篇》中出现多次。如第137首中有the songs of Zion(锡安的歌)。这首诗是古以色列人在"巴比伦之囚"(公元前586—539年)的生活和情绪的描绘,民族仇恨跃然纸上。古以色列人是以善于弹琴唱歌出名的,但在亡国之后,坐在敌国的河边,故国的情景尚记忆犹新,又怎能歌唱盛时欢愉的"锡安的歌"呢?第126首首句写道:When the LORD turned again the captivity of Zion, we were like them that dream(耶和华带我们回归锡安时,我们像从噩梦中醒来),诗人用"回归锡安"表现曾沦为俘囚的希伯来人获释回归故土的欢乐心情。

公元70年耶路撒冷城被罗马帝国摧毁后,犹太人常视"锡安"为民族以及圣城、圣殿的总象征。犹太复国主义者也因此自称为锡安主义者。

四、圣经文化专题

1.《诗篇》的宗教基调和世俗情调[2]

马丁·路德称《诗篇》是一部小圣经,是《旧约》的总和。恩格斯在《反杜林论》中指出:一切宗教都不过是支配着人们日常生活的外部力量在人们头脑中的幻想的反映,在这种反映中,人间的力量采取了超人间的力量形式[3]。这一点在《诗篇》中反映尤为突出。从文字表面看,赞美诗主要是对上帝的颂赞,但颂赞所使用的大量素材(物象、景观)以及运用的多种修辞手法(比喻、象征、拟人)使得赞美诗在文本功效上超越了神学的囿限,呈现出显著的艺术审美特征。如第104首是自然诗,诗人通过该诗歌抒发对上帝的无限敬畏之情,但是诗人所借用的光辉四溢的日月、高远无际的苍穹、雄奇秀丽的群山、浩瀚无边的大海等素材,都属于世俗的范畴。第10—13节写道:

> 耶和华使泉涌在山谷,流在山间;
> 使野地的走兽有水喝,野驴得解其渴。
> 天上的飞鸟在水边住宿,在树枝上啼叫。
> 他从楼阁中浇灌山岭,因他作为的功效,地也丰足。

诗人借景抒情、情寓景中,在歌颂上帝的同时也歌颂了美好的大自然,从而体现出世俗性。再如,《诗篇》119篇1—16节提及"耶和华的律法"及顺从的结果(第137—144节歌颂律法的公义,161—163节表达了对律法的喜爱)。这些律法内容与世俗伦理道德标准相叠合,只是以上帝的神圣面目出现。实际上,这体现了希伯来民族对世界的认知方式,是他们对日常生活感受和

---

1. R. Kevin Seasoltz, *A Sense of the Sacred: Theological Foundations of Christian Architecture and Art*. New York and London: the Continuum International Publishing Group Ltd., 2005, p.74.
2. 本项参考刘洪一著:《犹太文化要义》,北京:商务印书馆,2004年,第355页。
3.《马克思恩格斯选集》(第三卷),北京:人民出版社,1972年版,第353页。

自然生成法则所作的神圣化的艺术加工,对人们的现世行为产生了巨大的指导作用。

作为宗教抒情诗集,《诗篇》的基本精神是对上帝的崇拜和赞美。诗人咏颂和平年代人们与上帝的和谐关系,也表达他们在患难之际对上帝的信依。仔细分析这些诗篇的内容我们可以发现,祈祷民族欲得之物,诅咒敌人将失之物,称颂上帝之因,以及上帝教育子民和惩罚敌人所采用的方式,都体现出世俗的追求。在《诗篇》中,我们可以发现世俗的追求并感受到世俗的美。《诗篇》以宗教抒情诗的形式,生动地表现了希伯来民族复杂的经历和丰富的情感。有的诗篇气势恢宏,抒发对上帝的赞美,传达敬拜者同上帝、世界和谐相处的欢快情绪(如第145—150首);有的记录人生灰暗时刻的体验和遇难时的祈祷(第6、102首);有的吐露内心负疚忏悔的情感(如第51首大卫的忏悔诗);有的为无端受苦诉不平(第44首17—18节;第109首1—5节)。有的让读者窥见以色列民族面临动荡和灾难时的心理反应(如第44、74、80、83首);有的邀请读者参与他们民族生活中的重大庆典,如国王加冕礼、婚礼等(如第45首);有的饱含个人从人生试炼中蒙获拯救后对上帝的由衷感恩(如第65首)。通过对诸种情感的抒发,这些诗篇折射出希伯来民族历史的一幕幕,以诗意的语言再现了许多重大活动,而且几乎囊括了人生所有感受。

犹太民族的宗教学说是犹太民族早期历史生活的曲折反映,是一种以非理性的虚幻形貌出现、但又隐含了一定理性潜质的思想形式,也是早期犹太民族认知世界的一种复杂、特殊的方式,体现出独特的生存机智。从该意义上来讲,《诗篇》不愧为希伯来人浓缩的圣经,犹太民族的宗教正是犹太文化特质的重要体现。

2. 希伯来文学中"羊"的意象

希伯来人的始祖是幼发拉底河河畔的一支原始游牧民族,牧养一直是他们最重要的生产生活方式,无怪乎《旧约》中充满与牧人生活息息相关的语汇和风俗记录。"牧者"和"羊"的比喻便是带有游牧生活印记的一个典型,成为一个隐喻上帝与子民、耶稣与信徒关系的意义系统。

《旧约》作者熟知牧羊人眷顾、照料羊群的情况,他们从现实生活中深深感悟到,只有"牧者"才能表达上帝对子民的慈爱和关照。早在《创世记》第48章15节雅各就说 the God which fed me all my life long unto this day (上帝牧养我直到今日)。到了《诗篇》中,诗人将这一传统比喻具象化、场景化,赋予它浓厚的生活气息,一幅情景交融的田园风光跃然纸上:

耶和华是我的牧者,我必不至缺乏。
他使我躺卧在青草地上,领我在可安歇的水边。
他使我的灵魂苏醒,为自己的名引导我走义路。
我虽行过死荫的幽谷,也不怕遭害;因为你与我同在,你的杖,你的竿,都安慰我。
在我敌人面前,你为我摆设筵席;你用油膏了我的头,使我的福杯满溢。
我一生一世必有恩惠慈爱随着我,我且要住在耶和华的殿中,直到永远。[1]

《诗篇》第74首、第100首中也使用了上帝乃"牧羊人"的比喻。

---

1. 《诗篇》第23首"和合本"译文;英文参见本讲"选文与注释"部分。

《以赛亚书》第40章11节描述的是一幅尽心尽责的"牧人图":

He shall feed his flock like a shepherd: he shall gather the lambs with his arm, and carry them in his bosom, and shall gently lead those that are with young. 他(耶和华)必像牧人一样,牧养羊群,用他的手臂聚拢小羊,把它们抱在怀中;他温柔地引导那哺育羔羊的母羊。

《以西结书》第34章2—6节则对不负责任的"牧人"(以色列的首领)大加谴责:

Woe be to the shepherds of Israel that do feed themselves! should not the shepherds feed the flocks? Ye eat the fat, and ye clothe you with the wool, ye kill them that are fed: but ye feed not the flock. … And they were scattered, because there is no shepherd: and they became meat to all the beasts of the field, when they were scattered. My sheep wandered through all the mountains, and upon every high hill: yea, my flock was scattered upon all the face of the earth, and none did search or seek after them. (耶和华如此说)祸哉!以色列的牧人,只知道牧养自己。牧人岂不当牧养群羊吗?你们吃脂油,穿羊毛,宰肥壮的,却不牧养群羊。……因为没有牧羊人羊就分散;既分散,便成为一切野兽的食物。我的羊在诸山间,在各高岗上流离,在全地上分散,无人去寻,无人去找。

在《新约》福音书里,需要拯救的人被看做"没有牧人的羊",而耶稣自喻为"好牧人",且两者彼此"认识"。《马可福音》第6章34节记载:耶稣一下船,看见一大群人,就怜悯他们,因为他们好像没有牧人一样,就开始教导他们许多事。耶稣把自己比作好牧羊人:"我是好牧人;我认识我的羊,我的羊也认识我。"(《约翰福音》10:14)。

与"羊"有关的另一个著名隐喻是"迷途的羊"(lost sheep),喻指那些犯了错误、背离了上帝的信徒。在《以赛亚书》第53章6节,耶路撒冷的民众说:

All we like sheep have gone astray; we have turned every one to his own way; and the LORD hath laid on him the iniquity of us all. 我们好像迷路的羊,各人偏行己路,耶和华使我们众人的罪孽都归到他一个人身上。

从这段话中还引申出"替罪羊"(scapegoat)的比喻。不过,"替罪羊"的原始意象源自《利未记》第16章8—22节。摩西的哥哥、大祭司亚伦在耶和华神面前宰杀了一只公山羊,用羊血献赎罪祭。之后他双手按在一只活着的羊的头上,"承认以色列人诸般的罪孽、过犯,就是他们一切的罪衍,把这罪都归在羊的头上。"然后派人将这只羊带到旷野放生,因为"这只羊要担当他们一切的罪孽。"

五、圣经典故集锦

1. **with a rod of iron** (用铁杖):指"采用高压手段"、"铁腕统治"。典出第2首9节: Thou shalt break them with a rod of iron; thou shalt dash them in pieces like a potter's vessel. 你必用铁杖打破他们。你必将他们如同窑匠的瓦器摔碎。

2. **the valley of the shadow of death** (死荫的幽谷):指"恐怖之地"、"临死之际"。典出第23首4节: Yea, though I walk through the valley of the shadow of death, I will fear no evil: for thou art with me; thy rod and thy staff they comfort me. 我虽然行过死荫的幽谷,也不怕遭害。因为你与我同在。你的杖、你的竿,都安慰我。

3. **my cup runs over**（福杯满溢）：指"极为幸福"、"美满生活"。典出第23首5节：Thou preparest a table before me in the presence of mine enemies: thou anointest my head with oil; my cup runneth over. 在我敌人面前，你为我摆设筵席。你用油膏了我的头(君王加冕时被膏立，经常在事前进行，但宴会嘉宾也会以油膏头)，使我的福杯满溢。

4. **have clean hands and a pure heart**（手洁心清）：指"清白无辜"、"纯洁正直"。典出第24首3—4节：Who shall ascend into the hill of the Lord? Or who shall stand in his holy place? He that hath clean hands, and a pure heart; who hath not lifted up his soul unto vanity, nor sworn deceitfully. 谁能登耶和华的山，谁能站在他的圣所，就是手洁心清、不向虚妄、起誓不怀诡诈的人。

5. **lift the heel against somebody**（用脚踢人）：指"凌辱某人"、"欺辱某人"、"攻击某人"。典出第41首9节：Yea, mine own familiar friend, in whom I trusted, which did eat of my bread, hath lifted up his heel against me. 连我知己的朋友，我所倚靠吃过我饭的，也用脚踢我。

6. **in deep water**（深水之中）：指"处于水深火热之中"、"陷入困境"、"遇到危难"。典出第69首2节：I sink in deep mire, where there is no standing: I am come into deep waters, where the floods overflow me. 我陷在深淤泥中，没有立脚之地。我到了深水中，大水漫过我身。

7. **lick the dust**（舔土）：指"被人打倒"、"屈服于人"、"甘拜下风"。典出第72首9节：They that dwell in the wilderness shall bow before him; and his enemies shall lick the dust. 住在旷野的，必在他面前下拜。他的仇敌，必要舔土。

8. **Lift up the horn on high**（高举其角）：指"盛气凌人"、"趾高气扬"、"狂傲骄横"、"得意忘形"。典出第75首4—5节：I said unto the fools, Deal not foolishly: and to the wicked, Lift not up the horn: Lift not up your horn on high: speak not with a stiff neck. 我对狂傲人说，不要行事狂傲。对凶恶人说，不要举角。不要挺着颈项说话。

9. **Hallelujah**（哈利路亚）：指"赞美上帝"，颂词"你们要赞美上帝"的希伯来文译音，现已成为基督徒在祷告中常用之语，典出第106首1节、第135首1节：Praise ye the Lord. 你们要赞美耶和华。

六、课堂讨论题

1. 但丁曾经说《诗篇》第114首是令人快乐得发抖的诗，你如何理解？
2. 《诗篇》第137首是被广为传颂的"诗篇"之一，尤其是首句被许多文人墨客所引用或化用。试举例说明。

177

3. "象牙"牌香皂(Ivory soap)的商标与《诗篇》有何关系？
4. 谈谈《诗篇》中"舌如刀剑(tongue like a sword)"的比喻。

七、课后思考题

1. 你知道在北美大陆出版的第一本书是什么吗？
2. 后世译者在翻译《诗篇》时做过不少"艺术加工"。试以《诗篇》23首为例说明。
3. 谈谈你对《诗篇》第131首中"断奶的孩子"的隐喻的看法。
4. 你知道《诗篇》中译本《圣咏译义初稿》吗？

第十二讲 浪漫爱情歌集：《雅歌》

Song of Songs, Lyrics of Romantic Love

一、导读：《雅歌》的文体与结构

"爱情如死亡之坚强，嫉恨如阴间之残忍"(Love is strong as death; jealousy is cruel as the grave)，"爱情，众水不能熄灭，大水也不能淹没"(Many waters cannot quench love; neither can the floods drown it)。这两句名诗出自《雅歌》。"雅歌"的希伯来名称意为"歌中之歌"或"最美的歌"，指该卷所辑之歌是众歌中最优美者。中文译为"雅歌"，借用了《隋书·音乐志》中的语句："梁武帝有雅歌十二曲，为用于郊庙三朝之雅乐歌诗。"全诗情感纯真朴实，语言优美流畅，细腻地表现了爱情的欢乐和痛苦，赞美了纯洁、自然、炽烈、生死不渝、忠贞如一的爱情态度。诗中常用比喻、夸张、渲染、烘托、对比、反衬、双关、重叠等民间创作的惯用手法，具有浓郁的生活气息。

《雅歌》共8章，通篇诗体，采用情侣对话形式。当代学者认为，《雅歌》当属民间文学作品，成书前曾在民间长期传唱，直到公元前3世纪和公之前2世纪才由文人整理，形成定本。

我们把《雅歌》分成6支歌(选其精彩部分，标题为编者所加)：

第1支歌：思念之歌；女子热烈仰慕男子，用热烈、率直的诗句抒发久藏于心中的爱情；男子赞美女子。

第2支歌：相逢之歌；女子回忆心上人；在梦境中寻找情郎。

第3支歌：诉情之歌；迎亲队伍豪华、庄严；男子赞颂女子的容貌；一对恋人亲密交谈。

第4支歌：惊梦之歌；女子思念离别的情郎，第二次在梦中相会；女子赞美情郎。

第5支歌：赞美之歌；久别重逢的情侣抚爱对方，感慨万千；男子又一次禁不住赞美女子的美妙体态。

第6支歌：盟誓之歌；爱情如火燃烧，礼赞纯真爱情。

二、选文及注释

1. The Yearning for Love

The song of songs, which is Solomon's

The Woman:
Let him kiss me with the kisses of his mouth:
For thy love is better than wine.
Because of the savour of thy good ointments
Thy name[1] is as ointment poured forth,
Therefore do the virgins love thee.

---

1. Thy name 指人的魅力。魅力如香气四溢，芬芳怡人。

Draw me[1], we will run after thee:
The king hath brought me into his chambers:
We will be glad and rejoice in thee,
We will remember thy love more than wine[2],
The upright[3] love thee.

I am black, but comely[4],
O ye daughters of Jerusalem,
As the tents of Kedar[5],
As the curtains of Solomon,
Look not upon me, because I am black,
Because the Sun hath looked upon me:
My mother's children were angry with me;

They made me the keeper of the vineyards;
But mine own vineyard have I not kept.[6]

Tell me, O thou whom my soul loveth,
where thou feedest[7],
Where thou makest thy flock to rest at noon:
For why should I be as one that turneth aside
By the flocks of thy companions[8]?

The Man:
If thou know not, O thou fairest among women,
Go thy way forth by the footsteps of the flock,
And feed thy kids beside the shepherds' tents.

I have compared thee, O my love,
To a company of horses in Pharaoh's chariots.
Thy cheeks are comely with rows of jewels,
Thy neck with chains of gold.
We will make thee borders of gold[9]
With studs of silver[10].

The Woman:
While the king sitteth at his table,
My spikenard[11] sendeth forth the smell thereof.
A bundle of myrrh is my wellbeloved unto me[12];
He shall lie all night betwixt my breasts.
My beloved is unto me as a cluster of

---

1. Draw me 愿你吸引我。
2. remember thy love more than wine 意思是你的爱情胜似美酒。
3. The upright 指上面提到的"处女"(the virgins)。
4. comely *adj.* pleasing in appearance; attractive 秀丽的, 漂亮的
5. Kedar "基达"是阿拉伯以北的游牧民族, 居住在用黑羊毛织成的毛帐内。这里形容女子的肤色黑如毛帐。
6. But mine own vineyard have I not kept. 女子没有属于自己的葡萄园, 喻指没有嫁人、独立。
7. where thou feedest 在何处牧羊。
8. the flocks of thy companions 你同伴的羊群。
9. borders of gold 金辫, 指圆形装饰品, 垂在两腮, 增添光彩。
10. studs of silver 银片。能衬托人的雍容华贵。
11. spikenard *n.* 哪哒香膏, 产于印度及北部的名贵香膏
12. A bundle of myrrh is my wellbeloved unto me 这句话的意思是, 我爱的人好比馨香的没药, 在我怀中, 日夜陪伴我。a bundle of myrrh 一袋没药。

camphire[1]
In the vineyards of En-gedi[2].

The Man:
Behold, thou art fair, my love; behold, thou art fair;
Thou hast dove's eyes[3].

The Woman:
Behold, thou art fair, my beloved, yea, pleasant:
Also our bed is green.
The beams of our house are cedar,
And our rafters[4] of fir. (1)

I am the rose of Sharon[5],
And the lily of the valleys.

The Man:
As the lily among thorns[6],
So is my love among the daughters.

The Woman:
As the apple tree among the trees of the wood,
So is my beloved among the sons.
I sat down under his shadow with great delight,
And his fruit was sweet to my taste.
He brought me to the banqueting house,
And his banner over me was love[7].
Stay[8] me with flagons[9], comfort me with apples:
For I am sick of love.
His left hand is under my head,
And his right hand doth embrace me.
I charge you, O ye daughters of Jerusalem,
By the roes, and by the hinds of the field[10],
That ye stir not up, nor awake my love,
Till he please. (2: 1–7)

2. The Song of the Lover

The Woman:
The voice of my beloved! behold, he cometh
Leaping upon the mountains, skipping upon the hills.
My beloved is like a roe or a young hart;
Behold, he standeth behind our wall,
He looketh forth at the windows,
Shewing himself through the lattice.
My beloved spake, and said unto me:

The Man:
Rise up, my love, my fair one, and come away.
For, lo, the winter is past,
The rain is over and gone[11];
The flowers appear on the earth;
The time of the singing of birds is come,
And the voice of the turtle[12] is heard in our land:
The fig tree putteth forth her green figs[13],
And the vines with the tender grape give a

---

1. a cluster of camphire 一束凤仙花。
2. En-gedi (地名)隐基底,死海西岸的一片绿洲,以产葡萄著称
3. dove's eyes 鸽子的眼,比喻双目柔纯动人。
4. rafter *n*. 椽子
5. the rose of Sharon /ˈʃærən/ 沙仑的玫瑰。沙仑是靠近地中海的平原。"沙伦的玫瑰"比喻纯洁。
6. the lily among thorns 荆棘丛中的百合花,比喻容貌出众。
7. his banner over me was love 在我头上飘扬爱情的旗帜。也可以理解为: 飘扬在我头上的旗帜写满了"爱情"。"旗帜"象征爱情的宣言。
8. stay *vt*. to strengthen or sustain mentally or spiritually 支持
9. flagon *n*. 酒壶
10. By the roes, and by the hinds of the field (我)指着羚羊和田野的母鹿(吩咐你们)。roe *n*. 羚羊; hind *n*. 母鹿; 两种动物都是用来表达火热爱情的词汇。a young hart 小雄鹿,形容充满青春活力。
11. the winter is past, / The rain is over and gone 在中东一带,冬天就是雨季。
12. the voice of the turtle 斑鸠的声音。衬托爱的呼唤。
13. green figs 无花果树的果子渐渐成熟,衬托爱情的成熟。

good smell.
Arise, my love, my fair one, and come away.
O my dove, that art in the clefts of the rock in the secret places of the stairs[1],
Let me see thy countenance, let me hear thy voice;
For sweet is thy voice, and thy countenance is comely.
Take us the foxes, the little foxes' that spoil the vines:
For our vines have tender grapes.

The Woman:
My beloved is mine, and I am his:
He feedeth among the lilies.
Until the day break and the shadows flee away[2],
Turn, my beloved, and be thou like a roe or a young hart
Upon the mountains of Bether[3]. (2: 8–17)

3. The Wooing

The Man:
Behold, thou art fair, my love; behold, thou art fair;
Thou hast doves' eyes within thy locks[4]:
Thy hair is as a flock of goats,
That appear from mount Gilead[5].
Thy teeth are like a flock of sheep that are even shorn[6],
Which came up from the washing;
Whereof every one bear twins,
And none is barren among them.
Thy lips are like a thread of scarlet[7],
And thy speech[8] is comely:
Thy temples are like a piece of a pomegranate[9]
Within thy locks.
Thy neck is like the tower of David
Builded for an armoury[10],
Whereon there hang a thousand bucklers[11],
All shields of mighty men.
Thy two breasts are like two young roes that are twins,
Which feed among the lilies.
Until the day break,
And the shadows flee away[12],
I will get me to the mountain of myrrh,
And to the hill of frankincense[13].
Thou art all fair, my love;
There is no spot in thee.
Come with me from Lebanon, my spouse,
With me from Lebanon:
Look form the top of Amana,
From the top of Shenir and Hermon[14],
From the loins' dens,
From the mountains of the leopards.[15]

---

1. the clefts of the rock in the secret places of the stairs 陡岩隐秘处的磐石缝里。cleft *n.* 缝隙; stairs 指一层一层的岩石。
2. Until the day break and the shadow flee away 直到天起凉风，日影飞去。
3. the mountains of Bether 比特山，有岩隙的峻岭。
4. within thy locks 在头戴的帕子内。
5. mount Gilead 基列山。新妇的头发如同从基列山上倾涌下来的黑山羊群，漆黑光润，飘然垂下。
6. a flock of sheep that are even shorn 刚剪过毛的一群母羊。
7. a thread of scarlet 形容天生的朱红唇线，鲜艳动人。
8. thy speech 指你的嘴。
9. Thy temples are like a piece of a pomegranate /ˈpɒmgrænɪt/ 太阳穴或前额像石榴，颜色红润。
10. Thy neck is like the tower of David,/Builded for an armoury 你的颈项如同大卫的兵器库。形容颈项挺拔，充满生命力。armoury *n.* 兵器库。
11. buckler *n.* 圆盾
12. Until the day break,/And the shadows flee away 喻指男子盼望同新妇享受性爱的甜蜜。
13. I will get me to the mountain of myrrh,/And to the hill of frankincense 我要往没药山和乳香冈去。"没药山"、"乳香冈"比喻新妇的胴体。
14. Amana, Shenir and Hermon 山名"亚玛拿"、"示尼珥"、"黑门"。男子邀请新妇一同遨游各处，追寻理想天地。
15. From the loins' dens,/From the mountains of the leopards. 狮子洞、豹子山，指惊险之地。

Thou hast ravished[1] my heart, my sister, my spouse;
Thou hast ravished my heart with one of thine eyes,
With one chain of thy neck.
How fair is thy love, my sister, my spouse!
How much better is thy love than wine!
And the smell of thine ointments than all spices!
Thy lips, O my spouse, drop as the honeycomb[2]:
Honey and milk are under thy tongue;
And the smell of thy garments is like the smell of Lebanon.
A garden inclosed is my sister, my spouse;
A spring shut up, a fountain sealed[3].
Thy plants are an orchard of pomegranates[4],
With pleasant fruits;
Camphire, with spikenard,
Spikenard and saffron:
Calamus and cinnamon, with all trees of frankincense;
Myrrh and aloes[5], with all the chief spices:
A fountain of gardens,
A well of living waters,
And streams from Lebanon.

The Woman:
Awake, O north wind; and come, thou south;
Blow upon my garden, that the spices thereof may flow out.
Let my beloved come into his garden,
And eat his pleasant fruits. (4)

The Man:
I am come into my garden, my sister, my spouse:
I have gathered my myrrh with my spice;
I have eaten my honeycomb with my honey;
I have drunk my wine with my milk.[6]

Daughters of Jerusalem:
Eat, O friends;
Drink, yea, drink abundantly, O beloved. (5: 1)

4. A Dream

The Woman:
I sleep, but my heart waketh:
It is the voice of my beloved that knocketh, saying:
Open to me, my sister, my love, my dove, my undefiled[7]:
For my head is filled with dew,
And my locks with the drops of the night.
I have put off my coat; how shall I put it on?
I have washed my feet; how shall I defile them?
My beloved put in his hand by the hole of the door,
And my bowels were moved[8] for him.
I rose up to open to my beloved;
And my hands dropped with myrrh,
And my fingers with sweet smelling myrrh,
Upon the handles of the lock.
I opened to my beloved;
But my beloved had withdrawn himself, and was gone:
My soul failed when he spake:
I sought him, but I could not find him;
I called him, but he gave me no answer.
The watchmen that went about the city found me,
They smote me, they wounded me;

---

1. ravish *vt.* to seize and carry away by force 抢夺。形容新妇的美丽无法抗拒。
2. drop as the honeycomb 像蜂巢一样滴蜜。喻指甜蜜的私语和香吻的滋味。
3. a fountain sealed 我的妹子，我的爱人，乃是关锁的园，禁闭的井，封闭的泉。喻指处女的贞洁。此处把女人身体比喻成园子，身体的各部位则与园子中的各种果实相对应。这一比喻影响深远。
4. an orchard of pomegranates 石榴园。
5. aloe *n.* 芦荟
6. I have drunk my wine with my milk. 喻指初夜的甜蜜。
7. undefiled *adj.* 纯洁无瑕的(人)。 defile *vt.* to make dirty 弄脏。
8. my bowels were moved 动了心。

The keepers of the walls took away my veil from me.
I charge you, O daughters of Jerusalem, if ye find my beloved,
That ye tell him, that I am sick of love.

The Daughters of Jerusalem:
What is thy beloved more than another beloved,
O thou fairest among women?
What is thy beloved more than another beloved,
That thou dost so charge us?

The Woman:
My beloved is white and ruddy[1],
The chiefest among ten thousand.[2]
His head is as the most fine gold,
His locks are bushy, and black as a raven.[3]
His eyes are as the eyes of doves by the rivers of waters,
Washed with milk, and fitly set.
His cheeks are as a bed of spices, as sweet flowers:
His lips like lilies, dropping sweet smelling myrrh.
His hands are as gold rings set with the beryl[4]:
His belly is as bright ivory overlaid with sapphires.[5]
His legs are as pillars of marble, set upon sockets of fine gold:
His countenance is as Lebanon, excellent as the cedars.

His mouth is most sweet: yea, he is altogether lovely.
This is my beloved, and this is my friend,
O daughters of Jerusalem.

The Daughters of Jerusalem:
Whither is thy beloved gone,
O thou fairest among women?
Whither is thy beloved turned aside?
That we may seek him with thee?

The Woman:
My beloved is gone down into his garden, to the beds of spices,
To feed in the gardens, and to gather lilies.
I am my beloved's, and my beloved is mine:
He feedeth among the lilies. (5: 2–6: 3)

5. Praises of the Daughters of Jerusalem

The Man:
How beautiful are thy feet with shoes, O prince's daughter[6]!
The joints of thy thighs are like jewels[7],
The work of the hands of a cunning workman.
Thy navel is like a round goblet,
Which wanteth not liquor[8];
Thy belly is like an heap of wheat
Set about with lilies.[9]
Thy two breasts are like two young roes
That are twins;
Thy neck is as a tower of ivory;
Thine eyes like the fishpools in Heshbon,
By the gate of Bath-rabbim[10]:

---

1. white and ruddy 白里透红，充满青春活力。
2. The chiefest among ten thousand. 英武出众，超乎万人之上。
3. His locks are bushy, and black as a raven. 他的头发厚密，黑如乌鸦。
4. His hands are as gold rings set with the beryl 他的双手像金管，镶嵌着水苍玉。
5. His belly is as bright ivory overlaid with sapphires. 他的身体像象牙雕刻，周围嵌满蓝宝石。
6. prince's daughter 王女，对新妇尊贵的称呼。
7. The joints of thy thighs are like jewels 你的大腿圆润好像美玉。
8. Thy navel is like a round goblet,/Which wanteth not liquor 你的肚脐如圆环，不缺调和的酒。
9. Thy belly is like a heap of wheat/Set about with lilies. 你的腰如打捆的麦子，周围簇拥着百合花。形容新妇的纤腰。
10. Thine eyes like the fishpools in Heshbon,/By the gate of Bath-rabbim 你的双眸像希实本城巴特拉并门旁的水池。"水池"比喻眼睛清澈明亮。

Thy nose is as the tower of Lebanon
Which looketh toward Damascus.[1]
Thine head upon thee is like Carmel,
And the hair of thine head like purple;
The king is held in the galleries.[2]
How fair and how pleasant art thou,
O love, for delights!
This thy stature is like to a palm tree,
And thy breasts to clusters of grapes.[3]
I said: I will go up to the palm tree,
I will take hold of the boughs thereof:
Now also thy breasts shall be as clusters of the vine,
And the smell of thy nose like apples;
And the roof of thy mouth like the best wine.
For my beloved, that goeth down sweetly,
Causing the lips of those that are asleep to speak.[4]

The Woman:
I am my beloved's,
And his desire is toward me.
Come, my beloved, let us go forth into the field;
Let us lodge in the villages.
Let us get up early to the vineyards;
Let us see if the vine flourish,
Whether the tender grape appear,
And the pomegranates bud forth[5];
There will I give thee my loves.
The mandrakes give a smell,
And at our gates are all manner of pleasant fruits,
New and old,
Which I have laid up for thee, O my beloved. (7)

6. The Pledge of Love

The Woman:
Set me as a seal upon thine heart,
As a seal upon thine arm:
For love is strong as death;
Jealousy is cruel as the grave:
The coals thereof are coals of fire,
Which hath a most vehement flame.
Many waters cannot quench love,
Neither can the floods drown it:
If a man would give all the substance of his house for love,
It would utterly be contemned. (8: 6–7)

三、圣经文化知识链接

1. 对《雅歌》的不同诠释

对于《雅歌》的诗体性质，人们早就确信无疑。然而，《雅歌》究竟是何种类型的诗，论者引经据典，各执一端，一直没有达成共识。对《雅歌》的诠释主要有以下4种：

(1) 戏剧：有对白、有故事，但没有道具；一说有两个主角"所罗门与书拉密女；一说有3个

---

1. Thy nose is as the tower of Lebanon/Which looketh toward Damascus. 你的鼻子像朝向大马士革的黎巴嫩塔。比喻鼻子挺直。
2. Thine head upon thee is like Carmel, The king is held in the galleries. 新妇的头发像迦密山(茂密)，呈紫黑色(有光泽)。王的心被发绺系住了。比喻新妇的美发性感。
3. This thy stature is like to a palm tree,/And thy breasts to clusters of grapes. 你的身量好像一棵棕树，你的两乳如同其上的果实，累累下垂。stature *n.* the natural height of a human being 身材；"棕树"形容身材高大、壮实、笔直；clusters of grapes "串串果实"形容乳房结实、丰满。
4. For my beloved, that goeth down sweetly,/Causing the lips of those that are asleep to speak. (爱情如美酒)从爱人的嘴里流下，刺激唇齿，激发爱情。
5. bud forth (石榴花)萌芽；放蕊。

主角: 所罗门、牧羊女、牧羊郎。

(2) 牧歌: 有户外场景和田园意象，有两个主人公: 所罗门和书拉密女。

(3) 爱情诗集:《雅歌》是若干短诗汇集而成的爱情诗集，描写男女主人公从恋爱到婚姻生活的过程。

(4) 寓言:《雅歌》的男、女主角分别是上帝和人，犹太拉比把他们当作耶和华与子民以色列民族; 基督教把他们看成基督和教会的关系; 中国教会一向也采用寓言的方法来诠释《雅歌》。

(5) 礼仪歌: 是异教礼仪的诗章，采用酒、香料等词汇来表达异教神秘的经验。

抛开神学层面，以女性主义视角或从世俗的男女性爱出发,《雅歌》的爱情主题及整体结构突出的是女性的地位，表示出男女之间平等的关系。从女性形象的塑造、话语、乐园模式的隐喻来看,《雅歌》对女性性心理的直接袒露以及对女性在两性关系中的主动态度的描写，体现了非常强烈的女性意识。我们认为,《雅歌》是一部爱情诗集，它不仅是圣经诗歌中一枝独放异彩的奇葩，也是世界上古文学中不可多得的艺术珍品。

2.《雅歌》与世界三大爱情神话诗集

世界三大爱情神话诗集分别来自公元前3千纪中期的苏美尔、公元前1千纪前期的埃及和公元前1千纪中期的巴比伦。学者们把《雅歌》和这3部作品加以比较后发现，无论是内部语言还是外在结构，它们确实有相似之处。

苏美尔爱情神话诗用于当地每年一度的宗教仪式上，以庆祝牧羊王杜穆济和王后英安娜的圣婚。英安娜的职责是掌管性爱、丰产和生殖。她为欢迎情郎杜穆济到来而做准备:

> 她拿起头饰放在头上，
> 她拿起金丝带束住头发，
> 她拿起细长的金耳坠戴在耳朵上，
> 她拿起黑色的柳枝围住下腹……

埃及的爱情诗《果园之歌》的开头有:

> 石榴说:
> 她的牙齿像我的种籽，
> 她的双乳像我的果子。

巴比伦的爱情诗与其相似，描写巴比伦王马尔都克与情人伊什塔尔约会前所做的准备，以及伊什塔尔的服饰打扮。

上述爱情诗集有一个共同特点: 对异性的肉体吸引进行精心而具体详细的描述。这些诗与叙利亚民间新婚庆典期间演唱的名为"瓦斯弗"(Wasf)的诗极为相似。叙利亚人多在阳春三月举行婚礼，地点是打谷场，新郎新娘坐在特定的位置上，客人们围着他们又唱又跳，歌中唱的是新郎、新娘体态的美妙。新娘有时会站起来跳舞，以便让新郎观赏她的美色。新婚夫妇还化妆成国王和王后，村上的男女老少都要为他们服务。"瓦斯弗"在狭义上被限定为婚礼庆典仪式上以新郎、新娘名义演唱的诗，广义上包括任何描写女性装饰品和肉体的诗。《雅歌》中也有一些对自然意象和恋人美妙胴体的详细描绘以及对装饰品的指称，具有"瓦斯弗"诗歌的典型特征: 用于婚礼仪式，歌唱时有客人在旁，客人在庆典上发挥积极作用，新郎扮作国王。尤其值得注意的是，诗歌特别注重对新娘肉体的详致描述。因此，我们把《雅歌》理解为用于婚礼庆典的一组情歌:主人公以所罗门王和书拉密女自比——因为前者是最荣耀的王,后者是最美丽的少女,组诗用对唱、独唱、合唱、伴唱等形式表达热烈的追求、新人的美貌和真挚的爱情。

四、圣经文化专题

1. 《雅歌》所反映的希伯来民族审美意识

《创世记》开篇就写道:上帝说:"要有光",就有了光。这或许是希伯来民族对"光"情有独钟的根源。从上帝创造光到创造出太阳、月亮、星空,从上帝创造的宝石闪光,到健康的肉体的光彩,从象征生命之美的光明、白昼,到大自然五彩斑斓的色彩和人类制造的美丽服饰,这些都影响了希伯来民族的审美趣味和审美追求。《雅歌》中男女恋人用崇高美的比喻方式表达世俗爱情,从而形成了世俗美与崇高美相互渗透的审美情趣。

在希腊古典时代,美被认为是静止不变的,是安详与均衡的美。而在希伯来人看来,美是运动着的、富有生命力与充满活力的。《圣经》里所赞美的自然对象,都是在运动变化着的对象,都是显示出勃勃生机的对象。布满了树木、草地、果林的环境都被形容为动态的"流着奶和蜜"之地;伊甸园之美是以树木的苍翠、果实的繁茂和勃勃生机的形态来显现的。《雅歌》对人体的描写,更强调生机勃勃的动感。《雅歌》中所表现出来的活力美与动感美,具有西方浪漫主义因素。他们或展示情真意浓、心荡神怡的初恋时刻,或热烈地表达对对方的爱慕之情,并抒发沉浸于美妙爱情时期的内心感受。需要指出的是,从这个意义上来讲,《雅歌》更接近于现代理想的爱情观:注重彼此内心感受、追求纯真无邪的爱情、渴慕彼此外在美感、欣赏彼此内在品质,而不被社会地位和家庭财产等功利性因素所诱惑。《雅歌》中的一些植物已经被西方文学家看做是美好、吉祥、幸福的象征,具有美的意象,并被后代文学家称颂。这也是《雅歌》影响深远的原因之一。

2. 从《雅歌》看希伯来人对音乐的爱好

希伯来民族是喜好音乐的民族。《圣经》在相当程度上是一部音乐化了的文本作品。在《创世记》中有"犹八是一切弹琴吹箫之人的祖师"之说,而其中的《诗篇》、《雅歌》等原来就是歌曲。这部分诗文本身韵律规整、押韵上口,甚至在《诗篇》有些篇章中,还常标出特定的吟唱调名,诸如"百合花"、"远方无声鸽"、"流离歌"、"休要毁坏"、"募便拉"等等,颇类似中国的曲牌。

从《圣经》的很多章节中,我们可以看出古以色列人爱好音乐的传统。如对耶弗他的女儿,摩西的姐姐米利安的描写。《圣经》音乐要求人们用"赞美诗、赞歌、圣歌"的形式来歌唱和作曲。《历代志》保存了一批珍贵的文艺资料,多方面记载了犹太人的音乐活动。如大卫尚未建殿时,就确定了在殿中"唱歌、敲钹、弹琴、鼓瑟的人"(《历代志上》25:6);利未人在圣殿竣工典礼上"拿着亚卫的乐器,……祭司在众人面前吹号"(《历代志下》7:6)。国中每遇重大事件必定奏乐歌唱,如耶何耶大政变成功后"百夫长和吹号的人侍立在王左右,国民都欢乐吹号;又有歌唱的,用各样乐器领人歌唱赞美"(《历代志下》23:13)。《历代志上》第23章第5节记载"有四千人用大卫所作的乐器颂赞耶和华";《历代志下》第5章第11—14节在描写耶路撒冷圣殿落成之后举行的庆典,"他们出圣所的时候,歌唱的利未人亚萨、希幔、耶杜顿和他们的众子众兄弟,都穿细麻布衣服,站在坛的东边,敲钹、鼓瑟、弹琴,同着他们有120个祭司吹号;吹号的、歌唱的都一齐发声,声合为一,赞美感谢耶和华;吹号、敲钹、用各种乐器,扬声赞美耶和华"。从这些记载,我们可以看到希伯来音乐很早就发展起来,并趋于成熟。

这种音乐传统在《雅歌》中体现得更为突出。《雅歌》用来对唱,《雅歌》以情侣对唱形式写成。新娘唱道:"我的良人白而且红,超乎万人之上。他的头像至精的金子;他的头发厚密累垂,黑如乌鸦。"新郎唱道:"我妹子,我新妇,你夺了我的心!你用眼一看,用你颈上的一条金链,夺了我的心。"(《雅歌》5:10—11;4:9)

这种传统的形成有多方面的因素,但在很大程度上最根本地导源于古以色列人的宗教文化精神,特别是与在犹太文化生活中有着权威意义的摩西律法有关。摩西律法第二条规定:"不可为自己雕刻偶像,也不可作什么形象仿佛上天、下地和地底下、水中的百物"。犹太教这种反对偶像崇拜的神学思想的影响已经拓展到犹太生活的各个不同领域,特别是拓展到犹太人的艺术活动中去,由此我们可以理解犹太艺术中强烈的抽象精神的源泉。因为犹太教的神学思想在很大程度上又都是犹太民族的一种文化思想和传统精神,这一思想的影响是持续不断的,另一方面又是十分广泛的,它既影响着犹太教的忠实信徒,也影响到一般的世俗化的犹太人。

"一种文明标志着一种特定的审美情趣,表征了一种享受美感和想象美感的独特内涵。"[1]在犹太文化中,摩西律法反对偶像崇拜的思想可以说是犹太审美理想的主要特征,并制约着犹太艺术活动的各个领域。基于此,犹太传统中的艺术精神和审美理想具有注重抽象、摒弃具象的特征。作为古老的民族,希伯来人又极富抒情特质,但是,由于教规上不允许崇拜偶像,并禁止制作偶像,限制了造型艺术的发展,所以,他们的情感只有诉诸无形的形式——音乐和诗歌。

五、圣经典故集锦

1. **a lily among thorns**(百合花在荆棘内):指"姿色出众"、"鹤立鸡群"、"出类拔萃"、"压倒群芳"。典出《雅歌》第2章2节:As the lily among thorns, so is my love among the daughters. 我的佳偶在女子中,好像百合花在荆棘内。

2. **the palanquin of Solomon**(所罗门之轿):指"御驾龙乘"、"彩舆华轿"、"豪华车驾"。典出《雅歌》第3章7、9、10节:King Solomon made himself a chariot of the wood of Lebanon. He made the pillars thereof of silver, the bottom thereof of gold, the covering of it of purple, the midst thereof being paved with love, for the daughters of Jerusalem. 所罗门王用黎巴嫩木为自己制造一乘花轿。轿柱是用银作的,轿底是用金作的,坐垫是紫色的,其中所铺的乃耶路撒冷众女子的爱情。

3. **doves beside brooks of water**(溪水旁的鸽子):指"水汪汪的眼睛"、"明眸晶莹"、"秋波

---

1. 【美】摩迪凯·开普兰(Mordecai M. Kaplan) 著:《犹太教:一种文明》,第236页。转引自刘洪一《犹太文化要义》,第329页。

水灵"。典出《雅歌》第5章第12节: His eyes are as the eyes of doves by the rivers of waters, washed with milk , and fitly set. 他的眼如溪水旁的鸽子眼，用奶洗净，安得合适。

4. **beautiful as the moon, bright as the sun** (美丽如月亮，皎洁如日头): 指"珠辉玉丽"、"秀美绝伦"。典出《雅歌》第6章第10节: Who is she that looketh forth as the morning, fair as the moon, clear as the sun, and terrible as an army with banners? 那向外观看如晨光发现，美丽如月亮，皎洁如日头，威武如展开旌旗军队的是谁呢？

5. **a gazelle or a young stag on the mountains where spices grow** (香草山上的羚羊或小鹿): 指"心爱伴侣"、"如意郎君"。典出《雅歌》第8章第14节: Make haste, my beloved, and be thou like to a roe or to a young hart upon the mountains of spices. 我的良人哪，求你快来，如羚羊或小鹿在香草山上。

六、课堂讨论题

1. 比较《雅歌》中的"园"和"伊甸园"。
2. 结合所学《圣经》章节，谈谈《圣经》中的爱情观。
3. 中国文学作品中对女性的描写有类似《雅歌》的吗？
4. 谈谈《雅歌》所反映的希伯来民族自然观。

七、课后思考题

1. 中国古代文学中也有描写男女表达爱恋和纯真爱情的诗作，它们与《雅歌》有何异同？
2. 为什么把"大学"比作"象牙塔"？
3. 如果说《圣经》是西方文学之花，那么《雅歌》就是《圣经》之花。《雅歌》对现代中国文学家有什么影响吗？
4. 你知道美国电影《美国往事》和英国电影《保持缄默》对《雅歌》的引用吗？

第十三讲 以色列民族的绝唱:《哀歌》

Lamentations, a Poetic Peak of the Israel

一、导读:《哀歌》的文体特征

从内容来看,《哀歌》写于公元前586年耶路撒冷刚遭沦陷之后,公元前539年巴比伦帝国灭亡之前。《哀歌》共五章,每章为一首哀歌。

《哀歌》具有独特的诗体形式。前4首均采用"贯顶体"(Acrostic,又称"离合诗"或"藏头诗")写成。这是一种字面顺序诗(Alphabetic Poem),即每一句的头一个字母都按顺序排列。希伯来语有22个辅音字母,所以第一、二、四首都是22句,第一句用希伯来文第1个字母"Alph",第二句用第2个字母"Beth",依此类推,第22句用希伯来文最后一个字母"Taw"。由于第三首具有统领全诗的作用,每三个双行句开头的希伯来字母都是相同的,这样,诗节的数目就是22的3倍。第五首并非离合诗体,但也有22节。希伯来原诗这种煞费苦心、精雕细琢的体制能给人严密工整的视觉感受,同时为读者的阅读和记忆提供了极大方便。此外,每个诗节又采用了"气纳体"(Kinah,意思是"悲哀"),为古希伯来民族的独创。这是一种常用于哀悼的诗体,每行5个强音,分作前后两段,前段3个,后段2个,前后段之间出现表述哭泣吞声的短暂停顿,颇能造成悲哀不已、泣不成声的艺术气氛。

在希伯来圣经中,《哀歌》书卷并没有注明作者是谁。按照基督教传统,它的作者是耶利米,其主要根据是《历代志下》第35章25节这句话: And Jeremiah lamented for Josiah: and all the singing men and the singing women spake of Josiah in their lamentations to this day, and made them an ordinance in Israel: and, behold, they are written in the lamentations. 耶利米(犹大国第十六任国王)为约西亚作哀歌,所有歌唱的男女也唱哀歌,追悼约西亚,直到今日;而且在以色列中成了定例,这歌载在哀歌书上。在《希腊文七十子译本》和《拉丁通俗译本》中,《哀歌》开头附加了说明"以色列人被掳后,耶利米坐着为耶路撒冷哀哭,唱此哀歌。"因此,人们推断作者是耶利米,《哀歌》的全称因此变成 The Lamentations of Jeremiah(《耶利米哀歌》)。

本讲选取第1、2、4章:
第1章描写耶路撒冷劫后惨状,抒哀痛之情。
第2章历陈难民之苦,探究败亡原因。
第4章对照圣城今昔,倾诉灭国之仇。

二、选文及注释

Part 1

How doth the city sit solitary, that was full of people!

How is she become as a widow!

She that was great among the nations, and princess among the provinces[1],

How is she become tributary[2]!

She weepeth sore in the night, and her tears are on her cheeks;

Among all her lovers she hath none to comfort her:

All her friends have dealt treacherously with her,

They are become her enemies.

Judah is gone into captivity because of affliction, and because of great servitude[3];

She dwelleth among the heathen[4], she findeth no rest:

All her persecutors overtook her within the straits[5].

The ways of Zion do mourn, because none come to the solemn assembly[6];

All her gates are desolate, her priests do sigh:

Her virgins are afflicted[7], and she herself is in bitterness.

Her adversaries[8] are become the head, her enemies prosper;

For the LORD hath afflicted her for the multitude of her transgressions:

Her young children are gone into captivity before the adversary.

And from the daughters of Zion all her majesty is departed:

Her princes are become like harts[9] that find no pasture.

And they are gone without strength before the pursuer.

Jerusalem remembereth in the days of her affliction and of her miseries

All her pleasant things that were from the days of old:

When her people fell into the hand of the adversary, and none did help her,

The adversaries saw her, they did mock at her desolations[10].

Jerusalem hath grievously sinned; therefore she is become as an unclean thing:

All that honoured her despise her, because they have seen her nakedness:

Yea, she sigheth, and turneth backward.

Her filthiness was in her skirts; she remembered not her latter end[11];

Therefore is she come down wonderfully; she hath no comforter:

Behold, O LORD, my affliction; for the enemy hath magnified[12] himself.

The adversary hath spread out his hand upon all her pleasant things:

for she hath seen that the heathen entered into her sanctuary,

Whom thou didst command that they should not enter into thy congregation.

All her people sigh, they seek bread;

---

1. princess among the provinces 列国中的首领。
2. tributary *adj.* 从属的; 附庸的, 此处引申为 "成为奴隶"
3. servitude *n.* the state of being a salve or completely subject to sb. more powerful 劳役, 苦役
4. heathen *n.* 异族人, 外邦人。指不信奉耶和华的异教徒。
5. straits *n.* used in reference to a situation characterized by a specified degree of trouble or difficulty 困境; 窘迫, 危难
6. the solemn assembly 守节。
7. afflicted *adj.* affected advertently 受尽痛苦的
8. adversary *n.* one's opponent in a contest, conflict or dispute 敌人
9. hart *n.* 公鹿; 雄赤鹿
10. desolation *n.* great unhappiness or loneliness 悲哀; 忧伤; 不幸; 孤寂
11. latter end 结局。
12. magnify *vt.* to increase or intensify 加强

They have given their pleasant things for meat to relieve the soul:

See, O LORD, and consider; for I am become vile¹.

Is it nothing to you, all ye that pass by?

Behold, and see if there be any sorrow like unto my sorrow, which is done unto me,

Wherewith the LORD hath afflicted me in the day of his fierce anger.

From above hath he sent fire into my bones, and it prevaileth against them:

He hath spread a net for my feet, he hath turned me back:

He hath made me desolate and faint all the day.

The yoke of my transgressions is bound by his hand:

They are wreathed², and come up upon my neck: he hath made my strength to fall,

The LORD hath delivered me into their hands, from whom I am not able to rise up.

The LORD hath trodden under foot all my mighty men in the midst of me:

He hath called an assembly against me to crush my young men:

The LORD hath trodden the virgin, the daughter of Judah, as in a winepress³.

For these things I weep; mine eye, mine eye runneth down with water,

Because the comforter that should relieve my soul is far from me:

My children are desolate, because the enemy prevailed.

Zion spreadeth forth her hands, and there is none to comfort her:

The LORD hath commanded concerning Jacob, that his adversaries should be round about him:

Jerusalem is as a menstruous woman among them.

The LORD is righteous; for I have rebelled against his commandment:

Hear, I pray you, all people, and behold my sorrow:

My virgins and my young men are gone into captivity.

I called for my lovers, but they deceived me:

My priests and mine elders gave up the ghost in the city,

While they sought their meat to relieve their souls.

Behold, O LORD; for I am in distress: my bowels are troubled⁴;

Mine heart is turned within me; for I have grievously rebelled:

Abroad the sword bereaveth⁵, at home there is as death.

They have heard that I sigh: there is none to comfort me:

All mine enemies have heard of my trouble; they are glad that thou hast done it:

Thou wilt bring the day that thou hast called, and they shall be like unto me.

Let all their wickedness come before thee;

And do unto them, as thou hast done unto me for all my transgressions:

For my sighs are many, and my heart is faint. (1)

---

1. vile *adj.* of little worth or value 〈古〉微不足道的; 卑微的, 此处意为"被人藐视"
2. wreathe *vt.* to twist or entwine (sth.) round or over sth. 把……绕成一圈; 盘绕; 缠绕
3. winepress *n.* a press in which grapes are squeezed in making wine 压酒池
4. my bowels are troubled 我的心肠激动。
5. Abroad the sword bereaveth 街上有刀剑使人丧子 abroad *adv.* out of doors 〈古〉在室外; bereave *vt.* to deprive (sb.) of a close relation or friend through their death 使丧失亲人

Part 2

How hath the LORD covered the daughter of Zion with a cloud in his anger,

And cast down from heaven unto the earth the beauty of Israel,

And remembered not his foot-stool in the day of his anger!

The LORD hath swallowed up all the habitations of Jacob, and hath not pitied:

He hath thrown down in his wrath the strong holds of the daughter of Judah;

He hath brought them down to the ground:

He hath polluted the kingdom and the princes thereof.

He hath cut off in his fierce anger all the horn of Israel:

He hath drawn back his right hand from before the enemy,

And he burned against Jacob like a flaming fire, which devoureth round about.

He hath bent his bow like an enemy: he stood with his right hand as an adversary,

And slew all that were pleasant to the eye

In the tabernacle of the daughter of Zion: he poured out his fury like fire.

The LORD was as an enemy: he hath swallowed up Israel,

He hath swallowed up all her palaces: he hath destroyed his strong holds,

And hath increased in the daughter of Judah mourning and lamentation.

And he hath violently taken away his tabernacle, as it were of a garden:

He hath destroyed his places of the assembly:

The LORD hath caused the solemn feasts and sabbaths to be forgotten in Zion,

And hath despised in the indignation of his anger the king and the priest.

The LORD hath cast off his altar, he hath abhorred his sanctuary,

He hath given up into the hand of the enemy the walls of her palaces;

They have made a noise in the house of the LORD, as in the day of a solemn feast.

The LORD hath purposed to destroy the wall of the daughter of Zion:

He hath stretched out a line, he hath not withdrawn his hand from destroying:

Therefore he made the rampart and the wall to lament; they languished[1] together.

Her gates are sunk into the ground; he hath destroyed and broken her bars:

Her king and her princes are among the Gentiles[2]: the law is no more;

Her prophets also find no vision from the LORD.

The elders of the daughter of Zion sit upon the ground, and keep silence:

They have cast up dust upon their heads; they have girded themselves with sack-cloth:

The virgins of Jerusalem hang down their heads to the ground.

Mine eyes do fail with tears, my bowels are troubled,

My liver is poured upon the earth, for the destruction of the daughter of my people;

Because the children and the sucklings[3] swoon[4] in the streets of the city.

They say to their mothers, Where is corn and wine?

When they swooned as the wounded in the streets of the city,

When their soul was poured out into their mothers' bosom.

What thing shall I take to witness for thee?

What thing shall I liken[5] to thee, O

---

1. languish *vi.* to lose vitality, to grow weak 衰弱
2. Gentiles /ˈdʒentaɪl/ *n.* people that are not Jewish 非犹太人，常译为"外邦人"。犹太人中常用以特指基督教徒，同时也指不信犹太教和基督教的罗马人。
3. suckling *n.* an unweaned child 乳儿
4. swoon *vi.* to faint 昏厥，昏倒
5. liken *vt.* to point out the resemblance of sb. or sth. to 把……比作

daughter of Jerusalem?

What shall I equal to thee, that I may comfort thee, O virgin daughter of Zion?

For thy breach is great like the sea: who can heal thee?

Thy prophets have seen vain and foolish things for thee:

And they have not discovered thine iniquity, to turn away thy captivity;

But have seen for thee false burdens and causes of banishment.

All that pass by clap their hands at thee;

They hiss and wag their head at the daughter of Jerusalem, saying,

Is this the city that men call The perfection of beauty, The joy of the whole earth?

All thine enemies have opened their mouth against thee:

They hiss and gnash[1] the teeth: they say, We have swallowed her up:

Certainly this is the day that we looked for; we have found, we have seen it.

The LORD hath done that which he had devised;

He hath fulfilled his word that he had commanded in the days of old:

He hath thrown down, and hath not pitied:

And he hath caused thine enemy to rejoice over thee,

He hath set up the horn of thine adversaries.

Their heart cried unto the LORD,

O wall of the daughter of Zion, let tears run down like a river day and night:

Give thyself no rest; let not the apple of thine eye cease.

Arise, cry out in the night: in the beginning of the watches

Pour out thine heart like water before the face of the LORD:

Lift up thy hands toward him for the life of thy young children,

That faint for hanger in the top of every street.

Behold, O LORD, and consider to whom thou hast done this.

Shall the women eat their fruit, and children of a span[2] long?

Shall the priest and the prophet be slain in the sanctuary of the LORD?

The young and the old lie on the ground in the streets:

My virgins and my young men are fallen by the sword;

Thou hast slain them in the day of thine anger; thou hast killed and not pitied.

Thou hast called as in a solemn day my terrors round about,

So that in the day of the LORD's anger none escaped nor remained:

Those that I have swaddled and brought up hath mine enemy consumed. (2)

Part 3

How is the gold become dim! how is the most fine gold changed!

The stones of the sanctuary[3] are poured out in the top of every street.

The precious sons of Zion, comparable to fine gold,

How are they esteemed as earthen pitchers, the work of the hands of the potter!

Even the sea monsters draw out the breast, they give suck to their young ones:

The daughter of my people is become cruel, like the ostriches[4] in the wilderness.

The tongue of the sucking child cleaveth to the roof of his mouth for thirst:

---

1. gnash *vt.* to grind (one's teeth) together as a sign of anger (often used hyperbolically) 因(愤怒或痛苦等)咬(牙),磨(牙)
2. span *n.* a short distance or time 〈古〉一段时间(尤指人的一生); 短促的时间
3. sanctuary *n.* 圣所。此处指耶路撒冷的圣殿。
4. ostrich *n.* 鸵鸟

The young children ask bread, and no one breaketh it unto them.

They that did feed delicately are desolate in the streets:

They that were brought up in scarlet embrace dung-hills[1].

For the punishment of the iniquity of the daughter of my people

Is greater than the punishment of the sin of Sodom[2],

That was overthrown as in a moment, and no hands stayed on her.

Her Nazarites[3] were purer than snow, they were whiter than milk,

They were more ruddy in body than rubies, their polishing was of sapphire[4]:

Their visage[5] is blacker than a coal; they are not known in the streets:

Their skin cleaveth to their bones; it is withered, it is become like a stick.

They that be slain with the sword are better than they that be slain with hunger:

For these pine away[6], stricken through for want of the fruits of the field.

The hands of the pitiful women have sodden[7] their own children:

They were their meat in the destruction of the daughter of my people.

The LORD hath accomplished his fury; he hath poured out his fierce anger,

And hath kindled a fire in Zion, and it hath devoured the foundations thereof.

The kings of the earth, and all the inhabitants of the world, would not have believed

That the adversary and the enemy should have entered into the gates of Jerusalem.

For the sins of her prophets, and the iniquities of her priests,

That have shed the blood of the just in the midst of her,

They have wandered as blind men in the streets, they have polluted themselves with blood,

So that men could not touch their garments.

They cried unto them, Depart ye; it is unclean; depart, depart, touch not:

When they fled away and wandered, they said among the heathen,

They shall no more sojourn there.

The anger of the LORD hath divided them; he will no more regard[8] them:

They respected not the persons of the priests, they favoured not the elders.

As for us, our eyes as yet failed for our vain help:

In our watching we have watched for a nation that could not save us.

They hunt our steps, the we cannot go in our streets:

Our end is near, our days are fulfilled; for our end is come.

Our persecutors[9] are swifter than the eagles of the heaven:

They pursued us upon the mountains, they laid wait for us in the wilderness.

The breath of our nostrils, the anointed of the LORD, was taken in their pits,

Of whom we said, Under his shadow we shall live among the heathen.

Rejoice and be glad, O daughter of

---

1. dung-hill 堆积如山的肥粪。dung *n.* 动物的粪便。这两句诗的意思是：那些从前吃美食的，现今都流落街头，孤单凄凉；那些从前在豪奢生活中长大的，现今却在垃圾堆中打滚。
2. Sodom "罪恶之城"所多玛。最早出现在《创世记》，上帝用硫磺和火将其毁灭。
3. Nazarite /ˈnæzəraɪt/ *n.* 拿细耳人。曾出现在《士师记》，古希伯来人中的修行者，此处表示圣洁。
4. their polishing was of sapphire 他们的样貌像蓝宝石一样美丽。polish *v.* to improve; to refine 使(人、举止、仪表等)变得优雅; sapphire *n.* 蓝宝石
5. visage *n.* 脸，面容
6. pine (away) *vi.* to suffer a mental and physical decline, especially because of a broken heart 因悲伤而憔悴
7. sodden *vt.* to saturate (sth.) with water 〈古〉浸透，即烹煮
8. regard *vt.* to pay attention to; to heed 〈古〉看顾
9. persecutor *n.* 迫害者

Edom, that dewellest in the land of Uz;
　The cup also shall pass through unto thee:
　Thou shalt be drunken, and shalt make thyself naked.
　The punishment of thine iniquity is accomplished, O daughter of Zion;
　He will no more carry thee away into captivity:
　He will visit[1] thine iniquity, O daughter of Edom;
　He will discover thy sins. (4)

三、圣经文化知识链接

1. 希伯来圣经"五小卷"与希伯来节日[2]

所谓"五小卷"(The Megiloth, Five Scrolls),指的是希伯来圣经中篇幅较短的5部经卷:《路得记》、《以斯帖记》、《传道书》、《雅歌》和《哀歌》。按基督教对《圣经》的排列方式,它们被置于旧约的各个部分,《路得记》所载故事大概发生在士师时期,所以放在《士师记》之后,《撒母耳记》之前;《以斯帖记》中的故事发生在波斯统治时期,因此被归于流放时代的历史书之中,紧跟在《尼希米记》之后;《传道书》在文体上属于"智慧文学",和《雅歌》一样相传为所罗门所作,因此被放在《箴言》之后,而在基督教传统中归于"诗歌"部分,在天主教传统中则归于"智慧书"部分;至于《哀歌》,传统上被认为是由先知耶利米所写,记载耶路撒冷被攻陷的史实,所以放在了《耶利米书》后,归于"先知书"部分。然而,在希伯来圣经中这五卷书作为一个整体放在"圣卷"这一部分里。若以外在标准来看,将这五卷书归为一个整体,缺乏说服力。因为它们的创作时代可能跨越了几百年(约公元前1100—公元前450年);其次,它们的文体也各有不同。其中《路得记》和《以斯帖记》是"故事"(story narrative),《传道书》则是哲学式的沉思和感悟,《雅歌》是一部情歌集,《哀歌》则是忧伤的挽词。再者,它们的作者也不像"先知书"那样属于某一特殊的社会群体。那么,"五小卷"在希伯来圣经中为何具有整体性和独立性呢?

首先是礼仪(liturgical)的原因。这五卷书篇幅都比较短小,适宜于在公众集会时朗读。渐渐地,它们就成为犹太教五个重要节日期间必须朗读的经文[3]:

五小卷	朗诵节日	纪念意义
《雅歌》	逾越节(Passover)	纪念摩西在上帝庇护下带领以色列人出埃及
《路得记》	五旬节(Feast of Weeks)	纪念农业的丰收及上帝在西奈山颁布的律法
《传道书》	住棚节(Feast of Tabernacles)	纪念生命的变幻与短暂
《以斯帖记》	普珥节(Purim)	纪念以色列民族虎口脱险、战胜敌人
《哀歌》	圣殿节(Ninth of Av)	纪念耶路撒冷在公元前586年被毁

---

1. visit *vt.* to punish (a person or wrongful act) 〈古〉惩罚
2. 本项参考李炽昌、游斌著:《生命言说与社群认同——希伯来圣经五小卷研究》,北京:中国社会科学出版社,2003年版,第7—11页。
3. 需要注意的是,除《以斯帖记》和《哀歌》外,其他三小卷与节日之间并无明显的历史关系。

其次，五小卷被看做一个整体，还在于"五"这个数字在希伯来传统中的神圣性。我们知道，五卷律法书是希伯来信仰的基础，也是判定其他经卷的重要性、正统性的一个标尺。希伯来圣经中的另一个重要文本《诗篇》(*Psalms*)也被分成"五卷"。因此，"五小卷"被编订为一个整体，是为了与神圣的律法"五经"相呼应。弥散着虚无主义的《传道书》和宣扬男女情爱的《雅歌》得以纳入正典，"所罗门是其作者"是一个很重要的原因。其实，也许本来没有内在关联的"五小卷"被整合为一体，其本身即是一个诠释学的过程。希伯来圣经"五小卷"与这些节期相结合，以其丰富多彩的形式，弘扬着希伯来传统文化，潜移默化地影响着一代又一代的犹太人，从而强化了其民族特色。

2. 犹太历史的象征——哭墙[1]

圣殿山是犹太教徒最重要的一处圣地。约公元前1000年由大卫王的儿子所罗门，耗时7载，动用20万人在耶路撒冷一座小山，即后来著名的神庙山(也称圣殿山)上兴建了一座华丽的圣殿，作为朝拜犹太教的神耶和华的地方，这就是著名的耶路撒冷第一圣殿。公元前586年，巴比伦军队攻占耶路撒冷，第一圣殿被毁，后来犹太人两度重修圣殿，但又在罗马占领时期两次被毁坏殆尽。保护"至圣所"的著名大殿是公元前37年由希律一世大帝在所罗门建造的第一圣殿的废墟上重建起来的。希律圣殿被古罗马提图斯军团毁于公元70年，此后，犹太人在原来犹太圣殿废墟上，用约600块原来圣殿的巨石，垒起一堵50米长、19米高的大墙，称为"西墙"。犹太人称为"哭墙"(Wailing Wall)，成为当今犹太教最重要的崇拜物。

犹太人认为哭墙是当年圣殿留下的唯一遗迹，因而是犹太教最神圣的祈祷地方。许多世纪以来，犹太教徒都到这里来面壁祈祷，每当追忆历史上圣殿被毁情景，便不禁嚎啕大哭一场，"哭墙"因此而得名。以色列人发誓决不废弃"哭墙"。

哭墙看起来和一堵巨大的石墙无异。每天都可看见犹太人自动分成男女两拨，分别在哭墙的北南两段祈祷，他们常常手捧《圣经》，一边祈祷，一边点头(根据犹太教规，凡是念到圣人名字的时候必须点头)，有的人甚至搬把椅子面对哭墙，一整天都沉浸在与上帝的对话中；至于闻名世界的、把写着心愿的纸条塞入哭墙墙缝的行为，倒不是犹太人的习俗，而是旅游者们的发明。

1967年，"哭墙"所在的破败街区被拆除，成了一片宽阔的铺砌广场。虔诚的犹太教徒热切希望能重建这一圣殿，但那是不可能的，因为那将意味着要拆除后来在遗址上建起的穆斯林圣所。在圣殿地基附近还建有一座

---

1. 资料来源: http://news.xinhuanet.com/ziliao/2005-05/17/content_2964286.htm; 2009年5月6日读取。

犹太教堂和一座拉比学馆。

1981年,"哭墙"被列入《世界遗产目录》。(上页中上图为"哭墙"全貌;见"巴勒斯坦旅游商务网"。下图为2004年3月30日一名以色列男孩亲吻哭墙而祈祷。新华社记者 高学余 摄)

四、圣经文化专题

1. 从《哀歌》看希伯来诗歌的抒情性

希伯来诗人富于真挚、深沉而丰富的情感,他们对爱、憎、欢乐、悲伤、忧愁等的感受十分强烈。生动逼真地再现内心世界的真实和澎湃的激情是希伯来诗歌的最大特点。《哀歌》作为《圣经》中最杰出的诗歌,抒情性尤为突出,其情感主旋律为哀情,但在悲情的抒发之中,还糅杂着祈祷、赞美、诅咒、抱怨等情感。纵观《哀歌》,可以看出,其抒情特征有以下几点:

第一、抒情程度强烈,想象力丰富。借助自然万物加以想象,采用拟人、夸张等手法烘托气氛,是希伯来诗人增强抒情和诗情的常用技巧。如他们高兴时,日头、月亮、星宿、天上的天和天上的水、大山、小山,都与他们同乐,一同欢欣鼓舞,歌颂上帝(见《诗篇》148:3)。悲哀之时,群山、众水、丛林、乃至乡间的土路和圣殿的高墙似乎都和诗人一起流泪哭诉:"锡安的城墙啊,愿你流泪如河,昼夜不息"(《哀歌》2:18);"恐惧和陷坑,残害和毁灭,都临近我们"(《哀歌》3:7)。另外,诗人借助动词的频繁出现来增强诗歌的节奏感,通过对色彩、声音等感官描写加强了诗歌的生动性。

第二、抒情集个人情感与民族情感为一体。在《哀歌》中,诗人时而把自己作为上帝代言人,言说要惩罚敌人;时而把自己作为个人倾诉内心的忧患;时而把自己置之事外,客观描述圣城之凄惨。诗人身份的变化一方面可以使我们从不同视角感受人民的痛苦,另一方面可以强化个人和全民族的情感、体验、愿望及要求;这种视角的转换可以体现出个人与民族利益密不可分,个人利益即民族利益,民族利益即个人利益。从而突出了诗人的爱国情怀。如在开篇诗人以他者身份用拟人手法客观描述这座城市很孤独,如"先前满有人民的城,现在何竟独坐!……"(《哀歌》1:1—8);后来诗人以民族代言人身份出现,进而又以一个惩罚者的身份出现,有时又把抒情主体转化为"我"个人:"他从高天使火进入我的骨头,克制了我;他铺下罗网,绊我的脚"(《哀歌》1:13)诗人顺势强调悲哀之时,无人安慰,反倒遭人愚弄,所以"我因这事哭泣,我眼泪汪汪……"(《哀歌》1:16)。

第三、抒情与对话、哭诉相结合。在抒发悲情的同时,诗人常常哭诉,向上帝诉说他们的苦,如"耶和华啊,求你纪念,求你观看",然后诗人罗列凄惨之状,一气呵成,数十行,加快了节奏,并借用重复的技巧,使浓缩的悲情喷发而出,给人强烈冲击,牵动读者心魂。甚至向上帝抱怨,如"耶和华啊,求你观看,见你向谁这样行!妇人岂可吃自己所生育手里所要弄的婴孩吗?"(《哀歌》2:20)。这种抒情的对话性还体现在向上帝忏悔自己的罪过,然后又表明自己的信心同时祈祷上帝庇佑其子民,惩罚敌人(3:64—66)。这种抒情特点表明他们虽然痛苦,但并没有放弃希望,他们坚信上帝,寄希望于未来。这样,就从神学视角体现了古代希伯来人民悲观而不失望的民族特点。

除《哀歌》外,《圣经》中还有各种抒情诗歌,或对美好世界发出感叹,或对自然、智慧、律法、友谊、爱情由衷赞美;或处于情感的低谷而释放消极的人生态度,如《传道书》,或激情澎湃发出对敌人的诅咒等、或战胜敌人唱战歌，如《摩西之歌》。这些抒情诗契合着人类普遍存在的情感，对后世影响很大，如爱尔兰诗人、剧作家威廉·巴特勒·叶芝(William Butler Yeats 1865—1939)、英国著名现代派诗人艾略特(Thomas Stearns Eliot, 1888—1965)的抒情诗就受到了其影响。

2. 从《哀歌》看《圣经》中流浪母题的原型意义

几千年来，亚伯拉罕的子孙流浪四方，他们祈望返回锡安，重建圣殿。犹太民族远古的历史神话与后世犹太人的生活境遇一脉相承，展示了犹太民族典型的命运感受和精神观念："寻找"或"流浪"。《哀歌》中所诉说的犹太民族囚居巴比伦时期的痛苦经历，就是这种流浪历程的深刻写照。犹太民族的流浪体验包括时空意义上的流浪，即失去家园后的漂泊流浪，也包括情感意义上的流浪，即远离了圣殿、远离了上帝的精神流浪。《哀歌》作者在哀挽之时，发出对上帝的呼告，表达了在流浪状态下寻求精神归属的心声。这一流浪模式已经成为一种原型，不断出现在美国文学、尤其是美国犹太文学作品中。下面以美国犹太作家索尔·贝娄(Saul Bellow, 1915—2005)的小说为例加以说明。

在贝娄的小说中，主人公因这样那样的原因而到处流浪，不断寻找立足之地。这种反复出现的叙述结构形成了贝娄小说的统一模式：流浪模式。流浪模式一般表现为物理时空顺序流浪与精神流浪两种形式。前者具有明显的流浪汉足迹在现实意义上的时、空转换；后者不强调人物足迹在现实意义上的时、空转变，而是表达出一种强烈的情感流浪。在贝娄的小说中，这两种流浪模式同时出现，并且呈现出交合的趋势，如他的第一部长篇小说《挂起来的人》(*Dangling Man*, 1944)以日记的形式表现了一种强烈的感情危机。小说以约瑟夫的主观情感为主线，再现了他追求"自由"的心路历程。在记述约瑟夫情感历程的同时，贝娄融进了明显的时空顺序，每段顿悟之前注明的日记就是其重要标志。贝娄另一部作品《雨王汉德森》(*Henderson the Rain King*, 1955)则以"我要"的欲望引导汉德森的非洲之行和精神流浪，每一次旅行地点的变化与主人公的精神流浪之旅相对应。流浪的心理特质与现代人类的这种联系，反映出现代人的漂泊感、异化感及困惑状态。贝娄的作品对现代人类的情感世界进行了新的、全方位的重构与再现，具有深厚的历史感和道德寓意。

五、圣经典故集锦

1. **sow among thorns** (撒种在荆棘中)：典出《耶利米书》第4章3节上帝对犹大人的警告：Break up your fallow ground, and sow not among thorn. 要开垦你们的荒地，不要撒种在荆棘中。喻指种下恶果、引起后患。

2. **drink water of gall** (喝苦胆水)：典出《耶利米书》第8章14节：for the LORD our God hath put us to silence, and given us water of gall to drink, because we have sinned against the LORD. 耶和华我们的上帝使我们静默不言，又将苦胆水给我们喝，都因我们得罪了耶和华。喻指自食苦果，或过非人的生活。

3. **bend their tongues like their bow**（弯舌像弓）: 典出《耶利米书》第9章3节耶利米哀叹犹太人的罪孽: And they bend their tongues like their bow for lies. 他们弯起舌头像弓一样，为要说谎话。指摇唇鼓舌、谎话连篇。

4. **can the leopard change his spots**（豹子岂能改变斑点）: 典出《耶利米书》第13章23节耶利米的警告: Can the Ethiopian change his skin, or the leopard his spots? then may ye also do good, that are accustomed to do evil. 埃塞俄比亚人岂能改变肤色呢？豹子岂能改变斑点呢？若能，你们这些习惯行恶的也能行善了。此典指本性难移、恶习难改。

5. **stiff-necked**（硬着颈项）: 典出《耶利米书》第17章23节耶利米借上帝之口对犹大人的谴责: But they obeyed not, neither inclined their ear, but made their neck stiff, that they might not hear, nor receive instruction. 他们却不听从，不侧耳听，竟硬着颈项不听，不受教训。此典喻指执拗任性、顽固不化。

6. **the potter deals with his clay**（窑匠弄泥）: 典出《耶利米书》第18章4—6节耶利米借上帝之口所作的比喻: and the vessel that he made of clay was marred in the hand of the potter: so he made it again another vessel, as seemed good to the potter to make it. Then the word of the LORD came to me, saying, O house of Israel, cannot I do with you as this potter? 窑匠用泥做的器皿，在他手中做坏了，他又用这泥另做别的器皿；窑匠看怎样好，就怎样做。耶和华的话就临到我说：「以色列家啊，我待你们，岂不能照着窑匠弄泥吗？」此处上帝在维护人民，以示其威严，掌控人的命运就像陶匠掌控手中的泥那么随意。此典喻指随心所欲、得心应手。

7. **the glory of Israel**（以色列的华美）: 典出《哀歌》第2章1节: How hath the LORD covered the daughter of Zion with a cloud in his anger, /And cast down from heaven unto the earth the beauty of Israel. 主何竟发怒，使黑云遮蔽锡安城，将以色列的华美从天上扔到地上。此典喻指华美、繁荣或幸福如昙花一现、过眼烟云。

8. **the wormwood and the gall**（茵陈和苦胆）: 典出《哀歌》第3章19节: Remembering mine affliction and my misery, the wormwood and the gall. (耶和华啊)，求你记念我如茵陈和苦胆的困苦窘迫。喻指困苦窘迫的生活、令人憎恨之物或极不愉快的事。

9. **ostriches in the desert**（旷野的鸵鸟）: 典出《哀歌》第4章3节: The daughter of my people is become cruel, like the ostriches in the wilderness. 我民的妇人倒成为残忍，好像旷野的鸵鸟一般。喻指残忍之妇、冷酷女子。

10. **the cup of the bitterness**（苦杯）: 典出《哀歌》第4章21节: Rejoice and be glad, O daughter of Edom, that dewellest in the land of Uz;/The cup also shall pass through unto thee./Thou shalt be drunken, and shalt make thyself naked. 住乌斯地的以东民哪，只管欢喜作乐, /苦杯也必传到你那里, /你必喝醉，以致露体。喻指悲惨的命运。

六、课堂讨论题

1. 比较中国的哀歌传统和希伯来"哀歌"传统。
2. 从《哀歌》看《圣经》中比喻的特征。
3. 从人类学视角对比《芜城赋》与《哀歌》。

七、课后思考题

1. 从《哀歌》看希伯来人对身体的珍视。
2. 对比《哀歌》与屈原的《离骚》。
3. 赏析伦勃朗的油画《悲叹耶路撒冷灭亡的耶利米》(右图)。
4. 在《圣经》和西方文学中"巴比伦"常比喻"罪恶"。你知道为什么吗?

第十四讲

人生经验的浓缩:《箴言》和《传道书》
Proverbs and Ecclesiastes, a Treasure of Life Wisdom

一、导读

《箴言》(*Proverbs*)和《传道书》(*Ecclesiastes* /ɪkliːzɪˈæstiːz/)属于"智慧文学"。这里的"智慧",不仅指有知识,还指能达观人生所必需的道德、聪明睿智以及娴熟的社会技巧。

《箴言》计31章,汇集了不同年代有关处世为人的格言和谚语,有数字哲理诗、小型哲理论丛、贯顶体哲理诗。除了"题记"外,可归纳为三类主题:对智慧本身的认识和赞颂(第1—9章);各类箴言的汇编,包括简短的格言、言语和语录(第10—29章);"附录"(第30—31章),其中第31章10—31节的主题是对理想的贤慧妇女的赞颂。传统上认为《箴言》为所罗门所作,实际上应该是众多普通百姓和文学人士集体智慧的结晶,是经历了漫长年代陆续成文的,全书的编纂修订不可能早于公元前400年。

《传道书》用诗文相间的体裁写成,"传道者"从真实人生的种种困惑说起,考察了生命价值的虚无、死的虚空、智慧的虚妄以及智慧之源——上帝的不可测度,最后又回到现实,倡导喜乐的人生态度和对现实生活的执着。《传道书》计12章,除"序"(1:1—11)和"跋"(12:9—14)外,可分为3编:详述万事皆虚空;传道者的人生经验;智慧语录。涉及的专题计36个[1],相传《传道书》为所罗门或其宫廷中的无名哲人所作,成书时间约在公元前250年至公元前200年间。

本讲从《箴言》中选取5个主题:
1. 智慧的重要。
2. 勾引少年的淫妇。
3. 通奸的下场。
4. 所罗门的箴言。
5. 贤妇的写照。

从《传道书》选取4个主题:
1. 万物皆虚空。
2. 万事有定时。
3. 人生乃虚空。
4. 泰然对待人生。

---

1. 参见梁工著:《圣经指南》,沈阳:辽宁人民出版社,1993年版,第486–489页

二、选文及注释

Part 1 *Proverbs*

1. Importance of Wisdom

To know wisdom and instruction;
To perceive the words of understanding;
To receive the instruction of wisdom,
Justice, and judgment, and equity[1];
To give subtilty to the simple[2],
To the young man knowledge and discretion[3].
A wise man will hear, and will increase learning;
And a man of understanding shall attain unto wise counsels[4]:
To understand a proverb, and the interpretation;
The words of the wise, and their dark sayings[5].
The fear of the LORD is the beginning of knowledge:
But fools despise wisdom and instruction. (1: 2–7)

Happy is the man that findeth wisdom,
And the man that getteth understanding.
For the merchandise of it[6] is better than the merchandise of silver,
And the gain thereof than fine gold.
She is more precious than rubies:
And all the things thou canst desire are not to be compared unto her.
Length of days is in her right hand;
And in her left hand riches and honour.
Her ways are ways of pleasantness,
And all her paths are peace.
She is a tree of life to them that lay hold upon her;
And happy is every one that retaineth her.
The LORD by wisdom hath founded the earth;
By understanding hath he established the heavens.
By his knowledge the depths are broken up[7],
And the clouds drop down the dew. (3: 13–20)

2. A Strange Woman

For the lips of a strange woman drop as an honeycomb,
And her mouth is smoother than oil[8]:
But her end is bitter as wormwood[9],
Sharp as a two-edged sword.
Her feet go down to death;
Her steps take hold on hell.[10]
Lest thou shouldest ponder the path of

---

1. Justice, and judgment, and equity 正直、公义和公平。equity *n*. impartialness; fairness 公正
2. To give subtilty to the simple 让愚蒙者变得精明。the simple 愚蒙无知的人。
3. discretion *n*. ability or power to decide responsibly 谋略
4. a man of understanding shall attain unto wise counsels 聪明人获得可靠的智谋。
5. dark sayings 谜语。
6. merchandise *n*. goods bought and sold in business; commercial wares 商品; 货物。it 指上句 wisdom 和 understanding, 此句指获得智慧强于获得金钱。
7. By his knowledge the depths are broken up 耶和华以知识使深渊裂开。意思是上帝通过智慧掌管大自然，包括地下的泉水(深渊)和天空的雨露(下句的dew)。
8. smoother than oil 淫妇的口比油还滑，指善用花言巧语勾引人。
9. her end is bitter as wormwood (淫妇表面甜蜜的话)实质上苦若茵陈。wormwood 茵陈; 苦艾。巴勒斯坦的一种植物，味苦涩。《圣经》中常用此比喻痛苦、哀伤和灾害。
10. Her steps take hold on hell. 她的脚步踏在阴间。指淫妇能把人引向死亡和毁灭。

life[1].

Her ways are moveable, that thou canst not know them.

Hear me now therefore, O ye children,

And depart not from the words of my mouth.

Remove thy way far from her,

And come not nigh the door of her house:

Lest thou give thine honour unto others,

And thy years unto the cruel[2]:

Lest strangers be filled with thy wealth;

And thy labours be in the house of a stranger[3];

And thou mourn at the last[4],

When thy flesh and thy body are consumed,

And say, How have I hated instruction,

And my heart despised reproof[5];

And have not obeyed the voice of my teachers,

Nor inclined mine ear to[6] them that instructed me!

I was almost in all evil

In the midst of the congregation and assembly.

Drink waters out of thine own cistern,

And running waters out of thine own well.[7]

Let thy fountains be dispersed[8] abroad,

And rivers of waters in the streets.

Let them be only thine own,

And not strangers' with thee.

Let thy fountain be blessed:

And rejoice with the wife of thy youth.

Let her be as the loving hind and pleasant roe[9];

Let her breasts satisfy thee at all times;

And be thou ravished[10] always with her love.

And why wilt thou, my son, be ravished with a strange woman,

And embrace the bosom of a stranger? (*Proverbs* 5: 3–20)

3. The False Attraction of Adultery

At the window of my house

I looked through my casement[11],

And beheld among the simple ones,

I discerned among the youths,

A young man void of understanding,

Passing through the street near her corner;

And he went the way to her house,

In the twilight[12], in the evening,

In the black and dark night:

And, behold, there met him a woman

With the attire of an harlot, and subtil of heart.[13]

(She is loud[14] and stubborn;

---

1. the path of life 生命之途。
2. thy years unto the cruel 将你的岁月给残忍的人。thy years 指青春少壮的日子; the cruel 可能指淫妇或她的丈夫, 他们会索取钱财来赔偿损失, 也可以指因失足而带来的精神痛苦。
3. thy labours be in the house of a stranger 你凭劳碌所得的归入外人的家中。指因接近淫妇而倾家荡产。
4. thou mourn at the last 终究你会悲叹(自己的失足)。
5. reproof *n.* rebuke 责难
6. incline to (耳朵)想倾听。
7. Drink waters out of thine own cistern, And running waters out of thine own well. 喝自己池中的水, 饮自家井里的活水。cistern *n.* a tank for storing water 蓄水池。
8. disperse *vt.* to scatter 洒散。这句话的意思是, 你的泉水岂可溢到外面。
9. the loving hind and pleasant roe (妻子像)可爱的麀鹿, 可喜的母鹿。hind *n.* 雌性赤鹿。
10. ravish *vt.* to overwhelm with emotion 充满激情
11. casement *n.* a window of any kind 窗
12. twilight *n.* the time between sunset and dark 黄昏
13. With the attire of an harlot, and subtil of heart. 妓女的打扮, 诡诈的心。attire *n.* clothing or array; apparel 服装。
14. loud *adj.* vulgarly obtrusive; flashy 俗艳的, 招摇的

Her feet abide[1] not in her house:
Now is she without, now in the streets,
And lieth in wait at every corner.)
So she caught him, and kissed him,
And with an impudent[2] face said unto him,

"I have peace offerings with me[3];
This day have I payed my vows.
Therefore came I forth to meet thee,
Diligently to seek thy face, and I have found thee.
I have decked my bed with coverings of tapestry[4],
With carved works, with fine linen of Egypt[5].
I have perfumed[6] my bed
With myrrh, aloes, and cinnamon[7].
Come, let us take our fill of love[8] until the morning:
Let us solace[9] ourselves with loves.
For the goodman[10] is not at home,
He is gone a long journey:
He hath taken a bag of money with him,
And will come home at the day appointed."

With her much fair speech she caused him to yield,
With the flattering of her lips she forced him.
He goeth after her straightway,
As an ox goeth to the slaughter[11],
Or as a fool to the correction of the stocks[12];
Till a dart strike through his liver;
As a bird hasteth to the snare[13],
And knoweth not that it is for his life.

Hearken unto me now therefore, O ye children,
And attend to the words of my mouth.
Let not thine heart decline to her ways,
Go not astray[14] in her paths.
For she hath cast down many wounded:
Yea, many strong men have been slain by her.[15]
Her house is the way to hell,
Going down to the chambers of death. (7: 6–27)

4. The Proverbs of Solomon

A wise son maketh a glad father:
But a foolish son is the heaviness of his mother.

Treasures of wickedness profit nothing:
But righteousness delivereth from death. (10: 1–2)

---

1. abide *vi.* to remain in a place 停留
2. impudent *adj.* offensively bold 厚颜无耻的
3. I have peace offerings with me 平安祭在我这里。淫妇假借遵守宗教条例——吃祭肉为名要求无知少年到她家里。
4. decked my bed with coverings of tapestry 用绣花毯子铺好了床。说明淫妇家居奢华，或者善于勾引。
5. fine linen of Egypt 埃及亚麻布，是名贵的舶来品。
6. perfume *vt.* 洒上香水使(床)有香味
7. myrrh, aloes, and cinnamon 没药、沉香和桂皮。桂皮是制作香水的原料。
8. take our fill of love 尽情欢爱。
9. solace *vt.* to comfort or cheer as in trouble or sorrow 安慰；使人欢乐
10. goodman *n.* a husband（对一家男主人的敬称）丈夫
11. As an ox goeth to the slaughter 像一头牛走向被宰杀之地。slaughter *n.* the killing of animals for food 屠宰。
12. as a fool to the correction of the stocks 像愚昧之人去领枷锁之刑。stock *n.* (旧时刑罚用的)手枷; 足枷。correction *n.* punishment intended to improve 处罚。
13. As a bird hasteth to the snare 如同鸟雀急投罗网。snare *n.* a trapping device used for capturing birds and small mammals 罗网; 陷阱。
14. Go not astray 不要走歪路。astray *adv.* 歪斜。
15. For she hath ... slain by her. 这两句指有不少男人被淫妇毁掉了幸福。

He becometh poor that dealeth with a slack hand[1]:
But the hand of the diligent[2] maketh rich.

He that gathereth in summer is a wise son:
But he that sleepeth in harvest is a son that causeth shame. (10: 4–5)

The memory of the just is blessed[3]:
But the name of the wicked shall rot.

The wise in heart will receive commandments:
But a prating fool shall fall[4]. (10: 7–10)

Hatred stirreth up strifes,
But love covereth all transgressions[5]. (10: 12)

The rich man's wealth is his strong city:
The destruction of the poor is their poverty.

The labour of the righteous tendeth to life:
The fruit of the wicked to sin.

He is in the way of life that keepeth instruction:
But he that refuseth reproof erreth[6].

He that hideth hatred with lying lips[7],
And he that uttereth a slander, is a fool.

In the multitude of words there wanteth not sin:
But he that refraineth his lips is wise.[8] (10: 15–19)

Whoso loveth instruction loveth knowledge:
But he that hateth reproof is brutish[9]. (12: 1)

He that spareth his rod hateth his son:
But he that loveth him chasteneth[10] him betimes[11]. (13: 24)

A soft answer turneth away wrath:
But grievous words stir up anger. (15: 1)

Better is a dinner of herbs where love is,
Than a stalled ox and hatred therewith.[12] (15: 17)

A word fitly spoken is like apples of gold in pictures of silver.[13] (25: 11)

It is better to dwell in the corner of the

---

1. a slack hand 懒惰的手, 指懒惰的人。
2. the diligent 勤勉之人。
3. The memory of the just is blessed 纪念义人的行为是被称赞的。
4. a prating fool shall fall 嘴上愚妄的必要跌倒。prate *vi.* to talk foolishly or at tedious length about sth. 胡扯, 吹嘘, 空谈, 唠叨。
5. love covereth all transgressions 爱心能遮掩一切过错。
6. err *vi.* to stray 〈古〉走上歧途
7. He that hideth hatred with lying lips 隐藏怨恨的人, 嘴里必出谎言。
8. In the multitude ... lips is wise. 这两句的意思是, 多言多语难免有过错, 管住嘴巴才是明智。multitude of words 说话多。
9. brutish *adj.* rough; uncivilized 粗野的; 愚顽不化的
10. chasten *vt.* to correct by punishment or reproof 管教; 申斥
11. betimes *adv.* in good time; early 随时; 及早
12. Better is a ... and hatred therewith. 这两句的意思是, 吃素菜彼此相爱, 胜过吃肥牛彼此相恨。stall *vt.* to maintain in a stall for fattening 豢养长肥。
13. A word fitly ... pictures of silver. 意思是, 一句话说得合宜, 犹如金苹果落在银网里。"金苹果在银网子"可能是一件美观而贵重的艺术品。

housetop,
Than with a brawling[1] woman and in a wide house. (25: 24)

Whoso diggeth a pit shall fall therein:
And he that rolleth a stone, it will return upon him.[2] (26: 27)

Boast not thyself of to morrow;
For thou knowest not what a day may bring forth.

Let another man praise thee, and not thine own mouth;
A stranger, and not thine own lips. (27: 1–2)

Faithful are the wounds of a friend;
But the kisses of an enemy are deceitful.[3] (27: 6)

5. A Virtuous Woman

Who can find a virtuous woman ?
For her price is far above rubies.
The heart of her husband doth safely trust in her,
So that he shall have no need of spoil.
She will do him good and not evil
All the days of her life.
She seeketh wool, and flax[4],
And worketh willingly with her hands.
She is like the merchants' ships;
She bringeth her food from afar.
She riseth also while it is yet night,
And giveth meat to her household,
And a portion to her maidens.
She considereth a field, and buyeth it[5]:
With the fruit of her hands she planteth a vineyard.
She girdeth her loins with strength[6],
And strengtheneth her arms.
She perceiveth that her merchandise is good:
Her candle goeth not out by night.
She layeth her hands to the spindle[7],
And her hands hold the distaff[8].
She stretcheth forth her hand to the poor;
Yea, she reacheth forth her hands to the needy.
She is not afraid of the snow for her household:
For all her household are clothed with scarlet[9].
She maketh for herself coverings of tapestry;

---

1. brawl *vi.* to quarrel or fight noisily 争吵
2. Whoso diggeth a ... return upon him. 这两句的意思是，挖下陷坑者，必自己掉进其中；滚石头害人者，石头反而压在他身上。相当于汉语的"搬起石头砸自己的脚"。whoso *prep.* 无论是谁。
3. Faithful are the ... enemy are deceitful. 这两句的意思是，朋友造成的伤痛是出于真诚；仇敌给予的亲吻全是欺骗。
4. flax *n.* 亚麻
5. She considereth a field, and buyeth it 她看中一块田就把它买到手。
6. girdeth her loins with strength 用力量束腰，意思是贤惠妇人浑身是力量。
7. She layeth her hands to the spindle 她手拿纺锤。
8. distaff *n.* 纺纱杆
9. scarlet *adj.* of a brilliant red color 朱红色的

Her clothing is silk and purple.
Her husband is known in the gates[1],
When he sitteth among the elders of the land.
She maketh fine linen[2], and selleth it;
And delivereth girdles[3] unto the merchant.
Strength and honour are her clothing;
And she shall rejoice in time to come.[4]
She openeth her mouth with wisdom;
And in her tongue is the law of kindness.
She looketh well to the ways of her household,
And eateth not the bread of idleness.
Her children arise up, and call her blessed[5];
Her husband also, and he praiseth her.
"Many daughters have done virtuously, but thou excellest them all."
Favour is deceitful, and beauty is vain[6]:
But a woman that feareth the LORD, she shall be praised.
Give her of the fruit of her hands;
And let her own works praise her in the gates. (*Proverbs* 31: 10–31)

Part 2 *Ecclesiastes*

1. All Is Vanity

The words of the Preacher, the son of David[7], king in Jerusalem.

Vanity of vanities[8], saith the preacher, vanity of vanities; all is vanity. What profit hath a man of all his labour which he taketh under the sun? One generation passeth away, and another generation cometh: but the earth abideth[9] for ever. The sun also ariseth, and the sun goeth down, and hasteth to his place where he arose. The wind goeth toward the south, and turneth about unto the north; it whirleth about[10] continually, and the wind returneth again according to his circuits[11]. All the rivers run into the sea; yet the sea is not full; unto the place from whence the rivers come, thither they return again. All things are full of labour; man cannot utter it[12]: the eye is not satisfied with seeing, nor the ear filled with hearing[13]. The thing that hath been, it is that which shall be[14]; and that which is done is that which shall be done: and there is no new thing under the sun. (1: 1–9)

2. Everything Has Its Time

To every thing there is a season[15], and a time to every purpose[16] under the heaven: a time to be born, and a time to die; a time to plant, and a time to pluck up that which is planted; a time to kill, and a time to heal; a time to break down, and a time to build up;

---

1. known in the gates 意思是，丈夫因妻子的贤德内助在四邻五舍享有好名声。
2. fine linen 细麻布。希伯来文化中，穿细麻衣是高贵、美丽的标志。
3. girdle *n*. 腰带
4. Strength and honour ... time to come. 能力和威仪是她的衣服，她想到日后的幸福就欢笑。
5. call her blessed (女儿们)称她是有福的。意思是贤德之母得到上帝的赐福。
6. Favour is deceitful, and beauty is vain 艳丽是虚假的；美容是虚浮的。意思是女人之美不在外在容貌，而在心灵之美。
7. the Preacher, the son of David 人们认为传道书的作者为大卫之子所罗门。
8. Vanity of vanities 虚空的虚空。意思是虚空至极。这反映了传道者的虚无思想。
9. abide *vi*. 继续；保持某种状态
10. it whirleth about 风不断地旋转。
11. circuit *n*. 路线
12. All things are full of labour; man cannot utter it 意思是万事令人厌倦，人诉说不清。
13. nor the ear filled with hearing "耳听，听不足"，与上边的"口说，说不清"是同义重复。即，世上万事令人生厌，所看，所说，所听，皆令人生厌，空虚无比。这是《传道书》虚无主义的观点。
14. The thing that hath been, it is that which shall be 已有的事，以后必再有。
15. season *n*. 指定期
16. every purpose 指任何事物。

a time to weep, and a time to laugh; a time to mourn, and a time to dance; a time to cast away stones, and a time to gather stones together; a time to embrace¹, and a time to refrain² from embracing; a time to get, and a time to lose; a time to keep, and a time to cast away; a time to rend, and a time to sew; a time to keep silence, and a time to speak; a time to love, and a time to hate; a time of war, and a time of peace. (3: 1–8)

3. Life Is Vanity

He that loveth silver shall not be satisfied with silver; nor he that loveth abundance³ with increase: this is also vanity. When goods increase, they are increased that eat them: and what good is there to the owners thereof, saving the beholding of them with their eyes⁴? The sleep of a labouring man is sweet, whether he eat little or much: but the abundance of the rich will not suffer him to sleep.

There is a sore evil⁵ which I have seen under the sun, namely, riches kept for the owners thereof to their hurt⁶. But those riches perish by evil travail⁷: and he begetteth a son, and there is nothing in his hand. As he came forth of his mother's womb, naked shall he return to go as he came, and shall take nothing of his labour, which he may carry away in his hand. And this also is a sore evil, that in all points⁸ as he came, so shall he go: and what profit hath he that hath laboured for the wind? All his days also he eateth in darkness, and he hath much sorrow and wrath with his sickness. (5: 10–17)

4. Take Life as It Comes

Go thy way, eat thy bread with joy, and drink thy wine with a merry heart; for God now accepteth thy works. Let thy garment be always white⁹; and let thy head lack no ointment¹⁰. Live joyfully with the wife whom thou lovest all the days of the life of thy vanity¹¹, which he hath given thee under the sun, all the days of thy vanity: for that is thy portion in this life¹², and in thy labour which thou takest undet the sun. Whatsoever thy hand findth to do, do it with thy might¹³; for there is no work, nor device¹⁴, nor knowledge, nor wisdom, in the grave, whither thou goest.

I returned, and saw under the sun, that the race is not to the swift¹⁵, nor the battle to the strong, neither yet bread to the wise, nor yet riches to men of understanding, nor yet favour to men of skill; but time and chance happeneth to them all. For man also knoweth not his time: as the fishes that are taken in an evil net, and as the birds that are caught in the snare; so are the sons of men snared in an evil time, when it falleth suddenly upon them. (9: 7–12)

---

1. embrace *vt.* to hold closely as a sign of affection 拥抱。暗指男女体肤之亲。
2. refrain (from) *vi.* to stop oneself from doing sth. 克制; 忍住
3. abundance *n.* plentifulness 富足
4. saving the beholding of them with their eyes 不过是为满足眼目而已。saving *prep.* 除……外, 不过……而已
5. a sore evil 可悲的事。
6. riches kept for the owners thereof to their hurt 财主积存财富反害了自己。这说明了希伯来人的财富观, 教导人们不可过多贪恋财富。
7. travail *n.* painful or labourous effort 痛苦; 艰难
8. in all points 一切情形之下。
9. white *adj.* 洁白干净的。指体面的
10. ointment *n.* 油膏。意即头上不缺油膏须有好名声。
11. thy vanity 你虚空的日子。
12. thy portion in this life 生命中应得的份。
13. do it with thy might 尽你的力量去做。
14. device *n.* a plan, method, or trick with a particular aim 手段; 策略
15. the race is not to the swift 快跑的未必能赢。这种观点体现了传道者的悲观主义思想。

三、圣经文化知识链接

1. 希伯来人的"智慧文学"

"智慧文学"是圣经文学的基本文类之一,一般指《箴言》、《约伯记》、《传道书》和"后典"或"次经"中的《所罗门智训》(*Wisdom of Solomon*)、《便西拉智训》(*Wisdom of Ben Sirach*)等5卷书,还指散见于部分"历史书"、"先知书"和《诗篇》里的智慧作品(如《士师记》第9章8—15节;《以赛亚书》第28章23—29节;《诗篇》第37章10—11节;第85章10节等)。"智慧文学"是就其文学性质而言,而不是体裁而言。这些作品或总结某种生活经验,或探寻某一宇宙法则,通过优美的文学语言和形式,使读者从中得到精神的训导和心智的启迪,故称为"智慧文学"。表示"智慧"的希伯来文 Mashel 不仅指短小精悍的劝诫之语,还指篇幅较长的思辨性断论(如《箴言》中的"智慧颂"),甚至《约伯记》、《传道书》一类较长的诗文。圣经学者约德(S. C. Yoder)指出,这些由精辟语句表达的"智慧文学",目的是"引起人们的注意,唤起人们的共鸣,从而牢固地留在人们的记忆中",使闻者对各种实际问题做出聪慧的判断和处理。

2.《圣经》中的崇智观

智慧原本是一个世俗范畴的概念,但在《圣经》中,"智慧"却被赋予了强烈的神学和神圣色彩,智慧为上帝所造,因而成了上帝神性的一种流溢,敬畏上帝就是"知识的开端"、"智慧的开端"。可以说,崇尚智慧构成了犹太人的一个重要传统。

智慧作为《圣经》的重要论题,也是《圣经》所要着重宣扬的内容。在《圣经》中赞美智慧之人和歌颂智慧美德的诗行和论述比比皆是,比如,《箴言》在颂扬智慧的篇章中以"智慧的口吻"唱到:守得知识,胜过黄金。/因为智慧比珍珠更美;一切可喜爱的都不足与比较。透过这些格言,足见《圣经》对智慧的崇尚程度。《圣经》中大量有关智慧的类似论述散见于《圣经》的有关篇章中,详尽地论说了智慧之属性,智慧之重要性、功用以及通向智慧之路径等各个方面。除了在《箴言》、《诗篇》、《约伯记》等经典性的"智慧文学"篇章中,在《创世记》、《申命记》、《约书亚记》、《撒母耳记》(上、下)以及《以赛亚书》、《耶利米书》、《以西结书》等篇章中,也都有种种关于智慧的论题和论说。

四、圣经文化专题

1. 受希腊化影响的《传道书》[1]

《传道书》成书于希腊化时期,其作者不可避免地受到希腊哲学的影响。此时的学术界活跃着斯多葛派、伊壁鸠鲁学派和怀疑论学派,意识形态领域流行着世界主义观念和个人主义思潮。

---

1. 本项参考梁工、赵复兴著:《凤凰的再生——希腊化时期的犹太文学研究》,北京:商务印书馆,2000年,第200-202页。

怀疑论学派怀疑感性认识的真实可靠性，怀疑任何判别真伪的标准。他们认为，不可能对认识对象作出建立在其他判断之上的直接或间接的判断；对认识对象作出的正反两个判断都能等同地得到证明；这导致"既是又不是，既不是又不是不是"的结论，于是便只能放弃一切认识活动。《传道书》"凡事都是虚空"的主题，就是用怀疑论学说观察犹太教义与现实巨大反差的结果。伊壁鸠鲁学派以伦理学的快乐论而闻名，他们认为快乐是与生俱来的，是生活的目的，是最高的善；快乐分感官上"活跃的"和无痛苦而"平静的"两种。还认为最大的痛苦是对死亡和神的恐惧。《传道书》所谓"用酒使我肉体舒畅"(2:3)，"同你所爱的妻快活度日"(9:9)，"人活多年，就当快乐多年"(11:8)等，都明显受到伊壁鸠鲁哲学思想的影响。古希腊人特别注重物质享受，在地中海周围的文明古国中希腊人生活水平最高，有人把"过希腊人的生活"用为奢侈享乐或过度消费的比喻。在希腊英雄传说中，俄底修斯游地府时阿喀琉斯的阴魂曾向他表示，与其下阴间为王不如在人间为奴；赫拉克勒斯捉拿地府看门狗时，也觉得阴森森的地府不像光明温暖的现世那么欢乐。这种把死后永生视为不幸的观念反映在《传道书》中，就是多次提到死亡也是一种虚空；财富自己无法尽享，留给后人或别人，也是一种虚空。

显然，了解希腊化时期的哲学文化氛围对于我们理解《传道书》有很大的帮助。我们就可以理解《传道书》中所表达的怀疑、虚无、悲观等情绪是以色列人当时历史处境的真实写照，也是希腊化时期，希伯来文化与希腊哲学思想密切联系、相互渗透的表现。

2. 希伯来智慧文学与希腊智慧文学的区别[1]

由于历史、地理等多方面的原因，古代犹太人是一个弱小而多灾多难的民族，一直是周围列强掠夺的对象。相反，古希腊虽是小国，却是个强国，公元前2世纪中叶以前异族入侵很少有占便宜的。希腊人的物质生活水平在临近地区一直最高。这使两个民族的哲理诗文都表现出与其所在的社会大气候相适应的特点：

(1)以色列人偏重人际关系，常议论交友、妇女，并不时对国王提出警告。古希腊人则注重人与自然的关系，如称"人不能踏进同一条河流"(赫拉克利特)、"动物只要求它所必须的东西，反之，人则要求超过这个"(德谟克利特)等。由此古希腊哲学又与自然科学紧密相连，如欧洲第一位能预测日食的泰勒斯就是著名的哲学家，亚里士多德也有数本自然科学著作。除大量语录外，较早的哲学家也留下系统著述，如安提丰的《论真理》。稍晚些的柏拉图、亚里士多德等著述就更丰富了。

(2)犹太哲学强调智慧的重要性，除一般意义的智慧外，还把智慧与"信仰上帝"、"敬畏主"等同起来，基本上未超出宗教哲学的范畴。古希腊哲学也很重视智慧，可能因为哲学是智慧的结晶，是最高的智慧，早期哲学家一开始就重视对智慧的观察。他们的智慧语录和智慧故事举不胜举。公元前5世纪至前4世纪还出现过一个"智者派"，由一些演说家、作家和教师组成，教人在辩论中如何讲话、使用论据等。这是"希腊智者为了填补希腊教育生活中的一段空白，以达到较高级的教育而发起的一项创举"。但一般说来，希腊的智慧与宗教有着明确的分野。

(3)宏观犹太哲学思想——不论是关于智慧的论述还是关于人际关系的探讨——都与宗教信仰相联系，思维空间不算很大。希腊哲学的思维空间则非常开阔。苏格拉底之前已出现怀疑

---

[1]. 参考梁工、赵复兴著：《凤凰的再生——希腊化时期的犹太文学研究》，北京：商务印书馆，2000年，第195—197页。

论,"他们否认任何区分真理和谬误的标准,认为什么都不可认识"。由于怀疑论的每一次挑战都引起解决疑难问题的新尝试,人们至今也没有彻底否定过它。

通过比较可以看出,希伯来智慧文学与希腊智慧文学各有千秋,他们崇尚智慧的精神和探索的勇气是很珍贵的。

五、圣经典故集锦

1. **All is vanity**(凡事都是虚空):典出《传道书》第1章2节:Vanity of vanities, saith the Preacher, vanity of vanities; all is vanity. 传道者说:虚空的虚空,虚空的虚空,凡事都是虚空。指一切皆空,万念俱灰。在莎士比亚的名剧《奥赛罗》中,当苔丝狄蒙娜被奥赛罗指控为娼妓时,她的话可能是暗指着这段言语:我不愿意提起"娼妇"两个字,一说到它就会使我心生憎恶,更不用说亲自去干那博得这种丑名的勾当了;整个世界的荣华(the world's mass of vanity) 也不能诱动我。

2. **spare the rod**(惜了棍棒):典出《箴言》第13章24节:He that spareth his rod hateth his son: but he that loveth him chasteneth him betimes. 不忍心用杖打儿子的,是恨恶他。疼爱儿子的,随时管教。指"不管不成器"、"棒头底下出孝子","省了棍棒,害了儿女"。

3. **eyes on the ends of the earth**(向地极呆望的眼):典出《箴言》第17章24节:Wisdom is before him that hath understanding; but the eyes of a fool are in the ends of the earth. 精明的人,常面向智慧;愚人的眼,向地极呆望。比喻愚蠢之人眼光短浅,只顾眼前。

4. **golden apple in silver setting**(像金苹果镶嵌在银器上):典出《箴言》第25章11节:A word fitly spoken is like apples of gold in pictures of silver. 一句话说得合宜,就如金苹果在银网子里。形容搭配得当,相当于汉语的"珠联璧合"。

5. **heap coals of fire on one's head**(把炭火堆在某人头上):典出《箴言》第25章21—22节:If thine enemy be hungry, give him bread to eat; and if he be thirsty, give him water to drink: For thou shalt heap coals of fire upon his head, and the LORD shall reward thee. 若仇人饿了,你要给他吃的;若是他渴了,就给他水喝,这是将木炭堆在他头上,上帝也必要因此回报你。此典的意思是以德报怨,以善行消除仇恨。在英国诗人丁尼生的诗歌《罗姆尼的悔恨》(Romney's Remorse)中,画家罗姆尼因为艺术而遗弃了妻儿,后来又把她们领回来。在他老年半疯癫的时候,是妻子在身边照管他。罗姆尼感慨自己已经使:妻子成了寡居的新娘/难以拯救一个怪人。/我又疯了!/你堆在我头上的炭,/弄疯了我。

6. **lion in the way**(道上有猛狮):典出《箴言》第26章13节:The slothful man saith, "There is a lion in the way; a lion is in the street." 懒惰人说,"道上有猛狮,街上有壮狮。"指懒惰人的借口、搪塞之辞,转意为"前怕狼后怕虎"、"裹足不前"。

7. **earthenware covered with silver dross**(涂上银渣的陶器):典出《箴言》第26章23—26

节: Burning lips and a wicked heart are like a potsherd covered with silver dross. 嘴甜心坏之人，如同涂上银渣的陶器。指口蜜腹剑之人。

8. **a time for every matter under heaven** (天下万物都有定时): 典出《传道书》第3章1—8节: To every thing there is a season, and a time to every purpose under the heaven. 万事都有定期，天下万物都有定时。在乔叟(Chaucer)的《坎特伯雷故事集》(*The Canterbury Tales*)中，作者多次提及这个典故的含义，如在《学者的故事》(*The Clerk's Tale*)的开场语中即有此句: "这一整天我没有听见你讲一句话，我想你大概在研究修辞学罢；不过所罗门说得好，'每做一件事都应合乎时宜'。"哈代(Hardy)的《德伯家的苔丝》(*Tess of the D'Urbervilles*)中依茨对苔丝说："凡事都有定时。拥抱有时，不拥抱有时；这阵儿是俺拥抱的时候了。"亦引用了此典故。

9. **fly in the ointment** (膏油里的苍蝇): 典出《传道书》第10章1节: Dead flies cause the ointment of the apothecary to send forth a stinking savour: so doth a little folly him that is in reputation for wisdom and honour. 死苍蝇使香膏油发出臭气；一点愚昧也能败坏智慧和尊荣。形容令人扫兴的事情，如同"一粒老鼠屎坏了一锅汤"。查尔斯·兰姆(Charles Lamb)在《穷亲戚》(*Poor Relations*)对穷亲戚有一个定义，说他们在别的东西中间，就像是膏油里的苍蝇。在《美国经典文学研究》中，劳伦斯(D.H. Lawrence)说，麦尔维尔(Herman Melville)喜欢泰比(Type)但又不得不躲开它。"极度的自由对他简直是痛苦的折磨。自由的闲适慢慢变成他的一份恐怖。这时，它就是热带香膏中的一只苍蝇。"

10. **Cast thy bread upon the waters** (将粮食撒在水面): 典出《传道书》第11章1节: Cast thy bread upon the waters: for thou shalt find it after many days. 当将你的粮食撒在水面，因为日久必能得着。喻指"行善必得善果"、"好事定有好报"。

11. **As a tree falls, so shall it lie** (树倒在何处就躺在何处): 典出《传道书》第11章3节: If the tree fall toward the south, or the north, in the place where the tree falleth, there it shall be. 树若向南倒，或向北倒，倒在何处，就躺在何处。喻指听天由命、顺其自然、无为而治。

12. **The golden bowl is broken** (金罐破裂): 典出《传道书》第12章6节: Or ever the silver cord be loosed, or the golden bowl be broken, or the pitcher be broken at the fountain, or the wheel broken at the cistern. 银链折断，金罐破裂，瓶子在泉旁损坏，水轮在井口破烂。喻指生命终结、幻想破灭。麦尔维尔在《我和我的烟囱》(*I and My Chimney*)中讲述了妻子是如何讨厌他的烟斗和硕大的烟囱。"我的伴侣，她对烟丝的味道和煤灰同样的不悦，拼命攻击它们。我生活在持续的恐惧中，我的烟斗和烟囱像是那金罐总归要破裂毁坏。"

13. **a dog that returns to its vomit** (狗转过来吃它所吐的): 典出《箴言》第26章11节: As a dog returns to its vomit, so a fool repeats his folly. 愚昧人行愚妄事，行了又行，就如狗转过来吃它所吐的。这条典故是指愚蠢的人不知吸取教训，而是不断重复愚蠢的行径。类似汉语的"狗改不了吃屎"。在班扬(Bunyan)的《天路历程》(*The Pilgrim's Progress*)中，基督徒和忠信在谈论"柔顺"时,基督徒说道:"啊,我出发的时候,对他还抱有希望;可是现在恐怕他会跟那城市一起灭亡。因为那句古语已经在他身上应验了:'狗所吐的它转过来又吃,猪洗净了又回到泥里去滚。'"

六、课堂讨论题

1. 《箴言》中的思想对西方文学产生了巨大影响,请以"慎防淫妇"为例加以说明。
2. 《箴言》告诫人们审慎地对待自己所说的话语,同样的人生经验在世界各民族文化中都有反映,你能举出例子吗?
3. 试列举著名作家对《箴言》中的意象的使用。
4. 找出你认为与中国的谚语有相仿之处的《箴言》语句。

七、课后思考题

1. 《箴言》第31章赞美贤德妇女的言辞与中国的《论语》中对理想女性的描述有何相似之处?
2. 《传道书》第9章第4节言道: a living dog is better than a dead lion(活狗比死狮好)。你知道《一千零一夜》对它的引用吗?
3. 就《箴言》谈谈圣经智慧书对于自然规律的探索。
4. 你知道 The Sun Also Rises 的圣经渊源吗?请列举两部以"太阳照样升起"为题的中外作品?

第十五讲

耶稣形象的多维视角：福音书
Gospels, Multiple Perspectives of Jesus

一、导读：耶稣的传记

《新约》前四部书是著名的四大"福音书"，每部福音书的名称根据其作者的名字命名：《马太福音》(*Matthew*)、《马可福音》(*Mark*)、《路加福音》(*Luke*)和《约翰福音》(*John*)，记述了耶稣的生平、传道经历，以及受难、复活等传奇故事。

犹太青年木匠约瑟的未婚妻马利亚受圣灵而怀孕。时值罗马皇帝下令犹太人报名登册，马利亚随丈夫从家乡加利利的拿撒勒到犹太的伯利恒城注册登记。孩子就降生在伯利恒一家客店的马槽里。耶稣成年后，到施洗约翰那里受洗，接着在旷野经受撒旦的试探，遂开始宣讲天国的福音。耶稣选召了12位门徒，又多行神迹，追随者日益增多。耶稣的言论与行动触犯了犹太教中占统治地位的大祭司、法利赛人和撒都该人。在逾越节前夕，耶稣被门徒之一犹大出卖，犹太教大祭司的差役拘捕了耶稣，并交给罗马巡抚彼拉多，并迫使彼拉多下令将耶稣钉死在十字架上。耶稣受难死后于第三天复活，并向门徒和众人显现，第40日升天，第50日差遣圣灵降临。

"福音书"是很好的传记文学，既有纪实性，又有传奇性；既有人物间的对话和场景转换，又有人物内心的描写和戏剧性情节。耶稣及其门徒、罗马总督彼拉多和犹太大祭司的形象栩栩如生。耶稣被刻画成慈父、严师，一往无前的战士，视死如归的英雄。另外，耶稣具有哲人的头脑和诗人的气质，他的演讲充满诗意，他的譬喻形象、生动。耶稣受难一幕更是简繁相宜，既悲且壮，读之令人动容。

本讲选取耶稣生平中的5段经历：

1. 耶稣诞生在马厩。
2. 耶稣在约旦河受洗。
3. 耶稣用譬喻讲道。
4. 耶稣与12门徒最后的晚餐。
5. 耶稣在十字架受难。

二、选文及注释

Part 1

Jesus' Birth

Now the birth of Jesus Christ[1] was on this wise[2]:

When as his mother Mary[3] was espoused[4] to Joseph, before they came together[5], she was found with child of the Holy Ghost[6]. Then Joseph[7] her husband, being a just man, and not willing to make her a publick example[8], was minded to put her away privily[9]. But while he thought on these things, behold, the angel of the Lord appeared unto him in a dream, saying, "Joseph, thou son of David, fear not to take unto thee Mary thy wife: for that which is conceived in her is of the Holy Ghost. And she shall bring forth a son, and thou shalt call his name JESUS: for he shall save his people from their sins."

Now all this was done, that it might be fulfilled which was spoken of the Lord by the prophet[10], saying, "Behold, a virgin shall be with child, and shall bring forth a son, and they shall call his name Emmanuel[11], which being interpreted is, God with us."

Then Joseph being raised from sleep did as the angel of the Lord had bidden him, and took unto him his wife: And knew her not till she had brought forth her firstborn son[12]: and he called his name JESUS. (*Matthew* 1: 18–25)

Now when Jesus was born in Bethlehem of Judæa[13] in the days of Herod[14] the king, behold, there came wise men[15] from the east to Jerusalem, saying, "Where is he that is born King of the Jews? for we have seen his star in the east, and are come to worship him."

When Herod the king had heard *these things*, he was troubled, and all Jerusalem with him[16]. And when he had gathered all the chief priests and scribes of the people[17] together, he demanded of them where Christ should be born. And they said unto him, "In Bethlehem of Judæa: for thus it is written by the prophet,

---

1. Jesus Christ 耶稣基督。"耶稣"是名字，希腊文"耶稣"一名等于希伯来文的"约书亚"，含义是"耶和华拯救"。
2. wise *n*. the manner or extent of sth. 〈古〉方式；方法。on this wise 是这样的；如下所述。
3. Mary /ˈmeərɪ/（人名）马利亚(中国天主教写作"玛利亚"），耶稣的母亲，约瑟的妻子
4. espouse (to sb.) *vi*. to marry 〈古〉（与某人）订婚；结婚。按照犹太人的习俗，男女双方订婚之后便有夫妻的名分，如要离异就要办理正当手续。所以下文提到约瑟有休掉马利亚之心。
5. come together (结婚)同房。
6. with child of the Holy Ghost 由圣灵而感孕。
7. Joseph /ˈdʒəʊzɪf/（人名）约瑟，耶稣名义上的父亲
8. make sb. a publick example 让某人在公众面前丢人；公开羞辱某人。publick 是 public 的古语形式。
9. was minded to put her away privily 想要暗暗地把她休了。
10. the prophet 先知以赛亚(Isaiah；参见《以赛亚书》7:14—16)。以赛亚的预言中提到virgin(处女)，该词在希伯来文中还指年轻女子。
11. Emmanuel 又写作Immanuel；音译"以马内利"，意思是"上帝与我们同在"
12. her firstborn son 头胎的儿子。
13. Bethlehem /ˈbeθlɪhem/ of Judæa 犹太的伯利恒，是位于耶路撒冷南部8公里的一个小镇。"犹太"指古代巴勒斯坦南部地区，包括今以色列南部及约旦西南部。耶稣在世时，它是由希律王统治的王国，也是罗马帝国叙利亚行省的一部分。
14. Herod /ˈherəd/（人名）希律王，指大希律，公元前37至公元前4年间是罗马帝国内的藩王，管理犹太、以土买(以东)和加利利等地
15. wise men（东方来的）博士。可能是星象家，所以下文说 his star（耶稣的星）。
16. all Jerusalem with him 耶路撒冷全城的人和希律王一样也感到不安。
17. chief priests and scribes of the people 祭司长和民间的文士。"文士"是讲解与传授律法、在法庭上担任法律权威的专职人员。

'And thou Bethlehem, *in* the land of Juda,
Art not the least among the princes of Juda:
For out of thee shall come a Governor,
That shall rule my people Israel.'"

Then Herod, when he had privily called the wise men, inquired of them diligently[1] what time the star appeared. And he sent them to Bethlehem, and said, "Go and search diligently for the young child; and when ye have found *him,* bring me word again, that I may come and worship him also."

When they had heard the king, they departed; and, lo, the star, which they saw in the east, went before them, till it came and stood over where the young child was. When they saw the star, they rejoiced with exceeding great joy. And when they were come into the house[2], they saw the young child with Mary his mother, and fell down, and worshipped him: and when they had opened their treasures, they presented unto him gifts; gold, and frankincense, and myrrh[3]. And being warned of God in a dream that they should not return to Herod, they departed into their own country another way.

And when they were departed, behold, the angel of the Lord appeareth to Joseph in a dream, saying, "Arise, and take the young child and his mother, and flee into Egypt, and be thou there until I bring thee word: for Herod will seek the young child to destroy him."

When he arose, he took the young child and his mother by night, and departed into Egypt: and was there until the death of Herod: that it might be fulfilled which was spoken of the Lord by the prophet, saying, "Out of Egypt have I called my son.[4]"

Then Herod, when he saw that he was mocked of[5] the wise men, was exceeding wroth, and sent forth, and slew all the children that were in Bethlehem, and in all the coasts thereof, from two years old and under, according to the time which he had diligently inquired of the wise men. Then was fulfilled that which was spoken by Jeremy[6] the prophet, saying,

"In Rama[7] was there a voice heard,
Lamentation, and weeping, and great mourning,
Rachel weeping for her children, and would not be comforted,
Because they are not[8]."

But when Herod was dead, behold, an angel of the Lord appeareth in a dream to Joseph in Egypt, saying, "Arise, and take the young child and his mother, and go into the land of Israel: for they are dead which sought the young child's life."

And he arose, and took the young child and his mother, and came into the land of Israel. But when he heard that Archelaus[9] did reign in Judæa in the room of his father Herod, he was afraid to go thither: notwithstanding, being warned of God in

---

1. diligently *adv.* 仔细地；不懈地
2. the house 耶稣出生在马厩里(参见《路加福音》2:7)，此时已迁回"房子"里。
3. gold, and frankincense, and myrrh 黄金、乳香和没药。有黄金可使经济上不致有困难；乳香乃高级香料；没药有杀菌除秽作用，亦为产妇必需品。
4. Out of Egypt have I called my son. 这句话引自《何西阿书》第11章1节。指摩西带领以色列人出埃及一事(参见《出埃及记》4:22)。
5. of *prep.* 相当于by
6. Jeremy /'dʒerɪmɪ/ (人名)即 Jeremiah，先知耶利米
7. Rama (地名)拉玛。Rachel 即雅各的妻子拉结，葬于伯利恒以北、相传靠近拉玛的地方。
8. they are not (拉结的儿女)都不在人世了。这几句话引自《耶利米书》31:15，原以拉结在坟内的哀哭象征公元前586年犹太人经拉玛被掳往巴比伦王国破家亡的惨痛。如今希律王屠杀伯利恒四周的男婴，表明先知的话再一次适用。
9. Archelaus (人名)亚基老。希律王的三子之一，接管撒马利亚、犹太和以土买(以东)。他为人残酷而且统治无方，于公元后6年被罗马皇帝撤职放逐，其领土归由皇帝委派的巡抚直接统治。

a dream, he turned aside into the parts of Galilee[1]: And he came and dwelt in a city called Nazareth[2]: that it might be fulfilled which was spoken by the prophets, "He shall be called a Nazarene[3]." (*Matthew* 2)

Part 2

Jesus' Baptism

The beginning of the gospel[4] of Jesus Christ, the Son of God[5]; As it is written in the prophets, "Behold, I send my messenger before thy face, which shall prepare thy way before thee. The voice of one crying in the wilderness[6], 'Prepare ye the way of the Lord, make his paths straight.'"

John did baptize[7] in the wilderness, and preach the baptism of repentance for the remission of sins[8]. And there went out unto him all the land of Judæa, and they of Jerusalem, and were all baptized of him in the river of Jordan, confessing their sins.

And John was clothed with camel's hair, and with a girdle of a skin about his loins[9]; and he did eat locusts and wild honey; And preached, saying, "There cometh one mightier than I after me, the latchet[10] of whose shoes I am not worthy to stoop down and unloose. I indeed have baptized you with water: but he shall baptize you with the Holy Ghost.

And it came to pass in those days, that Jesus came from Nazareth of Galilee, and was baptized of John in the Jordan. And straightway coming up out of the water, he saw the heavens opened, and the Spirit like a dove descending upon him: And there came a voice from heaven, saying, "Thou art my beloved Son, in whom I am well pleased."

And immediately the Spirit driveth him into the wilderness. And he was there in the wilderness forty days, tempted of Satan[11]; and was with the wild beasts; and the angels ministered unto him.

Now after that John was put in prison, Jesus came into Galilee, preaching the gospel of the kingdom of God, and saying, "The time is fulfilled, and the kingdom of God is at hand: repent ye, and believe the gospel." (*Mark* 1: 1–15)

And he goeth up into a mountain, and calleth unto him whom he would: and they came unto him. And he ordained[12] twelve, that they should be with him, and that he might send them forth to preach, and to have power to heal sickness, and to cast out devils[13]. (*Mark* 3: 13–19)

Part 3

Jesus' Parables[14]

And he began again to teach by the

---

1. Galilee /ˈgælɪliː/ (地名)加利利。巴勒斯坦北部一多山地区, 现在的加利利是基督教徒的中心。
2. Nazareth /ˈnæzərɪθ/ (地名)拿撒勒, 位于巴勒斯坦北部, 本是约瑟和马利亚的故乡, 在当时是个无名小镇, 现代的拿撒勒是一个贸易中心和朝圣之地。
3. Nazarene /ˌnæzəˈriːn/ 拿撒勒人。the Nazarene 有时特指耶稣或基督教徒。耶稣被钉死在十字架上就有写着 "拿撒勒人耶稣" 的牌子(Jesus of Nazareth, King of the Jews; 希腊文简写为 INRI)。
4. gospel /ˈgɒspəl/ *n*. 福音, 关于耶稣的生平、死后复活及其教导的故事
5. the Son of God 上帝的儿子, 指耶稣基督。
6. wilderness *n*. 旷野, 指犹太境内、死海西面的荒漠地带
7. baptize *vt*. to water sb. on a religious ceremony 用水施洗礼
8. remission of sins 免除罪。
9. loin *n*. 腰部
10. latchet *n*. 鞋带
11. tempted of Satan /ˈseɪtən/ 被魔鬼撒旦试探。of 相当于 by。
12. ordain *vt*. to make (sb.) a priest or minister; to confer holy orders on 委任(某人)为牧师; 授以圣职
13. cast out devils 驱鬼, 指赶走附在病人身上的污灵。耶稣本人有此能力, 又赐予12门徒此种能力。
14. parable *n*. a simple story illustrating a moral or religious lesson 譬喻; 寓言。通过浅显的故事来说明道德或宗教道理, 为当时犹太教师常用的教导方法。

seaside: and there was gathered unto him a great multitude, so that he entered into a ship, and sat in sea; and the whole multitude was by the sea on the land. And he taught them many things by parables, and said unto them in his doctrine, "Hearken; Behold, there went out a sower to sow: and it came to pass, as he sowed, some fell by the way side, and the fowls of the air came and devoured it up. And some fell on stony ground, where it had not much earth; and immediately it sprang up, because it had no depth of earth: But when the sun was up, it was scorched[1]; and because it had no root, it withered away. And some fell among thorns, and the thorns grew up, and choked it, and it yielded no fruit. And other fell on good ground, and did yield fruit that sprang up and increased; and brought forth, some thirty, and some sixty, and some an hundred." And he said unto them, "He that hath ears to hear, let him hear."

And when he was alone, they that were about him with the twelve asked of him the parable. And he said unto them, "Unto you it is given to know the mystery of the kingdom of God: but unto them that are without, all these things are done in parables: that seeing they may see, and not perceive; and hearing they may hear, and not understand; lest at any time they should be converted, and their sins should be forgiven them." And he said unto them, "Know ye not this parable? and how then will ye know all parables? The sower soweth the word. And these are they by the way side, where the word is sown; but when they have heard, Satan cometh immediately, and taketh away the word that was sown in their hearts. And these are they likewise which are sown on stony ground; who, when they have heard the word, immediately receive it with gladness; and have no root in themselves, and so endure but for a time: afterward, when affliction[2] or persecution ariseth for the word's sake, immediately they are offended. And these are they which are sown among thorns; such as hear the word, and the cares of this world[3], and the deceitfulness of riches[4], and the lusts of other things entering in, choke the word, and it becometh unfruitful. And these are they which are sown on good ground; such as hear the word, and receive it, and bring forth fruit, some thirtyfold[5], some sixty, and some an hundred.

And he said unto them, "Is a candle brought to be put under a bushel[6], or under a bed? and not to be set on a candlestick[7]? For there is nothing hid, which shall not be manifested[8]; neither was any thing kept secret, but that it should come abroad. If any man have ears to hear, let him hear." And he said unto them, "Take heed what ye hear: with what measure ye mete, it shall be measured to you: and unto you that hear shall more be given[9]. For he that hath, to him shall be given: and he that hath not, from him shall be taken even that which he hath.[10]"

And he said, "So is the kingdom of God,

---

1. scorch *vt.* to wither or parch with intense heat 使枯萎
2. affliction *n.* a cause of pain or harm 苦恼，折磨
3. the cares of this world 世间的种种牵挂，即患得患失。
4. the deceitfulness of riches 财富的迷惑。
5. thirtyfold *n.* 30倍
6. bushel *n.* 斗，一种量器
7. candlestick *n.* 蜡扦，蜡烛架
8. For there is nothing hid, which shall not be manifested 因为想掩藏的事没有不显露的。
9. with what measure ... more be given 这句话的意思是：你们用什么器量量给人，也必得到什么器量量给的，甚至得到的还多。
10. For he that ... which he hath. 这句话的意思是：有的，还要给他；没有的，连他所有的也要夺去。耶稣这句话就是著名的"马太效应"的语义来源。

as if a man should cast seed into the ground; and should sleep, and rise night and day, and the seed should spring and grow up, he knoweth not how.[1] For the earth bringeth forth fruit of herself; first the blade[2], then the ear[3], after that the full corn in the ear. But when the fruit is brought forth, immediately he putteth in the sickle, because the harvest is come."

And he said, "Whereunto shall we liken the kingdom of God? or with what comparison shall we compare it? It is like a grain of mustard seed[4], which, when it is sown in the earth, is less than all the seeds that be in the earth: But when it is sown, it groweth up, and becometh greater than all herbs, and shooteth out great branches; so that the fowls of the air may lodge[5] under the shadow of it."

And with many such parables spake he the word unto them, as they were able to hear it. But without a parable spake he not unto them: and when they were alone, he expounded all things to his disciples. (*Mark* 4: 1–34)

Part 4

The Last Supper and Arrest of Jesus

And Judas Iscariot[6], one of the twelve, went unto the chief priests, to betray him unto them. And when they heard it, they were glad, and promised to give him money. And he sought how he might conveniently betray him.

And the first day of unleavened bread, when they killed the passover[7], his disciples said unto him, "Where wilt thou that we go and prepare that thou mayest eat the passover?" And he sendeth forth two of his disciples, and saith unto them, "Go ye into the city, and there shall meet you a man bearing a pitcher of water: follow him. And wheresoever he shall go in, say ye to the goodman of the house, The Master saith, 'Where is the guestchamber, where I shall eat the passover with my disciples?' And he will shew you a large upper room furnished and prepared: there make ready for us." And his disciples went forth, and came into the city, and found as he had said unto them: and they made ready the passover.

And in the evening[8] he cometh with the twelve. And as they sat and did eat, Jesus said, "Verily I say unto you, 'One of you which eateth with me shall betray me.'" And they began to be sorrowful, and to say unto him one by one, "Is it I?" and another said, "Is it I?" And he answered and said unto them, "It is one of the twelve, that dippeth with me in the dish[9]. The Son of man[10] indeed goeth, as it is written of him: but woe[11] to that man by whom the Son of man is betrayed! good were it for that man if he had never been born[12]."

And as they did eat, Jesus took bread, and blessed, and brake it, and gave to them, and said, "Take, eat: this is my body." And he took the cup, and when he had given thanks,

---

1. the seed should spring and grow up, he knoweth not how. 这句话的意思是：人对于种子发芽和成长秘密无从知道。
2. blade *n*. 叶片
3. ear *n*. 穗
4. mustard seed 芥菜籽。
5. lodge *vi*. to live in a place temporarily 住宿
6. Judas /ˈdʒuːdəs/（人名）出卖耶稣的门徒犹大；Iscariot /ɪsˈkærɪət/（族名）加略，犹大的族姓。
7. killed the passover 宰逾越节的羊羔献给上帝。
8. evening 逾越节晚餐从晚上开始，直到深夜（而犹太人平时的晚餐时间是黄昏）
9. dippeth with me in the dish 同我在盘子里蘸手(吃饭)的人。
10. the Son of man 人子，耶稣的自称。
11. woe (unto sb.) *interj*. used to express sorrow or dismay 感叹词，用于表达悲伤
12. good were it for that man if he had never been born 虚拟语气。这句话的意思是：那人不降生倒好了。

he gave it to them: and they all drank of it. And he said unto them, "This is my blood of the new testament[1], which is shed for many. Verily I say unto you, I will drink no more of the fruit of the vine, until that day that I drink it new in the kingdom of God."

And when they had sung an hymn, they went out into the mount of Olives[2]. And Jesus saith unto them, "All ye shall be offended[3] because of me this night: for it is written, I will smite the shepherd, and the sheep shall be scattered. But after that I am risen[4], I will go before you into Galilee."

But Peter said unto him, "Although all shall be offended, yet will not I." And Jesus saith unto him, "Verily I say unto thee, That this day, even in this night, before the cock crow twice, thou shalt deny me thrice[5]." But he spake the more vehemently, "If I should die with thee, I will not deny thee in any wise"[6]. Likewise also said they all.

And they came to a place which was named Gethsemane[7]: and he saith to his disciples, "Sit ye here, while I shall pray." And he taketh with him Peter and James and John, and began to be sore amazed, and to be very heavy; And saith unto them, "My soul is exceeding sorrowful unto death: tarry ye here, and watch." And he went forward a little, and fell on the ground, and prayed that, if it were possible, the hour[8] might pass from him. and he said, "Abba[9], Father, all things are possible unto thee; take away this cup[10] from me: nevertheless not what I will, but what thou wilt."

And he cometh, and findeth them sleeping, and saith unto Peter, "Simon[11], sleepest thou? couldest not thou watch one hour? Watch ye and pray, lest ye enter into temptation. The spirit truly is ready, but the flesh is weak." And again he went away, and prayed, and spake the same words. And when he returned, he found them asleep again, (for their eyes were heavy,) neither wist[12] they what to answer him. And he cometh the third time, and saith unto them, "Sleep on now, and take you rest: it is enough, the hour is come; behold, the Son of man is betrayed into the hands of sinners. Rise up, let us go; lo, he that betrayed me is at hand."

And immediately, while he yet spake, cometh Judas, one of the twelve, and with him a great multitude with swords and staves[13], from the chief priest and the scribes and the elders. And he that betrayed him had given them a token, saying, "Whomsoever I shall kiss, that same is he; take him, and lead him away safely." And as soon as he was come, he goeth straightway to him, and saith, "Rabbi[14];" and kissed him. And they laid their hands on him, and took him. And one of them that stood by drew a sword, and smote a servant of the high priest, and cut off his ear. And Jesus

---

1. my blood of the new testament 立新约的血。昔日在西奈山乃是用祭牲的血来确立人与神之间的"约"（参见《出埃及记》24:4—8），即"旧约"；耶稣用自己的血在人与神之间重新立"约"，即"新约"。
2. Olives （地名）橄榄山，耶路撒冷东面丘陵地带一狭长高地。它的西山脚就是耶稣蒙难地客西马尼花园。
3. offended 耶稣受难后门徒要遭受挫折，如失去牧羊人的羊群一般
4. risen 指耶稣死后复活升天
5. deny me thrice 三次不认我。耶稣预言门徒彼得在鸡叫三遍前将三次否认耶稣是自己的老师。
6. If I should die with thee, I will not deny thee in any wise. 就是和你一同赴难，也不会不认你。
7. Gethsemane /geθˈsemənɪ/ （地名）客西马尼，橄榄山脚下一座花园，是耶稣被捕之地
8. the hour 指耶稣借受难得升天荣耀的时刻。
9. Abba /ˈæbə/ 阿爸，犹太小孩对父亲的亲昵称呼。以此称呼呼唤神为耶稣首创。
10. this cup 这杯。比喻用法，指耶稣为人罪所担负的刑罚。
11. Simon （人名）西门，即彼得。有时称"西门彼得"。
12. wist 动词wit（知道）的过去式
13. stave n. 棍棒
14. Rabbi /ˈræbaɪ/ n. （音译）拉比，对犹太经师的称谓和称呼

answered and said unto them, "Are ye come out, as against a thief, with swords and with staves to take me? I was daily with you in the temple teaching, and ye took me not: but the scriptures must be fulfilled[1]." And they all forsook him, and fled. And there followed him a certain young man, having a linen cloth cast about his naked body; and the young men laid hold on him: And he left the linen cloth, and fled from them naked. (*Mark* 14: 10–52)

Part 5

The Crucifixion[2] of Jesus

And the soldiers led him away into the hall, called Prætorium[3]; and they call together the whole band. And they clothed him with purple, and platted[4] a crown of thorns, and put it about his head; and began to salute him, "Hail, King of the Jews!" And they smote him on the head with a reed, and did spit upon him, and bowing their knees worshipped him. And when they had mocked him, they took off the purple from him, and put his own clothes on him, and led him out to crucify him.

And they compel one Simon a Cyrenian, who passed by, coming out of the country, the father of Alexander and Rufus, to bear his cross. And they bring him unto the place Golgotha[5], which is, being interpreted, "The place of a skull." And they gave him to drink wine mingled with myrrh: but he received it not. And when they had crucified him, they parted his garments, casting lots upon them, what every man should take.

And it was the third hour[6], and they crucified him. And the superscription of his accusation was written over: THE KING OF THE JEWS[7]. And with him they crucify two thieves; the one on his right hand, and the other on his left. And the scripture was fulfilled, which saith, "And he was numbered with the transgressors." And they that passed by railed[8] on him, wagging[9] their heads, and saying, "Ah, thou that destroyest the temple, and buildest it in three days[10], save thyself, and come down from the cross." Likewise also the chief priests mocking said

---

1. **the scriptures must be fulfilled** 应验经上的话。《新约》作者在引用《旧约》时用 scripture 指代。
2. **Crucifixion** *n.* the killing of Jesus Christ on the cross 专指耶稣被钉十字架受难
3. **Prætorium** *n.* 管辖犹太人的罗马总督彼拉多(Pilate)在耶路撒冷的官邸
4. **plat** *vt.* plait (编)的变体
5. **Golgotha** /ˈgɒlɡəθə/ (地名)音译"各各他"，意思是"髑髅地"，距离耶路撒冷城墙不远，是罗马当局处死犯人的刑场。耶稣在此被钉死在十字架。
6. **the third hour** 巳初，即上午9时。下文的 the six hour 和 the ninth hour 分别是"午正"(中午12时)和"申初"(下午3时)。
7. **THE KING OF THE JEWS** "犹太人的王"，这是耶稣被处死的罪状。悬挂在耶稣头顶十字架上的牌子上是四个希腊字母：INRI 意思是"犹太人之王，拿撒勒人耶稣" (Jesus of Nazareth, King of the Jews)。
8. **rail** *vi.* to complain or protest strongly or persistently about 辱骂
9. **wag** *vi.* to move rapidly to and fro 摇头 (嗤笑耶稣)
10. 耶稣此前曾当着大祭司说过: I will destroy this temple that is made with hands, and in three days I will build another made without hands. (我要拆毁这人手所造的殿，三日内就另造一座不是人手所造的殿。《马可福音》14: 58)因此被大祭司们讥笑。

among themselves with the scribes, "He saved others; himself he cannot save. Let Christ, the King of Israel descend now from the cross, that we may see and believe." And they that were crucified with him reviled[1] him.

And when the sixth hour was come, there was darkness over the whole land until the ninth hour. And at the ninth hour Jesus cried with a loud voice, saying, "Eloi, Eloi, lama sabachthani?"[2] which is, being interpreted, "My God, my God, why hast thou forsaken me?" And some of them that stood by, when they heard it, said, "Behold, he calleth Elias[3]. And one ran and filled a spunge full of vinegar, and put it on a reed, and gave him to drink, saying, "Let alone; let us see whether Elias will come to take him down." And Jesus cried with a loud voice, and gave up the ghost[4]. And the veil of the temple was rent in twain[5] from the top to the bottom. And when the centurion[6], which stood over against him, saw that he so cried out, and gave up the ghost, he said, "Truly this man was the Son of God." (*Mark* 15: 16–39)

And when the sabbath was past, Mary Magd-alene[7], and Mary the mother of James[8], and Salome[9], had bought sweet spices, that they might come and anoint him. And very early in the morning the first day of the week[10], they came unto the sepulchre[11] at the rising of the sun. And they said among themselves, "Who shall roll us away the stone from the door of the sepulchre?" And when they looked, they saw that the stone was rolled away: for it was very great.

And entering into the sepulchre, they saw a young man[12] sitting on the right side, clothed in a long white garment; and they were affrighted[13]. And he saith unto them, "Be not affrighted: Ye seek Jesus of Nazareth, which was crucified: he is risen; he is not here: behold the place where they laid him. But go your way, tell his disciples and Peter that he goeth before you into Galilee: there shall ye see him, as he said unto you."

And they went out quickly, and fled from the sepulchre; for they trembled and were amazed: neither said they any thing to any man; for they were afraid.

Now when Jesus was risen early the first day of the week, he appeared first to Mary Magdalene, out of whom he had cast seven devils. And she went and told them that had been with him, as they mourned and wept. And they, when they had heard that he was alive, and had been seen of her, believed not. (*Mark* 16: 1–11)

---

1. revile *vt.* to criticize in an abusive or angrily insulting manner 辱骂；谩骂
2. "Eloi, Eloi, lama sabachthani" (音译)以罗伊，以罗伊，拉马撒巴各大尼？耶稣说的是亚兰语，意思是："我的神，你为什么离弃我？"
3. Behold, he calleth Elias 这句话的意思是：有人以为耶稣在叫以利亚的名字。Elias /ɪˈlaɪəs/ (人名) 以利亚，又写作Elijah，是《旧约》记载的伟大先知之一，他寻求废除偶像崇拜并重建公平。他并没有经历死亡，而是乘烈火马车升了天。
4. gave up the ghost 气绝而死。
5. twain *n.* term for two 〈古〉同 two，二；两个。窗幔顿时一分为二。
6. centurion *n.* 百夫长，古罗马的军官，指挥百人
7. Mary Magd-alene /ˈmæɡdəliːn, ˌmæɡdəˈliːnɪ/ (人名)抹大拉的马利亚
8. James (人名)雅各，耶稣的门徒之一
9. Salome /səˈləʊmɪ/ (人名)撒罗米；又译"莎乐美"
10. the first day of the week 星期日。犹太人以星期日为一周的开始。
11. sepulchre *n.* a small room cut in rock or built of stone in which a dead person is laid or buried 坟墓；墓窟
12. a young man 少年人，希伯来原文还可指"天使"。
13. affright *vt.* to arouse fear in 使惊恐

三、圣经文化知识链接

1.《新约》对《旧约》的接纳和引用

犹太教被人们称为基督教的"母亲宗教",两者共同构成西方文化的重要内核,被通称为"犹太—基督文化"[1]。因此,基督教的圣经与犹太文化的关系十分密切。基督教圣经含《旧约》与《新约》两部分,《旧约》本来就是犹太古典文化的集大成者——"犹太圣经"或称"希伯来圣经",而《新约》与犹太圣经也有着千丝万缕的联系。《新约》的基本观念如一神论、立约、救赎等,皆从犹太圣经脱胎而来,传达这些观念的各种故事,如耶稣的降生、受洗、传教、受难、复活、升天及教会的早期活动等,也都与犹太人的古老神话、传说和史传一脉相承。换言之,《新约》的成书离不开《旧约》,新约作者对旧约文本的接纳和引用痕迹十分明显。

(1) 引用的内容

《新约》对《旧约》的引用约有150处,这些引文涉及《旧约》的大部分书目,只有一些篇幅很短的先知书没有被引用。《希伯来书》(Hebrew)引用《旧约》经文是所有《新约》中最多的,直接引用的有39处53节;间接引用的有219处共270节,共258处323节,而《希伯来书》全书只有13章计303节。如此看来,《希伯来书》犹如《旧约》的注释书。

(2) 引用的方式

新约作者引用旧约文本时经常用"正如经上所写的"。但是因为被引用的文本没有使用引号,所以有时候很难对引文(Quotation)与暗指(Allusion)做出区别。成为犹太"习语"(Idiom)的旧约暗指如人名、地名、事件、习语,被引用较多;新约文本中的一节会同时暗指旧约文本若干个地方;新约作者在引用旧约文本时,有时逐字引用,有时则改写,或者加以说明。

(3) 暗指的例子

"盐":《马可福音》(9:49—50)暗指《利未记》(2:13);

"神的手指":《路加福音》(11:20)暗指《申命记》(15:9);

"眼睛就是身上的灯":《马太福音》(6:23; 20:15)暗指《申命记》(15:9);

"无花果树":《路加福音》(13:6)暗指《弥迦书》(4:4)。

2. "基督教"称谓的由来[2]

奉耶稣基督为救世主的各教派统称为基督教,亦称"基督宗教"。包括天主教、东正教和新教三大宗教。基督宗教虽脱胎于犹太教,但因为有了耶稣基督,基督徒对上帝、对世界、对人生、对未来有了新的了解,与犹太教传统大不相同。历史上发生的耶稣基督事件就是基督教与犹太教的分水岭。正是在这个意义上说,门徒承认耶稣是基督这一历史事件具有划时代的意义。它宣告了一种新宗教的萌芽。

"基督"(Christ)一词源于希伯来文 Messiah,音译为"弥赛亚",意为"受膏立者"(the Anointed),在《旧约》中特指以色列王。这个词后来可以指任何执行上帝使命的人。在耶稣去世

---

1. 梁工等译:《圣经犹太行迹——圣经文学概论》,上海:三联书店,1991年,见"译校前言"。
2. 本项参考刘光耀等著:《四福音书解读》,北京:宗教文化出版社,2004年,第182页;卓新平主编《基督教小辞典》,上海:上海辞书出版社,2001年,第1页。

后,很多人研究耶稣,跟随他的门徒认为耶稣就是犹太人正盼望等待的"弥赛亚"。当"耶稣是弥赛亚"这一信息越过巴勒斯坦进入罗马帝国希腊语地区时,耶稣被称为"基督"。从字面意思上看,"弥赛亚"与"基督"都指"受膏者";但在不同的语境中,其意义有所不同。犹太人的"弥赛亚"指的是人,给国家民族带来解放的救星。早期犹太基督徒承认耶稣是基督(Jesus, the Christ),意为"耶稣是我们等待盼望的那位基督"。此处的基督有特定的意思。在公元1世纪下半叶最早出现的有关耶稣的非基督教历史文献中,耶稣被称为"那位被称为基督的耶稣(Jesus the [so called] Christ)。但当基督教进入讲希腊语的"外邦人"中时,他们中的大多数对这个翻译过来的词语不甚了解,甚至将"基督"看做耶稣姓名的一部分,称他为"耶稣基督"或"基督耶稣",将两者合而为一作为信仰对象进行崇拜。

四、圣经文化专题

1. 耶稣形象的历史意义和文学魅力

福音书记载的核心角色是耶稣,他是一个历史人物,也是一个文学形象。

人性的耶稣是一个全然的现实社会中的人,他既有伟大的品行,也有平凡人的情感世界。说其伟大,是因为耶稣是他那个时代了不起的思想家、教育家、宗教改革家,更是一位勇于同保守势力、反动势力斗争的领导者;他有导师的禀赋、哲人的思维、演说家的口才、诗人的气质、讽刺大师的犀利。他能够开导和引导众人听信自己的主张,善于用生动的譬喻讲说深奥的哲理,采用丰富的意象和诗的语言阐明"天国的奥秘",巧用反诘和比喻反击对手的进攻。耶稣留给读者的印象是头脑清醒、体察人心、意志坚强、威武不屈。说其平凡,是因为他的表现一如世间凡人,有血肉之躯,充满爱心和怜悯,有喜、怒、哀、乐之情。比如他被钉上十字架上后发出疼痛的呼喊,承受着极刑的痛苦而断气。就神性而言,耶稣是太初就与上帝同体的"道",他的出生富有传奇色彩,传道过程中多行神迹、奇事。耶稣贵为上帝的独子,却取了仆人的形象;没有原罪,却被人钉死在十字架;他颠覆了凡人的生命规律,死而复活。从精神层面来看,耶稣的神性也非常突出,他有着不寻常的智慧,确实料事如神;另外,他有着非凡的忍受力,能忍常人所不能忍,比如他提倡爱仇敌,甚至在敌人打右脸时也让其打左脸。

从历史视角看,耶稣是犹太人理想追求和现实需求的折射,他既是民间传统中追求人性与灵性的统一和"神人"理想人格的代表,又是被压迫者对心有归属、民族解放、社会大同梦想的体现,满足了犹太人对"弥赛亚"的心理需求。从艺术视角看,耶稣的生平记述是一个完整的文学故事,以他的出生到离世三十余年的人生活动为叙事线索,以耶稣与一个反对者或一群反对者相对立的故事冲突为叙事情节,以耶稣最后受审和悲壮的死亡为高潮,以耶稣复活后人们的盼望作结尾。从叙事技巧来看,福音书没有对耶稣的外貌进行清晰、详细的描绘,这样在叙事上形成了空白,给读者留下丰富的想象空间。从主题来看,福音书通过耶稣的故事,谱写了一曲爱的赞歌,"上帝是爱",令人仰止。耶稣运用比喻的形式洞察并揭露人类内心世界的罪恶,同时也表征了犹太人对于罪恶的深恶痛绝和对人间真、善、美的探求。比如,耶稣通过"浪子回头"的譬喻(《路加福音》15:11—32),歌颂了父亲所代表的慷慨、宽容,抨击了长子所代表的狭隘、妒忌,颂扬了知错必改的勇气。再如,耶稣通过"好心的撒玛利亚人"的譬喻(《路加福音》10:25—37),倡导了互帮互助的美德和"四海之内皆兄弟"的道义。其实这些美德和道义是人类追求的普遍价值。读者之所以被吸引，是在于"善"本身的磁力，也是《圣经》文本高超的艺术性使然。因此可以说，福音书借用耶稣的形象表达了犹太民族乃至整个人类的内心追求。

福音书把耶稣刻画成一位兼具历史性和文学性的人物形象。看待耶稣，重要的不在于考证他到底是人还是神，而是在于深刻理解这一形象所浓缩的人类精神要素。揭去神学面纱，我们可以看出耶稣是一个文化符号，它将犹太人的传统美德和精神诉求融于一身。透过耶稣这一艺术形象，我们不但能领略人生哲理，感受福音书的文学魅力，还能领会基督教核心观念的内涵。

2. 作为宗教改革家的耶稣

耶稣是犹太人，从小受到严格的犹太教教育。作为一位伟大的思想家，耶稣对犹太传统做出了新的解释，而这些新见解的出现产生了革命性的后果，最终使基督教从犹太教中脱颖而出，发展成与犹太教有根本区别的新宗教。因此可以说耶稣是一个宗教改革家。他的宗教改革既体现在他的说教之中，也体现在他的行动上。

耶稣曾经宣告："就是到天地都废去了，律法的一点一画也不能废去，都要成全。"（《马太福音》5:18）耶稣对律法进行了纲领性总结，指出，律法的总纲就是爱：爱神与爱人。在登山宝训中，耶稣说爱人如己就是律法和先知的道理。在回答有关最大的诫命是什么的问题时，耶稣说："你要尽心、尽性、尽意爱主你的神。这是诫命中第一，且是最大的。其次，就是要爱人如己。"这两条诫命是"律法和先知的道理"（《马可福音》12:30—34）。耶稣的爱，不只是爱自己的族人，而是推广到所有人，甚至包括敌人。耶稣对于律法总纲的解释，与犹太教"以眼还眼，以牙还牙""爱朋友，恨仇敌"的原则有着本质的不同。

耶稣对律法的改革主要是强调要在内心深处约束自己，并以行动守法，而不是只注重外在形式。耶稣的根本态度不是反对律法，而是强调律法的内在价值。耶稣强调内在品质的完善与法利赛人强调遵守外在的律法形成对照。耶稣告诉信徒们："不仅杀人，就连愤怒和仇恨；不仅奸淫，就连不洁的念头，都是必须禁止的。只是我告诉你们，凡是向兄弟动怒的，难免受审判。"（《马太福音》5:22）这些思想蕴含在以下事例中：

(1) 关于安息日的规条。耶稣的门徒在安息日搓麦穗吃，在犹太人眼中就是"作工"。依照《旧约》规定，这触犯了安息日的规条。法利赛人指责他们"作工"犯了安息日的条例。耶稣说律法条例的根基是爱，条例是为了让人得益处，而不是要害人。所以，耶稣明确宣告说："安息日是为人设立的，人不是为安息日设立的"（《马可福音》2:28）。耶稣当然主张遵守安息日的律法规定，并且教导人们安息日救人性命是重要的。

(2) 税吏在犹太人眼中是卖国贼，如同罪犯，人们不与他们来往。然而，耶稣不仅收税吏利未为徒，而且在利未家中与好些税吏和犹太人眼中的罪人一起吃喝（《马可福音》2:13—17）。这引起文士的攻击。

(3) 耶稣治好有麻风病的人，他突破了人与人之间疾病与礼仪所导致的隔离，让文士知道"人子"耶稣在地上有赦罪的权柄。

(4) 摩西律法对什么洁净、什么不洁净，有详细的规定（《利未记》11），而耶稣却说，各样的食物都是洁净的（《马可福音》7:14—23）。耶稣一再强调：外表的不洁是次要的，内心的洁净才是真洁净。信仰在乎内心而不在乎外表的形式。

通过对照旧约传统可以看出，耶稣的教导具有"革命性"意义。耶稣招收税吏为徒，突破了人们因政治观念和品行不同所导致的隔离；耶稣关于禁食与安息日的新认识突破了旧有传统观念对人的束缚。他不仅反对"口头律法"，甚至对摩西律法也持批判、分析的态度。因此，耶稣的根本态度不是反对律法，而是强调律法的内在价值。

五、圣经典故集锦

1. **voice in the wilderness**（旷野的呼声）：指"没有得到反响的声音"，"无人理睬的改革口号"。典出《马可福音》第1章3节：The voice of one crying in the wilderness, prepare ye the way of the Lord, make his paths straight. 在旷野有人声喊着说："预备主的道，修直他的路。"施洗约翰在旷野宣传悔改的福音，疾呼人们改邪归正。

2. **the salt of the earth, the light of the world**（世上的盐、世上的光）：指"社会中坚"，"人世楷模"。典出耶稣要门徒在世上起盐和光的作用，带动众人防恶，指引大家为善。

3. **serve two masters**（事奉两个主人）：指"脚踏两只船"、"三心二意"、"幻想两全其美"。典出耶稣的言论："一个人不能事奉两个主，……你们不能又侍奉上帝，又侍奉玛门。"(mamman，玛门指"钱财"、"财富")

4. **cast pearls before swine**（把珍珠丢在猪前）：比喻同不明事理、不识好歹的人无法沟通。也有糟蹋珍贵之物的意思。典出耶稣的言论："不要把圣物给狗，也不要把你们的珍珠丢在猪前，恐怕它践踏了珍珠，转过来咬你们。"

5. **new wine in old bottles**（新酒装在旧皮袋里）：指"旧形式难容新内容"，"治标不治本"。在耶稣时代，用来装酒的容器是皮袋子，而没有"瓶子"。耶稣把福音比作新酒，不能装进犹太教的旧皮袋，而需要用新的方式来表达，只有把新酒装在新皮袋里，才能使形式、内容两样都得到保全。

6. **bear one's cross**（背十字架）：十字架是基督教信仰的标志。背负自己的十字架指"忍辱负重"，"经受磨炼"，"为了信仰不惜赴汤蹈火"。耶稣用背十字架告诉门徒，他们所受的磨炼和痛苦乃是对其忍耐、德性和信仰的考验："不背着他的十字架跟从我的，也不配做我的门徒。"

7. **a reed shaken with the wind**（风中的芦苇）：指"墙头草随风倒"，"随大流的人"，"没有主见的人"。耶稣在对众人讲论约翰的重要意义时顺便说道："你们从前出到旷野，是要看什么呢？要看风吹动的芦苇么？"

8. **sow tares among the wheat**（稗子撒在麦子里）：稗子是一种长在农田中的野草状植物。这个比喻指"坏种混入好种"，"阻碍事务健康发展的不良因素"。耶稣比喻说："天国好像撒种在田里，及至人睡觉的时候，有仇敌来，将稗子撒在麦子里就走了。到长苗吐穗的时候，稗子也显出来。"

9. **whited sepulchres**（粉饰的坟墓）：喻指虚假和伪善，和汉语的"金玉其外、败絮其中"相类。典出耶稣对法利赛人的斥责："你们好像粉饰的坟墓，外面好看，里面却装满了死人的骨头，和一切污秽。"

10. **Juda's kiss**（犹大之吻）：犹大在客西马尼园以亲吻耶稣为暗号出卖了耶稣。指"叛卖的行为"，"叛卖的信号"，"口蜜腹剑"。

六、课堂讨论题

1. 谈谈耶稣在演讲时所用的譬喻。
2. 有人说耶稣是教育家，谈谈其教育理念。
3. 你知道达·芬奇的名画《最后的晚餐》中描绘的人物吗(见右图)？
4. 耶稣和孔子都被其门徒称为"夫子"。他们的伦理道德教育思想有何相同之处？

七、课后思考题

1. 结合汉语成语"浪子回头金不换"，谈谈耶稣"浪子回头"的譬喻蕴含的教育理念。
2. 你知道提香的《基督与法利赛人》(又名《纳税钱》)吗(见右图)？
3. 谈谈圣母马利亚作为母亲的形象。
4. 你知道严复用文言文翻译的《马可福音》片段吗？
5. 谈谈中国现代文学里的耶稣形象。

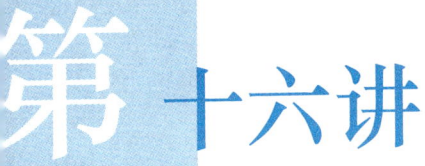

启示文学的典范:《启示录》
Revelation, a Model of Apocalyptic Literature

一、导读:《启示录》的内容和文体特征

《启示录》(*Revelation*)是《新约》最后一卷书,传统上认为作者是耶稣的门徒之一约翰(John)。取名《启示录》的意思是,约翰把来自耶稣基督的"启示",即将要发生的事传达给早期的基督教会,正如书卷开篇所言: The Revelation of Jesus Christ, which God gave unto him, to shew unto his servants things which must shortly come to pass. "世界末日"和"最后的审判"的说法都是源于《启示录》。

《启示录》由序曲、六个单元和尾声组成,总体上看有一个完整的故事框架,大致可分为三部分: 1. 约翰看到基督的异象; 2. 象征基督的羔羊揭开被封的七印(象征惩罚);第七印带来天使的七号(象征灾难); 3. 基督击败代表一切邪恶的兽和假先知、撒旦被捆绑同时基督作王一千年,以及最后的审判和新天新地的降临。善与恶的冲突是故事的情节主线。

传统上认为《启示录》写于公元 1 世纪末,按圣经里的时间算,就是耶稣死后 60 多年,正值罗马帝国对基督教迫害较为激烈的时期。这一时期,崇拜皇帝之风盛行,而教会刚刚兴起,还不够强大。使徒们要在这样的环境中传教,与不可一世的罗马帝国政府一决胜负。书中预言罗马帝国最后肯定要灭亡,且在其灭亡之前将要迫害教会。书卷以宇宙间基督与撒旦之间最后的战争为叙述背景,以意象和神话的方式表明,在这场战争中基督要战胜撒旦,寓意基督将对罗马帝国的罪行进行最后的审判。

本讲选取《启示录》5 部分内容:

1. 基督的异象: 约翰看到基督的全貌: 头发、眼目、手、足、衣着等,并听到他的声音。特写是基督口中含有一把双刃剑。

2. 七天使吹响七支号角: 号角依次吹响,各种天灾也依次降临人间。

3. 妇人和龙: 身披日头、脚踏月亮、头戴 12 星的临产孕妇象征上帝的选民; 她所生的男婴代表基督; 张牙舞爪的大红龙象征撒旦及其邪恶势力。天使长米迦勒与大红龙争战,并将其击败。

4. 大淫妇和兽: 朱衣淫妇被称为"大巴比伦"、"大城",影射罗马帝国; 七头十角的朱红兽充当撒旦的化身,代表罗马和一切抵挡上帝的国度。

5. 末日审判和新天新地: 撒旦最终被扔进地狱的火湖,死者都接受最后的审判; 新天新地出现,圣城新耶路撒冷从天而降; 生命水和生命树重现。

二、选文及注释

Part 1

The Vision of Christ

The Revelation of Jesus Christ, which God gave unto him, to shew unto his servants things which must shortly come to pass; and he sent and signified[1] it by his angel unto his servant John: Who bare record[2] of the word of God[3], and of the testimony[4] of Jesus Christ, and of all things that he saw. Blessed is he that readeth, and they that hear the words of this prophecy, and keep those things which are written therein: for the time is at hand[5].

John to the seven churches which are in Asia: Grace *be* unto you, and peace, from him which is, and which was, and which is to come[6]; and from the seven Spirits[7] which are before his throne; and from Jesus Christ, *who is* the faithful witness, *and* the first begotten of the dead[8], and the prince of the kings of the earth.

Unto him that loved us, and washed us from our sins in his own blood, and hath made us kings and priests unto God and his Father[9]; to him *be* glory and dominion[10] for ever and ever. Amen[11].

Behold, he cometh with clouds;
And every eye shall see him,
And they *also* which pierced him:
And all kindreds of the earth shall wail because of him.[12]
Even so, Amen.

"I am Alpha and Omega[13], the beginning and the ending," saith the Lord, "which is, and which was, and which is to come, the Almighty."

I John, who also am your brother, and companion in tribulation[14], and in the kingdom and patience of Jesus Christ, was in the isle that is called Patmos[15], for the word of God, and for the testimony of Jesus Christ. I was in the spirit on the Lord's day[16], and heard behind me a great voice, as of a trumpet, saying, "I am Alpha and Omega, the first and the last: and, what thou seest, write in a book, and send *it* unto the seven churches which are in Asia; unto Ephesus, and unto Smyrna, and unto Pergamos, and unto Thyatira, and unto Sardis, and unto

---

1. signify *vt.* to be an indication of 表明；晓谕
2. bare record 作见证。
3. the word of God 上帝的道。
4. testimony *n.* a solemn protest or declaration 〈古〉证言；证明
5. the time is at hand 日期临近了。"日期"指基督再次降临的时刻。
6. him which is, and which was, and which is to come 昔在、今在、以后永在的上帝。
7. seven Spirits （上帝宝座前的）七灵，指在七个教会中运行的圣灵。"七"是个神秘数字。
8. the first begotten of the dead 从死里首先复活的，指耶稣。begotten 是 beget 的过去分词，意思是超越，即耶稣进入死亡的领地又从中出来。
9. kings and priests unto God and his Father 国度和他父神的祭司。
10. dominion *n.* sovereignty or control 统治权；权柄
11. Amen *int.* （感叹词）阿门，用在祈祷或陈述的结尾表示承认、赞成
12. And all kindreds of the earth shall wail because of him. 此句意思是，地上的万族要因他哀哭。kindred *n.* one's family and relatives 家族；族人。
13. Alpha /ˈelfə/ and Omega /ˈəʊmɪɡə/ 阿拉法和俄梅戛，分别是希腊字母表第一个和最后一个字母，表示从头至尾。意思是耶稣代表永恒，与旧约中的耶和华自称"自有永有的（I am who I am）"的含义相似。
14. tribulation *n.* a cause of great trouble or suffering 苦难；磨难
15. the isle that is called Patmos 名叫"拔摩"的海岛，位于爱琴海。
16. in the spirit on the Lord's day 在主日被圣灵感动。"主日"即纪念耶稣复活的星期日。
17. seven golden candlesticks 七个金灯台。教会是黑暗世界里光的象征。

Philadelphia, and unto Laodicea." And I turned to see the voice that spake with me. And being turned, I saw seven golden candlesticks[17]; And in the midst of the seven candlesticks one like unto the Son of man, clothed with a garment down to the foot, and girt about the paps with a golden girdle[1]. His head and his hairs *were* white[2] like wool, as white as snow; and his eyes *were* as a flame of fire[3]; And his feet like unto fine brass[4], as if they burned in a furnace; and his voice as the sound of many waters. And he had in his right hand seven stars[5]: and out of his mouth went a sharp twoedged sword[6]: and his countenance was as the sun shineth in his strength[7].

And when I saw him, I fell at his feet as dead. And he laid his right hand upon me, saying unto me, "Fear not; I am the first and the last: I *am* he that liveth, and was dead; and, behold, I am alive for evermore, Amen; and have the keys of hell and of death. Write the things which thou hast seen, and the things which are, and the things which shall be hereafter; The mystery of the seven stars which thou sawest in my right hand, and the seven golden candlesticks. The seven stars are the angels of the seven churches: and the seven candlesticks which thou sawest are the seven churches." (1)

Part 2

The Seven Angels

And when he had opened the seventh seal[8], there was silence in heaven about the space of half an hour. And I saw the seven angels which stood before God; and to them were given seven trumpets. And another angel came and stood at the altar, having a golden censer; and there was given unto him much incense, that he should offer it with the prayers of all saints upon the golden altar which was before the throne. And the smoke of the incense, *which came* with the prayers of the saints, ascended up before God out of the angel's hand. And the angel took the censer, and filled it with fire of the altar, and cast it into the earth: and there were voices, and thunderings, and lightnings, and an earthquake.

And the seven angels which had the seven trumpets prepared themselves to sound. The first angel sounded, and there followed hail and fire mingled with blood, and they were cast upon the earth: and the third part[9] of trees was burnt up, and all green grass was burnt up.

And the second angel sounded, and as it were a great mountain burning with fire was cast into the sea: and the third part of the sea became blood; And the third part of the creatures which were in the sea, and had life, died; and the third part of the ships were destroyed.

And the third angel sounded, and there fell a great star from heaven, burning as it were a lamp, and it fell upon the third part of the rivers, and upon the fountains of waters; and the name of the star is called Wormwood: and the third part of the waters became wormwood; and many men died of the waters, because they were made bitter[10].

And the fourth angel sounded, and the third part of the sun was smitten[11], and the

---

1. girt about the paps with a gold girdle 胸间束着金带。girt 是 gird (*vt.* 束紧腰)的过去分词; pap *n.* 奶头。about paps 指胸间。金带象征高贵。
2. His head and his hairs were white 头与发皆白。象征智慧和尊贵。
3. his eyes were as a flame of fire 眼目如同火焰, 象征透视历史和人心的能力。
4. fine brass 发光的铜; 精铜。象征稳健且有力量。
5. he had in his right hand seven stars 右手擎七星, 象征对教会的掌管和护佑。
6. his mouth went a sharp twoedged sword 口中伸出一把双刃利剑, 象征无可抗拒的审判和权柄。
7. his countenance was as the sun shineth in his strength 面容如同烈日放光, 象征无上光荣和地位至高。
8. seal *n.* (书卷的)封印。象征权威。前文提到, 坐宝座者右手中有书卷, 里外都写着字, 用七印封严。
9. the third part 三分之一(部分)。
10. they were made bitter 河水变苦。
11. smitten 动词smite(击打)的过去分词

third part of the moon, and the third part of the stars; so as the third part of them was darkened, and the day shone not for a third part of it¹, and the night likewise.

And I beheld, and heard an angel flying through the midst of heaven, saying with a loud voice, "Woe, woe, woe, to the inhabiters² of the earth by reason of the other voices of the trumpet of the three angels, which are yet to sound!" (8)

And the fifth angel sounded, and I saw a star fall from heaven unto the earth: and to him³ was given the key of the bottomless pit. And he opened the bottomless pit; and there arose a smoke out of the pit, as the smoke of a great furnace; and the sun and the air were darkened by reason of the smoke of the pit. And there came out of the smoke locusts upon the earth: and unto them was given power, as the scorpions⁴ of the earth have power. And it was commanded them that they should not hurt the grass of the earth, neither any green thing, neither any tree; but only those men which have not the seal of God in their foreheads. And to them it was given that they should not kill them, but that they should be tormented⁵ five months: and their torment was as the torment of a scorpion, when he striketh a man. And in those days shall men seek death, and shall not find it; and shall desire to die, and death shall flee from them.

And the shapes of the locusts were like unto horses prepared unto battle; and on their heads were as it were crowns like gold, and their faces were as the faces of men. And they had hair as the hair of women, and their teeth were as the teeth of lions. And they had breastplates⁶, as it were breastplates of iron; and the sound of their wings was as the sound of chariots of many horses running to battle. And they had tails like unto scorpions, and there were stings⁷ in their tails: and their power *was* to hurt men five months. And they had a king over them, *which is* the angel of the bottomless pit, whose name in the Hebrew tongue is Abaddon, but in the Greek tongue hath his name Apollyon⁸.

One woe is past; *and,* behold, there come two woes more hereafter.

And the sixth angel sounded, and I heard a voice from the four horns of the golden altar which is before God, saying to the sixth angel which had the trumpet, "Loose the four angels which are bound in the great river Euphrates⁹." And the four angels were loosed, which were prepared for an hour, and a day, and a month, and a year, for to slay the third part of men. And the number of the army of the horsemen *were* two hundred thousand thousand¹⁰: and I heard the number of them. And thus I saw the horses in the vision, and them that sat on them, having breastplates of fire, and of jacinth¹¹, and brimstone: and the heads of the horses *were* as the heads of lions; and out of their mouths issued fire and smoke and brimstone. By these three¹² was the third

---

1. the day shone not for a third part of it 白昼的三分之一没有光。
2. inhabiter *n.* 居民
3. him 指代earth
4. scorpion *n.* 蝎子
5. torment *vt.* to cause to experience severe mental or physical suffering 折磨
6. breastplate *n.* 胸甲
7. sting *n.* 毒刺
8. Abaddon /əˈbædən/, Apollyon /əˈpɒljən/（音译）"无底坑"、"地狱"的使者或魔王亚巴顿和亚玻伦。喻指"毁灭者"。
9. Euphrates 幼发拉底河
10. two hundred thousand thousand 两亿。
11. jacinth *n.* 橘红色的宝石；红玛瑙
12. these three 指第五、六、七位天使。

part of men killed, by the fire, and by the smoke, and by the brimstone, which issued out of their mouths. For their power is in their mouth, and in their tails: for their tails *were* like unto serpents, and had heads, and with them they do hurt.

And the rest of the men which were not killed by these plagues yet repented not of the works of their hands[1], that they should not worship devils, and idols of gold, and silver, and brass, and stone, and of wood: which neither can see, nor hear, nor walk: Neither repented they of their murders, nor of their sorceries[2], nor of their fornication[3], nor of their thefts. (9)

And the seventh angel sounded; and there were great voices in heaven, saying, "The kingdoms of this world are become *the kingdoms* of our Lord, and of his Christ; and he shall reign for ever and ever."

And the four and twenty elders, which sat before God on their seats, fell upon their faces, and worshipped God, saying, "We give thee thanks, O Lord God Almighty, which art, and wast, and art to come; because thou hast taken to thee thy great power, and hast reigned. And the nations[4] were angry, and thy wrath is come, and the time of the dead, that they should be judged[5], and that thou shouldest give reward unto thy servants the prophets, and to the saints, and them that fear thy name, small and great; and shouldest destroy them which destroy the earth. And the temple of God[6] was opened in heaven, and there was seen in his temple the ark of his testament[7]: and there were lightnings, and voices, and thunderings, and an earthquake, and great hail. (11: 15–19)

Part 3

The Woman and the Dragon

And there appeared a great wonder in heaven; a woman[8] clothed with the sun, and the moon under her feet, and upon her head a crown of twelve stars: And she being with child cried, travailing in birth[9], and pained to be delivered. And there appeared another wonder in heaven; and behold a great red dragon[10], having seven heads and ten horns, and seven crowns upon his heads. And his tail drew the third part of the stars of heaven, and did cast them to the earth: and the dragon stood before the woman which was ready to be delivered, for to devour[11] her child as soon as it was born. And she brought forth a man child, who was to rule all nations with a rod of iron: and her child was caught up unto God, and *to* his throne. And the woman fled into the wilderness, where she hath a place prepared of God, that they should feed her there a thousand two hundred and threescore days.

And there was war in heaven: Michael[12] and his angels fought against the dragon; and the dragon fought and his angels, and prevailed not[13]; neither was their place found any more in heaven. And the great dragon

---

1. yet repented not of the works of their hands 仍旧对自己的亲手所为不悔改。
2. sorcery *n.* the use of magic, especially black magic 巫术；邪术
3. fornication *n.* 奸淫；乱伦
4. the nations 指外邦人。
5. the time of the dead, that they should be judged 审判死人的时候到了。行恶的人死后也不能逃避审判。
6. the temple of God 上帝的殿。
7. the ark of his testament 指(上帝的)约柜。
8. woman 这位妇人代表上帝的选民。下文所生男婴代表弥赛亚。
9. travailing in birth 妇人因生产的艰难而疼痛呼叫。
10. great red dragon 大红龙，下文所提到的古蛇、魔鬼、撒旦的代表，与上帝为敌。
11. devour *vt.* 吞吃，喻指攻击
12. Michael /ˈmaɪkl/ (天使长)米迦勒
13. prevailed not 不能取胜。

was cast out, that old serpent, called the Devil, and Satan, which deceiveth the whole world: he was cast out into the earth, and his angels were cast out with him. And I heard a loud voice saying in heaven,

"Now is come salvation, and strength, and the kingdom of our God, and the power of his Christ: for the accuser[1] of our brethren is cast down, which accused them before our God day and night. And they overcame him by the blood of the Lamb[2], and by the word of their testimony; and they loved not their lives unto the death. Therefore rejoice, *ye* heavens, and ye that dwell in them. Woe to the inhabiters of the earth and of the sea! for the devil is come down unto you, having great wrath, because he knoweth that he hath but a short time."

And when the dragon saw that he was cast unto the earth, he persecuted the woman which brought forth the man *child*. And to the woman were given two wings of a great eagle[3], that she might fly into the wilderness, into her place, where she is nourished[4] for a time, and times, and half a time, from the face of the serpent. And the serpent cast out of his mouth water as a flood[5] after the woman, that he might cause her to be carried away of the flood. And the earth helped the woman, and the earth opened her mouth, and swallowed up the flood which the dragon cast out of his mouth. And the dragon was wroth with the woman, and went to make war with the remnant of her seed[6], which keep the commandments of God, and have the testimony of Jesus Christ. (12)

Part 4

The Scarlet Woman and the Beast

And there came one of the seven angels which had the seven vials[7], and talked with me, saying unto me, "Come hither; I will shew unto thee the judgment of the great whore that sitteth upon many waters: With whom the kings of the earth have committed fornication, and the inhabitants of the earth have been made drunk with the wine of her fornication."

So he carried me away in the spirit into the wilderness: and I saw a woman sit upon a scarlet coloured beast, full of names of blasphemy[8], having seven heads and ten horns. And the woman was arrayed in[9] purple and scarlet colour, and decked with gold and precious stones and pearls, having a golden cup in her hand full of abominations and filthiness of her fornication[10]: And upon her forehead *was* a name written,

MYSTERY, BABYLON THE GREAT, THE MOTHER OF HARLOTS AND ABOMINATIONS OF THE EARTH.

And I saw the woman drunken with the blood of the saints, and with the blood of the martyrs of Jesus[11]: and when I saw her, I wondered with great admiration. And the

---

1. accuser *n.* 控告者；原告。喻指撒旦是上帝与其选民间的挑拨者。
2. the blood of the Lamb 羔羊的血，代表基督为人类而死。
3. two wings of a great eagle 大鹰的翅膀，象征拯救。
4. nourish *vt.* to provide with the food or other substances necessary for growth, health, and good condition 滋养；养活
5. water as a flood 恶龙吐出的水，象征撒旦要吞灭上帝的子民。
6. the remnant of her seed 妇人其余的儿女。
7. vial *n.* a small container 小瓶
8. blasphemy *n.* the action or offence of speaking sacrilegiously about God or sacred things; profane talk 亵渎(言语)
9. be arrayed in 穿着……衣服
10. abominations and filthiness of her fornication （朱衣妇人）淫乱的可憎之物和污秽之物。fornication *n.* a state of having sexual intercourse with sb. one is not married to 淫乱
11. the martyrs of Jesus 为耶稣殉教的人。

angel said unto me,

"Wherefore didst thou marvel? I will tell thee the mystery of the woman, and of the beast that carrieth her, which hath the seven heads and ten horns. The beast that thou sawest was, and is not[1]; and shall ascend out of the bottomless pit, and go into perdition[2]: and they that dwell on the earth shall wonder, whose names were not written in the book of life from the foundation of the world, when they behold the beast that was, and is not, and yet is[3]. And here is the mind[4] which hath wisdom. The seven heads are seven mountains, on which the woman sitteth. And there are seven kings: five are fallen, and one is, *and* the other is not yet come[5]; and when he cometh, he must continue a short space[6]. And the beast that was, and is not, even he is the eighth, and is of the seven[7], and goeth into perdition. And the ten horns which thou sawest are ten kings, which have received no kingdom as yet; but receive power as kings one hour with the beast[8]. These have one mind[9], and shall give their power and strength unto the beast. These shall make war with the Lamb, and the Lamb shall overcome them: for he is Lord of lords[10], and King of kings: and they that are with him *are* called, and chosen, and faithful." And he saith unto me,

"The waters which thou sawest, where the whore sitteth, are peoples, and multitudes, and nations, and tongues[11]. And the ten horns[12] which thou sawest upon the beast, these shall hate the whore, and shall make her desolate and naked, and shall eat her flesh, and burn her with fire. For God hath put in their hearts to fulfil his will, and to agree, and give their kingdom unto the beast, until the words of God shall be fulfilled. And the woman which thou sawest is that great city, which reigneth over the kings of the earth." (17)

Part 5

The Last Judgment and the New Heaven and New Earth

And I saw an angel come down from heaven, having the key of the bottomless pit and a great chain in his hand. And he laid hold on the dragon, that old serpent, which is the Devil, and Satan, and bound him a thousand years, and cast him into the bottomless pit, and shut him up, and set a seal upon him, that he should deceive the nations no more, till the thousand years[13] should be fulfilled: and after that he must be loosed a little season[14].

And I saw thrones, and they[15] sat upon them, and judgment was given unto them: and *I saw* the souls of them that were

---

1. was, and is not 先前有, 而如今没有了。
2. perdition *n.* a state of eternal punishment and damnation into which a sinful person passes after death 毁灭; 沉沦
3. that was, and is not, and yet is (那兽)先前在、如今不在、将来还要出现
4. mind *n.* 有才智的人
5. five are fallen, and one is, *and* the other is not yet come (七位王中)五位已经倾倒, 一位还在, 一位还没有到来。
6. continue a short space 存留一时。
7. is of the seven 与那七位王同列(都要归于沉沦)。
8. receive power as kings one hour with the beast 在一时之间要和兽同得权柄。
9. have one mind 同心合意。
10. Lord of lords 万主之主。下文万王之王均指(羔羊)基督。
11. tongues 指有人说话的每个地方
12. the ten horns 十角代表列国十王, 淫妇虽然利用列国, 但最终要被列国出卖、丢弃。大巴比伦最终要覆灭。
13. the thousand years 撒旦被捆绑一千年, 即下文所说信徒与基督做王的"千禧年"。
14. a little season 暂时。
15. they 指信徒、使徒和得胜者

beheaded[1] for the witness of Jesus, and for the word of God, and which had not worshipped the beast, neither his image, neither had received *his* mark upon their foreheads, or in their hands; and they lived and reigned with Christ a thousand years. But the rest of the dead lived not again until the thousand years were finished. This is the first resurrection[2]. Blessed and holy is he that hath part in the first resurrection: on such the second death hath no power[3], but they shall be priests of God and of Christ, and shall reign with him a thousand years.

And when the thousand years are expired, Satan shall be loosed out of his prison, and shall go out to deceive the nations which are in the four quarters of the earth, Gog and Magog[4], to gather them together to battle: the number of whom *is* as the sand of the sea. And they went up on the breadth of the earth, and compassed the camp of the saints about, and the beloved city[5]: and fire came down from God out of heaven, and devoured them. And the devil that deceived them was cast into the lake of fire and brimstone, where the beast and the false prophet *are,* and shall be tormented day and night for ever and ever.

And I saw a great white throne, and him that sat on it, from whose face the earth and the heaven fled away; and there was found no place for them. And I saw the dead, small and great, stand before God; and the books were opened: and another book was opened, which is *the book* of life: and the dead were judged out of those things which were written in the books, according to their works. And the sea gave up the dead which were in it; and death and hell delivered up[6] the dead which were in them: and they were judged every man according to their works. And death and hell were cast into the lake of fire. This is the second death. And whosoever was not found written in the book of life was cast into the lake of fire. (20)

And I saw a new heaven and a new earth: for the first heaven and the first earth were passed away; and there was no more sea[7]. And I John saw the holy city, new Jerusalem, coming down from God out of heaven, prepared as a bride adorned[8] for her husband. And I heard a great voice out of heaven saying, "Behold, the tabernacle of God is with men[9], and he will dwell with them, and they shall be his people, and God himself shall be with them, *and be* their God. And God shall wipe away all tears from their eyes; and there shall be no more death, neither sorrow, nor crying, neither shall there be any more pain: for the former things are passed away. (21: 1–5)

And he shewed me a pure river of water of life, clear as crystal, proceeding[10] out of the throne of God and of the Lamb. In the midst of the street of it, and on either side of the river, was there the tree of life[11], which bare twelve manner[12] of fruits, and yielded[13] her fruit every month: and the leaves of the

---

1. behead *vt.* to separate the head from 斩首
2. resurrection /ˌrezəˈrekʃən/ *n.* 复活
3. Blessed and holy ... hath no power 这句话的意思是, 在第一次复活有份的有福了、圣洁了, 第二次的死无权掌管他们。第二次死即下文所说的在地狱火湖受永罚。
4. Gog and Magog 歌革和玛各, 代表地上一切抵挡上帝的权势。
5. the beloved city 蒙爱的城, 象征选民的所在。
6. deliver up 交出; 移交。
7. sea 海, 象征动乱
8. adorn *vt.* to make more beautiful or attractive 装饰; 佩戴
9. the tabernacle of God is with men 上帝的帐幕在人间, 与人同住。
10. proceed *vi.* to originate from 源于
11. the tree of life 生命树。与伊甸园里的"生命树"呼应。区别是伊甸园中禁食生命树的果子, 而此处生命树的果子还有医治万民的奇效。
12. manner *n.* 样式; 种类
13. yield *vt.* to produce or provide 长出; 结(果实)

tree were for the healing of the nations. And there shall be no more curse[1]: but the throne of God and of the Lamb shall be in it; and his servants shall serve him: and they shall see his face; and his name shall be in their foreheads. And there shall be no night there; and they need no candle, neither light of the sun; for the Lord God giveth them light: and they shall reign for ever and ever. (22: 1–5)

三、圣经文化知识链接

1.《启示录》的现实基础

公元前63年，罗马大将庞培攻克耶路撒冷城，占领了圣殿，从此以色列民族的国家不再存在。后来，形成于该地区的基督教自然也受到罗马统治者的高压统治。面对这种时局，基督徒不能像从前的先知那样直抒胸臆。因而启示作品的作者往往构筑一个故事框架，通过异象、异梦或天使的话，来显示上帝隐秘的救世计划，以坚定信众的信仰。

启示文学与先知文学相同，都是犹太民族在面临危机、强敌入侵的动荡时代发展、繁荣起来的，其思想主旨最终都是指向有关末世的预言，简称"末世论"。《启示录》中以"穿红衣的女人"及"巴比伦淫妇"映射当时的罗马帝国。这是因为在当时的首都罗马，社会风气败坏，人们道德堕落，生活奢靡放荡；执政者不仅横征暴敛，荒淫无度，而且迫害基督教会，杀害基督教徒。《启示录》的现实基础就是那个时代深刻的社会现实，其历史根源就在于犹太民族的生存危机，文化背景则在于犹太文明与希腊文明的碰撞与交融。《启示录》结合了两种叙事倾向，兼具真实的现实主义和浪漫的传奇色彩，糅合了人类的两种冲动：理性与想象、事实与神秘。

2.《启示录》中的数字和象征

《启示录》的用语大多是象征性的。数字、颜色、矿物、宝石、野兽、星宿、灯台，全都用来代表人物、事物或真理。书中对一些象征有清楚的解释。例如，"七星"就是七个教会的使者(1:20)；大龙就是魔鬼撒旦(12:9)。四个活物(4:6)与《以西结书》第一章5—14节的四个活物差不多是完全相同的。《以西结书》第10章20节说明他们是基路伯。豹、熊和狮子(13:2)使人想起《但以理书》第7章，这些野兽分别代表希腊、波斯和巴比伦帝国。《启示录》里多次多处提到"7"，例如：信是写给7个教会的，神的7灵，7个金灯台，7印封严的书卷，吹号的7个天使，掌管末后7灾的7个天使，盛神大怒的7碗等等，7代表完全的数目，而777则是完全的完全。"666"出自第13章18节："凡有聪明的，可以计算兽的数目，因为这是人的数目，它的数目就是六百六十六"。"666"这个数字在基督教里就有了特别的意义，表示"邪恶"。有人甚至对666这个数字加以发挥，说每个世纪第一个第6年的6月6日是世纪凶兆。电影《天魔》(英文名 *Omen 666*)就选在2006年6月6日全球上映，取的就是这一"千年之叹"。

---

1. curse *n.* 诅咒。与亚当、夏娃被逐出伊甸园时受的咒诅呼应，区别是伊甸园中人类始祖遭到诅咒，此处在新天新地里，诅咒将永远消失。

3. "天堂"和"地狱"

"天堂"(Heaven)和"地狱"(Hell)是基督教教义中的常用语,前者为上帝的在天居所;后者乃不信基督、不悔改者死后灵魂受永罚的地方。

在《路加福音》第16章19—26节,耶稣讲了生前浑身生疮的乞丐死后被天使带去放在亚伯拉罕怀里得安慰,而享尽奢华宴乐的财主在阴间受痛苦的故事,其中就隐含了天堂和地狱两极世界的概念。在《启示录》中,天堂被描述成一座从天而降的圣城"新耶路撒冷",只有名字写在生命册上的人才能进去。在那里,上帝要"亲自与他们同在,作他们的上帝。上帝要擦去他们一切的眼泪;不再有死亡,也不再有悲哀、哭号、疼痛,因为以前的事都过去了"(21:3—4)。

在《新约》中,"地狱"一词的希腊文是 Gehenna,源自希伯来文 Gehinnom。Gehinnom 原是指耶路撒冷附近的"欣嫩子谷",犹大王亚哈斯和玛拿西曾在那里用火焚烧儿女向假神献祭(《历代志下》28:3; 33:6),这地方后来成了一个烧废物的垃圾场,也成了恶人将受刑罚的一个象征。在《马太福音》第25章41节,耶稣称地狱是"为魔鬼和它的使者所预备的永火"。《启示录》也用"火湖"和"第二次的死"来称呼地狱:"魔鬼被扔在硫磺的火湖里",在那里"昼夜受痛苦,直到永永远远"(20:10)。

四、圣经文化专题

1.《启示录》的蒙太奇手法

蒙太奇(Montage)原为法语名词,意思是剪接,指一些不同镜头恰当的组接,广泛使用在现代电影中。20世纪的试验小说借用了类似的表现手法,往往用它将一个个无明显逻辑联系的简短画面或印象组接起来,由此确定一定的场景或气氛。打开启示文学的书卷,映入我们眼帘的正是一连串迅速转换的不同画面。这些画面共同组成了通过人的感官就可以接受的形象的艺术世界,于是超验的、抽象的启示通过这种形式转化为人类思维更加容易接受、更易留下深刻印象的形象。例如《启示录》中接连打开的"七印封严"的书卷,七位天使所吹的号,将"盛神大怒的碗"倾倒于地上……

《启示录》第五章以天国为背景,以赞美基督为主题,并宣告基督才能揭开那书卷的"七印封严"的书卷。这个场景充满象征意义,而且没有一个一成不变的形象。基督分别被描写为一头狮子和一只羔羊(5:5—6),这些都是基督的象征。狮子象征力量和王权,而那只"像是被杀过的羊羔"却象征着基督的代赎。这一天国情景逐渐发展成为一个赞颂基督的最强音。该部分人物变化迅速,有四活物和宝座周围的二十四长老、周围的天使、在天上、地上、地底下、沧海里和天地间一切被造之物,他们都在唱歌,歌的曲调可能不同,歌词可能不完全一致,但是主旨却相同,可以想象这些歌颂者的颂歌此起彼伏,令人耳不暇接。

然后,我们看到揭开七印的篇章。前四个异象(6:1—8)有关马和骑马的场景,反映了一场盛会或赛会,这些异象以其视觉印象和象征的形式再现了耶稣所预言的争战和饥荒。接着,在描写人世间灾难的异象中,作者突然间把叙事的焦点转向天国。天国中那些殉道者被形象地描写成等待神对种种罪恶势力进行报复的人们(6:9—11)。第六印(6:12—17)笔锋从描写那充满着苦难的争战和饥荒的人类堕落史,转向描写人类历史的完美终结。我们看到了一个宇宙毁灭的异象,处处充满着毁灭世界的强大原型:大地震、黑太阳、血红的月亮、坠落的星辰、好像书卷被卷起来的天空,而且每一条山岭和每一个海岛都被挪移,等等。世间的居民所做出的反应就是逃离这羔羊的愤怒。我们不难看出一个用各种意象和象征手法描绘的现实世界。这就是我们在《圣经》中读到的历史的结束和最后的审判。第七印(8:1)令人吃惊:人们没有看到更多的异象,而仅仅是"天上寂静约有二刻"。回顾揭开七印的每个异象,我们能够看到《启示录》中发生了许多事情……

我们在阅读中可以感觉到这种运动不是从一个事件向另外一个事件平稳地过渡,而是酷似现代电影中的一些艺术效果:各种异象、图像、声音、意象就像一个万花筒式的连续体,千变万化。从天到地、从地到天,甚至以整个宇宙为背景,在辽远的时空范围内,把历史与未来,地上与天国连在一起,展示出一幅幅的海市蜃楼般的末世景观。作品因此具有场景变幻无穷、充满多层面寓意的特点,以及神秘、深奥、奇幻的色彩。这样,超验的世界与物质世界被巧妙地连接在一起,不仅把复杂的超验思想转化为易于理解的经验现象,而且有利于渲染罪恶、审判、死亡与拯救、宽恕、复活等相互对立的场景的气氛和色彩,从而给人留下立体而又色彩斑斓的生动印象。

2. 从《创世记》到《启示录》的U型叙事结构

通览《圣经》,我们发现其历史脉络呈现出一种清晰的结构:"喜剧→悲剧→喜剧",即从《创世记》美好的伊甸园开始,然后人类堕落,最后得救,到《启示录》出现了新天新地。弗莱称这种结构为"U型结构[1]"。

根据这种结构,我们可以将《圣经》记载的以色列古代史诠释成一种波浪式的运动过程:世界起源于一个美好的开端,《创世记》称之为"伊甸园";最后发展到一个理想化的未来,《启示录》称之为"从天而降的新耶路撒冷城"。在二者之间,世界经历了一个"败坏"的过程(《创世记》6:11—12),即神学家所谓的"堕落"、"疏离"或"异化"过程,于是就需要救赎,就导致所谓的"救恩史"或"圣史"。上帝在此过程中实现其创造世界的目的,而他将要带来的"新天新地"似乎又会开启一个新的历史程序。

大体来讲,《圣经》所记载的历史可以分成如下兴衰单元:

1)从伊甸园的完美世界开始,人类始祖亚当、夏娃偷吃禁果被逐出伊甸园后堕入低谷,直到上帝赐族长亚伯拉罕徙居迦南圣地,此为一个小高潮。

2)《出埃及记》中,以色列人被埃及法老奴役,在摩西和约书亚的带领下逃出埃及,再次到达应许之地迦南。

3)《士师记》中的侵略者如非利士人,断断续续统治以色列,到统一王国建立又进入高潮。

4)所罗门之后王国分裂,又一次灾难,至公元前6世纪初期犹太人被巴比伦人掳掠。

5)波斯的居鲁士允许巴比伦的犹太囚居之民回去重建圣殿,犹太人在几易其主后又出现了戏剧性下降,被打败波斯帝国的希腊(马其顿)王国统治。重压之下,犹太人在马加比领导下起义,建立犹太王朝。

6)公元前63年,希腊(马其顿)王国被庞培率领的罗马军团攻占,开始了罗马统治,基督徒遭受迫害,最后到《启示录》所描写,基督以他的启示——以色列的理想王国(一个精神王

---

1. Northrop Frye, *The Great Code: The Bible and Literature*, San Diego: Harcourt Brace & Company, 1982, p.169.

国)——使全人类获得了决定性的解放。

另外,《圣经》的许多书卷都呈现出这种U型叙事结构。《士师记》的英雄故事大体呈U型叙事结构:背叛之后是落入灾难与奴役,随之是悔悟,然后通过解救又上升到差不多相当于上一次开始下降时的高度;《约伯记》中约伯开始很富足,后来被撒旦考验,遭受财产损失和毒疮的折磨,最后又被上帝恩赐;《以斯帖记》中,以斯帖初入王宫堪称喜事,然而却面临着包括自己在内的族人灭绝的危险,但最终杀敌获救;《路得记》里,路得开始有一个美满的婚姻,丈夫去世后面临挨饿、守寡的苦境,结局是与波阿斯喜结良缘;《约拿书》中的约拿开始是上帝派的先知,后来因违抗上帝命令险些葬身大海,而后他祷告悔改,最后得救;福音书中,喜讯从救世主出生的"好消息"开始,然后耶稣被钉死在十字架,最后是耶稣的复活永生。不仅《圣经》中的独立书卷存在这样的U型结构,而且很多小故事也含有这种结构。如约瑟的成长故事,开始受父亲宠爱,继而被卖到埃及,最后位居宰相之位;在耶稣讲的"浪子回头"故事里,生于富足人家的浪子,得财产后外出闯荡,钱财挥霍尽光,结局却是被父亲接受。

清晰的U型框架不仅给我们理解《圣经》带来了方便,同时它作为一种叙事模式对西方文学产生了不小的影响。

五、圣经典故集锦

1. **hell**(地狱):福音书和《启示录》都提到"地狱",与"天堂"相对,指上帝惩罚恶人的处所,那里有烧着硫磺的火湖(lake of fire and brimstone),常常是无助、磨难、悲惨、恐怖的代名词。近代学者辜鸿铭在论及基督徒时指出:"真正的基督徒是因为爱好圣洁及基督教里面一切可爱的东西,而自然成为基督徒的。而那些因为害怕地狱之火而做基督徒的,是伪善的基督徒。那些只是为了想进天堂饮茶及与天使们共唱圣诗而做基督徒的,是下流的基督徒[1]。"无名氏的小说《海艳》第8章里,为了爱情而想彻底改变自己的女主人公瞿萦这样形容她所热恋的印蒂:"……从今夜起,你的胸膛即是一片刀山,我也要滚进去,让千万把刀子扎个透!我知道,你身上有天堂,也有地狱。你能给我天堂不朽的花朵,也能给我地狱永恒的鞭挞。……"在《简·爱》第3章中,简·爱被吓唬道:"撒谎的人个个都要到火和硫磺的湖里去受罪。"

2. **sharp, two-edged sword**(两刃的利剑):又译为"双刃剑",典出《启示录》第1章9—16节对基督异象的描写: ... and out of his mouth went a sharp two-edged sword: and his countenance was as the sun shineth in his strength. 他口中出来一把两刃的利剑,面貌如同烈日放光。"两刃的利剑"具有象征含义,表达基督的审判意识:一刃代表审判;一刃代表拯救。后来其意义扩展为一样事物利弊皆有,或表示对双方都不利的证据,或者表示某人言语刻薄,无论怎样说话都会伤害人。"感情是把双刃剑",因为感情可能伤了别人也伤了自己。

3. **the hidden manna**(隐藏的吗哪):典出第2章17节: To him that overcometh will I give to

---

[1] 见林语堂的文章《从异教徒到基督徒》第2章,载于张高明、范桥编《林语堂文选》(下),中国广播电视出版社,1990年。

eat of the hidden manna ... 得胜的，我必将那隐藏的吗哪赐给他。喻指天上的灵粮，前所未有的殊荣。活跃于20世纪70年代的一支美国摇滚乐队Bread发行过一个名叫*Manna*的专辑；2002年发行的Merve & Merla Watsond的歌曲专辑*Footsteps of Messiah*第一首歌名叫*Hidden Manna*.

4. **end of the world**（世界末日）：出自第4—19章，世界末日之前，基督将治理世界一千年，千年后，魔鬼被释放出来蛊惑人类，将人类引向毁灭，导致世界末日。此典常指人类自身因为堕落和罪恶走向覆灭的境地，或者象征无法抗拒的灾难或无法预知的未来。英文歌曲*The End of the World*把失恋比作世界末日，令人难以承受：Why does the sun go on shining?/Why does the sea rush to shore?/Don't they know it's the end of the world?/'Cause you don't love me anymore ...

5. **pale horse**（灰色马）：典出《启示录》第6章8节四活物之一"灰色马"的意象：And I looked, and behold a pale horse: and his name that sat on him was Death, and Hell followed with him. And power was given unto them over the fourth part of the earth, to kill with sword, and with hunger, and with death, and with the beasts of the earth. 骑在马上的，名字叫作死，阴府也随着他，有权柄赐给他，可以用刀剑、饥荒、瘟疫、野兽，杀害地上四分之一的人。因此"灰色马"象征死亡。俄国小说家卜洵路著有《灰色马》，郑振铎翻译后在1923年的《小说月报》上连载。美国女作家品特(K. A. Porter, 1890—1980)的小说集《灰色骑士灰色马》[1](*Pale Horse, Pale Rider*, 1939)就是借用骑灰色马的死神的典故，作品充满一种人无法与命运相抗衡的悲剧气氛。

6. **the bottomless pit**（无底坑）：最早见于《路加福音》第8章16—31节，指极端恐惧的受难之处。《启示录》中多次出现"无底坑"的意象，如"无底坑"（第9章1—2节），"从无底坑上来的兽(the beast that ascendeth out of the bottomless pit)"（第11章7节），"无底坑的钥匙(the key of the bottomless pit)"（第9章1节；第20章2节）等，这里的"无底坑"映射地狱。"无底坑"的引申义也很有趣。如苏格兰医生及作家阿巴思诺特·约翰(Arbuthnot John)1712年出版了一本讽刺英国维新党的小册子 *Law Is a Bottomless Pit*（《法律是个无底洞》）。再如，在上海访问的 Nike 公司首席执行官如是说: The Chinese market is a bottomless pit. 应该理解为"上海的市场无限巨大。"

7. **mark of the beast**（兽的印记）：典出第13章11—17节；第16章2节。长有两角、说话像龙从地中上来，迷惑地上的人类，拜兽的人无论大小贫富，都在右手或者额头上受一个印记。可见，接受兽的印记的人是在邪恶势力面前屈服的人，因此"兽的印记"是耻辱的标志。英国作家巴特(Samuel Butler, 1835—1902)的长篇小说《众生归途》(*The Way to All Flesh*, 1903)中，欧内斯特(Ernest)讨厌编辑们对他文章的关照，他说："编辑们就像是《启示录》中那些被买卖的人，没有一个额上没有兽的印记的。"

---

1. 参见鹿金等译:《灰色马，灰色的骑手》，上海:上海译文出版社，1997年。

8. **the great harlot of Babylon; Babylon as scarlet woman**（巴比伦大淫妇）：典出《启示录》第17章1—7节；第18章。其形象被描绘为：身着朱红色衣服、手拿盛满其淫乱的污秽的金杯骑在七头十角的怪兽上，本是借以映射罗马帝国政权。后来成为罪恶的化身，尤指妖艳淫荡的女人。在美国作家霍桑的小说《红字》(*The Scarlet Letter*, 1850)第8章《小精灵和牧师》中，海丝特带着女儿珠儿去见总督，总督眼见小姑娘特异的美貌便联想到其母亲："Nay, we might have judged that such a child's mother must needs be a scarlet woman, and a worthy type of her of Babylon!" "唔，那么我们可以判断，这样一个孩子的母亲肯定是个妖艳的女子，十足的巴比伦荡妇！"英国作家哈代的小说《苔丝》中，当苔丝出于报复的目的找到曾经侮辱了她的德伯时，德伯对苔丝的反应是："You temptress, Tess; your dear damned witch of Babylon, I could not resist you as soon as I met you again." "你这个迷人精，苔丝！你这个是亲爱的而又是冤孽的巴比伦女巫——我这次一看见你，就不论怎么，也摆脱不开你了。"

9. **the Last Judgment**（末日审判）：又译"最后的审判"、"大审判"，典出第20章11—15节对末日审判景象的描绘，背信弃义者以及同魔鬼同道者将遭到严厉的惩罚，而信义者将得到永恒。美国作家爱默生在《论自助》中指出：Speak your latent conviction and it shall be the universal sense; for the inmost in due time becomes the outmost, — and our first thought is rendered back to us by the trumpets of the Last Judgment. 如果把你隐藏的信念说出来，它一定会成为最外在的——我们最初的思想会被"最后的审判"的号角送到我们耳边。无名氏的小说《海艳》第6章《矜默》中，瞿萦对印蒂诉说刻骨铭心的爱恋时说："……从黑夜到天明，我的眼睛睁了十个小时。我在黑夜里徘徊，睁大眼睛凝望黑暗里的雪花，我对我这一生的命运，'最后审判'，'最后挣扎'……"

10. **streets of gold**（金街道）：典出《启示录》第21章21节对新耶路撒冷城的描绘：... and the street of the city was pure gold, as it were transparent glass. 城内的街道是精金，好像透明的玻璃。霍桑的小说《红字》第9章《医生》中，假装医生的海丝特的丈夫齐灵渥斯对陷入痛苦、不明真相的牧师丁梅斯代尔说："Youthful men, not having taken a deep root, give up their hold of life so easily! And saintly men, who walk with God on earth, would fain be away, to walk with him on the golden pavements of the New Jerusalem." "年轻人啊！根还没有扎深，怎么就那么容易放弃生命呢？与上帝同行的人间圣人们，都愿意跟随上帝一起路上通往耶路撒冷的黄金大道。"

六、课堂讨论题

1. 分析《启示录》的神话特征。
2. 结合以前所学章节谈谈《圣经》中的理想经验原型。
3. 有人把《启示录》列为史诗，你认同吗？
4. 阅读美国《独立宣言》中下面的段落，作者没有一律用God，而是采用不同的词汇(下划线)。你知道其中的原委吗？

When in the course of human events, it becomes necessary for one people to dissolve the political bands which have connected them with another, and to assume, among the Powers of the earth the separate and equal station to which … and of <u>Nature's God</u> entitle the …

We hold these truths to be self-evident, that all men are created equal, that they are endowed by <u>their Creator</u> with certain unalienable Rights, …

We therefore, the Representatives of … Assembled, appealing to the <u>Supreme Judge of</u> the world for the rectitude of …

With a firm reliance on the protection of <u>Divine Providence</u>, we mutually pledge to each other our Lives, our Fortunes and our sacred Honor.[1]

5. 谈谈"阿门"(Amen)的意思和用法。

七、课后思考题

1. 请阅读《双城记》的结尾段落，你能看出该段与《启示录》的关系吗？

   I see … long ranks of the new oppressors who have risen on the destruction of the old, perishing by this retributive instrument, before it shall cease out of its present use. I see a beautiful city and a brilliant people rising from this abyss, and, in their struggles to be truly free, in their triumphs and defeats, through long long years to come. 我看见，在社会压迫者的废墟上兴起压迫者们，将在这冤冤相报的机器被废除之前，一一被它毁灭；我看见从这深渊里，升起一个美丽的城市和卓越的民族，我看见，我为之献身的人们，生活在我来不及看到的英国大地上，过得宁静安详，幸福兴旺。

2. 你知道《启示录》对美国总统小布什的影响吗？
3. 你知道《七宗罪》的《圣经》渊源吗？
4. 你知道中国学者郑振铎对《圣经》的评价吗？

---

1. 王波主编：《美国重要历史文献导读——从殖民地时期到19世纪》，北京：北京大学出版社，2002年，第22页。

附录一 课程模拟试题

A卷

I. Translate the following biblical terms. (10 points)

1. Noah's Ark
2. The Tower of Babel
3. Jacob and Rachel
4. The first Passover
5. *The Song of Deborah*
6. Samson and Delilah
7. Hebrew prophets
8. Job's patience
9. Crucifixion
10. *Revelation*

II. Complete the following sentences by filling in the blanks. (10 points)

1. The Authorized Version of the Bible, which was published in 1611, contains about 780, 000 English words. The Old Testament consists of 39 books while the New Testament consists of _____ books.
2. The tree of knowledge and its fruit stand for wisdom and knowledge of _____.
3. There are _____ people in Noah's family who survived in the flood.
4. The story of _____ in *Genesis* is regarded as the first story of adolescent growth in western literature.
5. The Song on Moses, which is also called Song of Red Sea later, is a song of praise and a celebration on the Israel's successful escape from _____.
6. *Jephthah's Daughter*, one of Byron poems, is alluded to a biblical story from _____.
7. _____ and *Esther* are two books in the Old Testament which are respectively entitled by the name of the heroines.
8. The first four chapters of *Lamentations* are alphabetic poems which are charactered by _____ style.
9. Jesus was baptized by _____ in the River of Jordan.
10. Among his twelve disciples, _____ betrayed Jesus.

III. Explain the individual words in italics in the following sentences and translate them into Chinese. (20 points)

1. Now the serpent was more *subtil* than any beast of the field which the LORD God had made.
2. And the LORD God called unto Adam, and said unto him. "where *art* thou?"
3. And it shall be a token of the covenant *betwixt* me and you.
4. The LORD will pass over the door, and will not *suffer* the destroyer to come in unto your house to smite you.

5. And when the children of Israel saw it, they said one to another, "it's manna"; For they *wist* not what it was.
6. But every woman shall borrow of her neighbour, and of her that sojourneth in her house, jewels of silver, and jewels of gold, and *raiment*.
7. And the king said to Absalom, "*Nay*, my son, let us not all now go, lest we be chargeable unto thee."
8. What is man, that thou shouldest magnify him?/And that thou shouldest set thine heart upon him?/And that thou shouldest *visit* him every morning,/And try him every moment?
9. Vanity of *vanities*, saith the preacher, vanity of vanities; all is vanity.
10. John came who baptized in the wilderness and preached the baptism of repentance unto *remission* of sins.

IV. Comment on biblical metaphors based on examples. (10 points)

V. Identify the Biblical book which each selection is from and give a summary of its theme. (20 points)

1. Thou shalt have no other gods before me.
   Thou shalt not make unto thee any graven image, …
   Thou shalt not take the name of the LORD thy God in vain; for the LORD will not hold him guiltless that taketh his name in vain.
   Remember the sabbath day, to keep it holy …
   Honour thy father and thy mother: that thy days may be long upon the land which the LORD thy God giveth thee.
   Thou shalt not kill.
   Thou shalt not commit adultery.
   Thou shalt not steal.
   Thou shalt not bear false witness against thy neighbour.
   Thou shalt not covet thy neighbour's house, thou shalt not covet thy neighbour's wife, nor his manservant, nor his maidservant, nor his ox, nor his ass, nor any thing that is thy neighbour's.

2. Let the day perish wherein I was born,
   And the night which said, "there is a man child conceived."
   Let that day be darkness;
   Let not God regard it from above,
   Neither let the light shine upon it.
   Let darkness and the shadow of death claim it for their own;
   Let a cloud dwell upon it;
   Let all that maketh black the day terrify it.

As for that night, let thick darkness seize upon it:
Let it not come into the number of the months.
Lo, let that night be barren;
Let no joyful voice come therein.
Let them curse it that curse the day.

3. The LORD is my shepherd; I shall not want,
He maketh me to lie down in green pastures;
He leadth me beside the still waters.
He restoreth my soul;
He leadeth me in the paths of righteousness for his name's sake.
Yea, though I walk through the valley of the shadow of the death,
I will fear no evil: for thou art with me,
Thy rod and thy staff they comfort me.
Thou preparest a table before me in the presence of mine enemies;
Thou anointed my head with oil; my cup runneth over.
Surely goodness and mercy shall follow me all the days of my life,
And I will dwell in the house of the LORD for ever.

4. To know wisdom and instructions;
To discern the words of understanding;
To receive instruction in wise dealing,
In righteousness and judgment and equity,
To give subtilty to the simple,
To the young man knowledge and discretion,
And that the man of understanding may attain unto sound counsels;
To understand a proverb, and a figure;
The words of the wise, and their dark saying.
The fear of the LORD is the beginning of knowledge;
But the foolish despise wisdom and instruction.

VI. Write down your appreciation of the selected readings from the *Bible*. (30 points)

1. A virtuous woman who can find?
For her price is far above rubies.
The heart of her husband trusteth in her,
And he shall have no lack of gain.
She doeth him good and not evil
All the days of her life.

She seeketh wool and flax,
And worketh willingly with her hands.
She is like the merchant-ships;
She bringeth her food from afar.
She riseth also while it is yet night,
And giveth meat to her household,
And their task to her maidens.
She considereth a field, and buyeth it.
With the fruit of her hands she planteth a vineyard.
She girdeth her loins with strength,
And maketh strong her arms.
She perceiveth that her merchandise is profitable;
Her lamp goeth not out by night.
She layeth her hands to the distaff,
And her hands hold the spindle.
She spreadeth forth her hands to the poor.
Yea, she reacheth for her hands to the needy.
She is not afraid of the snow for her household;
For all her household are clothed with scarlet.
She maketh for herself carpets of tapestry;
Her clothing is fine linen and purple.
Her husband is known in the gates,
When he sitteth among the elders of the land.
She maketh linen garments and selleth them;
And delivereth girdles unto the merchant.
Strength and dignity are her clothing;
And she laugheth at the time to come.
She openeth her moth with wisdom;
And the law of kindness is on her tongue.
She looketh well to the ways of her house hold,
And eateth not the bread of idleness.
Her children rise up, and call her blessed;
Her husband also, and he praiseth her, saying;
"Many daughters have done virtuously,
but thou excellest them all."
Favour is deceitful, and beauty is vain;
But a woman that feareth the Lord, she shall be praised.
Give her of the fruit of her hands;
And let her works praise her in the gates.

2. And he (Jesus) taught them many things by parables, and said unto them in his doctrine,

"Hearken; Behold, there went out a sower to sow: and it came to pass, as he sowed, some fell by the way side, and the fowls of the air came and devoured it up. And some fell on stony ground, where it had not much earth; and immediately it sprang up, because it had no depth of earth: But when the sun was up, it was scorched; and because it had no root, it withered away. And some fell among thorns, and the thorns grew up, and choked it, and it yielded no fruit. And other fell on good ground, and did yield fruit that sprang up and increased; and brought forth, some thirty, and some sixty, and some an hundred." And he said unto them, "Know ye not this parable? and how then will ye know all parables? The sower soweth the word. And these are they by the way side, where the word is sown; but when they have heard, Satan cometh immediately, and taketh away the word that was sown in their hearts. And these are they likewise which are sown on stony ground; who, when they have heard the word, immediately receive it with gladness; and have no root in themselves, and so endure but for a time: afterward, when affliction or persecution ariseth for the word's sake, immediately they are offended. And these are they which are sown among thorns; such as hear the word, and the cares of this world, and the deceitfulness of riches, and the lusts of other things entering in, choke the word, and it becometh unfruitful. And those are they which are sown on good ground; such as hear the word, and receive it, and bring forth fruit, some thirtyfold, some sixty, and some an hundred.

B卷

I. Fill in the blanks to complete the following statements. (10 points)

1. The books in the Old Testament are written in ancient _____, with some chapters in Aramaic, while the New Testament is written in ancient Greek.
2. The Authorized Version, also called *King James Bible*, was completed in the year of _____.
3. There are _____ characters involved in the story of the Garden of Eden.
4. The story of the Tower of Babel tells about the origin of man's dialects from a philosophical viewpoint. It reviews the existence of three kinds of language, i.e. God's language, _____ language and man's plural or natural languages.
5. The father of the Twelve Tribes of the Israel is _____.
6. The Song on Moses, which is also called Song of Red Sea later, is recorded in the book of _____.
7. "Thou shalt not make unto thee any graven image" is the _____ commandment that Moses received from the Lord God on the Sinai Mountain.
8. The story of Samson and Delilah, which is frequently rewritten by poets, is from _____ of the Bible.
9. The festival of _____ is in honor of Jew's victory against Haman, their enemy.
10. The four books in the New Testament which record Jesus' life, teaching and revival, are also called _____.

II. Explain the individual words in italics in the following sentences and translate them into Chinese. (10 points)

1. In the beginning God created the heaven and the earth. And the earth was without form, and *void*.
2. And the Lord God said unto the woman, "What is this that thou hast done?" And the woman said, "The serpent *beguiled* me, and I did eat."
3. And Adam *knew* his wife; and she conceived, and bore Cain.
4. And Moses said, "Let no man leave of it till the morning." Notwithstanding they hearkened not unto Moses; but some of them left of it until the morning, and it bred worms, and stank: and Moses was *wroth* with them.
5. And she said unto her father, "Let this thing be done for me; let me alone two months, that I may go up and down upon the mountains and *bewail* my virginity, I and my fellows."
6. And she showed her mother-in-law with whom she had *wrought*, and said, "The man's name with whom I wrought today is Boaz."

7. Blessed is the man that walketh not in the *counsel* of the ungodly, /Nor standeth in the way of sinners, /Nor sitteth in the seat of the scornful.
8. If thou know not, O thou *fairest* among woman, /Go thy way forth by the footsteps of the flock.
9. And feed thy kids beside the shepherds' tents. /And he went the way to her house; /In the *twilight*, in the evening of the day, /In the blackness of night and the darkness.
10. Now when Jesus was *risen* early the first day of the week, he appeared first to Mary Magdalene, out of whom he had cast seven devils.

III. Explain the phrasal expressions in the following sentences. (20 points)

1. The LORD shall fight for you, and ye shall *hold your peace*.
2. Keep me as *the apple of the eye*, hide me under the shadow of thy wings.
3. And if any mischief follow, then thou shalt give life for life, *eye for eye, tooth for tooth*, hand for hand, foot for foot, burning for burning, wound for wound, stripe for stripe.
4. Thou shalt not *bear false witness* against thy neighbour.
5. *a land of promise*, land of memory/a land of promise flowing with milk/and honey, of delicious memories. (Alfred Tennyson: *The Lover's Tale*)
6. Behold now, I have taken upon me to speak unto the LORD, which am but *dust and ashes*.
7. My bone cleaveth to my skin and to my flesh, and I am *escaped with the skin of my teeth*.
8. And he shall judge among the nations, and shall rebuke many people: and they shall *beat their swords into plowshares*, and their spears into pruninghooks: nation shall not lift up sword against nation, neither shall they learn war any more.
9. And a man of understanding shall attain unto wise counsels: /To understand a proverb, and the interpretation; /The words of the wise, and their *dark sayings*.
10. Then Joseph her husband, being a just man, and not willing to *make her a publick example*, was minded to put her away privily.

IV. Explain the theme and style of the following biblical books. (30 points)

1. *Job* 2. *Ruth* 3. *Proverbs*

V. Comment on the motifs in biblical narratives. (10 points)

VI. Write down your appreciation of the selected readings from the *Bible*. (20 points)

1. How beautiful are thy feet with shoes, O prince's daughter!
   The joints of thy thighs are like jewels,
   The work of the hands of a cunning workman.

Thy navel is like a round goblet,
Which wanteth not liquor;
Thy belly is like a heap of wheat
Set about with lilies.
Thy two breasts are like two young roes
That are twins;
Thy neck is as a tower of ivory;
Thine eyes like the fishpools in Heshbon,
By the gate of Bath-rabbim:
Thy nose is as the tower of Lebanon
Which looketh toward Damascus.
Thine head upon thee is like Carmel,
And the hair of thine head like purple;
The king is held in the galleries.
How fair and how pleasant art thou,
O love, for delights!

2. By the rivers of Babylon,
  There we sat down, yea, we wept,
  When we remembered Zion.
  We hanged up our harps.
  Upon the willows in the midst thereof.
  For there they that carried us away captive required of us a song.
  And they that wasted us required of us mirth, saying,
  "Sing us one of the songs of Zion."
  How shall we sing the LORD's song in a strong land?
  If I forget thee, O Jerusalem,
  Let my right hand forget her cunning.
  If I do not remember thee,
  Let my tongue cleave to the roof of my mouth;
  If I prefer not Jerusalem above my chief joy.
  Remember, O LORD, the children of Edom in the day of Jerusalem;
  Who said, "raze it, raze it, even to the foundation thereof."
  O daughter of Babylon, who art to be destroyed;
  Happy shall he be that rewardeth thee as thou hast served us.
  Happy shall be he that taketh and lasheth thy little ones against the stones.

C卷

一、判断以下陈述是否正确（用T标记正确，F标记不正确）（每题1分；共10分）

1. 从学术的角度看，所谓的"圣经"文本只包括《旧约》和《新约》，不包括《圣经后典》。
2. 传说亚伯拉罕之子雅各曾与天使摔跤得胜，耶和华赐名"以色列"（Israel），意思是"与天使角力"。于是希伯来人有了"以色列人"的称谓。
3. 当代以色列国的国歌是《希望》（The Hope）。
4. 犹太教（Judaism）又称"摩西教"，是宗教史上最早出现的系统的一神教，是基督教的前身。因而基督教（Christianity）是犹太教的"女儿宗教"。
5. 《士师记》中，士师们的故事重要情节一再重复：以色列人作恶→上帝惩罚他们→他们求告耶和华→士师们兴起拯救民族，如此构成一个"作恶→惩罚→呼救→解救"的故事模式。
6. 《圣经》中的《启示录》与但丁的《神曲》及歌德的《浮士德》并称为人类探索自身与宇宙奥秘的三部曲。
7. "虚空的虚空，凡事都是虚空。人的一切劳碌，就是他在日光之下的劳碌，有什么益处呢？"——这句话出自《箴言》。
8. 荣获1905年诺贝尔文学奖的是托尔斯泰的《复活》，而不是波兰作家显克微支通过扩充和改编圣经历史故事而写的长篇小说《你往何处去》。
9. 电影《七宗罪》（Se7en）里的七种"罪"分别指：贪吃（Gluttony）；贪婪（Greed）；懒惰（Sloth）；嫉妒（Envy）；愤怒（Wrath）；虚妄（Pride）；淫行（Lust）。
10. 鲁迅的1924年发表的散文《野草·复仇》（其二），直接从《圣经》取材，相当忠实地依据了《马太福音》第27章，通过耶稣的形象表现了革命者的意志和对"庸众"的痛斥。

二、对应下列圣经引语及其出处的圣经卷名（每题1分；共10分）

圣经引语

1. "女儿啊，听我说，不要往别人田里拾取麦穗。"
2. "爱情，众水不能熄灭，大水也不能淹没；若有人拿家中所有的财宝要换爱情，就全被藐视。"
3. "敬畏耶和华，是智慧的开端；认识至圣者，便是聪明。"
4. "看哪！他们成为一样的人民，都是一样的语言，如今既做起这事来，以后他们所要做的事，就没有不成就的了。我们下去，在那里变乱他们的口音，使他们的言语彼此不同。"
5. "以色列人出埃及地以后，满了三个月的那一天，就来到西奈的旷野。"
6. "唯愿我的烦恼称一称，我一切的灾害放在天平里，现今都比海沙更重，所以我的言语急躁。"
7. "他从水里一上来，就看见天裂开了，圣灵仿佛鸽子，将在他身上。又有声音从天上来说：'你是我的爱子，我喜悦你。'"
8. "我们曾在巴比伦的河边坐下，一追想锡安就哭了。我们把琴挂在那里的柳树上。"

9. "先前满有人民的城,现在何竟独坐!先前在列国中为大的,现在竟如寡妇;先前在诸省中为王后的,现在成为进贡的。"
10. "我若在王前蒙恩,王若以为美,我所愿的,是愿王将我的性命赐给我;我所求的,是求王将我的本族赐给我,因为我和我的本族被卖了。"

圣经卷名

A. 《约伯记》　　　　　　　　　B. 《马可福音》
C. 《创世记》　　　　　　　　　D. 《雅歌》
E. 《以斯帖记》　　　　　　　　F. 《诗篇》
G. 《哀歌》　　　　　　　　　　H. 《箴言》
I. 《出埃及记》　　　　　　　　J. 《路得记》

三、对应下列圣经典故与圣经人物（每题1分；共10分）

圣经典故　　　　　　　　　　**圣经人物**

1. 一碗红豆汤　　　　　　　　　A. 约书亚
2. 为耶稣施洗　　　　　　　　　B. 施洗约翰
3. 方舟　　　　　　　　　　　　C. 犹大
4. 位及埃及宰相　　　　　　　　D. 亚伯拉罕
5. 崇拜金牛犊　　　　　　　　　E. 亚伦
6. 用独生子献祭　　　　　　　　F. 雅各
7. 娶拉结和利亚两姊妹为妻　　　G. 约瑟
8. 摩西的继任者　　　　　　　　H. 以扫和雅各
9. 出卖耶稣的人　　　　　　　　I. 大利拉
10. 引诱参孙的女人　　　　　　　J. 挪亚

四、单项选择题（每题1分；共10分）

1. 在"诺亚方舟"的故事中,洪水消落后,诺亚最先放飞出的鸟是:
   A. 鸽子　　　　B. 乌鸦　　　　C. 鹌鹑　　　　D. 喜鹊

2. "割礼"是耶和华神与谁立约的记号?
   A. 挪亚　　　　B. 雅各　　　　C. 亚伯拉罕　　D. 摩西

3. 在"亚伯拉罕献子"的故事中,"子"是指:
   A. 雅各　　　　B. 约瑟　　　　C. 罗得　　　　D. 以撒

4. 古希伯来民族十二支派源自:

A. 亚伯拉罕　　　　　　B. 雅各　　　　　　C. 大卫　　　　　　D. 约瑟

5. 在《出埃及记》中,"流奶和蜜的地方"是指:
   A. 西奈平原　　　　　　B. 迦南　　　　　　C. 伊甸园　　　　　　D. 两河流域

6. 摩西带领以色列民族出埃及后,在旷野流浪了多少年?
   A. 30年　　　　　　　　B. 50年　　　　　　C. 20年　　　　　　　D. 40年

7. "摩西十诫"之第一诫是:
   A. 不可崇拜偶像　　　　　　　　　　　B. 不可妄称耶和华的名
   C. 除了耶和华不可崇拜别的神　　　　　D. 当纪念安息日,守为圣日

8. 达·芬奇所绘的圣经名画是:
   A. 《蒙娜丽莎》　　　　　　　　　　　B. 《最后的晚餐》
   C. 《伊甸园》　　　　　　　　　　　　D. 《巴别塔》

9. 下列作品中哪一件不是米开朗基罗的作品?
   A. 雕像《大卫》　　　　　　　　　　　B. 雕像《摩西像》
   C. 穹顶壁画《创世记》　　　　　　　　D. 木版画《十字架上的基督》

10. "方鸿渐受到两面夹攻,才知道留学文凭的重要。这一张文凭,仿佛有亚当、夏娃下身那片树叶的功用,可以遮羞包丑;小小一方纸能把一个人的空疏、寡陋、愚笨都掩盖起来。自己没有文凭,好像精神上赤条条的,没有包裹。"这段话出自哪位中国作家的作品?
    A. 萧乾　　　　　　　　B. 郁达夫　　　　　　C. 钱钟书　　　　　　D. 许地山

五、《圣经》对西方文学和艺术影响深远。对应下列与圣经有关的西方文学艺术作品及其作者（每题1分；共10分）

作品　　　　　　　　　　　　　　作家

1. 油画《亚当和夏娃》　　　　　　A. 显克微支
2. 《失乐园》　　　　　　　　　　B. 丢勒
3. 《天路历程》　　　　　　　　　C. 斯坦贝克
4. 《复活》　　　　　　　　　　　D. 乔托
5. 《你往何处去》　　　　　　　　E. 班扬
6. 《愤怒的葡萄》　　　　　　　　F. 弥尔顿
7. 《马太受难曲》　　　　　　　　G. 托尔斯泰
8. 《书念的处女》　　　　　　　　H. 勃朗蒂
9. 油画《犹大之吻》　　　　　　　I. 阿莱唐多
10. 《简·爱》　　　　　　　　　　J. 巴赫

六、简述题（每题10分；共20分）

1. 解释"贯顶体"和"气纳体"。
2. 谈谈英国小说《简·爱》中的《圣经》痕迹。

七、论述题（任选一题；计30分）

1. 结合实例论述《圣经》对西方文学和艺术产生的深远影响。
2. 谈谈西方影视艺术对《圣经》的诠释方式。

D卷

一、填空（每空0.5分；共10分）

1. "两希文化"被称为西方文化的两个源头,它们分别指_____和_____。
2. 在希伯来圣经"伊甸园"的神话故事里,参与对话的角色共有____人。
3. 古希伯来人很早就对语言的起源进行了认真思考,他们的思想表述反映在《旧约》中"_____"的神话故事,英文写作_____。
4. 《旧约》里至少有4部书卷是诗歌性质的,它们分别是《约伯记》、《诗篇》、《雅歌》(和《耶利米哀歌》,这四部书卷的英文书名分别是_____,_____,_____,_____。
5. Acrostic和Kinah是古希伯来民族在诗歌方面的独创,这两个术语的中文意思分别是"_____"体和"_____"体。
6. 《旧约》中只有一部作品中没有提到"上帝"或"神"字样。这部作品是《_____》,英文写作_____。犹太人迄今还纪念的节日"_____"(又称"掣签节")就是源于该故事。
7. 《旧约》中有一部戏剧作品,主人公的名字叫_____。扮演主人公与上帝之间的中介者的角色是_____。
8. 《新约》是基督教的经典,但从文学的角度看,"福音书"是优秀的_____文学,《启示录》开创了_____文学的典范。
9. 在中国大陆,迄今被广泛使用的天主教《圣经》中文版本是出版于1968年的"_____"。
10. 《圣经》对中国当代文学也产生了一定影响。著名作家王蒙的作品《_____》便是一例。

二、对应下列圣经引语及其出处的圣经卷名（每题1分；共10分）

圣经引语

1. "你的国就是我的国,你的神就是我的神。"
2. "王女啊,你的脚在鞋中何其美好!你的大腿圆润好像美玉,是巧匠的手做成的。"
3. "敬畏耶和华是知识的开端;愚妄人藐视智慧和训诲。"
4. "他们说:'来吧!我们要建造一座城和一座塔,塔顶通天,为要传扬我们的名,免得我们分散在全地上。'"
5. "不可杀人。不可奸淫。不可偷盗。不可作假证陷害人。"
6. "愿我生的那日和说怀了男胎的那夜,都灭没。愿那日变为黑暗。"
7. "你们所听的要留心。你们用什么量器量给人,也必用什么量器量给你们。并且要多给你们。因为有的,还要给他;没有的,连他所有的也要夺去。"

8. "耶和华是我的牧者,我必不至缺乏。他使我躺在青草地上,领我在可安歇的水边。"
9. "我又看见一个新天新地,因为先前的天地已经过去,海也不再有了。"
10. "以色列啊,你尊荣者在山上被杀。大英雄何竟死亡!"

圣经卷名

A. 《约伯记》　　　　　　　　　　　B. 《马可福音》

C. 《创世记》　　　　　　　　　　　D. 《雅歌》

E. 《启示录》　　　　　　　　　　　F. 《诗篇》

G. 《路得记》　　　　　　　　　　　H. 《箴言》

I. 《出埃及记》　　　　　　　　　　J. 《撒母耳记下》

三、选择题（每题1分；共10分）

1. 下列人物中哪个与亚当无直接关系?
   A. 夏娃　　　　B. 亚伯　　　　C. 亚伯兰　　　　D. 该隐

2. "伊甸园"故事中夏娃被蛇引诱而吃了一棵树上结的果子,这棵树叫做:
   A. 无花果树　　B. 苹果树　　　C. 生命树　　　　D. 智慧树

3. "摩西十诫"中第二诫是:
   A. 不可敬拜偶像　　　　　　　　B. 不可妄称上帝的名
   C. 当守安息圣日　　　　　　　　D. 除上帝外不可敬拜别的神

4. "摩西五经"的排列顺序应该是:
   A. 《创世记》、《民数记》、《出埃及记》、《申命记》、《利未记》
   B. 《创世记》、《出埃及记》、《民数记》、《申命记》、《利未记》
   C. 《创世记》、《出埃及记》、《利未记》、《民数记》、《申命记》
   D. 《创世记》、《民数记》、《出埃及记》、《利未记》、《申命记》

5. 大卫和拔示巴所生的儿子是:
   A. 所罗门　　　B. 押沙龙　　　C. 暗嫩　　　　D. 他玛

6. 以下著名女性中哪个不是《圣经·旧约》中的人物?
   A. 以斯帖　　　B. 马利亚　　　C. 路得　　　　D. 利百加

7. "爱是恒久忍耐,又有恩慈;爱是不嫉妒;爱是不自夸,不张狂,不做害羞的事,不求自己的益处,不轻易发怒,不计算人的恶,不喜欢不义,只喜欢真理;凡事包容,凡事相信,凡事盼望,凡事忍耐。爱是永不止息。"这段话出自:
   A. 《马太福音》　B. 《启示录》　C. 《使徒行传》　D. 《哥林多前书》

8. 海明威的哪部小说取自《传道书》1:5:"一代过去,一代又来,地却永远长存。日头出来,日头落下,急归所出之地。"
   A.《太阳照样升起》 B.《老人与海》
   C.《丧钟为谁而鸣》 D.《永别了,武器》

9. 2001年中国国家广播电台记者关娟娟的新闻报道中有这样一句:"耶路撒冷什么都有,就是没有安全感。持续8个月的巴以冲突,已使这片被《圣经》誉为'流着奶和蜜的土地'再也找不到生活的安全感。"这里所谓"流着奶和蜜的土地"指的是《圣经》中哪个地方?
   A. 巴比伦 B. 迦南 C. 西奈 D. 锡安

10. 对"新文学运动"产生了一定影响、至今在中国依然很流行的中文《圣经》:
    A. "和合本"《圣经》 B. 天主教"思高本"《圣经》
    C.《现代中文译本》 D.《圣经新译本》

四、《圣经》对中国文学产生了不可忽视的影响。请对应下列中国作家与其作品内容或言论(每题1分;共10分)

作品或言论:

1. 成功十架血成溪,/百丈恩流分自西;/身列四衙半夜路,/徒方三背两番鸡;/五千鞭挞寸肤裂,/六尺悬垂二盗齐;/惨恸八埃惊九品,/七言一毕万灵啼。

2. 伊甸有树,一曰说生命,一曰知识。神禁人勿食其实;魔乃佗蛇以诱夏娃,使食之,爱得生命知识。神怒,立逐人而诅蛇,蛇腹行而土食;人则劳其生,又得其死,罚且及于子孙,无不如是。

3. 有上帝开天辟地的创造,又有《圣经》那样庄严简练的文字,所以我们才有空前绝后的《圣经》文学。

4. 古书的一个总集,被称为《圣经》(Bible)的,乃是具有无比的价值与重要的一部书。它的势力遍及于全世界,尤其是欧洲,它对于人类的道德的与宗教的发展的影响比任何文字都甚些。它记载千余年的人类文明的最显著的进步。其中的几篇,他们的艺术的精神直已到达了极峰。

5. 新旧约的内容正和中国的经书相似:《新约》是四书,《旧约》是五经,——《创世记》等纪事书类与《书经》、《春秋》,《利未记》与《易经》及《礼记》的一部分,《申命记》与《书经》的一部分,《诗篇》、《哀歌》、《雅歌》与《诗经》,都很有类似的地方。

6. 冰期世界太清凉,/洪水茫茫下土方;/巴别塔前一挥手,/人天从此感参商。

7. 近世基督教《圣经》的官话翻译,增富了我们的语言。

8. 伊人拣了一句山上垂诫里边的话作他的演题:
   "Blessed are the poor in spirit; for theirs is the Kingdom of Heaven."
   Matthew 5:2.
   "心贫者福矣,天国为其国也。"
   "说到这一个'心'字,英文译作 Spirit,德文译作 Geist,法文是 Esprit,大约总是作'精神'讲的。精神上受苦的人是有福的,……"

9. 这样我挨过许多煎熬的夜晚,于是我读《老子》,读《佛经》,读《圣经》,……我更恨人群中一些冥顽不灵的自命为"人"的这一类动物。他们偏若充耳无闻,不肯听旷野里那伟大的凄厉的唤声。……诚如《旧约》那热情的耶利米所呼号的,"我观看地,地是空虚的;我观看天,天也无光。"我感觉到大地震来临前那种"烦躁不安",我眼看着要地崩山惊,"肥田变为荒地,城邑要被拆毁。"在这种心情下,"我已经听见角声和打仗的喊声。"我要写一点东西,宣泄这一腔愤懑。我要喊"你们的末日到了!"对这般荒淫无耻,丢弃了太阳的人们。

10. 天上的星辰,骤雨般落在大海上,嗤嗤繁响。海波如山一般汹涌,一切楼屋都在地上旋转,天如同一张蓝纸卷了起来。树叶子满空飞舞,鸟儿归巢,走兽躲到它的洞穴。

中国作家:

A. 朱自清	B. 郑振铎	C. 梁实秋	D. 夏穗卿	E. 周作人
F. 冰心	G. 康熙	H. 郁达夫	I. 鲁迅	J. 曹禺

五、《圣经》对西方文学的影响深远。对应下列与圣经有关的西方文学作品及其作家(每题1分;共10分)

作品   **作家**

1. 《亚当和夏娃日记》   A. 显克微支
2. 《失乐园》   B. 马克•吐温
3. 《天路历程》   C. 斯坦贝克
4. 《复活》   D. 麦尔维尔
5. 《你往何处去》   E. 班扬
6. 《愤怒的葡萄》   F. 弥尔顿
7. 《卡斯特桥市长》   G. 托尔斯泰
8. 《押沙龙!押沙龙!》   H. 夏洛蒂
9. 《白鲸》   I. 福克纳
10. 《简•爱》   J. 哈代

六、《圣经》对西方艺术产生了深刻影响。请对应下列西方艺术作品和作者。（每题1分；共10分）

艺术作品：

1. 壁画《最后的晚餐》
2. 雕像《摩西》
3. 壁画《西斯廷圣母》
4. 人体油画《亚当与夏娃》
5. 油画《巴别塔》
6. 油画《路得拾穗》
7. 现代画《亚当与夏娃》
8. 油画《大利拉计诱参孙》
9. 油画《梳妆中的以斯帖》
10. 油画《犹大之吻》

西方艺术家：

A. 海耶兹
B. 勃吕盖尔
C. 沙塞里奥
D. 乔托
E. 米开朗基罗
F. 克里姆特
G. 鲁本斯
H. 拉斐尔
I. 丢勒
J. 达·芬奇

七、简答题（每题10分；计20分；每题要求不少于150字)

1. 简述《路得记》的宗教、历史、道德意义。

2. 谈谈美国小说《红字》(*The Scarlet Letter*, 1850) 中的圣经痕迹。

八、论述题（任选1题；计20分；不少于800字)

1. 论述《圣经》的文体特征和三重价值。

2. 看完影片《十诫》或《耶稣受难记》或任何一部与《圣经》有关的作品后, 你有何感想?

附录二 词汇表

1. 人名汇总

A
Aaron 亚伦
Abaddon 亚巴顿(无底坑之王)
Abel 亚伯
Abinoam 亚比挪庵
Abram 亚伯兰
Absalom 押沙龙
Adam 亚当
Ahasuerus 亚哈随鲁
Ammihud 亚米忽
Amnon 暗嫩
Amos 阿摩司
Anath 亚拿
Apollyon 亚玻伦(地狱之王)
Archelaus 亚基老
Asher 亚设

B
Barak 巴拉
Bath-sheba 拔示巴
Bilhah 辟拉
Boaz 波阿斯

C
Cain 该隐
Chilion 基连

D
Dan 但
Deborah 底波拉
Delilah 大利拉
Dinah 底拿

E
Edom 以东
Eglon 伊矶伦

Ehud 以笏
Elijah 以利亚
Enos 以诺士
Esau 以扫
Eve 夏娃
Ezekiel 以西结

G
Gad 迦得
Gershom 革舜
Gideon 基甸

H
Haman 哈曼
Heber 希百
Herod 希律王

I
Isaac 以撒
Isaiah 以赛亚
Issachar 以萨迦

J
Jacob 雅各
Jael 雅亿
James 雅各
Jephtath 耶弗他
Jeremiah 耶利米
Jeremy 即 Jeremiah
Jesse 耶西
Joab 约押
Jonadab 子约
Jonah 约拿
Joseph (雅各之子)约瑟；(耶稣名义上的父亲) 约瑟
Judah 犹大(民族)

Judas (耶稣门徒)犹大

L
Laban 拉班
Leah 利亚
Levi 利未
Lot 罗得

M
Mahlon 玛伦
Manoah 玛挪亚
Mary Magdalene 抹大拉的马利亚
Mary 马利亚
Michael (天使长)米迦勒
Miriam 米利暗
Mordecai 末底改

N
Naomi 拿俄米
Naphtali 拿弗他利
Noah 挪亚

O
Obed 俄备得

P
Phurah 普拉
Potiphar 波提乏

R
Rachel 拉结

Reuben 吕便
Reuel 流珥
Ruth 路得

S
Salome 撒罗米; 莎乐美
Samson 参孙
Sarai 撒拉
Satan 撒旦
Seth 塞特
Shamgar 珊迦
Shimeah 示米亚
Simeon 西缅
Simon 西门, 即彼得
Sisera 西西拉
Solomon 所罗门

T
Talmai 达买
Tamar (犹大的儿媳)他玛; (押沙龙之妹)他妈

U
Uriah 乌利亚

V
Vashti 瓦实提

Z
Zilpah 悉帕
Zipporah 西坡拉
Zubulun 西布伦

2. 地名汇总

A
Amalek 亚玛力
Amana 亚玛拿
Ammon 亚扪
Ararat 亚拉腊山
Aroer 亚罗珥

B
Baal-hazor 巴力
Babel 巴别
Bethel 伯特利
Bethlehem 伯利恒

C
Canaan 迦南

D
Dan 但

E
Eden 伊甸
En-gedi 隐基底
Ephraim 以法莲
Eshtaol 以实陶
Etham 以倘
Euphrates 幼发拉底河

G
Galilee 加利利
Gaza 迦萨
Gethsemane 客西马尼
Gibeah 基比亚
Gigal 吉甲
Golgotha 各各他
Gomorrah 蛾摩拉

H
Haran (地名)哈兰
Harod 哈律泉
Hebron 希伯伦
Hermon 黑门
Horeb 和烈山

J
Jericho 耶利哥
Jordan 约旦河
Judæa 犹太

L
Lebanon 黎巴嫩

M
Marah 玛拉
Meroz 米罗斯
Midian 米甸
Minnith 米匿
Mizpeh 米巴斯镇
Mizpeh 米斯巴
Moriah 摩利亚

N
Nazareth 拿撒勒
Nod 诺得

O
Olives 橄榄山
Ophir 俄斐

P
Pithom 比东

R
Rabbah 拉巴城
Rama 拉玛
Rameses 兰塞
Rephdim 利非订

S
Seirath 西伊拉
Seir 西珥山
Sharon 沙仑
Sheba 示巴
Shenir 示尼珥
Shinar 士拿平原
Shur 书珥
Shushan 书珊
Sinai 西奈
Sodom 所多玛
Sorek 梭烈山谷
Succoth (地名)疏割

T
Taanach 他纳
the hill of Moreh 摩利冈
the mountain of Bether 比特山
Tob 陀伯
Tyre 推罗

U
Ur 吾珥

Z
Zion 锡安山
Zorah 琐拉

3. 生词汇总

A

abate *vt.* (水势开始)回落
abhor *vt.* 憎恶; 痛恨
abhorred *adj.* 让人憎恶的; 令人讨厌的
abide *vi.* 继续;〈古〉耐心等候
abomination *n.* 可憎之物
abroad *adv.* 在室外
abundance *n.* 富足
accuser *n.* 控告者; 原告
acquit *vt.* 赦免
adorn *vt.* 装饰; 佩戴
adulterer *n.* 犯通奸罪者
adversary *n.* 敌人
adversity *n.* 逆境; 不幸
advertise *vt.* 告知; 提醒
afflict *vt.* 使……痛苦; 折磨
afflicted *adj.* 受尽痛苦的
affright *vt.* 惊恐
alas *int.* 哀哉
aloe *n.* 芦荟
aloes *n.* 沉香
anguish *n.* 痛苦
anoint *vt.* 涂油礼
apparel *vt.* 给某人穿上衣服
appease *vt.* 平息
appoint *v.* (上帝)赐给
armoury *n.* 兵器库
array *vt.* 给某人穿衣
artillery *n.* (一套)弓箭
ascribe sth. unto sb. 归于
asp *n.* 小毒蛇; 蝮蛇
assembly *n.* 人群
assuage *vt.* (洪水)退却; 回落
astray *adv.* 歪斜
athirst *adj.*〈古〉口渴的
atonement *n.* 补偿; 赎罪
attire *n.* 服装
avail *vt.* 有益于

B

balm *n.* 香脂
baptize *vt.* 用水施洗礼
barren *adj.*〈古〉不能生育的
beam *n.* 织布机上的织轴
beguile *vt.* 诱骗; 诱惑; 欺骗
behead *vt.* 斩首
bereave *vt.* 使丧失亲人
beseech *vt.* 恳求
besiege *vt.* 包围; 围困
betimes *adv.* 随时; 及早
betroth *vt.*〈古〉订婚
betwixt *prep.*〈古〉在……之间
bewail *vt.* 哀泣; 悲悼
bid *vt.* 命令; 吩咐
birthright *n.* 长子权
blade *n.* 叶片
blaspheme *vt.* 亵渎(上帝)
blasphemy *n.* 亵渎(言语)
bolt *vt.* 插(门)
bound *n.* 边界
bowels *n.*〈古〉怜悯之心; 慈悲之心
bracelet *n.* 把私印缚在颈项上的绳子或链子
brass *n.* 铜
brawl *vi.* 争吵
bray *vi.* 驴叫声, 指哀声
breach *n.* 裂口; 指港口
breastplate *n.* 胸甲
brutish *adj.* 粗野的; 愚顽不化的
buckler *n.* 圆盾
bud *vi.* 萌芽; 放蕊
bulrush *n.* 蒲草
bulwark *n.* 用作围城的堡垒
bushel *n.* 斗, 一种量器
by *prep.* 按照

C

camphire *n.* 凤仙花
candlestick *n.* 蜡扦, 蜡烛架
captain *n.* (战车)兵长
captive *n.* 战俘; 囚徒
carcase *n.* (动物)尸体
casement *n.* 窗

cedar *n.* 香柏
centurion *n.* 百夫长
chaff *n.* 秕糠
chamberlain *n.* (国王的)侍从
charge *vt.* 指示；吩咐
chargeable *adj.* 昂贵的；难以负担的
chasten *vt.* 管教；申斥
Cherubim *n.* (天使)基路伯
cinnamon *n.* 桂皮
circuit *n.* 周游；行程
circumcise *vt.* 割礼
cistern *n.* 蓄水池
clave *vt.* 〈古〉cleave 劈开
cleft *n.* 缝隙
cloven *adj.* 劈开的；分成两瓣的
clovenfooted *adj.* 有趾的
comely *adj.* 适时的；英俊的
comfort *vt.* 缓解；减轻
commit *vi.* 托付
compass *vt.* 包围
comprehend *vt.* 包含；包括
commune *vi.* 与某人谈心
conceal *vt.* 遮蔽
conception *n.* 怀孕
condemn *vt.* 判刑；定罪
confound *vt.* 〈古〉使羞愧；使不安；使狼狈
confusion *n.* 失去分辨能力
congeal *vi.* 凝结
congregation *n.* (犹太教)会众
consume *vt.* 消灭；毁灭
contend *vi.* 辩争；争论
convert *vt.* 更新；转变
cony *n.* (coney的变体)穴兔；石獾
correction *n.* 处罚
counsel *n.* 计策
counseller *n.* 谋士
covenant *n.* (立)约
covet *vt.* 贪念；觊觎
creditor *n.* 债主
crimson *n.* 深红色
crucify *vt.* 钉在十字架上处死
crucifixion *n.* (耶稣)十字架受难
cubit *n.*(长度单位)腕尺；一肘
cud *n.* 反刍的食物
curdle *vt.* 使变成凝乳；凝结

curse *n.* 咒诅
cymbal *n.* 钹

D

damsel *n.* 少女；姑娘
daub *vt.* 涂抹
dayspring *n.* 黎明；拂晓
deck *vt.* 打扮；装饰
decree *vt.* 颁令
defile *vt.* 弄脏
deliver *vt.* 分娩
den *n.* 兽穴；洞穴
desire *n.* 渴望；情欲
desolation *n.* 悲哀；忧伤；不幸；孤寂
destroyer *n.* 专司杀戮的天使
device *n.* 手段；策略
devour *vt.* 吞吃，攻击；消灭
diligently *adv.* 仔细地；不懈地
diminish *vt.* 减少；减量
discretion *n.* 谋略
disdain *vt.* 藐视
disperse *vt.* 洒散；分散
distaff *n.* 纺纱杆
dominion *n.* 统治权；权柄
dough *n.* 生面团
dowry *n.* 嫁妆
dress *vt.* 清洗收拾以备烹煮
dress *vt.* 整治(土地)
dung *n.* 动物粪便
dungeon *n.* 监牢；地牢

E

ear *n.* 穗
embrace *vt.* 拥抱
encamp *vi.* 扎营
enchantment *n.* 魔法；妖术
endue *vt.* 赋予
enmity *n.* 仇恨；敌意
entice *vt.* 引诱；诱惑
entil *n.* 小扁豆
entreat *vt.* 〈古〉对待
endue *vt.* 赋予
equity *n.* 公正
ere *prep.* 〈古〉在……之前
err *vi.* 犯错；走上歧途

espouse *vi.* 订婚; 结婚
evil *adj.* 不幸的
exact *vt.* 索要; 要求
expire *vt.* 期满
eye *vt.* 因嫉妒而怒视

F
fail *vt.* 疏忽; 忘记
fall *vi.* 跌倒; 喻指灭亡
famine *n.* 饥荒
fashion *vt.* 造就; 塑造成
fatling *n.* 肥壮的家畜
fence *vt.* 防护
fetter *n.* 脚镣
filthiness *n.* 污秽之物
fire *n.* 火石
firmament *n.* 苍穹; 天空
firstling *n.* 头生仔
flag *n.* 生长在尼罗河畔的高大青草
flagon *n.* 酒壶
flax *n.* 亚麻
fodder *n.* 饲料; 草料
forasmuch *conj.* 由于; 鉴于
fornication *n.* 奸淫; 乱伦; 淫乱
forsake *vt.* 抛弃; 离弃
fugitive *n.* 逃亡者

G
gender *vt.* 酿成
Gentiles *n.* 非犹太人; 非犹太教徒
gird *vi.* 腰佩; *vt.* 绑住; 束腰
girdle *n.* 腰带
gnash *vt.* 因(愤怒或痛苦等)咬(牙), 磨(牙)
goldsmith *n.* 金匠
goodliness *n.* 美貌
goodman *n.* 丈夫; 主人
gospel *n.* 福音
grind *n.* 推磨(碾米)

H
habitation *n.* 居所; 住处
haft *n.* (短剑的)柄
hallow *vt.* 使神圣
hap *n.* 运气; 偶然
harden *vt.* 使(自己)经得起考验

harlot *n.* 妓女
harness *n.* 〈古〉铠甲
hart *n.* 公鹿
haste *vt.* 催促; 逼迫
haughty *adj.* 傲慢的
hearken *vi.* 听; 倾听; 听从
hearth *n.* 炉膛
heathen *n.* (不信奉耶和华的)异族人; 不信上帝的人
heed *n.* 注意
henceforth *adv.* 从今以后
hew *vt.* 砍伐
highways *n.* 街市
hind *n.* 母鹿
hireling *n.* 雇工
hither *adv.* 到这
hoar *adj.* 灰白色的
hoarfrost *n.* 白霜
hollow *n.* (手)心
hold *n.* 〈古〉堡垒; 营寨
horsehoof *n.* 马蹄
host *n.* 军队; 许多; 一大群
howbeit *adv.* 然而
husbandman *n.* 农夫
hyssop *n.* 牛膝草

I
idle *adj.* 懒惰的
impoverish *vt.* 使贫穷
impoverished *adj.* 贫穷的
impudent *adj.* 厚颜无耻的
indignation *n.* 愤怒; 愤慨
inhabiter *n.* 居民
inheritance *n.* 财产
iniquity *n.* 邪恶; 罪恶
inquire *vt.* 询问
innocent *adj.* 无罪的; 免于犯罪的
intreat *vt.* 〈古〉祈求; 恳求
issue *vi.* 流出

J
jacinth *n.* 橘红色的宝石; 红玛瑙
javelin *n.* 长矛; 扫罗的武器
jeopard *vt.* 冒着危险

K

kid *n.* 小山羊
kindle *vt.* 点燃
kindreds *n.* 家族;族人
knead *vt.* 揉(面)
kneadingtrough *n.* 和面盆

L

lament *vt.* 哀悼;悲泣
languish *vi.* 衰弱
lap *vt.* 舔
latchet *n.* 鞋带
lattice *n.* 窗棂
lean *adj.* 消瘦的
liken *vt.* 把……比作
line *n.* 准绳
lintel *n.* 门楣
loathsome *adj.* 可恶的;讨厌的
lodge *vi.* 居住;住宿
lofty *adj.* 高傲的
loin *n.* 腰部
lordly *adj.* 高贵的;珍贵的
lothe *vt.* 厌恶
loud *adj.* 俗艳的;招摇的
low *vi.* 牛叫声
lusty *adj.* 健壮的;精壮的

M

magnify *vt.* 放大;加强
maid *n.* 处女
mandrake *n.* 风茄
manner *n.* 样式;种类
mar *vt.* 毁坏,损坏
mark *n.* 箭靶; *vt.* 打分;做标记
measure *n.* 尺寸;长度;斗;一斗约合公制15升
meditation *n.* 沉思
melt *vt.* 熔铸
merchandise *n.* 商品;货物
mete *vt.* 〈古〉测量;称量
minish *vt.* 〈古〉减少
minister *n.* 仆人
minister *vi.* 侍奉
morsel *n.* 冰雹;小块食物
morter *n.* 同 mortar, 灰泥
mount *vi.* 上升

multiply *vt.* 增加;繁殖
mustard *n.* 芥菜
myrrh *n.* 没药

N

nether *adj.* 下面的
nigh *adv.* 〈古〉靠近;接近
notwithstanding *conj.* 虽然;尽管
nourish *vt.* 滋养;养活
nourisher *n.* 养育者

O

oblation *n.* 祭品
observe *vt.* 遵守
offering *n.* 祭品
ointment *n.* 油膏
ordain *vt.* 授以圣职
ordinance *n.* 礼俗
organ *n.* 风
Orion *n.* 猎户座
ostrich *n.* 鸵鸟
ouch *vt.* 行凶;杀害
ought *n.* aught 变体。任何事;零
overlay *vt.* 覆闷致死
overseer *n.* 管家

P

pap *n.* 奶头
parable *n.* 譬喻;寓言
perdition *n.* 毁灭;沉沦
perfume *vt.* 洒香水
perish *vt.* 灭绝;毁灭
persecutor *n.* 迫害者
pertain *vi.* 属于
perverse *adj.* 不正当的
pestilence *n.* 瘟疫
pine *vi.* 憔悴
pitch *v.* 涂上树脂; *n.* 树脂;柏油
pitcher *n.* 陶瓶
plait *vt.* 编
Pretorium 官邸
pledge *n.* 抵押品
polish *vt.* 使(人、举止、仪表等)变得优雅
pomegranate *n.* 石榴
prancing *n.* (马蹄)腾跃

prate *vi.* 胡扯；吹嘘；空谈；唠叨
press *vt.* 再三请求
presumptuous *adj.* 专横的；放肆的
prevail *vi.* 泛滥遍地；占优势；强过
prey *n.* 掠夺
prince *n.* 君王
proceed *vi.* 源于
procure *vt.* 〈古〉招致
prophesy *vi.* 乱语；*vt.* 预言
psaltery *n.* 索特里尔琴，一种弹拨乐器
purification *n.* 洁净
purpose *vi.* 打算；企图；*vt.* 决心

Q

quench *vt.* 满足；熄灭
quail *n.* 鹌鹑
quite *adv.* 彻底地

R

Rabbi 拉比；经师
rafter *n.* 椽子
rail *vi.* 怒骂
raiment *n.* 〈古〉衣服
rate *n.* 份额
raven *n.* 乌鸦；渡鸦
revile *vt.* 辱骂；谩骂
ravish *vt.* 充满激情；抢夺
rebuke *vt.* 训斥
recompense *vt.* 补偿；*n.*〈古〉惩罚
redeem *vt.* 救赎；赎回
redeemer *n.* 赎身者；救主
refrain *vi.* 克制；忍住；*vt.* 禁止；阻止
regard *vt.* 看顾
rehearse *vt.* 颂扬
release *n.* 豁免，免债
remission *n.* 免除；宽恕
remit *vt.* 免除；宽恕
rend *vt.* 撕开
replenish *vt.* 充满
reproach *n.* 羞耻；耻辱
reproof *n.* 责难
reprove *vt.* 责备
respect *n.* 喜欢；纳悦
restore *vt.* 遣送
restore *vt.* 使苏醒

resurrection *n.* 复活
revenger *n.* 复仇者
reverence *vt.* 致敬；*n.* 尊敬
revile *vt.* 辱骂；谩骂
rigour *n.* 严格
roe *n.* 羚羊
ruby *n.* 红宝石
ruddy *adj.* 面色红润的

S

saddle *vt.* 放鞍子
sanctify *vt.* 洁净身体；使神圣
sanctuary *n.* 圣所
sap *n.* 树汁
sapphire *n.* 蓝宝石
saving *prep.* 除……外
scale *n.* 刻度
scarlet *adj.* 朱红色的
sceptre *n.* 权杖
scorch *vt.* 使枯萎
scorpion *n.* 蝎子
scribe *n.* 文士
seal *n.* (书卷的)封印
season *n.* 定期
seed *n.* 子孙；后代
seeing *conj.* 因为；鉴于
seethe *vt.* 〈古〉煮沸
sepulchre *n.* 坟墓；墓窟
servitude *n.* 苦役
shadow *n.* 暮影
sheaf *n.* (禾)捆；束
sheath *n.* 刀鞘
siege *n.* 围城；包围
sieve *n.* 筛子
sift *vt.* 筛撒
signify *vt.* 表明；晓谕
sinew *n.* 筋
slander *n.* 诽谤
slaughter *n.* 杀戮；屠宰
slayer *n.* 杀人者
sling *n.* 甩石机
smite *vt.* 击打；打架
snare *n.* 罗网；陷阱
sod *vt.* 〈古〉seethe 煮沸
sodden *vt.* 浸透

sojourn *vi.* 暂居；逗留
sojourner *n.* 寄居者
solace *vt.* 安慰；使人欢乐
sorcery *n.* 巫术；邪术
sottish *adj.* 迟钝的；愚蠢的
sound *vt.* 测探
span *n.* 跨度；一段时间(尤指人的一生)；短促的时间
spicery *n.* 香料
spikenard *n.* 哪哒香膏
spittle *n.* 唾沫
spoil *n.*〈古〉掠夺之物；战利品；〈古〉抢夺；毁坏；摧毁
spy *vt.* 看见
staff *n.* 象征家族权威的手杖
stain *vt.* 弄脏；玷污
stall *vt.* 豢养长肥
standard *n.* 旗；旗号
stature *n.* 身材
statute *n.* 律例
stave *n.* 棍棒
stay *vt.* 支持
stead *n.* 替代
sting *n.* 毒刺
stink *vt.* 发出恶臭
stock *n.* 手枷；足枷；树茎；鹳
straits *n.* 困境；危难
strangle *vt.* 窒息；扼死
stubble *n.* (植物的)断秸秆；茬
stuff *n.* 可以遮蔽的东西
subdue *vt.* 制服；慑服
substance *n.* 活灵；财产；财富
subtil *adj.*〈古〉阴险的；狡猾的
suck *n.* 喂奶
sucklings *n.* 乳儿
suffer *vt.*〈古〉允许；容许
supplant *vt.* 排挤
supplication *n.* 恳求
swoon *vi.* 昏厥；昏倒

T

tabret *n.* 小手鼓
tale *n.*〈古〉总数
talent *n.*(计量单位)他连得，1他连得约36公斤
tempt *vt.* 考验；试探

testimony *n.*〈古〉证言；证明
thicket *n.* 灌木丛；密林
tidings *n.* 音信；消息
till *vt.* 耕作；耕种
timbrel *n.* 手鼓；铃鼓
tithe *vt.* 献出十分之一
torment *vt.* 折磨
tossing *n.* 辗转反侧
touching *prep.* 关于
transgress *vt.* 违反
transgression *n.* 犯罪
travail *n.* 分娩；痛苦；艰难
tread *vt.* 踩踏；指压迫(穷人)
treasure *n.* 仓库；宝库
tribulation *n.* 苦难；磨难
tributary *adj.* 从属的；附庸的
trough *n.* 水槽
try *vt.* 考验；试炼
twain *n.* 同 two〈古〉二；两个
twilight *n.* 黄昏

U

unawares *adv.* 意外地
uncleanness *n.* 不洁；月经
undefiled *adj.* 纯洁无瑕的(人)
unsavoury *adj.* 难吃的

V

vagabond *n.* 流浪者
valour *n.* 勇猛；英勇
vanity *n.* 空虚
vaunt *vi.* 自夸
vengeance *n.* 报仇；复仇
venison *n.*〈古〉野味
vex *vt.* 使痛苦；遭受折磨
vial *n.* 小瓶
victual *n.* 食物；供给
vile *adj.*〈古〉微不足道的；卑微的
viol *n.* 一种古琴
virginity *n.* 处女之身
visage *n.* 脸，面容
vision *n.* 异象
visit *vt.* 降临；攻击；察看；监察；惩罚；报复
visitation *n.* 巡视；眷顾
void *adj.* 虚空的

W

wafer *n.* 薄饼
wag *vi.* 摇头
want *vt.* 缺乏
warfare *n.* 争战
wax *vi.* 变热; 衰老; 名声日隆
wayfare *vi.* 旅行; 步行
wean *vt.* 使断奶
weary *adj.* 厌烦的; *vt.* 使疲倦
wherefore *adv.* 为何
wherein *adv.* 在其中
whirlwind *n.* 旋风
white *n.* 蛋清; *adj.* 干净的
whore *vi.* 卖淫
whoredom *n.* 卖淫
wilderness *n.* 旷野

winepress *n.* 压酒池
winnow *vt.* 簸; 扬(谷)
wise *n.* 方式; 方法
wit *vt.* 〈古〉想知道
with *n.* 同 with 或 withy 柳条; 藤条
withal *prep.* 〈古〉用, 用以
withhold *vt.* 拒给; 保留
without *adv.* 在外面
wormwood *n.* 茵陈; 苦艾
wrath *adj.* 愤怒
wreathe *vt.* 把……绕成一圈; 盘绕; 缠绕
wroth *adj.* 愤怒的; 生气的

Y

yearn *vi.* 〈古〉怜悯
yield *vt.* 长出; 结(果)

责任编辑 / 张传根
封面设计 / 杨云青
版式设计 / 卞骐真

新世纪高等院校英语专业本科生系列教材（修订版）旨在打造完整的英语专业学科体系，全面促进学生的语言技能、学科素养和创新能力的培养，必将为我国培养国际化、创新型、高素质的英语专业人才奠定坚实的基础！

权威性和先进性的体现：

按照《高等学校英语专业英语教学大纲》提出的培养目标、课程设置、教学要求和教学原则精心设计，凝聚海内外英语专业教育界专家学者的智慧，反映英语专业教育、科研的最新成果。

前瞻性和创新性的结晶：

基于广泛的市场调研、详尽的需求分析和严谨的科学判断，梳理现有教程，优化教材结构，更新教学方法和手段，强化学生综合能力的培养。

专业素质和人文素养的同步提升：

专业技能、专业知识、相关专业知识的完美匹配，帮助学生打下扎实的语言基本功，增强其分析问题、解决问题的能力，提高专业素质和人文素养，使学生真正成为国际化、创新型、高素质的英语专业人才。

ISBN 978-7-5446-3311-6

定价：31.00 元

"十二五"普通高等教育本科国家级规划教材

新世纪高等院校英语专业本科生系列教材（修订版）
总主编 戴炜栋

圣经文化导论
An Introductory Course of Biblical Culture

学生用书

任东升　张德禄　马月兰 / 编著

上海外语教育出版社
SHANGHAI FOREIGN LANGUAGE EDUCATION PRESS
www.sflep.com